The American Football League

The American Football League

A Year-by-Year History, 1960–1969

by
ED GRUVER

McFarland & Company, Inc., Publishers
Jefferson, North Carolina, and London

British Library Cataloguing-in-Publication data are available

Library of Congress Cataloguing-in-Publication Data

Gruver, Ed, 1960–
    The American Football League : a year-by-year history, 1960–1969 / by Ed Gruver.
       p.   cm.
    ISBN 0-7864-0399-3 (softcover : 50# alkaline paper) ∞
    1. American Football League — History. I. Title.
GV955.5.A45G78   1997
796.332'64'0973 — dc21   97-22839
                                                                             CIP

©1997 Ed Gruver. All rights reserved

No part of this book, specifically including the table of contents and index, may be reproduced or transmitted in any form or by any means, electronic or mechanical, including photocopying or recording, or by any information storage and retrieval system, without permission in writing from the publisher.

Manufactured in the United States of America

McFarland & Company, Inc., Publishers
   Box 611, Jefferson, North Carolina 28640

To my mother, Roberta;
to the loving memory of my father, John,
and brother, Michael;
and to my family

Contents

Acknowledgments	1
Introduction	3
1. The Hunt for a New Beginning	7
2. New Frontiers	13
3. Founding the Foolish Club	21
4. 1960: Corralling a Loose Cannon	38
5. 1961: A Well-Oiled Offense	58
6. 1962: The AFL's Longest Day	73
7. 1963: Al, Sonny, and El Sid	96
8. 1964: The Turning Point	117
9. 1965: From Buffalo to Broadway	139
10. 1966: A Negotiated Peace	155
11. Super Bowl I: "Max"-imum Effort	172
12. 1967: Oakland's Angry Eleven	180
13. Super Bowl II: Oakland Gets "Starr"-struck	190
14. 1968: The Jet Age	195
15. Super Bowl III: Joe Guarantees It	216
16. 1969: A Wild West Show	225
17. Super Bowl IV: Hail to the Chiefs	246
Epilogue	255
Appendix A: AFL Yearly Standings 1960–69	258
Appendix B: Scoring Summaries for AFL Playoff, Championship, Super Bowl, and All-Star Games	266
Appendix C: AFL Team and Individual Honors, 1960–69	272
Index	277

Acknowledgments

ANY WORK of this length requires the efforts of not just one person, but many people. While it is impossible to name them all, following is a list of those who were most influential.

First of all, I'd like to thank my family members for their encouragement and support. Writing a book requires untold hours spent researching, interviewing, writing, and editing, and my family was gracious enough to understand the demands.

This book would not have been possible without the help of the owners, coaches, players, scouts, and media who made the AFL years such a memorable time. I list them all here, in alphabetical order, because they were kind enough to share their memories and opinions with me during phone interviews: Bud Adams, Bobby Bell, Phil Bengston, Buck Buchanan, Gino Cappelletti, Wray Carlton, Len Dawson, Weeb Ewbank, Larry Felser, Mike Garrett, Sid Gillman, Curt Gowdy, Larry Grantham, Charley Hennigan, Winston Hill, Mike Holovak, Joe Horrigan, Lamar Hunt, Joe Kapp, Ernie Ladd, Daryle Lamonica, Keith Lincoln, Al LoCasale, Paul Lowe, Jerry Magee, Don Maynard, Jerry Mays, Ray Nitschke, Jim Otto, Babe Parilli, Lee Remmel, Glenn Ressler, Johnny Robinson, Lou Saban, Steve Sabol, Billy Shaw, Bart Starr, Hank Stram, Mike Stratton, Billy Sullivan, Walt Sweeney, Lionel Taylor, Otis Taylor, Lloyd Wells, and Ralph Wilson.

When I first started researching this book in 1990, there had been only two major works published on the AFL: *Touchdown! The Picture History of the American Football League*, written in 1967 by George Sullivan; and *The Other League: The Fabulous Story of the American Football League*, written by Jack Horrigan and Mike Rathet in 1970. Both of these books were exceptional and proved valuable in my research.

Photos for the book were provided from numerous sources, and I'm particularly indebted to Vernon Biever, Al LoCasale, Berj Najarian, Jim Saccomano, Thom Vollenweider, Denny Lynch, and Leanne Thompson.

—Ed Gruver
Summer 1997

Introduction

PROFESSIONAL SPORTS MIRRORED SOCIETY in the 1960s, and the changes that were reshaping America's social and political landscape were felt in athletic venues as well. Major-league baseball, for example, established new frontiers via westward expansion. Through the 1950s, a trip west in baseball usually meant a game in Chicago or St. Louis, but the 1960s saw franchises relocating their teams to the far West, as cities like Los Angeles, San Francisco, Oakland, San Diego gained major-league clubs.

As baseball changed, so too did football, but in even more dramatic fashion. The increased popularity and availability of television did more than any other factor to make NFL football the nation's number-one spectator sport.

Lamar Hunt, the 27-year-old son of Texas billionaire oilman H. L. Hunt, recognized the increasing popularity of pro football and sought to become a part of the game's growth. Unable to buy into an existing franchise and rebuffed by NFL owners who had no desire for expansion, Hunt formed his own league in 1959. He placed his team in Dallas, called them the Texans, and invited other young entrepreneurs to join him.

Kenneth S. "Bud" Adams, a 38-year-old oil executive, founded the Houston Oilers. Thirty-two-year-old credit card and hotel magnate Barron Hilton created the Chargers, and situated his team in Los Angeles before moving them a year later to San Diego. Ralph Wilson Jr., a 41-year-old insurance and trucking executive from Detroit, started the Buffalo Bills. Forty-two-year-old baseball man Bob Howsam established the Denver Broncos. Chet Soda, operator of a construction company, became owner of the Oakland Raiders at age 52. Billy Sullivan, Jr., a late but fast riser in the business world who became the president of three different coal and oil companies, founded the Boston Patriots. Eccentric sports broadcaster Harry Wismer headed a New York franchise called the Titans.

Officially, they were known as the eight charter members of the American Football League. But as the fledgling owners sized up the overwhelming odds that faced them in their battle to win fan support from the established NFL, they gave themselves (out of public earshot) the unofficial title of "the Foolish Club."

The AFL's Original Eight were not reformists or activists, though their actions brought pro football to new cities and forever changed the face of their sport. Not only did the new league succeed in changing the structure of the game, it also popularized on-field strategies that thrilled fans and influenced a generation of coaches and players. The NFL establishment viewed "the Other League" as upstarts and rebels, but the success of AFL innovations through the years proved they were rebels with a cause.

The AFL's wide-open style of play and exciting young stars won the devotion of fans across the country, including youngsters like Terry Bradshaw and Joe Montana.

Bradshaw says his love affair with football began when he started watching AFL games as a youngster in Shreveport, Louisiana. As a youth he marveled at the sight of AFL quarterbacks like George Blanda, John Hadl, and Daryle Lamonica launching the long ball. To Bradshaw, the AFL represented fun, and the players seemed to be enjoying themselves more than those in the NFL. One of Bradshaw's most memorable Christmas presents was the J5-V Spalding, the official ball of the AFL, that his father gave him when he was nine years old.

Montana, too, enjoyed watching AFL games on TV. Growing up in the suburbs of Pittsburgh, Montana rooted for the Steelers. But his heroes were two AFL quarterbacks, Joe Namath of the Jets and Len Dawson of the Chiefs.

While the AFL appealed to young fans, the new league failed to gain the respect of its NFL elders. Nevertheless, in 1966, after just six years of operations, the AFL's success on and off the field forced the NFL to recognize it by pitting the champions of the two warring leagues in a final, climactic game that Hunt named "the Super Bowl."

Four years later, after defeating the NFL in two straight Super Bowls, the upstarts merged with the establishment. The AFL era ended in January 1970, but the league had come of age.

Hall of Fame wide receiver Don Maynard, who started for the Jets in their historic upset of the Baltimore Colts in Super Bowl III, looks back on the AFL and sees it as a symbol of the American Dream come true:

> The AFL is America. We had the opportunity to succeed, the freedom to expand, the freedom to explore. We fought all the negatives. It was a complete uphill battle all the way, until the Jets won the Super Bowl. When we won the Super Bowl, maybe a lot of people who were underdogs in their life said, "Hey, if the Jets can do it, maybe we can do it too."

Such is the allure of the AFL.

Al Davis, who built the Raiders into an AFL power and served as league commissioner in 1966, the year of the merger, refers to the AFL as "the greatest league of them all." No one, Davis said, can ever fully appreciate the obstacles the AFL overcame in its formative years.

The late Milt Woodard served as league president from 1966 to 1969. In 1970, Woodard said the AFL made a breakthrough in sports that allowed it to rival any success story.

Joe Horrigan, director of the Pro Football Hall of Fame in Canton, Ohio, agrees with Woodard's assessment:

> The AFL opened up a lot of doors. The league was a reflection of the mood of the country at that time. We had elected a Catholic president, the Civil Rights movement was alive and well. Americans wanted change. It was time to get out of the Eisenhower era and get into the Kennedy era. It was time to expand and grow.

The AFL's growth was measured on several fronts, as the league produced a series of dramatic changes that altered the game immeasurably. The AFL actively recruited black athletes from small southern colleges; instituted a revenue-sharing plan among the league owners; put nameplates on the backs of jerseys; and created additional excitement with the two-point conversion. All of the above measures have been adopted by the NFL.

The AFL's greatest resource however, was its personnel. Lamar Hunt ... Bud Adams ... Ralph Wilson ... Billy Sullivan ... Sid Gillman ... Hank Stram ... Lou Saban ... Jim Otto ... Ron Mix ... Buck Buchanan ... Billy Shaw ... Ernie Ladd ... Larry Grantham ... Gino Cappelletti ... Len Dawson ... Lionel Taylor ... Charley Hennigan ... Curt Gowdy.

They, along with hundreds of others, are the faces of the American Football League.

Chapter One

The Hunt for a New Beginning

"HERE COME THE COLTS to the line of scrimmage. Unitas over the center ... the ball is snapped, given to Ameche. He is over for a touchdown! The Colts are the world champions!"

The National Football League's ascension to the status of the nation's number-one spectator sport began precisely at 4:51 P.M. Eastern Standard Time on December 28, 1958. It was at that moment that NBC-TV announcer Chuck Thompson described to a nationwide audience Baltimore fullback Alan "the Horse" Ameche lowering his helmet and galloping through the gathering darkness and the New York Giants defense and into the end zone.

The drama was telecast live via NBC-TV to an estimated 10,820,000 homes, and the suspense and excitement of pro football captured the imagination of millions.

In NFL terms, Ameche's touchdown meant paydirt in more ways than one. A national television audience sat spellbound as Colts quarterback John Unitas, his white uniform illuminated against the gray mist by the Yankee Stadium floodlights, displayed the resourcefulness of a riverboat gambler as he drove his team to the winning score. When Ameche followed a crunching block by Lenny Moore on a 1-yard blast over right tackle, the Colts had a 23–17 victory in the first overtime in NFL championship history.

Tex Maule, writing for *Sports Illustrated*, began his story with the statement "Never has there been a game like this one..." In its January 5, 1959 issue, the magazine's editors titled it "The Best Football Game Ever Played." In 1976, Dave Klein, a sportswriter for the Newark (N.J.) *Star-Ledger*, devoted a book to the Colts–Giants classic called *The Game of Their Lives*. In it, Klein wrote that the game's drama and excitement "grabbed the nation by the nape of the neck, and shook.... When it was finished, nothing about pro football would ever again be the same."

The sport hasn't been the same. The NFL today bears only a faint resemblance to the pro game that began in the turbulent 1920s, when it grew from the restlessness that marked the post–World War I era. Pro teams sprang up in small towns like Pine Valley, Pennsylvania, and Decatur, Illinois, and whetted the fans' appetite for excitement with the spirited play of pioneers like Johnny Blood and Jim Thorpe.

Pro football emerged from its sandlot surroundings on a muggy night in September 1920, when a dozen men congregated in an automobile showroom in Canton, Ohio. Relaxing on Hupmobile running boards, they organized the town teams into a league. Initially, they called themselves the American Professional Football League. A short time later, the organization was renamed the National Football League.

Through the 1940s and '50s, the NFL grew from small towns and sandlots to major cities and expansive stadiums. The New York Giants moved into majestic Yankee Stadium; the Los Angeles Rams made the 100,000-seat Memorial Coliseum their home. The NFL expanded, surviving challenges from three separate American Football Leagues and the All-America Football Conference. Until 1946, a trip west for NFL teams meant Chicago. But the relocation of the Rams from Cleveland to Los Angeles and the absorption of the AAFC's San Francisco 49ers made the NFL a "national" game.

Under the intelligent guidance of commissioner Bert Bell, the NFL made maximum use of America's emerging television industry. Televised road games kept fans in touch with their favorite teams, so that on any given Sunday fans could watch Otto Graham coolly directing the Browns' precision passing attack, or Bob Waterfield and Norm Van Brocklin riding herd on the Rams' record-setting offense, the most explosive in NFL history.

"Television has had the greatest impact on pro football, more than anything else over the years," Cleveland Browns founder Paul Brown once said. "Television is what made the game. Television sold it."

Brown knew firsthand the impact TV had on pro football. When the Browns joined the NFL in 1950 after dominating the AAFC for four years, Brown approached the Cleveland Gas and Electric Company and offered to sell them exclusive TV rights for $5,000. Company officials balked, but Brown eventually convinced them of the profit to be made.

"They gave me the money," Brown said later, "but it was more to humor me than anything else."

By the mid–50s, as TV cables crisscrossed the country, pro football's fan base crossed all social and economic lines. In Detroit, the top executives of the country's motor industry owned season tickets to Lions games; in Baltimore, blue-collar fans bedecked Memorial Stadium with bedsheets declaring their territory, "Colts Corral."

The 1958 sudden-death championship signaled the start of the game's modern era. The marriage of major network television and pro football, born that December day, continues to the present. In 1959, NBC paid the NFL $200,000 for the TV rights to the championship game. Just six years later, the price had increased 10 times, to $2 million. Television influenced the growth of the game's live attendance. In 1950, the NFL's live gate total for the season was 1,977,556, a per-game average of 25,353; by 1960, the draw had increased to 3,128,296, or an average attendance of 40,106.

"I'm not sure whether [the '58 championship] was the greatest game ever played," former Dallas Cowboys head coach Tom Landry said, "but there's no question in my mind that it marked the time, the game and the place where pro football really caught on, where public attention was aroused and brought the game into the spotlight it enjoys."

Through television, pro football entered the homes of every town in the country. As Tex Maule noted in his 1960 book *The Pros*, "TV makes today's superstars — the Giffords and Huffs, Unitases and Berrys — familiar to a nation."

It was just the beginning. As Maule noted at the time, "The prospects for the next ten years are overwhelming."

In most NFL cities that was perhaps true, but not in Chicago. Beginning with the NFL's inception in 1920, Chicago had fielded two NFL teams, the Bears and Cardinals. As the 1950s wore on, however, it became increasingly clear that despite the NFL's increasing popularity, Chicago could not support two teams. Headed by George Halas, the Bears remained Chicago's dominant team on the field and at the gate. In the late 1950s, rumors circulated that the Cardinals would be sold and the franchise moved, with Houston being one of the cities under consideration.

Among those interested in buying the Cardinals was Lamar Hunt, the 26-year-old son of millionaire Texas oilman Haroldson Lafayette Hunt, one of the country's wealthiest men. In 1954, *Texas Monthly* reported that H. L. Hunt was the richest man in the country, worth $2 billion, with an estimated after-tax income of $54 million. The *New York Times* described Hunt as one of the five richest men in the world. *Fortune* and *Life* magazines listed him as the second-wealthiest man in the nation, next to J. Paul Getty. But no less an authority than Getty himself disputed the notion.

"In terms of extraordinary, independent wealth," Getty said in a 1957 interview, "there is only one man — H. L. Hunt."

H. L. himself liked to scoff at such talk, trivializing it as "stuff and nonsense." He was conservative in dress and manner, given to wearing blue business suits, white shirts with blue bow ties, and brown-bagging his lunch. But he clearly enjoyed the rumors of his immense wealth. When meeting new acquaintances, the oilman with the tousled white hair and sparkling blue eyes would extend his hand, smile graciously and say, "I'm H. L. Hunt. Some people say I'm the richest man in the world, and some say I'm only the second richest."

The cornerstone for the Hunt family fortune was cut at midnight on November 26, 1930, when H. L. bought a series of oil leases from a prospector named "Dad" Joiner. Among them was a gusher called Deep Rock Well, and upon that Rock, the Hunt oil dynasty was founded.

Lamar Hunt as he appears today. A member of the Pro Football Hall of Fame, Hunt founded the American Football League in 1959 and remains one of the league's most influential owners. (*Photo courtesy of Lamar Hunt.*)

Lamar was born August 2, 1932, in a brownstone home in El Dorado, Arkansas, the sixth and youngest child of H. L. and his second wife, Lyda. Margaret, the couple's oldest child, was 17 years old when Lamar was born. Hunt said he "grew up playing football." When he wasn't participating in athletics, he was studying the sports pages of daily newspapers.

"I read the box scores and attendance figures," Hunt said. "I was always interested in attendance figures at sporting events."

After graduating from Hill School in Pottstown, Pennsylvania, where he played halfback and was captain of the varsity, Lamar enrolled as a geology major at Southern Methodist University. At SMU, he was a substitute offensive end behind Raymond Berry, who went on to a Hall of Fame career with the Colts. SMU coaches said later that no one on the squad worked harder and talked less than Hunt.

Lamar's famous surname exposed him to good-natured critiques, on and off the field. Around the campus, the son of the millionaire oil man was known as "Poor Boy." At practice, teammates would knock him down, extend a hand, smile and say, "Here, Poor Boy, let me help you up."

Lamar took the ribbing in stride, and because of his good nature, was a popular student at SMU. He spent three years on the varsity, but never received a football letter. After red-shirting as a sophomore Lamar could have stayed one more year and gained his letter, since fifth-year varsity players were traditionally given letters. But he declined to stay; it was against his beliefs to accept something he didn't earn.

After graduating from SMU in 1956, Lamar often joked he had actually received *two* football letters: "One inviting me to join the squad," he laughed, "the other inviting me to leave."

Having been born and raised in a family that not only watched football but won large sums of money betting on it, Lamar knew the varied benefits inherent in the game. The on-field action satisfied his competitive nature; the sport's growing popularity promised huge financial gains.

"The growth of the game," Hunt said in his modulated, midwestern tone, "the game as was then played by the National Football League, was just becoming a major factor in American sports."

Hunt saw the pro game as more than sport. It was a lucrative entertainment enterprise destined to expand with the country's population. It was his belief that football-hungry Dallas would eagerly support an NFL franchise. Lamar's quest to own an NFL team was spurred by a conversation with his older brother Bunker, when both men agreed the Southwest would support an NFL team.

As a student at SMU, Hunt had owned two sports businesses. He set up a batting cage operation—10 swings for a quarter. The business was a success, but Hunt's next venture, miniature golf courses, failed. "We expanded too fast," he explained. Two years after the demise of his miniature golf business, Hunt began his search to buy into an NFL franchise. The trust his father had established for him in 1935 assured Lamar of a financial base reported to be more than $500 million. That income allowed Lamar to remain, as he put it, "self-employed."

Hunt's confidence that pro football could survive in Dallas was supported by the enthusiastic crowds he saw at high school and college games he frequented. "I have always been a football nut," Hunt said, "and I felt that the city of Dallas, being my home, should have a pro football team. I just felt I had a good understanding of the entertainment world. It was a challenge and I think I had some good ideas."

Despite his desire to field an NFL team in Dallas, Hunt failed to impress NFL officials enough to seriously consider the matter. In his book *The $400,000 Quarterback*, author Bob Curran wrote, "Few had ever heard of Lamar and even fewer were impressed by what they saw and heard." When Hunt called Bell in 1958 to inquire about NFL expansion, he was told the league was "not interested."

With his quiet personality, modest build, and thick, dark-rimmed glasses, the 6-foot, 175-pound Hunt was described by one observer as a ringer for Wally Cox, the mild-mannered star of *Mr. Peepers*, a TV show in the 1950s. Hunt was understated in dress as well; some would say frugal. He favored blue blazers and conservative ties. When he relaxed and propped his feet up, an associate was startled to see holes in both of the millionaire's shoes. The 1960 *AFL Press Guide* described Hunt as a man who "can be overlooked in the smallest gathering."

One thing about Hunt that was never overlooked was his personal integrity. Billy Sullivan, the founder of the Boston Patriots, once called Hunt "the cornerstone, the integrity of the AFL." Sullivan recalled league meetings in which Hunt would vote on proposals that helped the league, even if they didn't benefit Hunt's team, the Kansas City Chiefs. Hunt rarely swears, and when he does, *damn* is the strongest off-color word in his vocabulary. He doesn't drink, and once startled onlookers when he took a taste of champagne in a postgame locker room celebration following a championship game win.

Despite his mild manner, Lamar owned the same inner drive that marked his father's career. When friends of H. L. would remark, with a mixture of wonder and envy, that he was determined to do what he wanted to do, they could have been describing Lamar as well.

"I don't know what part of this is business and what part is personal," Hunt said in 1960. "I just know it is very important that I succeed."

Symbolic of his motivation to succeed on his own was Hunt's style of signature. A Dallas graphologist named Connie Gilmore noted in *D* magazine that the *L* in Lamar's first name was much larger than the *H* in Hunt. "The fact that the 'L' is much larger than the 'H' shows that he wants the recognition to be directed at him personally," Gilmore wrote, "disassociated from any laurels tied to the family name or heritage."

"He's emerging from the shadow of his father," a friend of Lamar's noted, "and he likes it."

Harry Hurt III, who authored a book on the Hunt family called *Texas Rich*, said Lamar's appearance masked his great ambition. "Those who dealt with Lamar firsthand," Hurt wrote, "quickly realized that he had much more going for him than his last name and his trust fund. Lamar was proving himself a shrewd and insightful businessman, a dreamer who could make his dreams become reality."

Texas Monthly called Lamar the "most preoccupied of the Hunt brothers, the one who is always off in his own world ... determined to make a name for himself apart from his family."

In 1959, Lamar Hunt was on the verge of not only making a name for himself, but changing the course of pro football history.

Chapter Two

New Frontiers

LAMAR HUNT RECOGNIZED clearly the plight of the Chicago Cardinals franchise. The team was a financial drain on the Wolfner family and a public embarrassment to the NFL. A relocation to the Southwest, Hunt believed, would solve both problems.

"It was widely known that the Cardinals were for sale," Hunt says now. "Bert Bell had put me in touch with the Cardinal owners, and with there being two teams in Chicago, there was interest in the NFL in moving the Cardinal franchise."

NFL owners cringed when they heard of Hunt's plan to buy the team and move it to Dallas. Memories of the last NFL franchise to call Dallas its home, the Texans, were all too vivid. The Texans went 1-11 in 1952 and finished the season on the road because of a lack of fan support. At season's end, the team was relocated to Baltimore and renamed the Colts.

Walter Wolfner himself wasn't above moving the Cardinals to another city, but he rejected the idea of selling controlling interest in the team. At the same time Wolfner was negotiating with Hunt, offers to buy the Cardinals were made by Kenneth S. "Bud" Adams, who was interested in moving the team to Houston, and Bob Howsam and Max Winter, who owned and operated sports franchises in Denver and Minneapolis, respectively.

Like Hunt, Adams was a Texas millionaire. The flamboyant, 38-year-old son of "Boots" Adams, the chairman of the Phillips Petroleum Company, Bud had founded the Ada Oil Company. Solidly built and quick to turn a phrase, Adams' passions included football, black cowboy hats, and full-length, white leather coats. His Houston office featured a barbecue pit, lily pond, and a desk one writer described as "long as a bowling alley."

Wolfner held firm in his negotiations with perspective investors. The most he would sell, he said, was a 49 percent share in the team. Unable to secure a controlling interest in the Cardinals, Hunt, Adams, and Howsam approached NFL commissioner Bert Bell on the question of NFL expansion. Like Hunt and Adams, Bell was a man of inherited wealth. But he turned his back on high society to devote time to his one overriding passion — pro football.

Elected commissioner in 1946, Bell successfully piloted the NFL through its draining financial war with the AAFC in the '40s. When the bidding for top collegiate players threatened to bankrupt both leagues, Bell stepped in and provided the lone voice of reason. His skillful negotiations helped the NFL survive, but he remained wary of further expansion, and told both Hunt and Adams the NFL was "not interested" in fielding new franchises.

With his dream of owning an NFL franchise seemingly over, Hunt boarded a plane in Miami, the sight of his final meeting with Wolfner, to head back to Texas. It was on that return flight home that Hunt hit upon the idea of forming a new league.

"On my return trip to Dallas," Hunt says, "the thought did occur to me that the Cardinal owners had asked me if I knew Bud Adams of Houston. All of a sudden it was like you see in the cartoons where a lightbulb comes on over a guy's head. It occurred to me that if all these people were trying to do the same thing I was, we could join together and form a new league."

At that moment, the American Football League was conceived.

"That was one of the few times in my life that I felt something like that," Hunt said. "The idea just came. I thought, 'Why not start another professional football league? Why wouldn't a second league work? All the basic information I needed had been supplied [by Walter Wolfner] in the four or five months we had tried to negotiate a sale. They had dropped the names of ... a bunch of people on the outside wanting in.... Why not start a new league? I had several motivations for forming a new league. I felt the city of Dallas should have a pro football team, Dallas being my home."

In Hunt's negotiations with Wolfner, the Cardinal executive disclosed that several others had been interested in purchasing the team and relocating it. Wolfner's casual disclosure spurred Hunt's idea of starting a new league.

Hunt's first step in forming a new league was to establish a cornerstone rivalry. He knew the NFL thrived on regional rivalries, like Giants–Browns in the Northeast, Packers–Bears in the Midwest, and Rams–49ers in the far West. Hunt thought a Dallas–Houston rivalry in the Southwest could form the cornerstone of his league. A phone call was placed to Adams, and the pair held their first meeting over lunch in March, 1959, at Adams' Charcoal Inn restaurant in Houston.

"We had a couple hours of conversation," Hunt recalled, "all one-on-one." Afterwards, the two men climbed into the back of Adams' chauffeur-driven limousine for the trip to Hunt's hotel. Throughout the initial meeting, Hunt had not mentioned his plans to form a new pro football league.

"We just talked about our attempts to get a pro team," Hunt said. "I never mentioned the new league, but during the conversation I became sure Adams was the man for a Houston franchise."

Gradually, Hunt broached the subject, giving a vague outline of what the new league would be like and being careful to point out the large role a Houston team would have in the league's makeup. Finally, Hunt asked Adams the question that had been on his mind for days.

"If I could get people in four other cities to sponsor teams in another professional football league, would you come in?"

"Hell, yes!" Adams roared.

Two factors prompted Adams' eager approval. The first was Hunt's belief that a Dallas–Houston rivalry would be the focal point in the league's development. The second was founded on Adams' frustration in trying to bring an NFL franchise to Texas. Like Hunt, Adams had met with Wolfner to discuss the sale of the Cardinals. Adams says today:

> I had been trying to buy the Cardinals, and I was not successful. I had talked to Mr. Bert Bell and he was under the impression that if I wanted to be in the NFL I would have to buy into a team. He said there wouldn't be any expansion. That's when I started talking with the Chicago Cardinals [management].
>
> I met with Mrs. Bidwill and Wolfner a couple of times, and we came to an agreement on price. The deal was I could move the team from Chicago to Houston and I would be president of the club.
>
> The problem was they wanted to keep 51 percent control of the club, and they would give me 49 percent. In February of 1959, we held our last meeting. I couldn't get them to put up an equal number of shares in the club, and that broke off the negotiations.

The addition of Adams to the new league was an important first step. Like Hunt, Adams had a solid background in sports; he had lettered in football at Culver Military Academy, Menlo College, and the University of Kansas. Following service as a U.S. Navy Air Force engineering officer in World War II, Adams went to Houston and though just in his 20s, founded the Ada Oil Company. He formed the Adams Petroleum Corporation and now owns the Adams Petroleum Center. Through the years, Adams' involvement in pro sports grew to include baseball — he was one of the original owners of the Houston Astros — basketball, and boxing.

Football, however, remains his primary sporting interest. "I played high school and college football and was a running back, really a blocking back, and a safety," Adams says. "So I knew the Southwest was a hotbed for football. And it looked to me like pro football would really go in the Southwest. I thought Houston would be a great place for a football team."

With Adams in the fold, Hunt turned his attention to Howsam and Winter. Since the 1940s, when their family business switched from beekeeping to sports, the Howsams were obsessed with the idea of bringing a sports franchise to Denver. By 1958, 39-year-old Bob Howsam was the son-in-law of Senator Edwin H. Johnson of Colorado. A civic leader himself, Howsam was the most notable figure on the Denver sports scene. As such, he represented Rocky Mountain Sports Enterprise, Inc. At the time the group was known mostly for operating what was widely regarded as the most successful minor-league baseball franchise in the country. Howsam had first gained control of the Bears in 1949, when they were members of the Class A Western League. During the next

12 years, Howsam was able to improve the team to such a degree that the Bears went from Class A to Class AAA, and Howsam was twice named minor-league Executive of the Year.

It was baseball, not football, that fueled the fire in the Howsams' passion for sports. The family owned the Denver Bears of the Pacific Coast League and were hoping to gain a franchise in Branch Rickey's proposed Continental League. Rickey, together with Howsam and New York-based attorney William Shea, was part of a group of wealthy businessmen whose dream was to make the Continental League a third major baseball league.

Howsam spent $500,000 to increase the seating in 12-year-old Bears Stadium by 8,100 seats. At the time of renovation, Bears Stadium was a bowl-shaped structure built into a natural land formation not more than five minutes from downtown Denver. One visitor termed Bears Stadium "the center of the metropolitan area." With baseball being the big show in town, Bears Stadium routinely sold out its 17,500-seat capacity.

Howsam's stadium additions included a new east wing added to the playing field and the 8,100 additional seats in the south stands. Eventually, the Howsams' plans to join the Continental League fell apart. Major-league baseball expanded, but the forces that pushed for a third league were induced to become part of the expansion plans; the cities that were envisaged as housing Continental League teams — New York, Los Angeles, San Francisco, and Atlanta — became part of the new major-league baseball map.

Missing from that map, however, was Denver; the Bears would remain a minor-league team. What was worse was the Bears' reduced fan base. The team's attendance slipped from a high of 500,000 to just 209,783 in 1960. Spurned by major-league baseball and the NFL, saddled with the costly improvements of a newly renovated stadium and a faltering baseball empire, Howsam turned an attentive ear to Hunt and his plans for a new pro football league.

"If I get commitments from other cities," Hunt asked Howsam, "would you come along?"

Howsam agreed, and Hunt now had three cities committed to the new league. A fourth soon followed. Recalling the names of those whom Bell had said were interested in owning a pro football franchise, Hunt contacted Max Winter in Minneapolis. Onetime owner of the Minneapolis Lakers of the National Basketball Association, Winter had been part of a group of investors who had been unsuccessful in attempting to lure the Cardinals to Metropolitan Stadium in Bloomington, a suburb of Minneapolis. Among those included in this adventure was Bill Boyer, a Minneapolis auto dealer. Unsuccessful in their negotiations with Wolfner, the group then applied for an NFL franchise. Snubbed a second time, Winter, Boyer, and Company welcomed Hunt's offer to buy into his league.

"I was trying to recruit people," Hunt said. "I went to Denver and Minneapolis. Nobody turned us down, so now we had four cities. The original thought was to field a six-team league and include New York and Los Angeles. You needed them from an image standpoint."

Hunt knew the difficulties in gaining a new foothold for football in New York. The Giants were one of the most popular teams in the NFL. Hunt sought out William Shea, who represented the AAFC New York Yankees. At the time of Hunt's overture, Shea was still involved in the idea of a Continental Baseball League and was seeking financing for a new stadium project in New York City's Flushing Meadows. A veteran of the NFL-AAFC wars, Shea had no love for the NFL. He also saw the need for a part-time tenant for his new stadium project. For these two reasons, Shea suggested Hunt talk to a friend of his, Harry Wismer.

Unlike most of his fellow owners, Wismer was already a well-known member of the national sports scene. As a student at Michigan State University, Wismer began his broadcasting career as a public address announcer for the Detroit Lions. He followed that with a daily program on Detroit radio station WJY, where he became known as the "Lions' Cub Reporter." Soon after, Wismer became director of sports at ABC.

By the mid-'50s, Wismer was one of the nation's leading sportscasters; in 1957, he did the play-by-play for the NFL title game, the NFL Pro Bowl game and the Sugar Bowl. In golf, he covered the Masters Tournament and the U.S. Open. Backing up his TV duties with radio commentary, Wismer broadcast Notre Dame and Washington Redskins football games, and handled a five-minute spot on the Mutual Radio Network.

Wismer's staccato announcing style produced some detractors. Jimmy Cannon, the late sportswriter, once wrote that Wismer announced football games "like a holdup victim hollering for a cop." Wismer's excitability sometimes got him into trouble. On one occasion, he announced a runner going from the 50 to the 55-yard line.

A onetime stockholder in the Lions, Wismer in 1959 held a 26 percent share of the Redskins. Knowing full well Wismer's diverse talents, Hunt spiced his offer of team ownership with a role in the new league's public relations as well. After Wismer agreed to head a New York-based franchise, Hunt asked him to "generate publicity" for the new league, a request Hunt would regret in coming years.

Following his meetings with Wismer, Hunt contacted Barron Hilton. The second of hotel magnate Conrad Hilton's three sons, Barron was vice-president of the Hilton Hotels Corporation and director of Carte Blanche, the Hilton's credit card subsidiary. Hilton's notoriety to that point stemmed from once having had Elizabeth Taylor as a sister-in-law and Zsa Zsa Gabor as a stepmother. But Barron had quietly made a name for himself in the financial world, turning a $25,000 investment in a citrus products firm into a $6 million profit. Hilton's Air Finance Corporation, which began operations in 1956, leased Electra

Jets to Pacific Southwest Airlines, and Barron also had financial interests in the MacDonald Oil Corporation, which in 1960 operated 130 producing wells.

Hilton was recommended to Hunt by Gene Mako. A former tennis star, Mako was a friend of the Hunt family, and when Lamar arrived in Los Angeles, Mako introduced Hilton to Hunt. An outdoorsman, Hilton's main sporting interests focused on hunting and fishing. The hotel heir's contact with football was limited mostly to time spent on the bench watching the Texas School of Mines football team. "I didn't know a field goal," Hilton said, "from a three o'clock checkout."

"He really didn't know a lot about football," Hunt says, "but within an hour, Barron was committed to the idea of a new league."

In early June, Hunt met with Washington Redskins owner George Marshall, the chairman of the NFL's expansion committee. The meeting lasted some 90 minutes, during which time Hunt listened as Marshall detailed the reasons why widespread expansion was not on the NFL agenda. Shortly thereafter, Hunt met with Bell. In a loud, rumbling voice that one acquaintance described as "frog-like," the NFL commissioner repeated the party line. Echoing Marshall, Bell told Hunt the NFL had no plans for expansion, least of all in Dallas, a city Bell said was "out of the question."

Hunt could have taken some delight from the NFL's stand on expansion. If NFL owners were true to their word, Hunt's new league would go unchallenged in the majority of their cities. Intent on maintaining good relations with the NFL, Hunt hit upon the idea of hiring Bell to act as a joint commissioner for both the NFL and AFL, a setup similar to major-league baseball, in which separate leagues operate under one commissioner. While Hunt would later characterize his thinking as "naive," he felt such a situation could prevent future warring between the leagues.

To act as a go-between, Hunt chose his friend Davey O'Brien, a onetime football star at Texas Christian University who had gone on to become a dealer in oil-drilling equipment. O'Brien was close to both Hunt and Bell; he had worked for H. L. in the oil business and played quarterback for Bell when the latter was coach of the Eagles in the late '30s.

"Davey O'Brien acted as an emissary for me," Hunt says. "He was a great quarterback who had played for Bell and he went and talked to Bell about serving as commissioner for the new league."

After getting O'Brien to agree to act as a third party, Hunt cautioned him to be discreet in his dealings with Bell. "There's a problem here, Davey," Hunt said. "You can't divulge the names of the other men involved."

O'Brien didn't, but when he phoned Hunt two weeks later to report on his meetings, he said that while Bell had dismissed the idea of a joint commissioner, he had spoken confidently of the new league's chances of success.

Given time to reconsider the matter, Hunt expected Bell's response. "It was an extremely naive idea to think Bert could serve both leagues as commissioner," Hunt admits. "I had figured that if major-league baseball operated under one commissioner, pro football could too."

Bell's tone with O'Brien was conciliatory. The commissioner told O'Brien the NFL had no desire to expand, and went so far as to invite him and a representative of the league to meet with him in Washington. Bell arrived in the nation's capital in July 1959 to testify before a Senate Anti-Monopoly Subcommittee investigating the NFL's seeming monopoly of pro football. Bell was there to prove the NFL innocent of monopolistic practices and keep the Anti-Trust Division of the federal government out of the league's business.

To assure the committee that the NFL was not monopolistic, Bell asked Hunt if he could reveal publicly that a new football league was being formed. Hunt named the six cities involved in the new league, and the contacts he had made. But he cautioned Bell not to go public with the names of his contacts, since no one had actually put up any money yet. Hunt was also uncertain whether Wismer and Hilton were really committed to the league.

Hunt and Wismer headed to Washington for the Congressional committee hearings, and they listened as Bell pleaded the NFL's case. It wasn't long before he divulged the information Hunt had given him.

"I want to tell you fellows about this new league, which would field eight or nine teams," he began. Bell named the six cities already involved, and told his listeners he was "all for the league and would help nurture it."

The next day, newspapers across the country headlined Bell's bombshell announcement. In Washington the story was considered front-page news.

"The news created an incredible stir," Hunt said. "This was the turning point for us. Our plans were out in the open. There could be no turning back."

Bell's testimony brought Hunt's fledgling league out of the closet and to the attention of the public. Hunt moved quickly to capitalize on his public relations boom. Within a week of Bell's testimony, Hunt was on the phone with Adams and the two men agreed to formerly announce the new league at a press conference in Adam's Houston office on August 2, the day of Hunt's twenty-seventh birthday. Nine days had passed since Bell's testimony when Hunt and Adams appeared before a media gathering of some 30 sportswriters to say that Houston was one of six cities involved, and the others would be named soon.

Hunt was now spending less time in his office in the Dallas Mercantile Bank Building and more time traveling coast-to-coast in his efforts to line up financial backers for the league. His hectic schedule often forced him to spend nights sleeping in airport lounges. Following a flurry of long-distance phone calls, it was decided by team owners to hold their first league meeting on August 14 at Chicago's Conrad Hilton Hotel. For the majority owners, it offered an opportunity to meet face-to-face for the first time. Apart from that, the talks held by Hunt, Adams, Howsam, Hilton, Wismer, and the Minneapolis troika of Winter, Boyer, and H. P. Skoglund yielded only one bit of official news: league play would officially begin in the fall of 1960.

Team nicknames were soon assigned. Dallas became the Texans, for obvious reasons. Houston was named the Oilers, Adams said, "for sentimental and social reasons." It was also because free-flowing oil was the primary reason Adams was in a position to start his own team. The Denver franchise became the Broncos, symbolizing the rugged nature of the American West. The New York team was named the Titans, because as Wismer said, "Titans are larger than Giants." In Los Angeles, Gerald Courtney of Hollywood submitted the nickname *Chargers* in a name-the-team contest and won a trip to Mexico. Hilton approved the moniker because of its various implications, not the least of which was a close identification with the new Hilton Carte Blanche charge card. The name was symbolized by a jagged bolt of lightning and a charging horse, and became instrumental in designing the team's uniforms.

For the fourth time in pro football history, an American Football League had been founded. To those who questioned Hunt's boldness in establishing a new pro league, it was simply a case of following the practices shaping pro sports at the time.

After half a century of sameness, baseball had become static. In 1953 the Boston Braves migrated to Milwaukee and the St. Louis Browns headed to Baltimore. In 1954 the Philadelphia Athletics moved to Kansas City. In 1958 New York was stunned by two franchise shifts — the Giants to San Francisco and the Dodgers to Los Angeles. In the '60s baseball welcomed three new franchises: the New York Mets, the Los Angeles Angels, and the Minnesota Twins.

Baseball set the tone for westward expansion in sports; Hunt and his colleagues were following the pattern. Joe Durso, a sportswriter for the *New York Times* in the 1960s, said Hunt's new league was merely a sign of the times. "[Hunt's] idea," said Durso, "which may have seemed radical at the time to some souls, actually was merely an expansion of the game of musical chairs that was taking hold in sports. The aim in all cases was to mine gold.... Hunt arrived just as a whole new frontier was being opened up to the gold rush: the upper Middle West."

New frontiers, yes; but for Hunt and his partners, what the new markets offered most of all was a new start.

Chapter Three

Founding the Foolish Club

POOR TIMING, MANAGEMENT, and attendance had combined to finish off the three previous American Football Leagues. Lamar Hunt felt he could avoid the first two, and the financial growth of the NFL in the 1950s allowed him to dismiss the third. In 1950, close to two million fans paid their way into NFL stadiums. By the end of the decade, the number of spectators at NFL games had grown to more than three million.

With fan support at an all-time high, with NFL commissioner Bert Bell's new television contract guaranteeing a hefty amount of added revenue — he established a TV "blackout" code that permitted only road games to be televised to home cities unless all tickets had been sold in advance — the NFL's financial gain for the '60s looked to be unlimited.

In his autobiography, Chicago Bears owner George Halas recalled the NFL's outlook at the beginning of the 1960s. "After thirty years, professional football was becoming a ... year-round business.... The prospect of big money from television brightened. Promoters and enthusiasts took new interest."

Still, Halas sounded a note of pessimism when he said the NFL was "vulnerable" to pro football's expansionists. Halas could see the growth of the game would lead to new markets. "I argued that football would spread into new cities," Halas said, "and past experience had shown the best course would be to have the growth come within the league."

Why, then, did Bell issue his support of Lamar Hunt's new league in the summer of '59? The implications of yet another challenger to the NFL were not lost on the commissioner. Still fresh in Bell's mind was the financial war engaged in 10 years earlier with the AAFC. Hunt's partners were wealthier than the AFC bosses, and Bell must have foreseen the coming clashes for territorial rights and college players.

Part of the reason for Bell's public support for the new league lay in his desire to free the NFL from a difficult legal situation. In 1959, the league was being investigated by a U.S. Senate subcommittee for antitrust violations. From Bell's standpoint, the arrival of Hunt's league could not have come at a more fortuitous time for the NFL. By openly embracing a direct competitor, Bell hoped to show the Senate that the NFL was not guilty of any federal violations.

Hunt understood this perfectly — more so than Bell's own brethren in the NFL, who, upon hearing the August 14 announcement of a new pro football league, immediately began a campaign of divide and conquer. Privately, Bell squelched dissent among club owners over his "peace pipe" policy with Hunt as he had done in the past, insisting things be done his way or he would resign.

Had Bell not been so popular among the owners, they might have held the door wide open for him. But his successful negotiations to end the AAFC way and eliminate a major competitor, his skillful handling of a gambling scandal in 1946, and his far-sighted TV blackout code had some observers speaking of him in reverent tones.

In his 1967 book *Touchdown*, a pictorial history of the AFL's early years, author Bob Curran wrote: "In thirteen years, Bell had done for the league what Kenesaw Landis, consciously, and Babe Ruth, unconsciously, did for baseball; and Bell had emerged from his ordeal more popular than Ruth and more respected than Landis."

While Bell sought to avoid open hostilities, factions within the NFL were carrying out their own war plans, aimed at isolating and undermining franchises in Hunt's league. The first shots in the new war were fired in early August by Halas. Arriving in Houston for an NFL exhibition game that Oilers founder Bud Adams was sponsoring, Halas, who was chairman of the NFL's Committee on Expansion, arranged to meet with Adams to discuss the AFL.

"The NFL almost went under in the forties with the All-American League," Adams says. "A lot of NFL teams were on the ropes financially back then. When I met with Mr. Halas, he was ready to give Houston an NFL franchise in 1960, for $650,000. I said, 'I gave my word to Lamar, and I can't go back on it.'"

At the same time he was feeling the pressure from Halas, Adams was being squeezed from the other side by Craig Cullinan of the Houston Sports Association. Cullinan called Adams on the phone and pleaded with him not to make any commitments to Hunt's league. Any temptation Adams may have felt about gaining an NFL franchise was cooled by a call he received from Max Winter in Minneapolis. When word spread that NFL representatives were playing the role of "block-busters" and that Adams was a prime target, Winter wasted no time in placing a call to Houston.

When Adams got on the phone, Winter's message was brief and to the point. "If you pull out," Winter said, "the whole thing will fold up."

To men like Hunt and Adams, the NFL's motives were readily apparent. "The idea was to get a couple of teams to bolt the AFL," Adams says, "so that the league would fold."

Similar tactics were being brought into play on other fronts. In Los Angeles, two officials of the Rams front office contacted Barron Hilton. Their offer was simple. Drop out of the AFL and become a shareholder in an NFL franchise. Ed Pauley, who owned stock in the Rams, invited Hunt to be his guest at a Rams–49ers exhibition game that summer. Hunt obliged, and the two men sat in the early summer heat watching stars like Hugh McElhenny and Ollie Matson perform on the field below. But when Pauley tried to dangle an NFL franchise in front of him, Hunt stiffened. He asked Pauley about the fate of his partners who had taken a financial gamble to form a new league. The NFL, said Pauley, was only interested in Dallas and Houston.

Hunt told Pauley it was a matter of honor. He had given his word to his partners, and there would be no turning back. "I cannot pull out now," Hunt said.

Halas warned NFL owners that the AFL was going to be trouble. Hunt, he said, had already started along the "dangerous, costly road" pioneered by the AAFC. Hunt was a "formidable rival," whose oil money "gave him a rare ability to absorb losses for a long time and to support other teams."

When Pauley relayed Hunt's message, NFL owners decided to go ahead with their own expansion. In Houston on Saturday, August 29, one week to the day after the AFL had been established, Halas called a press conference to announce that Dallas and Houston were being recommended for membership in the NFL and would begin operations in 1961. The Bears owner then produced a list of cities that the expansion committee was considering as potential hosts for NFL teams. The names were staggering: Minneapolis, Boston, Buffalo, Miami, Louisville, Denver, and New Orleans, or just about every AFL city.

Details of the NFL press conference stunned AFL owners. In Dallas, the normally mild-mannered Hunt was having trouble containing his rage. He heard the news on his car radio while driving home and quickly placed a call to Bell.

"This is an effort to sabotage us that will be apparent to 170 million people," Hunt charged.

The NFL commissioner brushed off Hunt's protests. "What can I do?" he asked. "They want to expand, how can I stop them?"

Bell didn't stay on the defensive for long. The next day, Sunday, August 30, the vacationing commissioner met the press in Atlantic City. "Nobody owns any city in this country," Bell said. "Any place is fair territory for our league, the second league and, if there's a third league, for it, too. That's what the antitrust laws provide."

It was beyond him, Bell said, why Hunt was disturbed at the expansion plans. "They're going into New York and Los Angeles," he said. "We have teams there but we didn't complain. Pro football is expanding to all parts of the country and there's room for everybody."

Hunt repeated his charge that the NFL wanted to sabotage his league. "It's pretty obvious to everybody," Hunt said, "and not just by this action but by several others, too. In our other cities they've tried some undercover tactics."

Despite the attempt by some NFL owners to break up the new league, Hunt still had hope that an all-out war could be averted. But on October 11, while watching a Steelers–Eagles game from the grandstands of Philadelphia's Franklin Field, Bell suffered a heart attack and died that same day. Hunt was saddened by the news, as much from a personal standpoint as a business one. Realizing that Bell represented pro football's best hope of peaceful coexistence between the leagues, Hunt said later that when Bell died, "the ball game blew up."

"I always felt," Hunt said, "Bell would've given us a fair shake."

While Hunt lamented Bell's untimely death, events soon demanded that he turn his attention to other matters. Hunt had a letter from Ralph C. Wilson, Jr., who had made millions in the trucking and insurance businesses, and in 1959 owned a minority share of the Detroit Lions. Wilson had first learned of the new AFL after reading about the league in New York newspapers. Wilson sat down and penned a note, only half expecting, he said later, to get a reply. But Hunt did reply, and the two men agreed to meet at Wilson's summer home in Miami.

Today, Wilson recalls how he first became involved with the AFL. "I've always been interested in football," Wilson says, "and I was up in Saratoga, New York, where I used to rent a house, when I read in the *New York Times* where a young man named Lamar Hunt was starting a new league. At that time I was living in Detroit, and I owned stock in the Lions."

Wilson's interest in the sport traced back to his childhood. As a boy, he had spent autumn afternoons accompanying his father to Detroit Lion football games. The Lions of Wilson's youth featured an unstoppable rushing offense that ground its way to an NFL title in 1935 and in 1936 set a league record for yards gained that stood until the Miami Dolphins broke it in 1972.

"I was an avid fan in the early part of my teens," Wilson said. "I could see the interest developing in professional football in the days of Leon Hart, Bobby Layne, and Doak Walker. We could see how popular the sport was becoming."

Wilson later bought a minority share of the Lions, but his real dream was to put a pro football franchise in Miami, where he owned a second home. In 1946, the AAFC had fielded a Miami franchise, the Seahawks. The Seahawks finished last in their division, winning just three of 14 games. Miami's largest home crowd in 1946 was just 9,700; their smallest a mere 2,250.

The situation was so bleak that head coach Jack Meagher bolted the team after six games. When the season mercifully ended, the AAFC was forced to pay $61,000 in player salaries and $19,000 more to United Air Lines. With that, the Seahawks were disbanded, but the dreadful memory of the team lingered in the minds of Miamians. Other cities could keep pro football and the raucous Sunday afternoons in autumn. The University of Miami brought the city to life in the fall. Wrote one observer, "The scene there on a game night is much the way it is in New York or Chicago on a Sunday afternoon when the Giants and Bears are hot, and one of the lucky ticket-holders considers the players his friends and the coaching his second business."

It wasn't surprising that Wilson and Hunt failed to make an impression on the city fathers when they met with them in Miami that August and discussed the possibility of establishing an AFL team there. University officials told the two men that the thought of pro football returning to Miami did not interest them. It would weaken the caliber of the University's football program, they said. Miami could not maintain the status of the college game in the face of competition from a professional team.

"The people in Miami didn't want to be involved in starting up a new league," remembers Wilson. "They had a bad experience with the AAFC, and they didn't want to go through that again."

Two days after their return from Miami, Hunt had Wilson on the phone. "We have six teams," Hunt said, "but we can't operate with that number. We need two more."

Hunt read the names of five cities he thought were prime candidates for membership in the AFL: Kansas City, Louisville, Cincinnati, St. Louis, and Buffalo.

"Pick one," Hunt said. The thought of starting a team in a city with which he had no connection did not appeal to Wilson. But Hunt persisted, and Wilson placed a call to Nick Kerbawy, a friend of his who had been general manager of the Lions. Wilson gave Kerbawy the names of the five cities Hunt had listed.

"Which one," Wilson asked Kerbawy, "would you take?"

To Kerbawy, the choice was clear. "Take Buffalo," he said.

Wilson chuckles when he remembers the turn of events that led to his picking Buffalo.

"Now, I had never been to Buffalo. But it turned out to be a very good sports town."

Wilson met with Paul Neville, managing editor of the *Buffalo Evening News*. Neville told him of the city's enthusiastic support of the AAFC Bills. The Bills' best season was 1948, when they beat Baltimore in a playoff game before losing to Cleveland in the championship.

Just as important as the team's success on the field was its success financially. In 1947, the Bills' average attendance was 31,099. When the Bills hosted the Browns that same year, a club-record 43,167 packed the stadium.

Buffalo's love affair with football predated the AAFC and the Bills. In 1921, a team known as the Buffalo All-Americans was part of the American Professional Football League, the forerunner of the NFL. Buffalo was a football town, and when the AAFC merged with the NFL in 1949, Bills fans wrote to Bell begging that their team be allowed to enter the NFL as a unit, in the same fashion as the Browns, the 49ers and the Colts. Noting the city's financial hardships, Bell declined to extend invitation to the Bills. Buffalo reacted by organizing a drive to raise money.

In just 24 hours, the citizens' drive raised $177,600, selling stock to those who felt Buffalo could become a great NFL city. Gene Ward of the *New York Daily News* sent Bell a petition signed by 25,000 Buffalo football fans — each one promising to buy a season ticket. The commissioner was impressed with the citizens' action, but in January of 1950, Bell turned Buffalo down.

When Wilson arrived in Buffalo in the summer of 1959, he asked Neville to show him War Memorial Stadium. Wilson knew the value of good publicity, and if Neville was behind it, an AFL team had a chance of surviving in Buffalo. On the return trip from the stadium, Wilson told the newsman, "I'll give the city a team for three years, if you'll support me."

Buffalo's mayor and city council showed its support by voting to increase the seating capacity of War Memorial Stadium from 22,500 to 36,500. Wilson phoned Hunt. "Count me in with Buffalo," he said.

With seven teams now in the AFL, club owners took up the business of filling their rosters. The first official college draft was held in November in Minneapolis. Presiding over it was Frank Leahy, the legendary ex–Notre Dame football coach, who was working for Barron Hilton's Los Angeles team.

Leahy was instrumental in helping the city of Boston break into pro football. William H. Sullivan Jr. had been lobbying unsuccessfully for an NFL franchise. The sports information director at Boston College from 1938 to 1941, Sullivan worked alongside Leahy when the latter coached BC to the Cotton and Sugar Bowls. When Leahy was hired by Notre Dame in 1941, Sullivan went along too, but not for long. With the outbreak of war, Sullivan entered the navy in 1942. By 1945 he was a member of the Naval Academy's football staff. From 1946 to 1952, Sullivan was public relations director for the Boston Braves baseball team, and in 1955 became assistant to the president at Metropolitan Coal and Oil Company. Some 34 months later, Sullivan became company president.

In 1959, Sullivan headed a 10-man syndicate determined to bring pro football to Boston. Among those involved with Sullivan was Dom DiMaggio, former outfielder for the Red Sox.

It was said of Sullivan that he had a remarkable record of getting Bostonians to do things they didn't want to do. With Sullivan's powers of persuasion at work on finding a stadium for his team, AFL owners, though they had never actually met him, gave Sullivan the green light to proceed with the franchise.

As the date for the AFL draft drew closer, Halas contacted Hunt and offered him 50 percent of the NFL's new Dallas franchise. Hunt turned down the deal:

> We'd conditioned everything in the AFL on the fact that everyone was a partner. I'd gone out and solicited these people to become part of the new league. Anything we did would have to take them all into consideration. That wasn't in the NFL's thinking.
>
> [The NFL] didn't want individuals, necessarily. They wanted cities. There

was some talk that Bud could have Houston, I could have Dallas, and Barron could possibly be brought into the Rams' ownership.

Of the NFL's tactics to target certain AFL owners and offer them franchises, Adams says now: "They were trying to break up the AFL. They figured if they could get two of eight teams [to leave the AFL] the whole league would break up. Mr. Halas tried very hard to persuade us not to start this new league. He said it would be very costly and wouldn't be very good for pro football."

In October, the NFL offered Hunt another olive branch. Clint W. Murchison, Jr., a 35-year-old East Texas millionaire oilman whose father had begun the family fortune with the region's oil boom in the heart of the Great Depression, was heading the Cowboys franchise. Involved with Murchison in the Cowboys was another Texas tycoon, Bedford Wynne, the son of Angus Wynne, who built his wealth through real estate, cattle, and oil dealings.

In a meeting initiated by Stewart Hunt, a man who was both Lamar's cousin and a distant relative of Clint's, Murchison made Hunt a surprising offer.

"Look," Murchison said, "I'll get out completely. My main goal is to see that Dallas gets an NFL team. Lamar, you take it. But you've got to take the NFL franchise."

"I said I couldn't [accept it]," remembers Hunt. "We were committed to the AFL people, and they were committed to us. We just couldn't pull out."

Still hoping for a settlement, Murchison asked Hunt to accompany him to New York, where the two men would meet with Colts owner Carroll Rosenbloom. Rosenbloom was willing to talk expansion with Hunt, but wouldn't one franchise be enough for both the Dallas and Houston areas?

Hunt remained firm in his stand. Over the next two weeks, the principal figures of the two leagues met twice. In Los Angeles the Saturday after his meeting with Rosenbloom, Hunt and Halas met before a Bears–Rams game. Hunt repeated his demand that all of the AFL's franchises be accepted into the NFL. Halas said the NFL had no interest in fielding new teams in New York, Los Angeles, and Denver. The stalemate continued three days later in Chicago. Hunt, Adams, and Howsam met with Halas again, and Halas' final proposal was to bring Minneapolis and Dallas into the NFL in 1960, and add Buffalo and Houston in 1961. When the idea was rejected, Halas sought out the principals in the Minneapolis franchise—Winter, Boyer, and Skoglund. He told the trio the NFL was planning on expanding into the Twin Cities.

On November 22, the AFL's first meeting to discuss the college draft was held in Minneapolis. On the afternoon of the first day, Winter and Ralph Wilson of Buffalo were heading to the meeting room when Winter told Wilson he might pull out of the AFL. The reason, he said, was the NFL's expansion plans. "I can't buck an NFL franchise in this city," Winter said.

As the principal figures in the host city, Winter, Boyer, and Skoglund had arranged for a reception banquet to be held at the Cedric Adams Hotel. That night, as Hunt, Adams, and a host of people sat talking, the doors to the meeting room burst open. In strode Harry Wismer, a stack of 10 newspapers bundled in his arms. Earlier in the day, Wismer had received a long-distance phone call from Mims Thomason, the president and general manager of United Press International news service. Calling from New York, Thomason told Wismer, "You've been had, Harry. We've received a tip that the NFL has offered a franchise to your people in Minneapolis and they've accepted."

Wismer couldn't believe it. But Thomason proceeded to read excerpts of a column written by Harold Weissman in that day's *New York Mirror*. Weissman reported that sources close to the club were ready to break from the AFL as soon as they had received written assurance from the NFL they would be granted a franchise.

Wismer dropped the newspapers on a tabletop. The papers, early Monday morning editions, trumpeted the staggering news: "Minneapolis to Get NFL Franchise."

Glaring at Winter, Wismer shouted, "Boys, it looks like it's the Last Supper."

Radio reports updated the breaking news. Austin Gunsel, onetime league treasurer and acting NFL commissioner after the death of Bell, told reporters the owners of the Minneapolis franchise had applied for NFL membership. Heated exchanges followed between Wismer and Winter, Wismer referring to Winter as "Judas" and Winter denying reports of defection.

AFL owners recovered from the shocking news and proceeded with their draft, which Hunt remembers as "an out-of-the-hat" deal. Will Walls, a talent scout hired by the owners, huddled in one room at the Cedric Adams Hotel with Leahy, Don Rossi of the Dallas franchise, Dean Griffing of Denver, and a committee of employees from each team. Because the league would be starting from scratch, AFL teams figured to suffer an identity crisis with fans in their home states. With an eye to appealing to as many hometown fans as possible, league owners decided to establish "territorial claims." What these claims did was allow the owners to choose one player from the team's own area.

"It wasn't a very intelligent draft," 49ers scout Lynn Waldorf said at the time. "How could it be? They had a few guys looking around and they pooled their information. It will be years before their scouting system can compare to ours. They got a little jump on us by drafting first, but all the top kids will wait to see who drafts them in our league before doing any business."

Despite the shortcomings in their draft system, Hunt defended this initial groundbreaking. "We feel that we accomplished exactly what we wanted to do," he told reporters. "We were striving primarily for equalization, and we feel that we did a good job in that respect."

The November meetings yielded two more substantial announcements. The first was a cooperative television plan. Unlike the NFL's TV deal, which left teams to fend for themselves by allowing them to sell their rights individually — thus creating a severe imbalance in revenue money between major market cities like New York, Chicago, and Los Angeles and smaller cities like Green Bay and Baltimore — AFL owners put together a package policy that would benefit everyone. The far-sighted plan worked extraordinarily well, and helped insure the league's survival through the difficult early years. At the close of the 1960 season, each of the eight AFL teams earned more TV money than the NFL champion Philadelphia Eagles.

As chairman of the television committee, Wismer, the onetime director of sports for ABC, sought to sell the TV rights to AFL games for one set price. The lump sum would then be divided up equally among the teams.

"It worked as we thought it would," said Hunt. "During our first year of operation, there were five NFL clubs that received less TV money than our AFL teams."

Though Wismer gets credit for advancing the TV policy, a similar policy had been set up by New York attorney Bill Shea for the Continental Baseball League. Its ultimate worth may have been the fact that one year after its implementation in the AFL, new NFL commissioner Pete Rozelle borrowed the policy and instituted it in the NFL — a move Rozelle would say later was "the most important thing I have done as commissioner."

The art of the TV deal, as described by ABC's vice-president of Television Programming and Talent Tom Moore, was "cloak-and-dagger stuff."

Jay Michaels, an agent with the Music Corporation of America and father of ABC broadcaster Al Michaels, represented the AFL in its bid to secure a TV contract. At both CBS and NBC, Michaels had been abruptly turned away. Wismer contacted Harry Haggerty in the summer of 1960 and asked him to arrange a meeting between officials from the AFL and ABC. Haggerty, the vice-chairman of Metropolitan Life Insurance Company, had dealt with ABC before, lending the cash-starved company the necessary capital to effect a merger with United Paramount Theatres. Haggerty telephoned Leonard Goldenson, the president of Paramount Theatres, to arrange the meeting, but Goldenson referred him to Moore. The meeting took place at the Ambassador Hotel in New York. Moore listened to Hunt and Wismer and said he was interested, but he declined to make any agreements.

A second meeting was held, this time at Wismer's apartment in the Park Lane Hotel. Representing the AFL were Wismer, Hunt, Adams, Hilton and Leahy, Sullivan and Winter. Moore brought with him Edgar Scherick, ABC's head of programming. After they arrived at staggered appointment times to avoid detection by the media, Wismer opened the meeting by offering to sell ABC the TV package for $2 million. Moore had to fight to keep from laughing. He told Wismer ABC was "talking about two hundred thousand, at most."

Wismer exploded in rage. Banging his fist on the table in front of Moore, Wismer screamed that he was "absolutely insulted" and said if Moore and

Scherick didn't leave the room immediately, he would. "Harry always was a bit theatrical," Hunt said later.

Ignoring Wismer's threats, Moore turned to talk to Adams. With that, Wismer jumped from his chair, turning it over in the process, and stormed out of the room. What everyone knew was that Wismer, instead of stepping out, had just stepped into his own closet. For 10 minutes, everyone in the room waited for Harry to reappear. He finally did, sitting in his chair and resuming negotiations as if nothing had happened.

Eventually, a deal was struck on June 9 calling for ABC to pay the AFL $8.5 million for TV rights over the next five years; first-year revenue was set at $1,785,000. Included in the deal was a contingent package protecting ABC; sliding scales were constructed for ratings and sales slippage. Moore estimated that ABC actually paid $400,000 for first-year rights to AFL games.

On November 30, one week to the day after the announcement of the AFL's new TV policy, Joseph Jacob Foss, 45 years old and former two-term governor of South Dakota, signed a three-year contract as AFL commissioner. The choice was a curious one, since Foss had a limited sports background. As a lineman on the University of South Dakota football team, Foss saw little playing time. He spent most of his time as a messenger guard, carrying in plays to the offensive huddle, staying in for one play, and then returning to the sideline. The coach would lean on Foss' shoulder pads, and yell, "Tell that idiot to keep his hands down." In later years, Foss would tell friends his best position in college was "sitting on the bench."

Whatever athletic abilities he lacked, Foss more than made up for them when it came to leadership. He grew up on a Sioux Falls (South Dakota) farm, under the guidance of his parents, Frank, a charismatic, storytelling Norwegian, and Mary, a stern, no-nonsense woman of Scotch-Irish descent. In his autobiography, *A Proud American*, Foss points out the differences in his parents' personalities:

> Pop was gregarious and loved an audience. He'd sing and spin yards at the drop of a hat. My mother was dead serious. She had absolutely no sense of humor. I can't remember her ever telling a funny story, or even cracking a smile when someone else told one.

Frank Foss died in an electric storm when Joe was 18, and to help his family survive, Joe on more than one occasion took a break from continuing his education to work the farm. At the University of South Dakota, Foss majored in business administration and developed an interest in planes that changed his life.

When the United States entered World War II, Foss enlisted as a U.S. Marine Corps pilot. In 1942 he was assigned to a carrier squadron headed for Guadalcanal. Aerial reinforcements were needed to combat Japan's daily bombing raids. Over the next four months, Foss' squadron shot down 135 Japanese planes. Foss was credited with 26 enemy kills, and his squadron soon became known as "Joe's Flying Circus." For his distinguished service in the Pacific Theater, the 28-year-old Foss was decorated with the Congressional Medal of Honor by President Franklin D. Roosevelt.

Foss' reputation as a war hero was so great that in the spring of 1943, he was brought stateside for a war bond tour. One of the drives took place on the steps of New York's City Hall and involved a humorous incident that illustrated Foss' frank honesty. When Mayor Fiorello LaGuardia enthusiastically introduced him as "the only man ever to survive a head-on crash with a [Japanese] Zero," Foss took his place at the microphone and said, "I don't know who the hell the Mayor is talking about, but I'm Joe Foss."

After the war, Foss returned home to South Dakota, where his fame, rugged good looks, and pleasing personality made him a natural for local politics. Foss was elected to two terms in the South Dakota House of Representatives, and in 1954, at the age of 42, he was elected governor.

In the fall of 1959, Foss was in Los Angeles on business during the AFL meeting. He had flown there with Skoglund, who was a major investor in Raven Industries, a company that manufactured high-altitude research balloons. Foss at the time was working for Raven, and he and Skoglund flew to Los Angeles together on Skoglund's company plane. After arriving at the Beverly Hilton, Skoglund said to Foss, "They're having a cocktail party for this football thing. Why don't you drop in if you haven't anything better to do."

The AFL owners knew of Foss and his spotless reputation. It was mentioned to Foss that the new league needed a commissioner, and they were looking for a well-known face to promote the league. Foss had decorated the cover of *Life* magazine, and had appeared in newspaper photos with the likes of FDR, Charles Lindbergh, Bob Hope, and Gary Cooper. Might Foss be interested in the job?

Foss told the owners he wasn't informed enough about the league to know if he was interested or not. But he would, Foss said, submit to an interview. Foss loved football, and the thought of being the commissioner of one of his favorite sports intrigued him. The interview was set for the following evening. In the meantime, Foss decided to investigate the backgrounds of the AFL owners.

"I checked around," Foss said, "and found that the owners were solid citizens. But a lot of people told me the new league couldn't help but flop. That meant it was a big challenge and I'm a sucker for a challenge."

While some doubted the availability of football talent for two pro leagues, Foss didn't. "I was firmly convinced," Foss said, "that there was room for a second league. It would have been hard to believe that there was only enough national manpower for a dozen teams."

When Foss met with the owners the following evening, their line of questioning focused on Foss' knowledge of the game.

"How much football have you played, Mr. Foss?

"What position did you play?"

"Have you ever coached?"

"How many pro football games have you seen?"

"Why do you think you would be qualified?"

Foss quickly figured that the owners were trying to decide if this former South Dakota farmer could distinguish, as he put it, "a football from a bale of hay." Nonetheless, he answered each question with his honest, straightforward style, occasionally bringing a laugh from the owners. He then paused, stared at the faces before him, and startled them with his candor.

"Seems to me," Foss said, "what you need is somebody who has the ability to open doors and pump life into a dead horse. From what I've heard, the National Football League has a forty-year head start.... If you're going to be successful, you've got to have somebody who's willing to travel the length and breadth of this land to talk to people in person and get attention for this league."

That ended the interview, and left some AFL owners, like Wismer and Hilton, grumbling. Wismer called Foss "a hick," and argued that the former politico wasn't "a football kind of guy." Hilton told his associates Foss was out of the running, and the following day, the *Los Angeles Times* ran a story that read: "According to Thomas Eddy, administrative assistant to Barron Hilton, owner of the Los Angeles Chargers, the American Football League is certain of one thing and that is that Joe Foss will not be commissioner."

Angry with the *Times* story, Foss told Skoglund he was no longer interested in the position, and returned to Raven Industries. A few weeks later, however, Hunt called and asked Foss if he would reconsider.

"I might," Foss said, "if certain conditions are met."

Hunt arranged for a 4 P.M. conference call between Foss and the owners' selection team of Hunt, Adams, and Howsam. During the call, Foss asked for and received a $30,000-a-year contract for three years, and the freedom to decide where the AFL commissioner's office would be located. Most importantly, Foss had the owners' assurance that they were committed to the goal of operating a successful league.

On November 30, 1959, Foss was officially announced as commissioner of the AFL. The decorated World War II flying ace, who had commanded Captain Joe's "Flying Circus," the most successful airborne fighting unit in marine history, was now the squadron leader for a group known as "The Foolish Club."

As soon as the announcement was made, sportswriters across the country played up the contrast between the cowboy pilot and the wealthy young owners. Foss took it in stride. In Guadalcanal, his pilots had referred to him as the squadron's "quarterback," and Foss often used football terms when outlining combat strategy. Be it combat or football, Foss had one simple philosophy: "If you get into something, get into it all the way."

Foss believed that strong public relations held the key to the AFL's survival. Almost immediately after his appointment as league commissioner, he set up league headquarters in Dallas and then took wing. He arranged speaking engagements at every outpost, appearing, as he said, "anywhere they'd have me." Small-town booster banquets, Rotary, and Kiwanis clubs were all part of Foss' hectic agenda. He crisscrossed the country, logging more than 200,000 miles in his attempt to sell the AFL.

Said Foss, "I talked to anyone who would listen — hair-burners, riveters, plumbers, political conventions, the Elks, the Moose, or the Owls."

His speeches, one listener noted, were "part Sioux Falls simplicity, part Madison Avenue public relations." In his rumpled business suits, Foss appealed to many small-town citizens as a commoner, a circumstance that helped them identify with the underdog AFL.

When a reporter told Cowboys executive Clint Murchison that many members of the sporting public looked upon Hunt and the AFL as underdogs, Murchison shook with laughter. "Well, I'll be damned," he said. "You're the first person I ever heard call a Hunt an underdog!"

As head of the newly formed Dallas Cowboys, Murchison and Wynne were in direct competition with Hunt. The two sides sniped at each other through the press. When Wynne said that the chances of survival for Hunt's league "are very problematical, with the lack of players available and the caliber of players he'd have to go with," Hunt responded with gusto from his office in the Dallas Mercantile Bank Building.

"It'll be an accident," Hunt told newsmen, "if any new NFL club finishes out of the cellar." The implication was clear. Dallas football fans could choose between the Cowboys, who had almost no chance of contending in the NFL, or they could follow the Texans, who could immediately challenge for a championship in the fledgling AFL.

Murchison countered with a suggestion that Hunt's new league was nothing more than a case of a rich man not getting what he wanted in the first place. "I think that Lamar would have preferred an NFL franchise himself," Murchison said. "Formation of a new league was more or less a last resort."

In early January, Foss named his chief lieutenants. Milt Woodard, the executive secretary of the Western Golf Association, was named assistant commissioner. Distinguished in appearance, Woodard had previously served as general manager for two minor-league baseball teams, and had been an award-winning sportswriter for a Chicago daily. Another former sportswriter, Al Ward, was named publicity director.

Through the early weeks of his administration, Foss exhibited strong leadership. "I am the boss man," he declared, and treated the NFL like they were Japanese Zeros. In March, Foss told the media he had secured a deposition with the Department of Justice asking for an antitrust suit against the NFL. Foss accused the NFL of trying to run the AFL into the ground. His chief complaint was with the NFL's new desire for expansion, particularly into cities that already were home to AFL teams, and specifically in Dallas.

Though the Justice Department failed to find suitable reason to act, Foss announced on June 17 that the AFL would file a $10 million "private" antitrust suit against the NFL. The suit called for $180,000 in damages; the Texans were seeking $1.5 million in reparation. Said Hunt, "The lawyers feel that Dallas is where all the teams will be hurt — on TV when they play here, since the AFL club will be competing against the NFL's Cowboys."

The antitrust suit was debated in court for the next two years, but the Justice Department's official decision stood. In Baltimore on May 21, 1962, a U.S. district court judge ruled against the AFL.

While Foss sparred in the public spotlight, a flurry of activity kept the league owners busy. On January 26, the opening day of the AFL's first annual meeting in Dallas, Hunt was named league president for a one-year term. The following day, the owners approved the withdrawal of the Minneapolis franchise. The reason listed was "stadium problems," but Minneapolis' city fathers buckled under the influence of NFL owners, who had promised the city an NFL franchise if a stadium was made available. Charley Johnson, the city's most influential sportswriter, supported the NFL, and so did many of Minneapolis' business leaders. Fearing a civil war in their city, Winter, Skoglund, and Boyer simply backed out of the AFL.

Foss said later he didn't know why Skoglund didn't just admit to having negotiated an NFL deal with Bears owner George Halas. Perhaps it was because Halas' dealings with Skoglund violated the NFL's bylaws requiring unanimous approval by team owners for expansion. At the time, the NFL was split on the topic of expansion. Redskins owner George Preston Marshall told Frank Blauschild of the *New York Mirror*: "The only reason for expansion I've heard from other owners is that we could destroy the new league. If that's the only reason, then we are guilty of monopolistic practices. No one can give me an intelligent reason for adding a couple of more franchises."

With Minneapolis gone, the AFL needed to fill a vacancy. Presentations were made by representatives from Atlanta, Oakland, San Francisco, St. Louis, and Miami. On January 30, AFL owners granted the final franchise to Oakland, largely because of the lobbying done by Barron Hilton. Hilton's push for Oakland was done for obvious reasons, the most important being the immediate and natural rivalry an Oakland team would present for his Los Angeles Chargers. So strong were Hilton's feelings on the issue that he delivered an ultimatum to his fellow owners: Give Oakland a franchise, or the Chargers would withdraw from the AFL.

The new franchise was an eight-man syndicate headed by Y. C. (Chet) Soda. Included in the group were Ed McGah, Robert Osborne, and Wayne Valley. Oakland inherited the Minneapolis draft list, and was given permission to select five players from each of the other teams. The plan put forward allowed each team to effectively freeze 11 players of choice, making the rest of the team available to be drafted by Oakland.

For Valley and McGah, the Oakland franchise was a 17-year-old dream come true. Since 1943, the two men had been trying unsuccessfully to bring a pro football team to the Bay Area. In 1943, the NFL offered to sell franchise rights to investors in Oakland, but the deal fell through with the emergence of the AAFC, which had the San Francisco 49ers. In 1954 Valley and McGah had put in bids to buy the 49ers, but changed their minds when they learned they could purchase only a half interest.

Valley's main contributions to the new league often came about during closed-door meetings of the league's executive committee. Valley, who played football at Oregon State, was blunt and direct; a gruff, growling man lacking in matters of diplomacy.

"He has a lumberjack's skill," one writer said, "when it comes to cutting through the heavy layer of bullshit present at all American Football League meetings. When indecision threatens the AFL, he is a virtuoso at bullying the other owners into actually doing something."

It was Valley who helped establish the AFL's dubious identity. "Wayne Valley commented at that time," Sullivan said, "that he thought instead of being known as the executive committee of the league the club owners should instead be known as 'The Foolish Club.'"

With eight teams on board, league owners adopted rules revolutionary for the time. They instituted the first 14-game schedule in pro football history, adopted the two-point conversion rule after touchdowns that college football used, made the game clock the official timekeeper, and gave the media a free hand in game coverage. The AFL also put nameplates on the back of player jerseys. Chicago White Sox owner Bill Veeck had introduced the idea to major-league baseball earlier that spring, promoting it with a wire photo of Ted Kluszewski with his name on the back of his shirt. The photo appeared in newspapers across the country, prompting Woodard to call Veeck.

"We want to adopt it as a league rule," Woodard said.

"Of course," Veeck answered. "It's not copyrighted."

In his book, Foss looked back on the AFL's new ideas with pride. The AFL, Foss said, "took the lead in transforming the way football was presented on television.... In fact, we began a whole set of traditions."

They were traditions, Foss said, that had the NFL "playing catch-up." Through the years, the NFL has validated the worth of the AFL's ideas by adopting jersey nameplates, revenue sharing, official timing, TV coverage, and the two-point conversion.

From the start, the AFL sought to make itself "fan-friendly." Jersey nameplates were one step in that direction, and the official timing of the game was another. Through 1960, the NFL's practice had always been to use two clocks — one for the crowd and one for officials. The practice was confusing to fans, since the official time left in the game was kept on the field by officials, and only they knew how much time actually remained.

Elinor Kaine, a nationally syndicated football columnist, published a book in 1970 called *Pro Football Broadside*. In her book, Kaine wrote that since NFL scoreboard clocks were rarely exact, the situation confused coaches, players, officials, announcers, and fans. "Especially," wrote Kaine, "the fans, who can't be sure when it's time to rush out and tear down the goalposts."

By making the game clock the official timepiece, AFL owners enhanced the excitement of late-game drives for the fans, who were aware for the first time of how much time was officially left in the game.

Foss also announced that at ABC, cameras would be given freedom of action. At the time, CBS practiced what Foss called "censorship restriction." That is, TV viewers were not shown disagreements and fights between players.

"I think the public is a mature body," Foss said at the time, "and realizes that players of professional football are mature men and professional men.... Some impurities of conduct may naturally develop in a closely played game, but I do think my position as AFL Commissioner gives me the right ... [to prevent] the censoring of these instances from the game's fans."

The commissioner's announcement was hailed by various sportswriters. In a column headed "AFL Rules Made for Man in Stand," sportswriter Charles Burton wrote, "The American Football League now has the most exciting set of rules in the game — pro, college, or high school. It has free substitutions, of course, and it wisely adopted the extra-point rule after touchdown, meaning that the fans will have an opportunity to watch the quarterback call for a kick for one point, or a pass or run for two."

John Hanlon, a columnist for the *Providence Journal Bulletin*, wrote that the AFL was proving itself a big-league operation:

> The new American Football League ... is soundly organized and financed, apparently in each of its locations. As a league, it has played its television hand cleverly, getting a rich nest egg from that source....
> The latest bit of evidence that the outfit has the adult, intelligent approach is its announced intention to show on its telecasts that sometimes-part of the game's action the National Football League bans.... A small item, to be sure, but a sign that grownups are running the [AFL].

As the AFL prepared for its inaugural season, opinions on the league's chances for survival came from various sources. At a banquet in Philadelphia to receive that city's sportswriters award as America's outstanding athlete, Colts quarterback John Unitas gave a ringing endorsement of the AFL. Unitas told his startled audience:

> The more teams the better. I don't think the [NFL] will be hurt as much as everybody says. With more pro teams and a greater demand for players, it means that some of the veterans will be able to play two more years than they normally would.

I'll tell you something. If the AFL was looking for players when I was getting out of the Louisville University, I'd probably be playing in the AFL today.

Los Angeles Rams general manager Elroy Hirsch said the AFL would survive where other leagues failed because it was much better organized.

Dallas Cowboys coach Tom Landry said the AFL's "enthusiasm and efficiency" would make it a success. NFL commissioner Pete Rozelle agreed. "I'll say that they [the AFL] have done a tremendous job in getting organized in one year."

"It will take [the AFL] three years to organize and field solid teams of 22 or 33 men who play as a unit," said Joe Kuharich, a former NFL coach. "If the AFL holds out that long, and battles for top names, it can survive profitably. The pro market is there."

A writer for the *Pasadena Star-News* sized up the league's chances perhaps better than anyone. "The new league is a Capricorn, which is good. Capricorns are stubborn, materialistic, occasionally foolish, but always ready to correct faults. They are also accomplished at the art of survival."

Under such an advantageous sign from the stars, the Foolish Club opened for business.

Chapter Four

1960: Corralling a Loose Cannon

TO OUTSIDERS, THE MEN OF THE AFL were a curious collection, a spectrum of personalities that differed depending upon the light in which they were viewed. From the NFL's vantage point, they were viewed solely as a threat. Paul Brown disparaged AFL owners as "the sons of rich men, not football men."

In his book *Hit the Sign and Win a Free Suit of Clothes from Harry Finklestein*, author Bert Randolph Sugar took an entertaining look at the history of sports promotions in the United States and the relationship between sports and big business. In the opinion of Sugar, the AFL was as much a cotillion as a consortium.

"When the NFL denied a few petitioners admission," wrote Sugar, "momentarily depriving them of their prospective toys, they did the only thing any red-blooded little rich boys would do: they went out and bought a league of their own."

Not everyone shared Sugar's opinion. Joe Foss, the decorated World War II hero and former governor of South Dakota, worked with the AFL owners after being named commissioner in 1960. While Foss acknowledged that the prevailing attitude toward the new league's ownership was that they represented a group of "wealthy young swashbucklers," Foss grew to respect the owners' determination and courage in turning a dream into reality—particularly Lamar Hunt.

"No new league had succeeded since the turn of the century," Foss wrote in his autobiography, *A Proud American*. "Hunt was not, however, the sort of man to abandon a dream just because no one was selling what he wanted to buy."

From the start, AFL owners had a strong desire to establish their own identity. The influx of former NFL coaches like Sid Gillman and college coaches like Hank Stram, and the emphasis on offensive talent in the college draft, allowed the AFL to adopt strategies that gave the league its own distinct flavor.

"We had new people in the AFL, and we didn't want to do what the NFL was doing at the time," says former Kansas City head coach Hank Stram, the winningest coach in AFL history and a former football analyst for CBS radio. "We did what we had to do to take advantage of the personnel in the AFL at that time."

This sense of change was evident by the owners' choice of front office and coaching personnel. AFL management teams consisted of men whose football experience lay in the NFL, Canadian Football League, or college ball. On February 9, Oakland owners officially named Eddie Erdelatz as their head coach, completing the front office staffs for each of the AFL teams.

In 1959 Erdelatz was coming off a highly successful eight-year reign as head coach at the Naval Academy. Under Erdelatz, Navy became a national power. In 1955, Navy beat Southeast Conference champion Mississippi in the Sugar Bowl; in 1958, Erdelatz guided Navy to a triumph over Southwest champion Rice.

In Boston, Billy Sullivan named Lou Saban. Saban had been an All-America player at the University of Indiana, and for four years he was Paul Brown's defensive captain for the Cleveland Browns. In 1959 Saban coached Western Illinois University to an unbeaten record. He was approached by general manager Ed McKeever, whose background in football included a stint as Frank Leahy's backfield coach at Boston College in 1939–40. He also had experience in the old AAFC, where he had been general manager and head coach of the Chicago Rockets. At the time of his hiring by the Patriots, McKeever was supplementing his income as backfield coach at LSU by scouting for the New York Giants. A strong-willed Texan, McKeever was known as "a dynamo with a drawl." Mike Holovak, who was coming off nine years as head coach at Boston College, was named Boston's director of player personnel.

Buffalo's choice of head coach was Garrard "Buster" Ramsey. Ramsey had been a member of the Chicago Cardinals title teams in the 1940s, and by 1959 he was an eight-year veteran of the Detroit Lions' defensive staff. Under Ramsey, the Lions became a formidable defensive team in the 1950s, earning the tag "Ramsey's Wreckers." The club won NFL titles in 1952, 1953, and 1957, and a conference championship in 1954. Ramsey balked at the idea of coaching the Bills. He was happy in Detroit, and ranked as the NFL's highest-paid assistant coach. But he was won over by Wilson's promise of complete control over the playing operation. Ramsey took the job and hooked up with club GM Dick Gallagher to put together a team. An assistant coach and director of player personnel for the Browns, Gallagher was given the task of recruiting and signing players.

To coach his Dallas Texans, Lamar Hunt selected Stram, a stocky, self-styled disciplinarian who was serving as assistant coach at the University of Miami. "Show me a good loser," Stram liked to say, "and I'll show you a loser, period."

Born and raised in Gary, Indiana, Stram was an all-state halfback at Lew Wallace High School, and his first choice of colleges was Notre Dame. Leahy, however, was less than enamored with 5-foot-8, 165-pound tailbacks, so Stram went to Purdue University, where he earned three letters as a single-wing back and the Big Ten award as Scholar and Athlete. Upon graduation, he joined the Boilermakers' coaching staff, putting in eight years as an offensive backfield coach under Stu Holcomb. Stram moved on to SMU for the 1956 season, then to Notre Dame for the 1957–58 seasons. When Terry Brennan's entire Notre Dame staff was fired in December 1958, Stram joined the Hurricanes' staff.

By 1959 Stram had earned a reputation as an astute and imaginative coach. The possibilities of offensive football fascinated Stram. He tinkered with formations, often interrupting a meal to sketch plays on the tablecloth. Stram joined scout Will Walls and administrative director Don Rossi as part of the Texans' front office.

To lead the Denver Broncos, the Howsam group named Dean Griffing general manager and Frank Filchock head coach. The combination seemed a natural as the two men had worked together in the Canadian Football League. Griffing, who played football at the University of Kansas, had been GM for the Saskatchewan Rough Riders, and his frugality attracted the attention of the financially shaky Howsams.

"If you want to run an operation at the lowest possible cost," said one Griffing associate, "you hire Dean Griffing."

Griffing in turn hired Filchock as field boss. A standout quarterback for the University of Indiana, Filchock signed with the Washington Redskins in 1938. He was traded to the New York Giants in 1944 and quarterbacked the team to the Eastern Conference title in 1946. When his career ended in 1950, Filchock headed north and became head coach of the Rough Riders, where he remained until the Broncos came calling.

In Houston, Bud Adams' first move was to hire John Breen as director of player personnel. A tall, genial man in his mid-50s, Breen had NFL experience, having once scouted for the Chicago Cardinals. He was considered an astute judge of football talent. To coach the team, Adams and Breen signed Lou Rymkus. Like Breen, Rymkus was a product of the NFL. An All-America at Notre Dame in the 1940s, Rymkus had learned his football from the leathery Frank Leahy. After graduation, Rymkus spent the next 17 years first as a player for the Redskins, then as an assistant coach on the staffs of the Packers and Rams, at every stop following the Leahy precepts of discipline and conditioning. Upon being introduced to the press, Rymkus announced, "I'm hardnosed. I'm controversial."

As his chief lieutenant, Rymkus chose Mac Speedie, the former all-pro end from the Cleveland Browns, to help design the Oilers' offense. Though Rymkus eventually became his choice for head coach, Adams had interviewed a host of other possible candidates. Chief among them was Tom Landry. The defensive coordinator for the NFL's New York Giants, Landry had strong ties with the Southwest, where he had grown up and graduated from the University of Texas.

"I agreed to meet with him," Landry said later, "more out of curiosity than any real interest. He gave me a big sales pitch on the AFL. An exciting new league, a chance to get in on the ground floor, and an opportunity to create football furor in Houston the way the Giants had in New York."

In Los Angeles, Hilton selected Sid Gillman as the Chargers' head coach. A graduate of Ohio State University, Gillman played end for the Cleveland Rams of the second AFL in 1936. As a coach at Miami University of Ohio, Gillman owned a 31-6-1 record; at the University of Cincinnati, his record was 50-13-1.

Like Stram, Gillman earned a reputation as an imaginative offensive coach. The father of the modern passing game, Gillman is recognized by many for popularizing "rule" or option blocking. Gillman's reputation as an innovator led to his hiring as head coach of the Los Angeles Rams in 1955. Gillman guided the Rams to the NFL title game his first year, but the team struggled its next four seasons and Gillman resigned at the end of '59 season. On January 7, 1960, he was named head coach of the Chargers.

In New York, Harry Wismer's search for a new coach was built on his finding a "name," a high-profile person whom the fans would instantly recognize. While watching a TV broadcast of an Old-Timers' Day game at Washington's Griffith Stadium, Wismer saw Sammy Baugh on the screen. Wismer picked up the phone, placed a call to the Griffith Stadium press box and implored Baugh to fly to New York to talk about the Titans coaching job.

Tall and lanky, Baugh had gained national notoriety as a single-wing tailback at Texas Christian University, where he achieved All-America status in 1935-36. Drafted by the Washington Redskins in 1937, Baugh's rifle passes earned him the nickname "Slingin'" Sammy. In his 16-year career, he led the NFL in passing six times and led the Redskins to two NFL titles.

When Wismer called to discuss coaching the Titans, Baugh was head coach at Hardin-Simmons University in Abilene, Texas. Baugh demanded a substantial part of his first year's salary in advance. Wismer agreed, and on December 18, Sammy Baugh was introduced to the New York media as the Titans' head coach.

Thousands of hopefuls flocked to AFL training camps in the summer of 1960 seeking a spot on a pro football roster. In Los Angeles, Gillman, who became general manager of the Chargers following Leahy's resignation due to ill health, opened camp in Burbank and some 350 prospects showed up. Among them was Ron Mix, an All-America offensive tackle out of USC. The number-one draft choice of both the Colts and Patriots, Mix chose the AFL for two reasons: the Patriots dealt their rights to Mix to the Chargers, and he preferred San Diego's climate and financial offer.

"The Colts offered me $8,500 to come play in cold Baltimore," said Mix, who went on to be recognized as the best offensive tackle in AFL history. "The Chargers offered me $12,000 to play in my home town. It was one of my easier decisions. It didn't bother me that the AFL at that time had no guarantee of success, that it might last only a few years. I had planned to play only two years of pro ball and then go into teaching."

Apart from Mix and a few other budding stars, the Chargers' early tryout camps offered a collection of what Gillman remembers as bartenders, truck drivers, and boilermakers. "Every bartender in Los Angeles," Gillman said, "thought he could play football."

One ex-bartender who didn't disappoint was Boston's Gino Cappelletti. A graduate of the University of Minnesota, where he was a blocking back in a single-wing offense, Cappelletti in 1959 was earning $80 a week tending bar in his brother's Minneapolis lounge when he heard about the AFL. After his graduation, Cappelletti spent five years trying to break into pro football, and was in a city touch-football league when the AFL appeared.

"I had just about given up my hopes [of playing pro football]," said Cappelletti, who became the league's all-time leading scorer. "The AFL gave me that final chance to make it."

In New York, more than 100 players were in Sammy Baugh's Titans camp. Among them was Larry Grantham, an undersized linebacker from the University of Mississippi who was drafted by the Titans and the Baltimore Colts, but went with the Titans.

"The Colts had just won the NFL championship," Grantham says, "and they brought thirty rookies to camp. They told us they were only going to keep three rookies to fill spots. I figured I had a better chance to play in the new league."

In Oakland, the Raiders discovered a future Hall-of-Famer when they invited Jim Otto, a center from the University of Miami, to their summer camp. NFL scouts were unimpressed by Otto's size — 6-foot-2, 205 pounds — and durability — he was hampered by knee and shoulder injuries in college. But Otto bulked up to 227 pounds for his tryout with the Raiders and impressed head coach Eddie Erdelatz enough to win a job — though not the one Erdelatz imagined. The former Navy coach remembered Otto's outstanding play at linebacker for the Hurricanes, and Erdelatz, who specialized in defensive strategy, was anxious to see if Otto could play the position in the pros.

Otto, however, had other ideas.

"When I started in this league, I had to try harder," Otto said. "There were about eight centers at the 1960 Oakland camp, and they told me to line up on defense. I said, 'Look, I can block and I want to last. I was hurt all through college by blindside and angle blocks.' So they put me on offense."

Otto, nicknamed "Double Zero" because his uniform number, 00, signaled the first and last letters of his name, went on to become the best center in AFL history.

A onetime star defensive lineman for the Los Angeles Rams, 32-year-old Lewis "Bud" McFadin was talked out of retirement by the Denver Broncos.

Gino Cappelletti of the Boston Patriots was one of the AFL's greatest success stories. The one-time bartender was one of just three players, along with George Blanda and Jim Otto, who played in all 140 AFL games. Cappelletti gained all-pro honors as a wide receiver and placekicker, and retired as the AFL's all-time leading scorer. (*Photo courtesy of the New England Patriots.*)

McFadin had retired to his ranch in Humble, Texas, following an accidental off-season shooting in 1957 that left a .44 caliber bullet in his stomach. A friend was showing McFadin his pistol when it discharged. McFadin, who nearly died from the wound, spent the next three years recovering.

Drafted by the Rams in 1951 following an All-America career at the University of Texas, the 6-foot-4, 280-pound McFadin impressed the Broncos with his strength and lateral pursuit. McFadin was named to the all–AFL team from 1960 to 1962, and was considered the finest defensive tackle in the AFL's formative years.

In Dallas, the Texans held their first training camp at New Mexico Military Institute in Roswell. Among the 129 players who showed up in Roswell was Smokey Stover, a free-agent linebacker out of Northeast Louisiana University. Stover would go on to play seven years with the Texans and help them win two AFL titles, but in 1960 he was just one more player out to prove himself in the new AFL.

The Dallas free agents were put through a rigorous first day of camp that saw 30 players quit at day's end. Walt Corey, the former Bills defensive coach, was a linebacker with the Texans in 1960. Corey remembers the players being lined up in two rows and going head-to-head. If you whipped the man across from you, Corey said, you were invited back the next day. Players didn't dare show pain from injuries. Corey said if any free agent got hurt, he was immediately cut.

Conditions at the camp were just as harsh as the coaches. The temperature was 110 degrees in the daytime and 85 at night, with not an air conditioner in sight. The mosquitoes that plagued the camp were so large that wide receiver Chris Burford, in just a slight exaggeration, said six or seven of them were capable of carrying off a player. It was too hot to sleep with sheets, Burford said, but the players needed the sheets just to keep the mosquitoes off.

The Texans' lone relief was provided by irrigation ditches near the practice field. Stover said players would run to the ditches after practice and fall in just to get cool. The combination of long practices and oppressive heat saw Stover's weight fall to 188 pounds, extremely light for a linebacker. In order to prevent being cut, Stover hid 10-pound weights under his arms at team weigh-ins.

In an era when black athletes were just beginning to fully integrate pro football, Abner Haynes and Paul Lowe took the opportunity to build memorable careers. The two were alike in size but differed in style. A 6-foot, 190-pound All-America halfback out of North Texas State, Haynes electrified AFL audiences with his running style — shuffling, side-stepping, and seemingly changing direction in mid-air — to be named all-pro from 1960 to 1962.

While Haynes flowed like liquid through enemy defenses, Lowe galloped through them with a high-knee action that stemmed from his time spent on the track as a hurdler at Oregon State College. Taking the ball on San Diego's patented toss sweeps, Lowe would start wide, stutter-step, and accelerate into the secondary. A product of the Watts section of Los Angeles, Lowe was cut by the San Francisco 49ers and called Barron Hilton at the Charger offices to request a tryout. When Hilton mentioned Lowe to his coaching staff, the resourceful Al Davis recalled Lowe as a game-breaker in college, and the Chargers signed him.

Lowe's first game in a Charger uniform saw him return the opening kickoff 105 yards for a touchdown. He went on to be named all–AFL in 1960 and '65, and his 4.88 career yards-per-carry average is the highest in AFL history.

Because the AFL had established "no tampering" verbal pacts with the NFL on February 9 and CFL on February 11— agreements that prevent the raiding of teams for star players— the new league had to be content with signing ex-pro and college players they could afford. Many of the AFL's quarterbacks in 1960 had NFL experience. L.A.'s Jack Kemp, who had been signed by Leahy before his resignation, was a 25-year-old NFL veteran who had played with the

Lions, Steelers, and Giants. Dallas' Cotton Davidson was a former Colt; Oakland's Vito "Babe" Parilli once played for the Packers and Browns; Buffalo's Tom O'Connell with the Bears and Browns; the Titans' Al Dorow with the Redskins and Eagles.

But it was Houston that made the most important quarterback signing in 1960. Early in the year, when Adams and Breen sat down to discuss the building of their team, Adams asked, "What will be the basic weakness [of first-year teams]?" Breen answered in two words. "Pass defense." With that, Adams gave Breen the go-ahead to sign the best available quarterback.

Apart from Leahy, who didn't last long in the AFL, John Breen was perhaps the most competent general manager the league had in its formative years. Breen believed that in a new league, an accurate quarterback was a necessity, because it takes at least two years before defenses would be sophisticated enough to stop a strong passing game. Breen's choice of 33-year-old George Blanda was typical of the AFL's mix of scouting and luck in the early days. Drafted in 1949 out of the University of Kentucky by the Bears, Blanda played backup to Johnny Lujack his first three years in the NFL. After Lujack retired in 1952, Blanda led the league in pass completions in 1953, and in 1954, combined with rookie Zeke Bratkowski to help the Bears to an 8–4 record.

Despite his on-field success, Blanda and Halas clashed. Observers judged them too much alike in their personalities. It wasn't uncommon for Blanda to walk up to Halas on the sidelines during a game the Bears were losing and chide the "Papa Bear" by saying, "Why the hell don't you put me in, you're such a great coach?" When Wrigley Field crowds would chant, "We want Blanda!" Halas would call Blanda over and tell him, "Hey kid, you better get up in the stands. They want you."

A shoulder injury slowed Blanda the next three seasons, and after throwing just seven passes in the 1958 season, he retired. Between his passing, place-kicks, and field goals Blanda was the Bears' all-time leading scorer. Still, it was Halas' belief that Blanda's injury had ruined his arm.

In the early 1950s, Breen coached at Chicago's Lake Forest College and later became a Chicago Cardinals executive. He knew Blanda, his talent, and his competitive nature. He was just the kind of experienced quarterback who could flourish against the inexperienced defenses the new league would field.

"While he is not the greatest quarterback in the world in some departments," Breen said at the time, "he really knows how to take a defense apart."

Breen told Adams that Blanda was the man around whom the Oilers could build their offense. Adams told Breen, "Go get him." Following two weeks of negotiations, Blanda signed with the Oilers for $20,000 a year, with a signing bonus and stock options.

While the Blanda signing was important to the league's development, it was overshadowed by the Oilers' attempt to sign LSU All-America halfback and Heisman Trophy winner Billy Cannon.

A 6-foot-1, 208-pound back from Baton Rouge, Cannon burst onto the national scene as a junior in 1958. A unanimous All–America choice that season, Cannon averaged six yards per rush and scored 11 touchdowns to help LSU go 10–0. With a national title on the line, Cannon threw for the game's only score, a nine-yard TD pass, as LSU beat Clemson 7–0 in the Sugar Bowl.

Cannon finished third in the Heisman voting in '58, but came back to win it the following year after averaging 4.3 yards per carry and scoring seven TDs as LSU went 9–1. The most memorable play of Cannon's collegiate career came on a rainy Halloween night in '59. LSU trailed Mississippi 3–0 in the fourth quarter when Cannon took a punt on his 11-yard line and ran through the mud and seven tackles on an 89-yard TD run that won the game. The win helped LSU return to the Sugar Bowl, but the Tigers fell to Mississippi 21–0. Again Cannon was named All-America, and what impressed scouts was his breakaway speed. During his career at LSU, Cannon had 19 runs of 40 yards or more.

"Cannon is the best football player I've ever seen," LSU head coach Paul Dietzel said at the time. "No matter what you ask him to do — run, pass, receive, punt, block, tackle, cover passes or fake — he is superlative."

The rush to draft Cannon began with Pete Rozelle, who was then still general manager of the L.A. Rams. "First choice in the draft was between the Rams and Cardinals," Rozelle said. "We knew the Cardinals wanted George Izo of Notre Dame, a quarterback. We planned to draft Cannon, but we wanted assurance that he would play for us."

On November 30, Cannon, who was in New York as a member of the Kodak All-America Team, received a phone call from Rozelle, who was staying at the Warwick Hotel in Philadelphia. Rozelle told Cannon that the Rams were planning to draft him, and laid out the figures: $15,000 a year for three years and a $5,000 signing bonus. Cannon agreed to terms, and following a press conference introducing Cannon to the media, Rozelle typed a contract calling for Cannon to receive a $10,000 signing bonus, a $10,000 salary for the first season, and two more seasons at $15,000 a year. The contract, Rozelle pointed out, was not dated — it was just a written offer that would go into effect after Cannon's collegiate career ended on New Year's Day.

Rozelle finalized the transaction by handing Cannon two checks. The first was the $10,000 signing bonus. The second was a $500 expense check. Cannon thanked him and headed back to Baton Rouge, fully expecting to make his pro debut with the Rams.

Not long after returning to Louisiana, Cannon took a call from Bud Adams. The two men talked, Cannon explaining the nature of his signing with the Rams. One month later, Adams called again, offering Cannon a better deal: $100,000 guaranteed over three seasons, a gift of $10,000 to Cannon's wife, and the possibility of ownership in service stations that would carry Cannon's name.

Feeling he had been too quick to sign with the Rams, Cannon told his lawyer to send a letter to Rozelle. In the letter Cannon told Rozelle he didn't care to enter into any contract, predated or otherwise, with the Rams. Cannon sent a copy of the letter to Austin Gunsel, interim commissioner of the NFL. He also returned the two checks, totaling $10,500, to Rozelle. Cannon waited for a response, but never got one. Instead, Rozelle attended the Sugar Bowl game and told Cannon the Rams would dispute the matter — in court if necessary. Cannon, meanwhile, put on a postgame show that grabbed the nation's attention.

Immediately after the game, Cannon walked to the end zone, stood between the goalposts, and in full view of the thousands in attendance and the millions watching on TV, took a personal service contract from Adrian Burk, a former Eagles quarterback working for Adams, and signed on the dotted line.

"Actually, I had already signed a three-year personal services contract with Adams," Cannon said. "The bit under the goalposts was just for show."

Rozelle returned to Los Angeles, where he angrily told reporters that Cannon would play for the Rams or he would not play at all. The case went before an L.A. court in June. Cannon complained that the contracts he signed with Rozelle were undated, and that the date listed on them, November 30, was added afterwards. Rozelle said that signing undated contracts was common practice in the NFL. "A contract is never dated until the player signs it," he said.

On June 20, a Los Angeles court ruled Cannon's contract with the Rams invalid, thus freeing him to officially join the Oilers. In a parting shot, the judge admonished Rozelle for attempting to hide the facts beneath what he called "a shroud of secrecy."

"Billy came to us under strange circumstances," Adams said. "He admitted to me that he signed the contract with the Los Angeles Rams, and I agreed to double the salary that he would receive from the Rams. And then the Los Angeles Rams filed a lawsuit against Billy, [and] naturally we had to defend him in the Los Angeles courts. We won the case, on the basis [that] the judge said he thought Billy should have the maximum amount of money, and we had offered him the maximum amount, so he should play with the Oilers. And we [the AFL] got our first superstar."

Throughout the spring and summer, AFL teams scrambled to find bodies to fill their rosters. Each team did manage to secure some name players.

For many of these men, the AFL offered a last chance to make something of their careers. Babe Parilli summed up the feelings of many AFL players when he said, "I was at the point in my career where I had to take over or get out of the game."

Charley Hennigan, who still holds Oiler club records for receiving, echoed Parilli's feelings. "I'm not being maudlin when I say 'Thank God for the American Football League.' I mean it sincerely," says Hennigan. "You know damn well that if it hadn't been for the AFL, even our neighbors back home wouldn't have heard of us."

Vito "Babe" Parilli of the Boston Patriots was one of several former NFL quarterbacks who became stars in the early years of the AFL. Parilli is one of just 19 players whose career spanned the 10-year existence of the AFL. (*Photo courtesy of the New England Patriots.*)

To some, the AFL offered little more than a collection of castoffs and misfits. Some NFL people heaped scorn upon the new league — Bears owner and coach George Halas among them.

"That damn Mickey Mouse league doesn't even own a football," Halas said. Foss responded to that statement by stopping at a Dallas sporting goods store on his way to a league meeting, buying a football, and then brandishing it to reporters.

Breen refuted the claim that the AFL's players were something less than real athletes. "[Johnny] Unitas was a castoff, too, remember," he said, reminding some that the starting quarterback of the world champion Baltimore Colts had once been cut from the NFL. "So was Big Daddy Lipscomb. There's nothing wrong with castoffs."

From the first draft, the AFL had a distinct advantage over the NFL in signing players considered on the bubble of making it in pro football. NFL rosters were filled with established players; AFL teams lacked a talent base and signed as many as 12 to 15 rookies per team. In the 1960 college draft, the AFL signed six of the NFL's 12 first-round draft choices and 75 percent of the college players both leagues went after — including the 1959 All-America backfield of Billy Cannon, Ron Burton, Charlie Flowers, and Richie Lucas.

Much of the success for these early signings can be traced to men such as Breen, Don Klosterman, and scouts like Lloyd Wells and Will Walls. Titans head coach Sammy Baugh called Walls "the best recruiter there is. He knows every kid in the country and they all like him."

More so than their counterparts in the NFL, AFL scouts, general managers, and head coaches took to recruiting players from black college campuses.

"It was an untapped market," Klosterman told Michael Hurd, author of the book *Black College Football*. "The AFL could give those players a chance to play right away. They hadn't had exposure, and we could give that too."

Hurd believes that if ever there was a perfect match, it was the AFL and black players, both of whom were emerging on the pro scene at precisely the same time. "Both [the AFL and black athletes] were seeking exposure," Hurd writes, "and an opportunity to prove themselves at the highest level."

Stram, whose Super Bowl IV squad was the first league champion to have more black athletes than whites on their roster, agreed with Hurd. "The desire to prove they were worthy of playing in the NFL was always very impressive," Stram said. "We were the underdog and they were too. It was a good mix."

Finding a suitable place to play their games was the final obstacle AFL owners faced before the exhibition season began. Denver used its minor-league baseball facility, Bears Stadium; the Bills moved into War Memorial Stadium. The Oilers leased a high school field called Jeppesen Stadium and spent $200,000 renovating it and increasing seating from 22,000 to 36,000. The Texans shared the Cotton Bowl with the Cowboys; the Chargers and Rams shared the L.A. Coliseum. The Patriots leased University Field, a 27,000-seat stadium that had once been home to the Boston Braves baseball team. The Raiders played *outside* their home city, sharing San Francisco's Kezar Stadium with the 49ers.

To showcase his Titans, Wismer leased the Polo Grounds, which had stood abandoned since 1957. Once the home of some of baseball's greatest moments — such as Bobby Thomson's ninth-inning homer to beat the Dodgers for the pennant in 1951 and Willie Mays' over-the-shoulder basket catch in centerfield in the 1954 World Series — the Polo Grounds had deteriorated into a decrepit old haunt. Rust caked the steel girders; many seats were broken or missing. "People don't like this place," Wismer told his team. "Even the Giants couldn't make money here."

Since 1959, AFL owners had been busy building a pro football league from scratch. Rarely did they have time to sit back and assess their progress. The magnitude of what he had accomplished didn't occur to Hunt until he was driving home from his office at the Dallas Mercantile Bank Building the final week of July. Hunt turned on his car radio, tuned in a sports program, and was startled to hear odds on the weekend's football games:

In their first exhibition game this weekend in Tulsa, the brand-new Dallas Texans of the brand-new American Football League are two-and-a-half-point favorites over the Houston Oilers.

When he got home, Hunt hurriedly placed a call to Adams. "We've arrived," Hunt said. "The bookies made odds on us. I heard it on the radio. They know about us in Las Vegas."

In Buffalo on July 29, over 100,000 fans were on hand to welcome the Bills to their new home the night before the team's preseason opener against the Boston Patriots in the first-ever AFL game. On a brutally hot evening, 16,474 fans showed up as curious witnesses to history. The Patriots beat the Bills 28–7 as Butch Songin completed 13 passes and threw for two scores. A Boston newspaper the next morning declared, "Songin like Unitas." A delighted Saban shook hands with every member of the Patriots team and had each one autograph the AFL's official game ball, the J5-V Spalding.

The AFL's first weekend of exhibitions offered a mix of high drama and low comedy. On a desert-dry night in Tulsa, the Texans beat the Oilers 27–10. Events surrounding the game, however, were straight out of a Hal Roach classic. An open-car cavalcade scheduled to carry the two teams through the middle of Tulsa wound its way through the wrong end of town. At the stadium on game night, the Oilers, victimized by thieves, had to take the field in mismatched uniforms — half the team wearing their Columbia-blue home jerseys, the other half fire-engine red jerseys on loan from the Texans, who dressed in road whites. To cap matters off, the stadium's public address system failed.

The Denver Broncos, bereft of sweat suits or sideline jackets, did at least have game jerseys — one set, for home and away. The jerseys shrank after one washing, forcing Tripucka to cut holes under the arms so he could have freedom to pass the ball. Bronco helmets were equipped with used, paint-scraped facemasks. Even worse were the team's socks. Supplied by Dean Griffing, the long hose were an ugly brown and gold combination of *vertical* stripes. The players cursed the offensive hose, and Griffing too, for buying them.

The AFL's regular season inaugural was Friday, September 9, when the Patriots hosted the Broncos in an 8 P.M. start. Some 21,597 curious onlookers at Boston University watched Patriots offensive tackle Tony Discenzo step up to the tee and perform the AFL's first kickoff. Gino Cappelletti, the ex-bartender from Minnesota, gave Boston a 3–0 lead with a 35-yard field goal late in the first quarter. The Broncos took a 7–3 halftime lead as Tripucka hit Al Carmichael with a short swing pass, and the 30-year-old halfback carried it 59 yards for the first official touchdown in AFL history.

Denver increased its lead to 13–3 when Gene Mingo returned a third-quarter punt along the sideline 76 yards for a touchdown. "About three guys grabbed me," Mingo said later with a smile, "but I just ran past them."

The Patriots rallied in the final period as end Jim Colclough scored on a

Wearing the infamous vertical-striped socks that marked his team's 1960-61 season, Denver Broncos quarterback Frank Tripucka fires a pass to wide receiver Lionel Taylor against the Boston Patriots in 1960. (*Photo courtesy of the Denver Broncos.*)

10-yard TD pass from Songin. Cappelletti's extra point cut Denver's lead to 13–10, but Boston, which had been favored by 16 points, was shut out the rest of the way. The AFL had its first upset victory.

"I'm not a good loser," Patriots owner Billy Sullivan told reporters. "But tonight I have to say I was content."

When Sullivan looks back at that first game today, he recalls the deep feelings he experienced when the Patriots took the field.

"I really lack the vocabulary to portray with any degree of factuality the ecstasy which surged through my body when I sat with the members of my family at Boston University Field," Sullivan says. Sullivan's feelings stemmed from the fact that his wife and son Billy Jr. each received degrees from the University, and Bill's brother Paul had been captain of the 1939 B.U. football team.

There was also a feeling of having proved wrong the critics who insisted the AFL would never get off the ground. "The local critics who predicted that it couldn't be done seemed somewhat surprised that we were able in short order to put together a fine team," Sullivan says, "and that we were able to provide the fans with plenty of action for their money."

Like his fellow owners, Sullivan's route to pro football had been a circuitous one that involved public relations jobs in college football and major-league baseball. Today, Sullivan looks back at each job as an important learning process toward ownership in the pioneer AFL. Sullivan's story is one of unrelenting determination to fulfill a dream, a tale that was the central theme of the AFL:

> The early part of my career was spent at Boston College, at the University of Notre Dame, and at the Naval Academy as a sports information director for those schools and particularly as a personal publicity man for Frank Leahy at Boston College.
>
> Despite the fact that after my Navy career was ended I went into professional baseball as the public relations director of the Boston Braves, I was fortunate enough to be on hand when the Braves won the pennant in 1948.
>
> While with the Braves, we presented exhibition NFL football games each summer because of my desire to try to get an NFL franchise in Boston. The NFL had failed twice in this community. The Redskins began here but they left in 1937 to go to Washington, and frankly, they had not done well in Boston. This seemed like the end of any chance that the NFL would ever try to compete against Boston College, Boston University, Harvard, Tufts, [or] Holy Cross, because college football did have a firm footing in this area.
>
> After the end of World War II, the Boston Yanks came in and gave it a try but it also failed. Despite these failures it was always my view that if local ownership had the team — which had not been the case with the Redskins or Yanks — we would have a good chance of making a go of it.
>
> We staged several preseason exhibition games, and while none of them exactly set the world on fire, I thought that they were paving the way for possible entry of a Boston franchise in the [NFL].
>
> Through my dear friends, Frank Leahy and Jack Mara of the New York Giants, I did get an appointment with Bert Bell, who was then commissioner of the National Football League. Interestingly enough, the appointment took place on Patriots' Day, the 19th of April in 1958. While Mr. Bell was not enthusiastic about the chance of the team coming to Boston, he did like the idea that when and if it occurred ... local ownership would have a better chance of getting the ball across the goal line than people from the outside world, so to speak.
>
> He did say, however, that one of the teams was considering moving and it was no secret at all that the Cardinals happened to be that team. They just couldn't compete against the Bears successfully, and it was Mr. Bell's thought that if the team moved to another town, if there could be some local ownership involved, that Boston would be a primary locale if the situation was developed properly.
>
> With that in mind, I happily left his office and started to dream about the future. A few months later I was listening to a Giants–Packers game on the radio when I learned that Bert Bell had died of a heart attack while sitting in his favorite locale, the end zone, while the Eagles and the Steelers played against each other. Mr. Bell had been associated with both of those teams at one time or another and with his passing, I thought that our chances might well be behind us.
>
> Nevertheless, I tried to get an opportunity to chat with the Maras to see if they might still be interested in endeavoring to get a franchise in the Boston marketplace. When I met with Jack Mara at his office in New York, he told me that it was highly unlikely that at the next meeting of the league, which was scheduled for the latter part of January in 1960, that there would be much talk about expansion or about the move of the Cardinals to St. Louis because the major topic would be the selection of a commissioner. Mr. Mara rather sardonically

remarked, "It seems that there are twelve candidates for the job, and obviously, only one can be chosen." I asked who the candidates were and he said, "The twelve league presidents, because the commissioner's job was a better job than that of president of any of the teams."

That was the meeting at which Commissioner Rozelle was elected. I then said, "Well, if I can't get into your league, perhaps I should take a shot at the American Football League." He suggested that I should have my head examined because the league, in his opinion, would never get off the ground.

Nonetheless, I left his office and went to the home of Harry Wismer, who headed a group that was going to own the New York Titans. I knew Harry quite well because while I worked at Notre Dame he was broadcasting our football games, and we did have a very fine relationship.

It didn't take me long to start moving in the right direction with Harry because he told me that, while at that time there were seven teams in place, the league would like to have an eight-team circuit providing home-and-away games for each team in the league. He also advised that the expansion committee, which would select the eighth team, consisted of Lamar Hunt, Frank Leahy — who was then the general manager of the Los Angeles Chargers — and Harry.

Since I had been associated with Coach Leahy for the better part of fifteen years, and since I was generally regarded as his best friend, and he in turn, mine, it didn't take long to get in touch with Frank and tell him that I was ready, willing, and anxious to get a franchise. With his customary thoughtfulness, Coach Leahy called around and recommended me to all of the members.

I am not quite sure how Lamar stood, but I do know that he eventually acceded to the recommendation. He did so because he was quite impressed by Frank Leahy's comments [to the effect] that, "My friend Bill doesn't have much money and he has no place to play but I can tell you that he will outwork all of you fellows that are so well-set financially."

Shortly after that conversation, I had a call from Lamar advising that if I would have $25,000 on deposit at the Mercantile Trust Bank in Dallas by the close of the business 48 hours after the call was made, we would then have the eighth franchise. I did so, and Lamar still refers frequently to the Patriots as "The phone order franchise."

The AFL's three-day grand opening climaxed in New York, where the Titans hosted the Bills in a 2 P.M. Sunday game at the Polo Grounds. Van Miller, who has been the voice of the Bills since their inception, recalls that first weekend, which saw the Bills lose 27–3.

"I was the original broadcaster for the Bills," says Miller, who called Bills games on WBEN in 1960. "We did the first exhibition game ever played in the AFL, the game between the Bills and Patriots, and the Bills' first regular season game, when they played the Titans in New York. I remember Harry Wismer put us in a baseball press box that was at one end of the stadium. It seemed like every point that was scored was at the far end of the field. We could hardly see anything."

No one knew what to expect as the AFL's first season unfolded, but veteran football writer Tex Maule predicted the new league would generate wide-open offenses.

"Although the new American Football League is far behind the National league in the number of good players it has, the new clubs can match the NFL in excitement and might even produce a more wide-open game," Maule wrote in *Sports Illustrated*. "This is not because they have better runners, passers or receivers; it is because it is almost impossible to develop a cohesive, intelligent and dependable defense using 11 players who met as strangers on the opening day of training camp."

Houston linebacker Dennis Morris, who had played two seasons with the 49ers before joining the Oilers, agreed with Maule's assessment. Speaking of the AFL's lack of good defensive players, Morris shrugged and said, "We'll just have to develop them as we go along."

The AFL's lack of defense was painfully obvious in 1960. Four teams scored as many or more points than the NFL's Cleveland Browns, who led their league with 362 points. The Oilers scored a combined total of 75 points in winning their first two games; the Chargers rang up more than 50 twice. Under Baugh, the Titans both scored and surrendered points at a dizzying pace; New York led the AFL in points scored (382) and points allowed (399). Symbolic of this was the Titans' season finale in Los Angeles, when they lost to the Chargers, 50–43.

With Blanda launching rockets to receivers Bill Groman and Charley Hennigan, and with Cannon rebounding from a slow start to lead the club in rushing, the Oilers won the Eastern Division title with a 10-4 mark. Houston's 3,371 passing yards ranked tops in the league; their 379 points ranked second only to the Titans. Blanda ran a wide-open offense that featured a double-wing set and quick posts to Hennigan.

The Oilers emerged as the AFL's first dominant team, and while their play was artistic, their surroundings were not. Jeppesen Stadium smelled like a septic tank, and its playing surface was terrible. Texans head coach Hank Stram said the field was like concrete — "Poorly laid concrete," Stram noted.

As the AFL's first superstar and drawing card, Cannon played the 1960 season under the microscope. Defenses took special delight in stopping the rookie All-America. "This is a different league, Cannon," one Dallas defender said after dropping him for a loss. "You better grow up." Even Cannon's teammates, some of whom were jealous of his $100,000 contract and All-America status, were skeptical of his ability. They chided him as "All-American," and when Cannon fumbled the ball away in the regular season opener, one Oiler player advised him to shape up.

"You're playing with men now, All-American." At times, Cannon's teammates would mockingly ask him, "You trying to make that hundred thousand on one run, boy?"

"It wasn't easy," Cannon said, "for an All-American breaking into a new league where there are no established stars. After the papers had built me up pretty good, the people all expected me to be a crowd pleaser."

Fortunately for Cannon, he came under the tutelage of the experienced

Blanda. The pair roomed together in training camp, and stayed up late talking football. Blanda explained to Cannon how Frank Gifford ran the Giants' sweep, and how Ollie Matson performed his patented sideline steps.

Cannon struggled early, gaining just 21 yards against Dallas and nine against New York before being benched in the second half by Rymkus. "That was the low point," Cannon said of the Titan's game. "I couldn't do anything right."

Before the Oilers' next game against Buffalo, Rymkus called Cannon into his office and told him the benching might be permanent if he didn't improve. The sharp warning turned Cannon's season around. "I didn't do anything different," Cannon said, "but maybe that's when I started to do things instinctively."

Cannon's improvement was immediate. He rushed for 60 yards and scored two touchdowns against the Bills, then ran through Denver for 105 yards. He followed with two TD receptions against the Chargers, and beat Boston with a 24-yard TD pass. Though he was unhappy with the fact that his longest run from scrimmage in the 1960 season was 39 yards, Cannon was pleased with the final numbers of his rookie campaign — 664 yards rushing, 187 receiving, six touchdowns.

"It bothered me that I hadn't broken loose for more than a 39-yard gain," he said, "but the reason was no mystery. I was simply running against bigger, faster, more experienced players."

But for their nonexistent defense, the Titans might have made a run at the title. Only 9,607 showed up for the home opener against Buffalo, a 27–3 New York victory. Onlookers at the crumbling Polo Grounds thrilled at the sight of a scrambling Al Dorow heaving long passes to the sprinting Don Maynard and Art Powell. The Titans had the offense, but a midseason slump saw them drop four in a row, and they finished the season in second place at 7–7. Not that anyone in New York noticed.

"We didn't have any fans in the stands," Grantham says. "Harry Wismer used to announce 20,000 fans, but there used to be a hot dog vendor for every customer. They used to let us go up into the stands after games and shake people's hands. But it was a lot of fun. I always felt at home in the Polo Grounds. There was so much history behind it. I remember standing out in center field where Willie Mays made his catch."

The Bills were an oddity in the early days of the AFL — a team trying to win with defense. Headed by all-pros LaVerne Torczon, Archie Matsos, and Richie McCabe, Buffalo led the league in pass defense. The offense was headed by fullback Wray Carlton and receiver Elbert "Golden Wheels" Dubenion, but the Bills were inconsistent and finished third in the East at 5–8.

In Boston, the Patriots upset both the Chargers and Texans to reach the .500 mark late in the season, but losses in their final four games dropped them to 5–9 and last place in the East.

In the West, superlatives abounded as the Chargers won the division with a 10–4 record. Jack Kemp threw for 3,018 yards and 20 touchdowns and was the AFL's top-ranked quarterback. Lowe rushed for 855 yards and nine TDs and led all AFL runners with a 6.3 yards-per-carry average. After losing three of their first five games, the club's explosive offense kicked into gear and overwhelmed opponents. Over their final nine games, the Chargers scored 41 points or more five times. In their final four games, L.A. *averaged* 46 points per game. But they remained a tough sell.

"The Coliseum in L.A. was so empty for our games and the stands so empty the people looked like flies sitting in buttermilk," Lowe remembers with a laugh. "They'd move everyone in the stands to one side of the field to make it look crowded."

In Dallas, the Texans finished second at 8–6, and showcased one of the AFL's most exciting players in halfback Abner Haynes. Head coach Hank Stram geared his flashy I-formation offense to Haynes, and Haynes responded by averaging 5.6 yards per carry and leading the AFL in rushing with 875 yards. Haynes also led the league in punt returns, picking up 215 yards and a 15-yard per attempt average.

Because of their late arrival on the AFL scene, Raider management was forced to play catch-up. Oakland dropped three of its first four games, but rebounded with wins over Dallas and Boston to fashion a .500 mark. A 34–28 loss to Boston started a three-game losing streak that dropped Oakland from contention.

The Broncos had offensive heroes in Gene Mingo, who returned a punt 76 yards to beat Boston in the season opener, and end Lionel Taylor, who joined the team in the third week of the season and led the league in receiving.

As the Broncos lost games, they also lost fans. After drawing more than 18,000 for their home opener against Oakland, attendance steadily declined until just 5,861 came out to see the team's final home game against the Titans.

Total attendance for the AFL its first season was 926,156 for 56 games, an average attendance of 16,000. At season's end, Foss announced losses as high as $2 million. The Texans lost $400,000, but Hunt laughed when an NFL owner said the AFL would survive as long as the Texas oil money holds out. "I hope," Hunt said, "he doesn't hold his breath until we go broke."

When reports of the Texans' financial losses put the figure at close to half a million for 1960, H.L. Hunt said, "At that rate, he can't last much past the year 2135 A.D."

To a man, the members of the Foolish Club were certain the AFL would survive. "Next year our operating costs will go down," Hilton said. "Teams which have had to pay for the expansion of stadiums will not be faced with that again. We can carry much smaller preseason squads, since by then we will have a solid base upon which to build; this year everyone had to look at every football player he could get in order to find enough good ones. And our attendance should rise. In three years, we'll be operating in the black."

With the league title game between the Oilers and Chargers set for January 1, and with cautious optimism abounding among most team owners, 1961 did indeed offer a brighter future.

Chapter Five

1961: A Well-Oiled Offense

THE FRESH COAT OF PAINT on old Jeppesen Stadium gleamed in the early morning sunlight as New Year's Day, 1961, dawned bright and warm in Houston. By early afternoon, the temperature hovered in the mid–50s, and some 32,183 fans were on hand for the championship game showdown between the Houston Oilers and Los Angeles Chargers.

ABC-TV touted the AFL game as a matchup of the league's two most exciting offenses. The clash of quarterbacks featured the Oilers' experienced George Blanda against the Chargers' youthful Jack Kemp. During the season, Kemp led the league in passing, but Blanda had thrown for more touchdowns and fewer interceptions. The matchup at running back was just as intriguing. Houston was led by Heisman Trophy winner Billy Cannon, the AFL's most recognizable player; L.A. had Paul Lowe, who rose out of obscurity to lead the league in rushing.

It was also a matchup of head coaches Lou Rymkus and Sid Gillman. It was a showdown Rymkus was desperate to win. The two teams had split their regular season games, each winning a close game at home. Rymkus was hoping the home-field trend would continue one more time.

"[Rymkus] developed this big thing about Sid Gillman and the Chargers," Blanda said in his autobiography *Still Kicking*. "He had to beat Sid. They'd been together in the National League and it kind of carried over into the AFL."

In Houston's cramped dressing room prior to kickoff, Rymkus told his team the Oilers had *earned* the honor of winning the AFL's first title game.

"Gentlemen," he said, "after all we've been through, the heat and the mud and the mosquitoes, we deserve to be champions of the AFL. We do. They don't. Nobody is going to beat us."

The Chargers controlled the early going, scoring on their first two drives. Four minutes into the game, Ben Agajanian, L.A.'s 41-year-old kicking specialist, hit a 38-yard field goal for a 3–0 Charger lead. At the 8:16 mark, Agajanian added a 22-yarder to boost L.A.'s lead to 6–0.

The Oilers took a 7–6 lead early in the second quarter when Blanda keyed a 12-play, 40-yard drive with eight consecutive passes, including a 17-yard touchdown to fullback Dave Smith. Blanda's 18-yard field goal later in the quarter boosted Houston's lead to 10–6. Behind the running of Lowe, who averaged just under 8 yards per carry on the afternoon, the Chargers rallied late in the quarter. With five seconds to go in the half, Agajanian's 27-yard field goal cut the Oilers' lead to 10–9 at the half.

In the third quarter, a seven-yard scoring pass from Blanda to Bill Groman gave Houston a 17–9 lead, but the Chargers countered when Lowe scored from 2 yards out to bring L.A. to within one, 17–16, heading into the final period.

The game turned for good in the fourth quarter when on third down from his own 12, Blanda bent low in the huddle and called, "Pass Z, Slant Four, Swing and Go." The play was designed to isolate Cannon on a fly pattern against strong safety Jim Sears, who kept creeping up to the line of scrimmage. At the snap, Cannon slanted for the sideline, running a 45-degree angle that mirrored the pattern wide receiver Charley Hennigan was running on the same side of the field. As Sears closed, Cannon broke off the pattern and headed upfield. Sears, caught up with Hennigan and Charger cornerback Charlie McNeil, fell behind. Cannon pulled in Blanda's pass at the Houston 35, and went in for the TD.

The 88-yard score gave Houston an eight-point lead. The Houston defense secured the 24–16 win by stopping the Chargers on downs at the Oilers' 35- and 22-yard lines. When the game ended, Oiler captain Orville Trask cradled the game ball next to his muddied jersey. Cannon was named MVP after totaling 259 yards of offense. A photographer moved in as the dirt-covered Cannon accepted congratulations from team owner Bud Adams, who was dressed in a snow-white Stetson hat and long white raincoat.

The drama of the AFL championship prompted some bold remarks, most of them directed at the rival NFL. Rymkus told a reporter, "If that wasn't just as good a brand of football as they play in the *other* league, I'll kiss your ass!"

Blanda, who threw for three touchdowns and 301 yards, had some biting comments for his old employers. "I've waited eleven years for this moment," he said. "I've waited eleven lousy years. This is my first championship. The damn Chicago Bears never won one during my ten years. Maybe if Halas had let me play, they might have. How about that?"

New York Titans owner Harry Wismer said the Chargers–Oilers title game surpassed the NFL championship waged a week earlier by Green Bay and Philadelphia.

"Some forty or fifty million people saw the best professional football playoff game of the season," Wismer remarked. "The American League game was far better than the one between Philadelphia and Green Bay in the other league. I'd say that the Houston Oilers could easily beat the Chicago Bears, the Los Angeles Rams, the Washington Redskins and the Dallas Cowboys, to name some of the weaker clubs in the NFL. And the Oilers could play a representative game against either of the NFL divisional championship teams. Our prestige is on the rise."

Through the years, Blanda has insisted the AFL would have *won* a showdown game with the NFL in 1960. "That first year, the Houston Oilers or Los Angeles Chargers could have beaten — repeat, *beaten* — the NFL champion in a Super Bowl," Blanda said. "The pass receivers on the Oilers were every bit as good as those I've thrown to before and since. They had the same quickness and ability to get open. I think the AFL was capable of beating the NFL in a Super Bowl game as far back as 1960 or 1961. I just regret we didn't get the chance to prove it."

The NFL hard-liners scoffed at such a notion. To them, the AFL was pure minor league, barely worthy of notice. "The American Football League can't be anything but a Mickey Mouse League," Bears coach George Halas snorted. "How can it be anything else? Isn't George Blanda a first-string quarterback over there?"

The late Tex Maule, who covered the NFL for *Sports Illustrated*, also took a dim view of Blanda, the Oilers, and the quality of AFL football in general:

> No player on the Houston Oilers could break into the starting lineup of any of the four top teams in either division of the NFL, and only one or two could break into the starting lineups of any team in the NFL," Maule wrote. "The only reason George Blanda, who threw only 50 touchdown passes in ten years in the NFL, can hope to succeed in the American Football League, is because he can expect to find his receivers less adequately covered.
>
> The question is: how good are the Oilers (and for that matter, how good is the rest of the league)? Unquestionably, the Oilers are better than Missouri or Minnesota or Mississippi. They are smarter and more versatile than these college teams; but they are not as good as the Dallas Cowboys, the newest and weakest team in the National Football League. The Cowboys, who are smarter and more versatile than the Oilers, would beat them, and easily.

Joe Foss wasn't sure how the Oilers would have fared against the NFL's weaker teams, but the AFL commissioner laughed off Wismer's notion of a playoff game between the league champions.

"If the NFL had paid attention to Ole Harry's cries for a championship game in those first couple of years, we'd never have lived to see the day of the merger," said Foss, who shuddered at the thought of the Oilers playing the 1960 Eagles or '61 Packers.

"They'd have handed us our heads," said Foss. "The AFL would have been left in the dust for the buzzards to pick at our bones."

While football fans debated the relative merits of the AFL and NFL over hot stoves through the winter, Barron Hilton and Gillman set about improving the conditions of their team. For Hilton, the concern was purely financial. The Chargers had failed in their attempt to secure a faithful following in Los Angeles. In 1959, Redskins owner George Preston Marshall told Hilton, "You've got no worries. Your team will draw in L.A. just like everything else draws. They go for anything out there."

The Rams led the NFL in attendance if not in wins, and the Dodgers did the same in major-league baseball. In 1960, Hollywood Park was the most successful race track in the country. But apathy, rather than enthusiasm, best described the Chargers' following. When Wismer brought Joe Arcuni, one of the Titans' stockholders, to the Coliseum for the season finale, only 11,457 were on hand in a stadium that seated more than 100,000. The figure represented a 50 percent drop in attendance since the start of the season, when the Chargers had played to Coliseum crowds of 17,724 for the season opener against Dallas, 18,226 for Boston, and 21,085 for Houston. Arcuni looked at the empty seats and demanded a return of his investment.

When Hilton first decided to buy the Charger franchise, the hotel magnate figured he was purchasing his own personal gold mine. "When we build a hotel," Hilton said, "we have to put in $18 to $20 million before we even open the doors. For the football franchise, we needed no land, no bricks, no cement — nothing except a few balls, uniforms and a staff."

The 1960 season saw Hilton's team lose $910,000. The team's financial problems were common knowledge; at the 1960 World Series between the New York Yankees and Pittsburgh Pirates, *San Diego Union* sports editor Jack Murphy heard that Hilton was pondering moving the team from Los Angeles. After Murphy returned to San Diego at the conclusion of the Series, he asked Gene Gregston, a sports columnist on the *San Diego Tribune*, to help talk civic leaders into inviting the Chargers to San Diego.

San Diego's mayor and city council embraced the idea. "We're a Green Bay with climate," one city council member said. Plans were drawn up to add a second deck to San Diego's Balboa Stadium, thereby boosting seating capacity from 20,000 to 34,500. Abe Polinsky, a San Diego sports enthusiast who sported a Salvador Dali–style mustache, helped form the Greater San Diego Sports Association, a group of more than 200 of the city's business leaders. General Dynamics, San Diego's massive aircraft plant, established ticket booths on its grounds. Charger players were promised off-season jobs, and further support came from local newspapers, TV, and radio stations.

San Diego's enthusiastic response to the Chargers convinced Hilton his team would profit there. On February 10, AFL owners gave formal approval for Hilton to transfer his franchise from L.A. to San Diego. With his team situated only 15 miles from the Mexican border, Hilton said, "I hope things work out here. We're about as far south as we can go."

Jerry Magee, a sportswriter for the *San Diego Tribune*, has covered the Chargers since they moved to San Diego in 1961. Magee believes the Chargers and the AFL are responsible for the stunning growth of the city of San Diego:

> I covered the city council meetings that led to the Chargers coming to San Diego. At that time, San Diego was kind of a sleepy little city. It was a naval town, but it had settled into the doldrums following World War II. Geographically, it's kind

of an isolated place. You go west from San Diego, and there's mountains. You go south and there's Mexico. My house is only 13 miles from the Mexican border. But the Chargers sort of represented a catalyst for bringing people together. Today, San Diego is the sixth-largest city in the U.S.

The Chargers' franchise shift wasn't the only high-level jockeying going on in the AFL. On January 17, three members of Oakland's eight-man syndicate bought out their five partners. Ed McGah, Wayne Valley, and Robert Osborne were the survivors; McGah was named team president.

On May 14, Denver ownership underwent a facelift when Bob and Lee Howsam sold their shares in the club to a syndicate headed by Cal Kunz, Jr. Like the Chargers, the Broncos had failed to build a solid following in their initial season. Only 91,332 had paid to see the Broncos in their seven home games, an average of 13,047 per game. Just 5,861 saw Denver play New York in the twelfth game of the season.

Kunz offered to buy out the Howsams when rumors spread that the team might be moved out of Denver. Such a move was unlikely, since the Howsams owned Bears Stadium, but Kunz was taking no chances.

Owning a fondness for crewcut haircuts and Ivy League clothes, Kunz's style was in keeping with his background; he was a former marine colonel and a graduate of the Harvard Business School. Gerald H. Phipps was named the team's new chairman of the board. Phipps had gained notoriety in Denver as the man who built the city's glass, granite, and steel skyline.

As the 1961 regular season approached, it was clear that the Oilers and Chargers remained the strongest teams in the AFL. The Oilers were an offensive-minded machine, with George Blanda at quarterback, Cannon and Charley Tolar at running back, and Bill Groman and Charley Hennigan at wide receiver. Tolar and Hennigan were two of the more interesting examples of pro careers that would not have been if not for the AFL.

A 5-foot-6, 200-pound fullback, Tolar had appeared in a few exhibition games for the Steelers in 1959. When he joined the Oilers, Tolar's size and low center of gravity made it difficult for AFL defenders to find him, much less tackle him. He was called the "Human Bowling Ball," and his uniform number, 44, often disappeared in the crowd.

"He's so short," Dallas Texans linebacker E. J. Holub said, "that when he bends low you just can't get under him. When you tackle Tolar, you butt helmets.

Said Boston Patriots linebacker Tony Sardisco, "Whenever I couldn't see where the ball went, I figured they gave it to Charley."

Tolar's size ultimately became an advantage to him. He had the upper body of a 250-pound man, and ran with balance and instinct. When he retired after playing seven seasons in the AFL, he was the fifth-leading rusher in league history. His best season was 1962, when he rushed for 1,012 yards. He was equally effective catching swing passes out of the backfield — he had eight TD catches in 1962 — and cutting down blitzers. During one AFL telecast, ABC sportscaster Curt Gowdy referred to Tolar as "a kneecap blocker."

In college, Tolar and Hennigan played in the same backfield at Northwest Louisiana State. They were both living in Robiline, Louisiana, when they heard news of a new pro football league being started in 1960. Tall and thin with flat palms, Hennigan was described by one writer as having the build of a flamingo. Cut by the Edmonton Eskimos of the Canadian Football League, Hennigan was teaching high school biology when the AFL began.

When he first heard of the new league, Hennigan scoured the local papers for additional information. When none was forthcoming, he called the sports editor of the Shreveport newspaper and was told that the closest franchise city was Houston. Hennigan phoned the Oilers' head coach Lou Rymkus, who told him the team was interested in any players they could find. Hennigan contacted Tolar, and the odd couple set out for Houston in a car both knew could only make it one way.

Throughout the course of their trip, Tolar, an oil field firefighter, kept telling Hennigan the pros wouldn't be interested in guys like them, that they ought to turn around. But Hennigan, who had earned exactly $2,734.18 to that point as a teacher, wouldn't hear of it. In Hennigan's pocket was his final teacher's paycheck stub — $270.62 — a piece of paper that served as a constant source of inspiration to him his first year in Houston. When Hennigan got to the Oilers camp, he taped his teacher's pay stub to the inside of his helmet. Hennigan says today:

> I wanted to play football so bad. I drove down with Charlie Tolar and there were 62 guys in the Oilers camp when we got there. We trained at the University of Houston in an old baseball stadium, Buff Stadium, and some of the big guys they had in camp were out of shape; they literally crawled in there. Within two weeks, they had eliminated all but 50 of us. At that time, they only kept 33 ballplayers on the roster. Making the final cut was something everyone wanted to do.
>
> I was in awe of Billy Cannon, the Heisman Trophy winner. He was a great athlete and an outstanding player. And George Blanda was obviously the best quarterback I ever played with. He always had the ball to you right on the break. I remember we played an exhibition game in Mobile, Alabama, and George called a corner route. Well, the defense had zoned us and there was no one in the middle of the field, so I ran in the middle and he hit me with the pass. But when I got back to the huddle, George just said, "Run where I tell you."

Thanks in part to the coaching of former Cleveland Brown greats Dub Jones and Mac Speedie, whom Rymkus had brought in as receivers coach, Hennigan did make it. Speedie taught him how to pull the ball to his chest when making a reception, and despite the protests of the rest of the Oilers staff, Hennigan survived the final cut. Hennigan explains:

> Some of the other guys could catch, but they didn't have my speed. I was really lucky. Before I got to the Oilers I called Dub Jones, who owned a lumber yard in

Louisiana, and asked if he would work with me. He taught me finesse and moves, how to release from the line and turn my man, how to carry a defensive back until I turned and made my move.

We played the Raiders in Kesar Stadium in our first (regular season) game, and I scored the first Oiler touchdown. But I got flipped on the play, and I broke my collarbone. I missed the next three weeks. I should have had an operation, but the motto then was to have the operation in January. We couldn't afford to have them during the season.

Hennigan became one of the AFL's greatest rags-to-riches stories. He caught 44 passes as a rookie, and in 1961 had 82 receptions for 1,746 yards, a club record. In 1964 Hennigan set a pro record with 101 catches. Like Tolar, Hennigan retired after the 1966 season, and he remains the club's all-time leading receiver with 410 catches for 6,823 yards and 51 TDs.

Hennigan thrived in an era when defenders used a physical bump-and-run coverage. "They could hold us up anywhere on the field or cut us down," he says. "We'd run shoulder-to-shoulder with those guys. We were taught where to make our moves."

Hennigan says that receivers in the 1960s learned to use the playing field to their advantage. One of Hennigan's favorite moves near the goal line was to reach out with one hand and grab the goalpost, which in the 1960s was situated on the goal line.

"We'd use the pitcher's mound, the goalposts," he recalls. "We were taught anytime we were eight yards from the goalpost, we would run a quick slant, and brush the guy defending us against the post. Or else we'd grab the post with one hand and swing around and go the other way. Groman had hands like a frog's, with long fingers that were like suction cups. He ran great patterns. We scored a lot of touchdowns on that play."

Receivers in the 1960s often used the goal posts the way basketball players use "picks." Miami Dolphins halfback Joe Auer once ran a deep pattern against the Bills. When he got close to the end zone, Auer cut towards the middle of the field and ran parallel with the goal line. Trailing Auer was Buffalo outside linebacker Mike Stratton. Auer could hear Stratton pounding behind him, when suddenly the sound was interrupted by a noise that Auer described as "BUHH-WANNNG!! *Oof!*"

"I turned around," Auer said later, "and it was just like the Tom and Jerry cartoon where the cat runs into a wall because Stratton had just run into the goalpost.... It must have hurt Stratton, but he and I just stood about ten yards away from each other laughing our heads off."

As the Oilers disembarked in Boston in the season's fifth week, the defending champions found themselves in last place in the Eastern Division with a 1-3 record; in 1960, they had never spent a day out of first place. Owner Bud Adams asked head coach Lou Rymkus for the team's game films so he could study their strategy. Rumors spread that Rymkus' job was on the line.

"A new coach would at least focus attention away from the Oilers," wrote Jack Gallagher in the *Houston Post*. "Adams thinks he sees a number of opportunities where his high-priced talent could be better used."

For the Patriots game, Rymkus went with backup quarterback Jacky Lee. Ignoring a gathering fog that rolled in from the nearby Charles River, Lee completed 27 passes for an AFL-record 457 yards. Hennigan hauled in 13 of those passes to set another league mark. Still, Houston trailed 31–28, with five seconds left in the game. With the ball on the Boston 14-yard line, Rymkus sent Blanda in to attempt the game-tying field goal.

In the Houston huddle, an Oiler player who had been benched by Rymkus offered advice. "Miss, it George," he whispered to Blanda. "Teach the son of a bitch a lesson he'll never forget."

Incensed, Blanda grabbed the player by the jersey. "Don't ever say that to me again." Blanda's ensuing field goal was good, and the Oilers left Boston with a tie.

Rymkus didn't survive the week as Oilers head coach. Citing differences in philosophy, Adams fired Rymkus and named former assistant coach Wally Lemm, who had left the team after the 1960 season to spend more time with his sporting goods company.

"I questioned some of Coach Lou Rymkus' strategy and asked to see some game films," Adams said, explaining the move. "I studied them and decided we needed a coaching change."

Lemm's personality was a complete turnaround from Rymkus. "Football," Lemm said, "is supposed to be fun. I try to make it clear, straightforward, and as pleasurable as I can."

"Lou was intense, always irascible," Hennigan says. "He was an old Notre Damer, and he called himself 'the Great Northern Buffalo.' I remember when we won our first AFL championship. Our take home pay was $800. Lou groused about it. He felt we should've gotten more. Wally came over from the defense, and he let the offense run itself. We ran double and triple wing sets, we'd send five guys out on passes. We had a ball. It was fun.

Lemm's easygoing approach helped the Oilers reel off 10 straight wins. The team was white-hot on offense, scoring 49, 45, 33, 48, and 47 points over their final five games. They also scored 55 points on two occasions and became the first pro team to score more than 500 points and gain more than 6,000 yards.

Blanda set AFL records with 464 yards passing in a game and 36 touchdown passes in a season. He threw seven TDs in one game, hit a league-high 62 percent of his field goals, and was named AFL Player of the Year. Hennigan's 1,746 yards receiving set a pro record; Groman led the AFL with 17 TD catches. Running Lemm's draw play, Cannon led the AFL in rushing yards with 948, and accounted for 331 yards and five TDs. Tolar rushed for an additional 577 yards on the year behind a line that included all-pro-caliber players in tackles "Dirty" Al Jamison and Rich Michael and guard Bob Talamini.

Houston quarterbacks aired it out in '61, attempting nearly 500 passes. With such a heavy dependence on the passing game, it was up to the offensive line to protect Blanda and Lee. Varying their pass-blocking techniques, the Oilers allowed just 14 sacks in '61 and only 11 in '62. Talamini, who joined the Oilers in 1960, said the line had three methods of pass protection: drop back and absorb the blow; fire out to simulate run blocking and then recoil; helmet-butt the defender and cut him low.

"I always [went] into a game with one main plan for my moves," Talamini said, "and a couple of countermoves in case the first plan [didn't] work."

While the Oilers won with offense, the Chargers excelled on defense. Behind a unit that allowed an AFL-low 219 points and intercepted a pro-record 49 passes, San Diego started the season with 11 straight wins, including a 24–14 win over Dallas before a record crowd of 33,788. For the Chargers, who had drawn just 9,000 to the Coliseum the year before, the Dallas game marked their third straight home attendance of more than 32,000.

The Chargers had great offensive talent in Jack Kemp, Paul Lowe, and Ron Mix, but in 1961 it was their defense that opponents feared most. Gillman had drafted a pair of defensive giants to anchor the front four. From Grambling College came Ernie Ladd, a 6-foot-9, 317-pound tackle nicknamed the "Big Cat." From the University of Indiana, Gillman drafted 6-foot-5, 262-pound defensive end Earl "Tree" Faison. Combined with Ron Nery, a 6-foot-6, 247-pound end, and 6-foot-5, 275-pound tackle Bill Hudson, the Chargers owned the West Coast's original "Fearsome Foursome."

Originally from Orange, Texas, Ladd came from a household where size was a family trait. His father was 6-foot-4, 265 pounds. His mother was 6-foot, 245. Ernie, too, grew to be a man of immense size — and appetite. He had 22-inch calves and wore size 17 EEE shoes. He once lost a pancake-eating contest to a husband-and-wife *team*, 137–124. "I want to set that record straight," Ladd said. "I got there 30 minutes late and was already 53 pancakes behind."

Ladd's daily menu went as follows:

Breakfast: a dozen eggs, a dozen pancakes, a pound of bacon, half a loaf of toast, half a jar of jam, half a gallon of juice.

Lunch: 10 pork chops, three servings each of green beans and rice, half a gallon of milk, three peach cobblers, three dishes of ice cream.

Dinner: four 16-ounce steaks, three baked potatoes, three servings of spinach, three dishes of cole slaw, eight rolls and a half-pound of butter, two shrimp cocktails, three desserts, and a half-gallon of milk.

At Grambling, Ladd was part of a team that included future all-pros Buck Buchanan, Willie Brown, and Roosevelt Taylor. He was drafted by the Chargers and the Chicago Bears, and to improve their chances of signing the young giant, San Diego dispatched Brad Pye, a local black sportswriter, to meet Ladd. Pye took him to Houston for the 1960 AFL title game. It was there, on New Year's Day, when Ladd met Al Davis for the first time.

"There was a knock on the door," said Davis, an assistant coach with the Chargers at the time, "and in walked Brad. And behind him this giant of a man. I couldn't believe it. Well, we didn't let him out of our sight. We tried to sign him right after the game, but he said the Bears had made him a good offer and he wanted time to think about it."

Davis put Ladd on a plane to Los Angeles and sent him out to meet Gillman. A week later, Davis, who had signed the huge Bill Hudson, called Gillman to inquire about Ladd.

"You know what?" Gillman said. "This big SOB wants a no-cut contract."

"Give it to him, Sid," Davis responded. "Can't you just see it now? We'll have the biggest damn defensive line in football."

Ladd says that despite his contract demands, there was never much doubt which team he was going to sign with. "I didn't like the cold weather," Ladd says today, "and I didn't want to play in it. California to me was much better than Illinois. Really, I was kidnapped [by the AFL]. They talked me into going on a plane to California. I was just a kid from Grambling, and they said, 'Go out to California for a couple of days.' They were romancing me, and I was overwhelmed."

Before long, it was Ladd who was overwhelming others. His teammates called him "Big Man"; opponents called him "Sir." Ladd used a straight-ahead, forearm-flailing charge capable of caving in helmets. "He broke my nose," Jets tackle Dan Ficca said, "and then he broke my cheekbone. Then he broke the cheekbone on the other side, but by then my head was numb."

Patriots center Jon Morris said Ladd blocked out the sun when he lined up over him. "It was dark," Morris said, recalling a game against Ladd. "I couldn't see the linebackers. I couldn't see the goalposts. It was like being locked into a closet. He comes out there, and you can't get your eyes off his arms. He has those long arms and all over them he has these pads and bandages. He keeps hitting you with the right forearm over and over again."

Guard Charley Long, who lined up next to Morris, said the only way to handle Ladd was to compliment him. "After each play, Ladd cracked either me or Jon. He hit us on the helmet so hard ... I didn't know if I was conscious. The noise was terrible, bells were ringing.... What could we do? I told him how great he was — just praying he wouldn't get mad and hit any harder."

Oakland's Jim Otto, the AFL's all-time center, remembers Ladd's great presence on the field. "Ernie Ladd," Otto says, "was a *dominating* person."

Ladd's size, strength and speed — he was fast enough to run down a sweep — made him one of the premier defensive tackles in the game. Davis called him "the most dynamic defensive force in football." Buffalo back Wray Carlton, who played behind one of the premier guards in the league in Billy Shaw, says teams had to devise special blocking schemes — not all of them legal — to handle Ladd.

Oakland Raiders center Jim Otto was known as "Mr. AFL" because of his fierce allegiance to the league. Otto was distinguishable on the field not only by his double-zero uniform number but by his style of play, which earned him AFL all-pro status for 10 straight seasons. (*Photo courtesy of the Oakland Raiders.*)

"Billy Shaw doesn't like to talk about it," Carlton says, "but you had to play tricks with [Ladd]. You couldn't really handle him one-on-one. Billy had experience, and he knew some of things you could do, holding without being seen, things like that."

AFL quarterbacks kept an eye out for Ladd. The Patriots had a slogan for him — "No, Ernie, no!" — which is what quarterback Babe Parilli yelled whenever Ladd got loose in the pocket. Houston's George Blanda said, "Every time I felt that damned Ernie Ladd near me, I just got rid of the ball."

While Ladd was the "Big Cat," Faison was the "Tree." He was impressive physically, with a huge chest and sloping shoulders that branched out from his columnar neck. San Diego strength coach Alvin Roy, who was also an Olympic trainer, called Faison "the most magnificent physical specimen I've ever seen."

Born and raised in Newport News, Virginia, Faison was the youngest of four children who were raised by their mother alone. He matured physically at an early age. When he was 12, Faison walked into a classroom for the new school year and was told by the teacher, "Sorry mister, we don't allow visitors here."

Faison earned an athletic scholarship to Indiana University, where he played the line on both offense and defense. In 1960 he was named Lineman of the Year by the Washington Touchdown Club. Drafted in the first round by the Chargers, Faison made a profound impression on his teammates. When a Houston lineman got into a fight with Ladd, Faison picked the 300-pound Oiler off his feet and threw him to the ground.

As much as opponents feared Ladd, they respected Faison. "Ladd's the biggest," Titans running back Charlie Flowers said at the time. "But Faison is their bull."

Faison didn't have great pursuit ability, but he was tough to handle when the play came to his side. "They shouldn't ever run over Earl Faison," Gillman said. "At his best he's the absolute best in the league.... He's very tough to hold in a block."

Even double-team blocking schemes were futile. Blanda recalled the Oilers trying to run at Faison behind a tackle *and* guard. "You pull a guard out to help the tackle block him and he doesn't blink," Blanda said of Faison. "Just blows through both."

The Chargers initially put Faison at left end and Ladd at left tackle, but changed their minds when offenses began sending plays in the other direction. "Ernie and I egged each other on to get to the quarterback," Faison said. "We had a real rivalry going to see which one would get more ink. They started him next to me, and then they found out I could cover my side of the line by myself, so [Ernie] played the rest of the time on the other side at right tackle."

The Chargers' record-setting pass defense was predicated on the penetrating rush of the front four. "They were a zone team," said Lee Grosscup, who quarterbacked the Titans in the early 1960s. "They blitzed rarely. Sid Gillman's pass defense was built mainly on four very big men up front who rushed the passer while seven other men took their pass drops."

The height of San Diego's pass rushers created sight problems for quarterbacks and clogged their passing lanes. Kansas City head coach Hank Stram devised his famous "moving pocket"—a quarterback rollout behind pulling linemen—specifically to neutralize the San Diego rush. "Ladd and Faison would invariably knock down six or seven balls every game," Stram said, "if you tried to throw from the normal pocket."

Helping coach the great Charger defense was a young assistant named Chuck Noll. "He had a great way with the players," Gillman said. "If a guy didn't do the job expected, Chuck could climb on his back."

Ladd was one of those who felt the sting of Noll's low-key criticism, but he holds his former coach in high regard. "Chuck was a real fiery guy," Ladd says. "But he was the best teacher I ever played under. He and I were always fighting, always squabbling, but he had a great way of teaching. I take my hat off to Chuck. He was one of the main reasons for our success."

Lining up opposite Faison was Ron Nery, a 6-foot-6, 247-pound speed rusher who liked to number his moves. When Nery was having a good day, he would toy with the offensive lineman across from him. "Here comes Move

Number One," Nery would say. "Here comes Move Number Three." The '61 Charger defense ranked first in the AFL against the pass, second against the run, and first in total defense.

The success of the Oilers and Chargers helped dispel the negative publicity the AFL received in 1961 that resulted from some highly publicized feuds. In the middle of most of the wars was New York Titans owner Harry Wismer. Wismer was described by one AFL observer as the "mad pitchman of the league." The Titans played their home games in the grimy, near-empty Polo Grounds, and the team's front office was situated in Wismer's New York apartment. Wismer himself sold what tickets he could out of his bedroom.

During the '61 season, Wismer was involved in public squabbles with AFL Commissioner Joe Foss, Bills owner Ralph Wilson, and even his own head coach, Sammy Baugh. Baugh returned the verbal sniping with Wismer and New York quarterback Al Dorow, who complained about the Titans' lack of playbooks.

"Before you can have playbooks," Baugh snapped, "you have to have paper."

The two incidents that proved most embarrassing to the AFL involved a secret November draft the owners held behind the back of Joe Foss. The secret draft was done to get a jump on the NFL, but it represented a challenge to Foss' authority. When word about the draft leaked, AFL owners initially declared it was less an actual draft than a "negotiation list" for choosing players to whom they would later have the rights.

Foss vetoed the November draft, but had little control over the Boston Patriots' decision on Friday, October 20, to postpone their scheduled home game that night against the Buffalo Bills. The Bills were riding a two-game win streak, but when they arrived in Boston, they were told Hurricane Gerda posed enough of a threat that the Patriots were going to postpone the game. Buffalo GM Dick Gallagher thought the postponement was a joke. "Who ever heard of a football game being called off?" Gallagher asked.

Bills linebacker Archie Matsos told reporters, "I've seen girls' softball games played in worse weather than this." Bills coach Buster Ramsey looked up at the clear skies over Boston, and called the postponement "a bush-league trick." The Patriots responded by bombing the Bills 52–21.

Van Miller, the Bills' radio announcer, laughs when he remembers the incident:

> Billy Sullivan was the owner of the Patriots at the time, and I was sitting with Dick Gallagher in Billy's office when we were told of this "hurricane alert." I told Billy, "You can't postpone this game because of an alert." He got mad and threw me out of the office.
>
> Well, they ended up playing five or seven high school games that Friday night. It turned out to be a nice, breezy night. When we kicked off on Sunday, we ended up playing in a typhoon.

On Christmas Eve, 29,556 filled the stone seats of San Diego's Balboa Stadium for the championship game rematch between the Chargers and Houston Oilers. The sun shone brightly and the temperature stood at 59 degrees as the AFL's showcase teams met for the fifth time, including exhibition games, in 1961.

A national TV audience settled in to watch an offensive showdown between the Oilers, who set a pro football record with 513 points, and the Chargers, whose 12-2 record was the best in the league. Instead, the defenses dominated. Looking to shut off Gillman's passing game, the Oilers instituted a series of blitzes designed at pressuring Kemp. The strategy forced the Chargers to often keep both backs in to block on passing downs, allowing the Houston secondary to double the receivers. Even with the extra blocking, Kemp was sacked six times.

"Our rushes worked so well at the beginning," Lemm said, "we stuck to them through the whole game."

The game settled into a bruising defensive battle. Some 13 players had to be helped off the field. Oiler ends Hennigan and Groman were both sidelined with injuries; a peelback block sent Ladd to the hospital. San Diego picked off six passes, Houston four, and the teams combined for seven fumbles.

Blanda's 46-yard field goal in the second quarter gave Houston a 3-0 lead at the half. With just over four minutes left in the third quarter, Houston faced a third-and-five at the San Diego 35. Running to his right, Blanda threw across the field to Cannon, who made a leaping catch at the 17. Cannon skipped through a tackle, picked up a block from end Bob McLeod and scored for a 10-0 lead.

George Blair's 12-yard field goal 39 seconds into the final quarter finally got the Chargers on the board. Down 10-3, San Diego needed a touchdown to tie. But like the 1960 title game, the Oilers' defense made the key plays when it counted. A pass interference call against the Oilers put the Chargers at the Houston 37. On first down, Kemp threw over the middle to his 6-foot-5, 250-pound tight end Dave Kocourek. Enter 5-foot-9, 153-pound safety Julian Spence. The smallest man on the field, Spence made the biggest defensive play of the game, stepping in front of Kocourek to intercept Kemp's pass.

In their locker room, the Oilers sounded less like champions than survivors. Blanda called the '61 title game the "roughest game I ever played in."

Lemm, who shuttled between the AFL and NFL during the 1960s as a head coach, recalled the 1961 title game as the most fiercely contested game of his career. "I have to rate this game as the most vicious, hard-hitting football game I have ever seen," Lemm said. "That game was played with more ferocity than I had ever seen before. The game became more violent as it progressed and the hitting could literally be heard in the stands."

Not only in the stands, but in the press box as well. Covering the game for the *San Diego Tribune*, sportswriter Jerry Magee was struck by the ferocity of both defenses. "Offense was the thrust of the old AFL," says Magee, who still writes for the *Tribune*. "The league relied on a lot of big plays. But the 1961 championship was a real hard-hitting game."

In the end, the difference between the two teams was Blanda, who shook off six interceptions to make the big play when he absolutely had to. Later, Lemm called Blanda "probably the fiercest competitor it has ever been my pleasure to coach."

Gillman agreed. "Blanda's an old pro and a real money man. Under pressure, he's at his best."

In winning their second straight AFL championship, the same could be said for the Oilers as a team.

Chapter Six

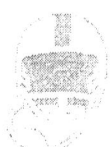

1962: The AFL's Longest Day

A LATE-AFTERNOON WIND WHIPPED jam-packed Jeppesen Stadium on December 23, 1962—fickle 15-mile-per-hour gusts that blew north to south in the direction of the scoreboard clock behind the end zone. A misting rain and four quarters of championship football had turned the crabgrass floor of the old high school stadium into muddy patches.

At midfield, Dallas Texans halfback Abner Haynes and linebacker E. J. Holub stood opposite Houston Oilers captain Al Jamison and Ed Husmann. To Haynes' left was ABC announcer Jack Buck. Buck was describing the scene to his broadcast partners in the ABC booth, Curt Gowdy, who was doing play-by-play, and color commentator Paul Christman. In his right hand, Buck held a microphone extended toward Haynes, a maneuver that allowed a national television audience to eavesdrop on the coin toss for the first overtime period of this historic AFL championship game.

To Haynes' right, referee Harold "Red" Bourne held a silver dollar in his hand. "We're in sudden death now, men," Bourne said. "Call it while it's in the air and call it loudly." Bourne flipped the coin into the sodden turf as Haynes made his call.

"Heads," Haynes said.

"Dallas won the toss," Bourne said. "You'll have your choice of kicking or receiving."

The gap-toothed Holub grinned behind his facemask. Dallas had led 17–0 at the half before the Oilers rallied to tie before the end of regulation play. Before Haynes and Holub left the Dallas sideline for the coin toss, Texans head coach Hank Stram called Haynes over to discuss strategy. Unwilling to have his offense test both the tricky winds and the stifling Houston defense, and wary of Oiler kicker George Blanda's abilities to kick a game-winning field goal with the wind at his back, Stram opted for the unorthodox. He would give the Oilers the ball in exchange for the wind. His instructions to Haynes were precise.

"If we win the toss," Stram said, "we don't want to receive. We want the wind. If they win the toss and elect to receive, we want to kick it to the clock. We want the wind."

Haynes nodded, and began to say something when official Bob Finley, who was standing at midfield with Bourne, interrupted. "We're ready for the toss," Finley shouted.

"Okay," Haynes replied, "but coach wants to talk for a second."

Finley wouldn't hear of it. "Abner," he yelled, "get your butt out here or it's fifteen yards."

In the press box in Jeppesen Stadium, Gowdy told his nation of listeners that it was rare for a football game to go into overtime. It was, in fact, just the second time in pro football history that a championship game had not been decided during regulation play. In 1958, the Baltimore Colts defeated the New York Giants 23-17 in overtime in what was at the time the longest pro game in history.

As the coin lay heads up on the wet grass, Haynes had only to make his call. He didn't hesitate. "We'll kick to the clock."

For a moment, Bourne was stunned. "You're going to kick?"

"Yeah," Haynes said, "to the clock."

Aghast that Haynes had given the Oilers both the ball and the wind at their back, Bourne said, "Captain Haynes, you made the choice and said you'll kick."

Jamison slapped his helmet as if he couldn't believe what he had heard. "We'll take the wind," he said.

Buck told his TV audience that Haynes had just fumbled the coin toss.

BUCK: *Well I'll tell ya, over on that Dallas bench they're going wild, Curt. They don't know what's going on. Abner Haynes elected to kick off and I'm sure that's not the unanimous opinion of the bench.*

On the Texans' sideline, Stram was frantically pointing toward the Oiler end zone, indicating he wanted the wind at the Texans' back. On the Houston sideline, Blanda, armed now with both the ball and the wind, strapped on his helmet. "We thought they were crazy," he said of the Texans' call.

"When we went into overtime," Haynes explained, "Coach Stram called me to the sideline and told me that we did not want to receive.... Our plan was to kick the ball to them, hold them, try to get a good runback on the punt return, and get on the board with a field goal."

For the second time that afternoon, it appeared the Texans were throwing away their chances at an AFL title. Dallas had dethroned the San Diego Chargers as champions of the league's Western Division, building an 11-3 record that tied Houston for best in the league.

The teams were well matched. The Oilers had the AFL's best offense, the Texans the best defense. The Texans had the second-best offense, Houston the number-two defense. They had split their two previous meetings in 1962, and this interstate showdown between Houston and Dallas was just the kind of rivalry Texans owner Lamar Hunt had in mind when he founded the AFL in

1959 and made Bud Adams his first contact in fielding a franchise. The game was sold out just three hours after tickets were made available the week before the game, and demand for seats was so large that Gowdy told viewers the Oilers could have sold 60,000 tickets. Yet neither Hunt nor Adams, who met on the field for a photo before the game wearing their respective team blazers, could have foreseen the epic about to unfold.

Dallas was a young team, averaging just 23 years of age, and appeared too inexperienced to defeat the two-time defending champion Oilers before a hostile Houston audience. An AFL championship game record crowd of 37,981 fans, some 2,500 more than capacity, wedged into Jeppesen Stadium, unfurling banners that read, "Go Big H, Crush Little D."

The Oilers were a study in self-confidence. Head coach Frank "Pop" Ivy, who had taken over the reins from the departed Wally Lemm, beckoned his team to a date with destiny. "If we win the championship three years in a row," Ivy told his squad, "we'll be considered one of the great teams in all of football, not just the AFL."

Houston started fast, but it was Dallas that made the first big play of the game.

GOWDY: *Third down, nine to go for Houston. They're on the Dallas nine. Hennigan goes wide right, Dewveall split end left. Blanda fading on third down.... The pass is intercepted at the goal line! Up to the five, the ten is E. J. Holub.... To the twenty, the thirty, and Holub is tripped up.... E. J. Holub nearly broke away.*

Holub's interception allowed the Texans to score first, rookie Tommy Brooker kicking a 16-yard field goal. Dallas made it 10–0 in the second quarter on a spectacular pass play between quarterback Len Dawson and Haynes.

GOWDY: *Second down, nine to go for Dallas on the Houston 28. Abner Haynes flanked wide right, the two big fullbacks are deep. There's a fake to McClinton, Dawson throwing to Haynes, he's got him at the twenty! He's to the five and he's over! Haynes scores! Abner Haynes, a remarkable performer, caught that ball on the 20 and you saw him stay in bounds and go over for the touchdown.*

Late in the half, Dave Grayson's interception of Blanda set up Haynes' 2-yard TD run for a 17–0 lead. Throughout the first half, the Oilers' famous offense was frustrated by Stram's innovative defenses. The Texans employed an early version of the 3-4 front, made popular by the University of Oklahoma. In the Texans' 3-4, 6-foot-7 rookie Bill Hull doubled as a defensive end and linebacker, alternating between rushing the passer and dropping into coverage. The move paid off late in the game when Hull, who was named "Giraffe" by his teammates because as Jerry Mays said, "he looked like a basketball player," came up with a key interception. Stram also used a triple stack, with three linebackers positioned directly behind down linemen. The remodeled defense confused Blanda, who threw five interceptions in the game.

Under scudding clouds that moved in from the gulf and darkened the skies over Houston, the Oilers took the second half kickoff and drove 68 yards in six plays. A change in strategy saw Blanda use all–AFL end Charley Hennigan as a decoy and focus on tight end Willard Dewveall. The Oilers also revamped their defense, pressuring Dawson with an array of blitzes that sent linebackers Gene Babb, Doug Cline, and Mike Dukes in waves after Dawson.

The moves paid dividends for the Oilers in the third quarter, beginning with the Houston offense, which received the second half kickoff.

GOWDY: *Second down, ten to go for Houston at the Dallas 15. Blanda's pass ... touchdown to Willard Dewveall!"*

Blanda had the Oilers driving, and only an end zone interception by Johnny Robinson prevented Houston from scoring again in the quarter. Blanda's 31-yard field goal early in the fourth cut Dallas' lead to 17–10, and Blanda followed by driving his team to the 1-yard line.

GOWDY: *A touchdown and a point can tie this game up. Charley Tolar scores! Little Charley Tolar, only five-foot-six, scores ... and now it's 17–16. Now, will Houston go for one or two? They're going for the point ... Blanda will attempt to tie it, holding is Groman ... and the kick is good, it's a tie game. The score at Jeppesen Stadium, the Dallas Texans 17, and the Houston Oilers 17.*

With Houston's defense pitching a second-half shutout, Blanda moved the Oilers into position for a 42-yard, game-winning field goal. Across the line, Sherrill Headrick took his position in the middle of the Dallas defense. Normally, the Texans linebacker did not have rush responsibilities on field goal attempts, but as he settled into position he noticed a gap in the Oiler line. Headrick blew into the Houston backfield and blocked Blanda's kick.

Late in the first overtime period, the Oilers were at the Dallas 35. On second down, Blanda dropped back and looked for Hennigan on an out pattern. Out of the mist rose Hull. Dropping back into coverage, Hull had slipped between Blanda and Hennigan. He intercepted the ball and returned it to midfield.

"I'm just second-guessing myself," Blanda said later, "but if I had called a hook-in pass instead of a down-and-out, we'd have made it."

The fifth quarter ended with the Texans at the Houston 48. On the first play of the sixth quarter, Dawson passed to Jack Spikes for 10 yards. When Dawson read a strong-side blitz, he handed off to Spikes, who hit the weak side for 19 yards. With the ball at the 19, the Texans lost a yard on two plays before

Dawson kept it himself on third down, gaining a yard on a keeper as he positioned the ball in the middle of the field.

On fourth down, Tommy Brooker, the Texans' 22-year-old rookie kicker, headed onto the field. Stram, in a long white raincoat and felt fedora, paced the Dallas sideline, his game plan clenched in his right fist. Across the field, "Pop" Ivy was looking for ways to rattle the rookie kicker. Ivy called timeout to freeze Brooker, then called linebacker Tom Goode to the sideline. "Put all eleven men up on the line," Ivy said.

During the time-out, Brooker grabbed a towel and wiped mud from the toe of his kicking shoe. "Don't worry about it," he told his mates. "It's all over now."

GOWDY: *Fourth down. Dallas on the 18-yard line of Houston in the second overtime period, can win the game if this field goal is good. Dawson to hold on the 24. The big rush is on, the kick is up, the kick is ... good! Dallas wins the championship! Dallas wins it on a 24-yard field goal by Tommy Brooker. They had to go into the second overtime period to win it ... and this has gotta be one of the greatest football games I've ever seen, Paul.*

CHRISTMAN: *That was about the wildest finish we'll ever see. Hank Stram is beside himself.*

Pro football's longest game was over, 77 minutes and 54 seconds after it had begun. Fans who had been crowding the end zones poured onto the field. Brooker was carried off the field on the shoulders of his teammates. Inside the Texans' champagne-soaked dressing room, Brooker said, "There wasn't anything to do but kick. I kept my eyes on the ground. When I finally looked up, I saw the ball going through the goal posts."

Stram, his raincoat soaked with champagne, was still clutching his game plan as he accepted congratulations from Hunt and AFL commissioner Joe Foss. "I just can't say what was the big play of the game," Stram said, "or what was the deciding point.... There were just too many big plays."

In the Oiler clubhouse, Al Jamison, whose bad back would soon force him into retirement, sat slumped over, tears welling in his eyes. Blanda stood in front of his locker, talking quietly with reporters. Somebody asked him about the Oilers' quest for a third straight title.

"Maybe we got too keyed up for this one," he answered. "That can happen and you can get sluggish. I didn't play my best, that's for sure."

The '62 AFL title game, the longest game in pro football history at the time, was a coming-out party for the young league. "We couldn't have written a script like that," Foss said.

New York Daily News columnist Gene Ward wrote that the game was indicative of the AFL's growth. "The American League," Ward wrote, "still has some growing to do, but it has earned the right to hold its head high in National League company."

Gowdy says today that the '62 title game sold his ABC broadcast partner Paul Christman on the value of AFL football. Gowdy, the legendary broadcaster who did numerous Super Bowls and World Series, and Christman, former Missouri quarterback who was a member of the Chicago Cardinals' famed "Million Dollar Backfield" of the mid-1940s, were in their first year of broadcasting AFL games on ABC. While Christman started out a skeptic, Gowdy never doubted the AFL would survive:

> They had a lot of rich, young owners. Lamar Hunt, Bud Adams, Barron Hilton, Ralph Wilson ... these guys had money. I knew they were going to hang in there and hang in there tough.
>
> Paul Christman and I started doing the games in 1962. He didn't want to do them. He had been the quarterback of the Dream Backfield with the Chicago Cardinals and he thought [the AFL] was below him. We had a year left on our [ABC] contracts, and CBS offered me the job of doing NCAA football that they got away from ABC, which we had done in '60-'61. But I had a contract with ABC and couldn't leave, so there we were, and we were put on the AFL.
>
> I was disappointed we had lost the college package because that was a great package. So we came up with the AFL and it was football, and I talked to Paul and said, "Come on, we'll get through this thing. These guys will get better." And he got into it and he rather liked it. It was sort of his kind of football. It was the wide-open passing game. They went to the skill players, the receivers and quarterbacks, and they had high-scoring games. It was like basketball on stripes. It was entertaining. So we got into it and we could see the AFL got better.

Gowdy recalls the 1962 AFL championship as one of the most memorable games of his broadcast career. "When the regulation was over, they went down to the field for the toss of the coin," he says. "Abner Haynes represented the Texans, and he said, 'We'll kick to the clock.' He gave them the ball, the wind, and it looked like the game. Christman about fell off his stool. Dallas came back and won, and I always kidded Hank Stram about it. And he always says, 'No, no. Abner made a great decision.' And I said, 'Bull. You don't give a team the ball and the wind in overtime.'"

Broadcasters like Gowdy, Christman, and Charlie Jones were known nationally as the voices of the AFL. But each AFL team had its own distinctive voice as well. In Buffalo, Van Miller broadcast Bills games on WBEN Radio. Oakland had Bud Foster on KNBC and Bill King on KNEW; the Chargers were covered by Lyle Bond on KFMB; the Chiefs by Bill Grigsby on KCMO; the Titans by Bob Murphy and later Merle Harmon on WABC. All were essential to the success of the AFL. So were members of the print media, like Larry Felser of the *Buffalo Evening News*, Will McDonough of the *Boston Globe*, Jerry Magee of the *San Diego Tribune*, and Paul Zimmerman of the *New York Post*. They helped bring the AFL to the public, and made household names of Hank Stram and Sid Gillman, and Lance Alworth and Buck Buchanan.

"We had a lot of great games and saw a lot of outstanding individual players," says Gowdy. "The AFL couldn't have made it without the TV money and the exposure."

The coverage of AFL and NFL games polarized pro football fans across the country. Because the NFL was viewed as the superior league, AFL writers and broadcasters had to endure a patronizing attitude by NFL media and fans. When he covered the Jets, Paul Zimmerman used to get angry at constantly being told by people in his neighborhood what a "crummy" league he covered.

"There was great animosity between the two leagues," Miller says. "I remember sitting in the press box in Miami before Super Bowl III when the Jets played the Colts. Norm Van Brocklin walked into the press box and announced for all the world to hear, 'Joe Namath is about to play his first pro game.' As it turned out, nobody ate bigger words than the Dutchman."

When the Packers played the Chiefs in Super Bowl I, NBC and CBS shared the same telecast feed of the game. Members of the rival networks met a few days before the game to discuss their shared hookup. Curt Gowdy, who would broadcast the game for NBC, the AFL network, remembers feeling like he was walking, as he put it, "into the camp of the enemy" when he entered CBS' production meeting.

McDonough said AFL writers did not take put-downs of their league lightly. "It was a personal thing for us," said McDonough. AFL writers often had to bite their tongues when confronted by NFL media types like the late Tex Maule of *Sports Illustrated*. Maule gloried in the NFL's supposed superiority.

"I thought for the first five or six years of its existence, the AFL was clearly not up to the standard of play in the NFL, and I never hesitated to say so in my magazine stories," Maule wrote in his 1970 book, *The Pro Season*.

In his travels around the country covering the NFL, Maule also noticed the depth of feeling concerning AFL and NFL teams. Maule wrote:

> They polarized football fans in this country. The fans in the AFL cities believed wholeheartedly in their teams; in NFL cities, the fans looked on the younger clubs as upstarts.
> I must admit that for a long time, I was an NFL adherent. I was raised in the NFL; I didn't think that the upstarts could match NFL teams.

To his credit, Maule would later admit he was wrong in underestimating the level of talent and coaching in the AFL. But at the time, AFL writers took exception to what Bills beat writer Larry Felser called NFL "propaganda." Felser points out:

> You have to remember that there were only 12 teams in the entire NFL when the AFL started. The Canadian Football League was at its absolute zenith at that time, and there were a lot of people who could have been playing football who weren't. There was a helluva player pool when the AFL started.

I think there were presentable teams in the AFL [in the early years]. They were able to compete in the draft, so you had presentable talent. In Dallas and Houston and San Diego, the football was very presentable.

The AFL began the new year of 1962 with its first all-star game. Played on January 7, the game was a showcase for Dallas Texans stars Cotton Davidson and Abner Haynes. Davidson threw for three touchdowns and Haynes ran for two more, including a 66-yard punt return, as the West beat the East 47–27.

The war between the two leagues to sign top college players intensified in 1962. The San Diego Chargers made headlines when they signed two blue-chip college players away from the NFL. Through a gentlemen's agreement with the Oakland Raiders, the Chargers obtained the rights to Arkansas halfback Lance Alworth. Because the AFL draft would be held in inverse order of the league standings, the Chargers traded four players to Oakland in exchange for the Raiders' second-round choice, which they used to draft Alworth.

An All-America halfback at the University of Arkansas, Alworth had been a member of Razorbacks teams that went 24–6 during his career and won three consecutive Southwest Conference championships from 1959 to 1961. Born in Houston, Alworth earned 16 letters as an all-around athlete at Brookhaven High School in Mississippi. Both the New York Yankees and Pittsburgh Pirates offered Alworth bonus-laden baseball contracts, but he elected to play football for Frank Broyles at Arkansas.

A lithe 6 feet, 178 pounds, Alworth was installed at halfback and used as the Razorbacks' outside running threat. "He's an 'even and leavin' man," Broyles said. "When he's even with you, he's left you."

Because of his lack of size, Alworth was out of place on Broyles' ground-oriented offenses. In three years, Alworth carried the ball 301 times but had only 38 receptions. Still, Alworth averaged 20.3 yards per catch in 1960 and 17.8 in 1961. It was enough to convince Sid Gillman and his scouts, chief among them Al Davis, that Alworth's talents were well suited to the Chargers' passing game.

Along with Alworth, the Chargers drafted John Hadl, a versatile offensive threat who played both quarterback and halfback at the University of Kansas. In his three years at Kansas, Hadl passed for 1,277 yards and ran for 1,016 more. To sign Alworth and Hadl, Gillman assigned two of his top scouts, Davis and Don Klosterman, to act as emissaries.

"We assigned Klosterman to Hadl," Gillman says, "and Davis was assigned to Lance. They both stayed on 'em pretty good."

Drafted by both the Chargers and the NFL's San Francisco 49ers, Alworth wanted a no-cut contract. Though both the 49ers and Chargers agreed to his demands, it was the personality of Davis and the class of the Charger organization that finally convinced Alworth to sign with the AFL.

"Lance liked Al," Gillman says, "and he liked our organization."

Still, the Chargers almost lost Alworth to the 49ers at the last moment. Just moments after Arkansas lost to Alabama, Alworth walked through a crowd to the end zone to meet Davis.

"I knew it wasn't safe to let Alworth go to the dressing room," Davis said. "But I figured he could at least make it to the goal posts without being stopped."

"After the game there was a big mix-up and I didn't see Al," Alworth said. "But I did see a guy whom I thought was a Charger scout. It ended up he was with San Francisco, and he helped me over there under the goalpost. I almost signed, but I didn't, and Al came over and saved me."

The Chargers' signing of Hadl, who had been drafted by the Detroit Lions, was only slightly less dramatic. When the Lions told Hadl they saw him as "the next Paul Hornung," Hadl, who wanted no part of being a pro halfback, decided to accept the Chargers' offer. Klosterman signed Hadl on the field at the end of the Bluebonnet Bowl.

"The Lions wanted to make a running back out of Hadl," Gillman recalls, "but John wanted to be a quarterback. We promised him he would play there for us."

Klosterman hadn't expected to sign Hadl. But after the Kansas quarterback joined the Chargers, he told Klosterman, "You know, there was never any question that I wasn't going to sign with you and San Diego."

"Why?" Klosterman wanted to know.

"Do you remember when Loyola played Kansas and an 11-year-old kid stopped you after the game and asked a hundred questions about throwing a football? You hadn't showered, but you spent a half hour talking about playing quarterback and the importance of hard work?"

"No," Klosterman said, "I don't remember."

"I was the kid," Hadl said, "and I was going to sign with any team you were associated with."

Klosterman was a force in the AFL, and one of the main reasons the young league signed blue-chip college players away from the NFL. A onetime quarterback at Loyola College, Klosterman set NCAA records in a game against Florida and was the nation's leading passer. He was drafted by the Browns, played backup to Otto Graham, and then was traded to the Rams, where he backed up Bob Waterfield and Norm Van Brocklin.

Klosterman left the NFL to play in the Canadian Football League. The move north also allowed Klosterman to indulge in another sport — skiing. But in March of 1957, while skiing down a mountain in Banff en route to a St. Patrick's Night party, Klosterman rounded a turn, saw a woman in his path, and swerved to his right to avoid her. Traveling close to 45 miles per hour, Klosterman crashed into a thicket of trees, sustaining multiple injuries to his head, rib cage, legs, and chest.

Paralyzed from the waist down, the 27-year-old Klosterman was told by a neurosurgeon he would never walk again. Klosterman fired the doctor on the spot, then spent the next four months doing daily exercises. Klosterman's weight dropped to 130 pounds, but he continued his rehab, exercising to the point where his bed linen would be soaked in sweat.

Using braces and crutches, Klosterman eventually taught himself how to walk again, but then was faced with another challenge. Medical expenses had wiped out his savings. Jobless and virtually penniless, Klosterman got a job selling life insurance. He was lifting weights in a Los Angeles gym frequented by USC athletes when he met Ron Mix, the Trojans' All-America offensive tackle. Mix was drafted in 1960 by both the Colts and the new L.A. Chargers. Klosterman gave advice to Mix on contractual matters, and it was at that point that Chargers general manager Frank Leahy asked Klosterman if he would help the new franchise recruit players. Klosterman signed Mix to a two-year contract, and the Chargers hired him full-time.

Klosterman's low-key, likable personality was instrumental in the Chargers' signing stars like Mix, quarterbacks Hadl and Jack Kemp, and fullback Keith Lincoln. In 1962 Texans' owner Lamar Hunt hired Klosterman as director of player personnel. Later, as the Kansas City Chiefs went on to win three AFL titles and one Super Bowl, Klosterman played a major role in the team's success. He was instrumental in the Chiefs' signing stars like Buck Buchanan, Bobby Bell, Otis Taylor, and Aaron Brown. The '63 draft that Klosterman was part of has been called the best in franchise history, yielding such talent as Buchanan, Bell, guard Ed Budde, punter Jerrel Wilson, and tackle Dave Hill. Each man was a starter on the Chiefs' 1970 Super Bowl championship team.

Frank Gifford, a close friend of Klosterman, said Klosterman was part talent scout and part undercover agent in the years when the AFL was competing for talent against the NFL.

In his book *Gifford on Courage*, the ABC broadcaster called Klosterman "a major force in the birth and success of the AFL and its eventual merger with the National Football League."

Klosterman left the Chiefs to become executive vice president and general manager of the Oilers in 1966, and the Oilers responded by winning a division title in '67 and reaching the AFL playoffs two of the next three years. In 1970, Klosterman joined the Baltimore Colts as GM. Baltimore instantly won the Super Bowl and the following year advanced to the AFC title game.

While Klosterman helped build the Texans into champions, the Oilers and Chargers entered the '62 season as prohibitive favorites to repeat as division champions, but both were hurt by unexpected losses. The Chargers organization was rocked by a series of losses, the most tragic being linebacker Bob Laraba's death in an off-season car accident.

Injuries also took their toll on the Chargers. Halfback Paul Lowe suffered a fractured forearm and was out for the season; Alworth missed 10 games due to a thigh injury; quarterback Jack Kemp ruptured a finger joint on his right hand, was placed on the injured reserved list by Gillman, and then was signed by the Bills for $100 — the biggest steal in AFL history.

Much controversy has surrounded Gillman's placing of Kemp on the waiver wire, a move that paid off handsomely for the Bills. AFL commissioner Joe Foss recalled the inner workings of the transaction:

> What happened was that Jack, who was with the Chargers, had broken the middle finger on his right hand and had to be pulled off the squad. Not wanting to lose him, Sid Gillman tried to hide him so he was not listed on the official squad. When we found out at the league office, we said they had to put Kemp up for any team that wanted him. The Broncos, the Dallas Texans, and the Buffalo Bills tried to claim him, but I felt the Bills needed a promising young quarterback, so I awarded him to them — for one hundred dollars! And Kemp brought them a championship.

As the season got underway, it became clear that while the Chargers could not overcome their setbacks, the Oilers remained the class of the AFL's Eastern Division. The team emerged from its training camp and underwent a typical slow start that saw them go 4–3. In Houston, head coach Wally Lemm abruptly announced he was leaving to become head coach of the St. Louis Cardinals. Though Lemm publicly freed Bud Adams of any blame in his decision — it was a business move, Lemm said, to keep him closer to his sporting goods operation in Chicago — Oiler fans were outraged and hung Adams in effigy. Adams hired Frank "Pop" Ivy, who had been fired as head coach of the Cardinals. The Oilers rebounded to go unbeaten the rest of the season, due in part to Ivy's triple-wing offense, which confused defenses with its formations and counter plays.

The imaginative offense helped juice up a team slowed by injuries. Cannon was playing with a painful bad back and managed just 474 yards rushing; Bill Groman struggled to overcome off-season knee surgery; and Blanda was nursing cracked ribs suffered against the Raiders. Stabilizing the offense was fullback Charley Tolar, "The Human Bowling Ball" who bulled his way to 1,012 yards rushing and a 4.1 yards-per-carry average. The team's 387 points ranked second in the league, and their 11–3 record was the club's best of the decade.

Cannon, Tolar, and Charlie Hennigan were stars, but the undisputed leader of the Houston offense was George Blanda. In his Columbia-blue Oilers jersey and high-top cleats, the 34-year-old Blanda appeared unimposing enough. But down on the field, Blanda's hawkish features and hard-edged personality gave him the look and language of a longshoreman. He sniped at opponents and teammates alike. One writer said Blanda had "a busy tongue and vast vocabulary." Cannon called Blanda's approach to football "all business," and Blanda didn't downplay his role as a leader. "Coach Ivy has confidence in me and allows me to run the offense," Blanda said.

Steve Weller, a columnist for the *Buffalo News*, said Blanda was the dominant quarterback in the AFL's early years. "Blanda was a class quarterback when the AFL had no other class quarterbacks," Weller wrote. "Yapping at defensive players who brushed his usually spotless uniform, barking at teammates who didn't perform as expected, nagging officials who overlooked what he considered flagrant breaches of the rules by enemy cornerbacks, Blanda made sure that nobody went to sleep."

Under Blanda's whip, the Oilers of the early '60s set an AFL record by leading the league in passing yards four times. Blanda twice threw more than 60 passes in a game, and he bombed the Bills in one game with 68 attempts and 37 completions. One AFL defender said, "Blanda throws like every game is his last."

High-profile stars like Blanda, Hennigan, and Alworth gave the AFL glitz. But it took a 246-pound fullback named Carlton "Cookie" Gilchrist to give the league grit.

The AFL's first great power runner, Gilchrist's intimidating size and demeanor made him a terrifying figure, both to defenders and head coaches. Along with tales of his dragging defenders across the frozen tundra of the Canadian Football League were rumors of Gilchrist's near-brawls and confrontations with front-office brass. Gilchrist was eventually banned from the CFL, prompting one NFL coach to say at the time that while the entire league knew Gilchrist's abilities, his reputation prevented them from signing him.

Gilchrist never played college football. As an 18-year-old junior at Har-Brack High School in Breckenridge, Pennsylvania, Gilchrist was projected as one of the top college prospects in the country. Because he was too old to play football his senior year, Gilchrist dropped out of high school and enrolled at Cheshire Academy to improve his grades for Michigan State. But when the Cleveland Browns offered him a contract for $5,500, Gilchrist opted to head to Cleveland.

"That money," Gilchrist said at the time, "was more than my father made in a year. [The Browns] teased me when I joined the club. They told me they had seen all–Army, all-pro, and all-world players, but this was the first time they had seen all-schoolyard."

Browns head coach Paul Brown liked what he saw of Gilchrist, but felt the 19-year-old needed more experience. Brown tried to hide Gilchrist by sending him to the CFL for seasoning, but Cookie became a star, playing with Ontario-based teams Sarnia, Kitchener, and Hamilton. Following Hamilton, Gilchrist migrated to Regina, Saskatchewan, and finally to the Toronto Argonauts, where he was eventually suspended for breaking curfew.

Ultimately, Gilchrist's long-running battles with assorted CFL brass, his near-fights with coaches, his protracted holdouts, and his flaunting of team curfews finished his career in Canada. When Toronto put Gilchrist on waivers, not a single CFL team claimed him. In the spring of 1962, Harvey Johnson, the Bills' director of player personnel, signed Gilchrist to a $30,000 contract. When

Gilchrist told Johnson, "Just give me the ball, Harve," new head coach Lou Saban knew he had the perfect fit for his ball-control offense.

Gilchrist dominated defenses in 1962, running for 1,096 yards to become the AFL's first 1,000-yard back. He scored 15 touchdowns and averaged 5.1 yards per carry, despite playing with a pulled leg muscle that limited him to an average of 10 minutes per game over the last four games. The Bills finished 7–6–1, the first winning season in franchise history.

"Cookie was a tremendous fullback," says Bills owner Ralph Wilson, who deserves credit for signing Gilchrist in spite of rumors concerning Cookie's off-field antics. "He was big and strong, a great blocker, and for 250 pounds, he was fast. He wasn't a straight-ahead runner. He would start towards the line, and then cut back."

Though every NFL owner was aware of Gilchrist's outstanding talents and on-field achievements in the CFL, none showed an interest in signing him. The main reason pro clubs shied away from Gilchrist, says Wilson, stemmed from Cookie's troubled off-field reputation.

"Cookie had a great reputation in Canada," says Wilson, "but he had some financial difficulties or something."

Gilchrist's reputation as a malcontent and an eccentric was a strange match for blue-collar Buffalo. Yet while the Gilchrist legend has been blown out of proportion — the Bills' public relations department once fictionalized a report that Cookie drove a white limo with the slogan "Lookie, Lookie, Here Comes Cookie" painted on the side — Gilchrist rarely tried to dispute the tall tales.

"You've got to be more than a football player," he said at the time. "You've got to have character, be colorful — *be* a character. Maybe," the big Cookie mused, "that's what's responsible for my reputation."

"He was an unusual fellow," remembers Wilson, "and he had a lot of off-field problems. But Cookie Gilchrist was a terrific player."

In New York, the 1962 season started under ominous conditions and grew worse. Of the five picks the team made in the revamped AFL draft, team owner Harry Wismer was able to sign only one. With Wismer financially strapped, head coach Sammy Baugh often covered for Wismer by financing players out of his own pocket.

"I think Sammy took a pretty good beating financially," linebacker Larry Grantham says today. "I know for a fact that if a kid was having problems Sammy would slip him something out of his own pocket."

By 1962, Wismer's financial losses were approaching the $2 million dollar mark. For years, Wismer had been running the Titans like a bargain-basement production. The floor of the team locker room was littered with broken glass. Showers produced cold water only, and the mirrors above the sink were covered with crusted shaving cream that spelled out obscenities directed at Wismer. Team trainer Buddy Leininger ran low on adhesive tape and used it sparingly, reserving it only for the most needy.

While every pro team used two projectors to scout opponent's game films, the Titans tried to get by with only one. There were no chairs in the film room, so players huddled on the cold concrete floor. While the offense watched the game films, the members of the defense shot craps and dozed off in a nearby room. Five weeks into the season, the overworked projector burned out. It wasn't replaced.

Rather than pay to have press releases with team logos and letterheads printed up, Wismer told Titans press agent Ted Emery to scour local stores and request free samples of stationery. Instead of sending scouts to recruit players, Wismer relied on a 50-cent copy of *Street & Smith's College Football Yearbook* for information. He told his general manager, Steve Serbo, "Watch the other teams' cut lists. You'll do all right."

Baugh railed against Wismer's tactics. "There's no way," Baugh argued, "you can win games by using people who aren't good enough to make the teams you're trying to beat."

To get out of paying dinner bills for his team, Wismer arranged 8 P.M. flights for all trips west. Rather than pay plane fare for games to the Midwest, he booked his team to ride the rails — in nonairconditioned cars, of course. Before a game in San Diego, Wismer had his team practice on a field 45 minutes away from the team's motel. The field's surface was dried clay, "baked so solid," one observer said, "that it would have been a perfect training ground for the Afrika Corps."

The final day of practice in San Diego saw Titan players scattered along the highway, holding helmets and pads and hitching rides back to their hotel; Wismer didn't pay the bus company to pick the players up.

Wismer used his apartment at 227 Park Avenue as the Titans' business office. The Titans' ticket office was Wismer's bedroom, and thousands of dollars worth of tickets routinely lay strewn on the bed. It wasn't uncommon for people to walk in off the street, pick up two tickets, drop $10 on the bed, and walk out. The coaches' office was in the kitchen and the press agent's office in the butler's pantry next to the bathroom. When the Chargers wrote the Titans requesting team pictures, Wismer returned an envelope stuffed with 100 head shots of himself.

Subway walls carried posters trumpeting "Harry Wismer's Titans of New York," and Wismer hired a band to play "I'm Just Wild About Harry" at all home games, but the Titans were an embarrassment. Players found their cars vandalized in the parking lot outside the Polo Grounds, and the press ridiculed them. The team that Wismer bragged was named after the Titan missile was laughed off by the media as "the Miss-iles."

"We were just like guys opening up a new business," Don Maynard says. "We were going up against guys who had been in the business for forty years. Wismer didn't get many good writeups. He tried to demand it from the press, but he was always bucking them anyway. But I couldn't understand why the press didn't help our league more. We were providing new jobs and teams for the fans to support. But I guess you always have somebody who wants to knock new things, and that's the way it was then."

"We didn't have any fans in the stands," says Grantham. "Wismer used to announce a crowd of 20,000, but we used to look around and there'd be a hot dog vendor for every customer. The Giants owned New York then. What really hurt was the disparity between players from both teams. We'd go to speaking engagements and we'd get fifty dollars and the Giants players would get five hundred. But that's the way it was. We couldn't draw flies, and they were the established team."

Wismer tried to give the appearance of fan attendance by throwing open the doors of the Polo Grounds to kids and then exaggerating the number of people in the seats. Even that didn't help. "The announced attendance of twenty thousand refers to arms and legs," one reporter wrote. "Or else fifteen thousand of the twenty thousand people came disguised as empty seats."

New York Daily News sports columnist Dick Young wrote that Wismer counted fingers instead of noses in setting attendance figures for Titan games at the Polo Grounds. Foss still maintains he's the only commissioner in any sport who ever shook hands with every spectator in the stands during a regular season game.

> It happened on Thanksgiving Day in New York that first season, when less than a thousand people huddled in the Polo Grounds as the wind howled and the snow whipped around the stands. I was freezing solid, so I decided to warm up by walking around and talking with the fans. As usual I was wearing my cowboy hat ... and people recognized me immediately as I thanked every one of the spectators for coming to the game.
> "At least you all got good seats," I told them.
> Some said, "I'm here on a comp ticket."
> "I don't care how you're here," I said. "Thanks for coming."

On September 18, the players angrily announced their paychecks to be "194 hours late," and voted to go on strike unless they received money before noon the next day. The checks arrived at 1 P.M., but so did a telegram from Wismer. Upset that his players threatened a strike, Wismer wired his staff that they would be fired if they conducted practice. Assistant coach George Sauer told the team, "Prepare yourselves."

"I remember when they came out to Dallas to play us," Texans defensive lineman Jerry Mays says. "They had no coaches. The players were coaching themselves."

The players weren't the only ones complaining. Before a game in Boston, the Titan team bus driver went on strike, refusing to drive unless he was paid first. "In cash," he demanded. Titan paychecks had more bounce than team footballs. Players learned not to change after practice; overcoats were thrown over their practice sweats as they engaged in a wild run to the team bank, the Irving Trust Company, to cash their checks before funds ran out. Eventually, the bank set a policy that allowed for only one teller to cash Titan checks. As each player submitted his overdue earnings, the amount was deducted from the club's dwindling balance. When word of the Titans' money problems got around, local businesses grew wary. Laundromats and sporting goods stores refused Wismer credit; clean socks were available for game days only. Wismer cut costs at every corner. He refused to turn on the stadium lights at the Polo Grounds; Titan games were often concluded in the dark.

Finally, with Wismer bankrupt, with the team operating without a coaching staff, with the players threatening mutiny, and with virtually no fan following at all, Foss stepped in to save the franchise. On November 8, he announced the league's headquarters would meet the club's financial obligations.

"I was smart enough to know then that the league needed a team in New York," said Grantham. "So I picked up the phone and called Lamar Hunt and told him we hadn't been paid."

Hunt recalled the Titans as "an underfinanced club with a very poor image." Yet he knew that the success of the AFL's New York franchise was a necessity if the league was to survive.

"We had to have a New York franchise with a good public image," Hunt said. "Unfortunately, at that point the Titans were our weakest club. It was the most miserable operation imaginable. We were worried they might drag the whole league down with them."

As the Titans prepared to host Houston in the final game of the regular season, Wismer called the team together. "There probably won't even be any New York Titans next year," Wismer said. "So most of you are playing in your last pro game. Most of you aren't good enough to play anywhere else."

With that stirring pep talk, the Harry Wismer era in New York closed in fitting style, with a 44–10 loss at home. A grand total of 70 people were on hand to verify the fact.

"I looked around," Grantham says, "and felt like going up into the stands and introducing myself to everyone there."

Despite the humiliation and the bounced checks, players like Grantham and Maynard harbor no ill feeling towards Wismer.

"I was close to Mr. Wismer," Grantham said. "I got out of school in midterm and I spent the first few months in New York around him. He had his faults. He'd go into an airport and page himself, just so everyone knew he was there. He was colorful."

Said Maynard, "He helped give pro football teams to cities that couldn't get NFL teams. He gave jobs to players, to coaches, to personnel in the front office."

In the Western Division, the Dallas Texans wrapped up their division title in November. One of the key reasons for the team's success was the addition of Len Dawson at quarterback. After being drafted number one by the Steelers in 1957, Dawson had spent three years in Pittsburgh backing up Bobby Layne and an additional two years with the Cleveland Browns. Through five NFL seasons, Dawson had attempted just 45 passes. When the AFL started in 1960 and Hank Stram was selected as head coach of the Texans, Dawson made plans to meet with Stram, his former position coach at Purdue, who was in Pittsburgh for a coaching convention. "If you get your release," Stram told him, "I'd love to have you at Dallas."

After the 1961 season, which saw him attempt only 15 passes, Dawson went to Cleveland head coach Paul Brown and asked if he could be put on waivers. When no NFL team claimed him, Dawson contacted Stram, who was in Buffalo for the Coaches' All-America team. Aware that both the Bills and Raiders were interested in Dawson, Stram took a plane to Pittsburgh where he met Dawson at the airport and signed him on the spot.

Years of inactivity in the NFL had eroded Dawson's skill; the polished and poised quarterback Stram had known at Purdue was tarnished in his skills and tentative in his actions. "He was like sterling silver," Stram said. "The silver was there, but it was tarnished."

"I was terrible," Dawson said. "If my coach had been anyone but Stram, who knew me from the past, I'm sure he'd have cut me."

Dawson's performance in the Texans' preseason opener against Oakland in Atlanta did little to encourage support. His first three plays in a Dallas uniform saw him throw an interception, fumble the ball, and overthrow a wide-open receiver. He regained enough composure to help the Texans earn a 13–3 win.

"I was shocked at how bad he was at first," Stram said, "but I couldn't help but realize that five years of sitting on the bench or manning telephones didn't make a man sharp. I stuck with him and he swiftly smoothed out the rough spots."

Under Stram's guidance, Dawson regained his lost skills. The spiral on his passes grew tighter, and his footwork and techniques improved. By season's end, Dawson set a new league record by completing 60.9 percent of his passes, and he was named AFL MVP after throwing for 2,759 yards and 29 touchdowns. Dawson also proved to be a team leader. Dawson, Chargers coach Sid Gillman said, became "the heart and soul of his team."

With league MVP Dawson at quarterback, AFL Rookie of the Year Curtis McClinton at fullback, and all-pro Abner Haynes at halfback, the Texans in 1962 owned one of the most talented backfields in league history.

Haynes' stop-action runs and long strides gave him a distinctive style. Sportscaster Elmer Angsman said Haynes "runs like a fox." Blackie Sherrod of the *Dallas Times-Herald* wrote of one Haynes run: "He stopped, gave a guy change for a quarter, picked up a paper at the corner, dealt a hand of stud and ambled off to happy land."

The public address announcer at Texan home games told fans leaving the Cotton Bowl, "Drive carefully on your way home. The life you save may be Abner Haynes."

Haynes' superb skill was the primary reason Stram adopted the I-formation as his base offense. "Abner Haynes was a very skillful runner," Stram said. "He had a great capacity to find seams, running room, and daylight."

Born in Denton, Texas, Haynes became the all-time leading rusher at North Texas State College. He was drafted in 1960 by both the Steelers and the AFL's Minneapolis franchise. Unimpressed with either team's contract offer, Haynes was ready to sign with Winnipeg of the CFL when Texans GM Jack Steadman reached him by phone. "Wait," Steadman implored. "Don't sign until you talk to Lamar Hunt."

Haynes agreed, and after meeting with Hunt decided to sign with the Texans. Haynes' desire to play in his home state of Dallas and his feelings for Hunt were key reasons for his decision to sign with the AFL.

"He seemed so determined," Haynes said of Hunt, "that I wanted to help him. Everybody would ask me why I didn't go NFL. They said I'd have a lot more prestige. And I'd say that I wanted to play right away, which I could do in the AFL, and that I couldn't put prestige on my dinner table and eat it."

The Texans overwhelmed the AFL with all-pro performances. Dawson led the league by completing 61 percent of his passes and Haynes was second in the AFL in rushing with 1,049 yards. End Chris Burford had a league-high 12 TD catches.

Dallas' defense was built around four all-pro caliber players: tackle Jerry Mays, linebackers E. J. Holub and Sherrill Headrick, and safety Johnny Robinson.

Mays, who later in his career switched to defensive end and was named to the All-Time All-AFL team, signed with the Texans as a fifth-round draft choice in 1961. Co-captain and an all–Southwest Conference tackle at Southern Methodist University, Mays resisted his father's initial desire for him to quit pro football and go into the family engineering business.

"My father thought it was time I quit playing games," Mays said. "And I wasn't proud of the image I had of a pro football player. A lot of the people I associated with looked down their noses at pro sports. Then, all of a sudden, after I played a full game, I was proud to be a football player."

Mays, who died in 1994 from cancer, was an emotional man who wore his heart, and his football past, on his sleeves. After retiring in 1970, Mays had cufflinks made with his uniform number — "75" — on them. His permanently displaced knuckles were clear reminders of his AFL career.

Mays was drafted by both the Texans and the NFL's Minnesota Vikings. Because the AFL draft was held in November and the NFL's draft day wasn't until after Christmas, rumors abounded that Mays had already signed with the Texans. "I got maybe 15 calls the night the NFL was drafting," Mays said. "All night long, first one club, then the other ... things like, 'Don't do a thing until you've signed with us.' Minnesota finally drafted me, and I talked to them."

Even though the Vikings promised to trade his draft rights to Dallas so he could be near his home, Mays opted for the AFL and signed with the Texans' general manager. Though the AFL had an inferiority complex in its early days, Mays enjoyed the camaraderie that prevailed throughout the young league.

"That's what made the AFL so enjoyable," Mays said. "We not only wanted to beat other clubs, we worried about them. When the New York Titans' paychecks started bouncing, our players started asking, 'What can we do?' When Denver burned its vertical brown and yellow striped socks, we were happy because we were part of it."

While Mays was the ultimate professional, Sherrill Headrick was an unpredictable character who played with pain and once took the practice field in a Beatles wig, floppy hat, and bathing suit. His teammates called him "psycho."

After flunking out of Texas Christian University, Headrick showed up for tryouts with the new Dallas Texans in 1960 because the camp was close to his home in Fort Worth. He signed as a 210-pound middle linebacker, a position perfectly suited to Headrick's free-spirit personality.

Before the 1960 season was over, Gillman was calling Headrick "the finest (linebacker) in the AFL." Ray Collins, who had played 10 years in the NFL before joining the Texans, said Headrick was one of the best linebackers in the game.

"I've never seen a linebacker in any league who can do what he does," said Collins. "He's not just the best linebacker in the league, he's the best player."

Stram said Headrick, who refused to wear hip pads, had the highest pain threshold he's ever seen in an athlete. Headrick played with a broken neck, infected gums, broken hand, and a fractured thumb. When an injury left the bone in his finger protruding from the skin, Headrick popped the bones in place without missing a play.

While Headrick was a surprise starter, E. J. Holub was a sure thing. Nicknamed "the Beast" because of his fierce tackling, Holub was a two-time All-America linebacker at Texas Tech who in one game made 25 individual tackles for the Red Raiders. Drafted by the Cowboys and Texans, Holub signed with the AFL and in his first year played both center and linebacker. In a November game against the Titans, "the Beast" logged 58 minutes of playing time.

Holub's proper given name was Emil Joseph, but he shortened it to E. J. in the third grade. "I got fed up," he said. "'Til then, people called me Eemo and Nemo and Emily, so I said one day, 'I'm E. J.' I was big enough to make it stick."

When 36-year-old Jack Faulkner arrived in Denver as the team's new head coach and general manager, the first thing he addressed was the Broncos' shabby image. The 1960–61 Broncos may have had the ugliest uniforms in pro football history. The team helmets were brown with a white logo of a ragged cowboy chewing a toothpick and riding a bucking bronco. The jerseys were mustard yellow; the pants brown. Some of the pants had a satin sheen, some didn't. The socks, which have grown in infamy, were alternating brown and yellow *vertical* stripes.

Broncos general manager Dean Griffing, who purchased the uniforms *used* from the Copper Bowl College All-Star game, said the socks made Denver players look taller. His players thought otherwise. Defensive tackle Bud McFadin called the socks "the most ridiculous things I ever saw in my life." Safety Goose Gonsoulin said the vertical stripes made the players look like pegs. "You had these real broad shoulders because of the pads," Gonsoulin said, "and then you had these up-and-down striped socks.... It was unique, put it that way."

Jerry Mays of the Dallas Texans said the entire AFL was glad when the Broncos got rid of the hose because they made the league "look bush."

In hiring Faulkner, the Broncos announced, "There's Lots New in '62." Faulkner changed the team's uniform colors from brown and gold to their current orange, blue, and white, and held a public burning of the team's vertically striped socks. Players ran around the field at Bears Stadium before the game, holding the ugly socks aloft. The offending hose were then dropped into an Olympic-style flame that was blazing at one end of Bears Stadium, bringing a cheer from the 8,377 people on hand. Some of the socks have survived; one is on display at the Hall of Fame in Canton. Their current worth to collectors begins at $500.

"They had bought those uniforms from a semi-pro team," Faulkner recalls today, "and they were ugly. Especially those vertical-striped socks. So we burned them. But Denver was a great town. I knew that from the start. We just needed some players."

Faulkner not only designed the team's new uniforms, he also designed their plays. Like the Titans, the Broncos had gone the first two seasons without any playbooks. Faulkner coached the Broncos to a 6–1 start and a 7–7 finish, their best in AFL history. At season's end, Faulkner was named Coach of the Year.

The Broncos began the season with a stunning 31–21 win at home over the Chargers before a record crowd of 24,928. The victory marked the first time Denver had ever beaten San Diego. With quarterback Frank Tripucka leading the league in completions (240) and yards (2,917), the Broncos went from burning socks to burning enemy defenses. End Lionel Taylor, fresh off his record 100-reception season, had 77 catches to lead the league for the third straight year.

Taylor, the most prolific pass receiver in AFL history, was another of the league's Cinderella stories. He went from New Mexico Highlands University, where he played halfback and linebacker, to the Chicago Bears in 1958. The

Bears tried him at linebacker and defensive back, kept him on the taxi squad as a tight end in 1959, then put him at wideout before cutting him in 1960.

"I was playing semi-pro ball in Bakersfield, California, and I had met Dean Griffing, and he had a [semi-pro] team in Tucson, the Tucson Rattlers," says Taylor, whose 567 receptions are the most in AFL history. "He talked to me about going to Canada the next year, and then when the AFL started in 1960, he became the general manager of the Denver franchise and he called me."

At a Bronco tryout camp, then-head-coach Frankie Filchock put Taylor at defensive back. It wasn't until the players chose up sides for a touch football game that Taylor's real talent was noticed. "I had Lionel on my side that day," quarterback Frank Tripucka said, "and it didn't take me long to see what he could do as a receiver. He really stopped us when he made one of those one-handed grabs of his. That was it. I looked at Filchock and he looked at me. Taylor started for us the next Sunday."

At 6-foot-2, 215 pounds, Taylor wasn't blazing fast. Nor did he own a lot of moves. But he had great hands and an even greater work ethic. "He caught passes," Tripucka said, "like pro basketball players rebound and he practiced harder than the rawest rookie."

Tayor led the league in receiving five times, but what teammates remember most about him was his ability in the clutch. He was unstoppable when the Broncos went to the hitch pass inside the red zone or in short-yardage situations.

"Our hitch pass," Tripucka said, "wasn't a certain number of yards, like 6 or 11. It was whatever yardage we needed for a first down. And Lionel would catch the ball, covered or not, fall down, leap up, or whatever he had to do to get it." Taylor says:

> We put on a decent show offensively. We put a lot of points on the board. The NFL was playing three yards-and-a-cloud-of-dust. We couldn't come in and do the same thing. That wasn't going to get the fans. I don't know if it was the owners who approached the head coaches or if it was the head coaches who realized, "Hey, we have to do something different." But we had better skill people at that time than we did offensive and defensive linemen, because it takes a little more time for [line play] to mature. The AFL had guys like Don Maynard and Art Powell, so you put it in the air and let them see what they could do with it. You have to remember that there were just 12 teams in the NFL then, and if you got cut from the NFL, there was nowhere to go. There were a lot of guys who wanted to play.

The Broncos' neighbor in the AFL West, the Oakland Raiders, began the 1962 season in their new home, Frank Youell Field, a high school-sized stadium named after a local undertaker and located in the shadows of the Oakland courthouse. Owner Wayne Valley's "build or we move" demand to city fathers prompted plans for a new facility—Alameda County Stadium. In the meantime, Youell Field was renovated with temporary stands added to boost attendance capacity to 20,000. The Raiders' first game in Youell Field attracted

Quarterback Frank Tripucka and wide receiver Lionel Taylor formed one of the AFL's most potent passing combinations in the early years of the league. In 1961, Taylor became the first player in pro football history to catch 100 passes in a season and holds the AFL record for most receptions in a career. (*Photo courtesy of the Denver Broncos.w*)

17,000 fans for a preseason meeting with the Chargers. But just 13,000 were on hand for the regular season opener against the Titans, a game Oakland lost 28–17 to extend their losing streak to seven straight, dating back to '61. Season attendance steadily declined as the Raiders' losing streak reached an all-time league-record 19 straight, including their first 13 games of the '62 season.

"I wanted to toss the ball in the stands," Oakland middle linebacker Tom Louderback said after returning an interception 46 yards for a score, "but there wasn't anyone in the stands."

The Oakland franchise lost more than a million dollars in its first three years of operation. Worried that the team would either fold or move, the *Oakland Tribune* combined with the mayor's office on a fund-raising campaign to keep the organization in Oakland. The ticket campaign was titled "Operation DRIVE," and its goal was to sell 7,300 season tickets for a package of Raider home games.

Behind the scenes, another campaign was being launched to save the team. Wayne Valley and Ed McGah were recruiting a young assistant coach from the San Diego Chargers. On January 18, 1963, 33-year-old Al Davis became head coach and general manager of the Oakland Raiders. Few recognized it at the time, but the future of the Raiders — and pro football — was heading in a new direction.

Chapter Seven

1963: Al, Sonny, and El Sid

TOMMY BROOKER'S DRAMATIC FIELD GOAL in the dusk of a late December afternoon served to do more than just give the Dallas Texans an AFL championship. The six-quarter, 77-minute classic helped give the AFL a new identity as well. Gene Ward wrote in the *New York Daily News* that the AFL had finally come of age. Shirley Povich of the *Washington Post* agreed, and like Ward, credited the '62 title game for the league's rise in stature.

"The AFL was born at the age of three, so magnificent was the game," Povich wrote. "Viewers were even given to wonder if Joe Schmidt or Sam Huff could excel E. J. Holub."

Interest in the AFL was on the rise in 1963. Fan attendance at AFL stadiums was improving every season, and thanks to the NFL's "blackout" rule that prohibited NFL games from being televised in host NFL cities, the AFL was gaining much-needed TV exposure. Says Curt Gowdy, who broadcast AFL games for ABC from 1962 to 1964 and then from 1965 to 1969 for NBC:

> The NFL made a crucial mistake in 1962. The NFL had a blackout routine where, if the New York Giants were at home, there were no games on TV in that area. They opened the door for us. On Sundays, we were the only pro football game on TV in those areas where NFL teams were playing at home.
>
> In other words, if you were in New York and the Giants were at home, you couldn't see the Giants on TV and you couldn't see an NFL game, but you could see an AFL game. That's like opening the door to a vacuum cleaner salesman and letting him in. And that's what the NFL did.
>
> The AFL ratings shot up and suddenly people were talking about the AFL. The NFL realized after the season was over they had made a bad mistake. They rescinded their blackout rule, so if the Giants were at home, and you lived in New York, you couldn't see the Giants on TV but you could see a Packers–Bears game. But in that one year that the NFL had their blackout rule, the AFL was the only game on in some of those big cities. And that was a bad strategical error by the NFL.

The other factor in the AFL's increased popularity was their style of play. In an era when NFL coaches modeled their teams on the Green Bay Packers' ground-oriented "Run to Daylight" offense and the New York Giants' 4–3, middle linebacker-dominated defense, AFL coaches stood apart as original thinkers.

"The sixties were the decade of simplicity," Kansas City head coach Hank Stram said. "During the sixties the great teams came out in the same set play and wham, bam, here they came. Teams like the Green Bay Packers didn't really try to fool you."

In contrast, each AFL team sought to create its own identity. In San Diego, Sid Gillman's Chargers burned up the track with blistering speed. In Dallas and then Kansas City, Stram confused opponents with camouflage offenses and odd-front, stack defenses. Oakland put running backs out on deep pass patterns and instituted a 3-4 defense. Houston opted for a spread offense. Buffalo used a big-back, double-tight end offense and five-man defensive front. Boston popularized the blitz. Says Gowdy:

> The emphasis was on offense. The owners knew they had to sell this league to new people, and you're not going to sell it with a 10–7 game or a 7–0 game. AFL coaches deserve a lot of credit. They were much more imaginative than NFL coaches. They could afford to be. They could gamble, and be unpredictable and exciting, and I think it was poured into everybody, "Listen, we've got to entertain people if this league's gonna go. We have to be an entertainment factor." And they were. We had some great games — 50–48, 62–50. It was basketball on stripes. But if you liked defense, you liked the NFL more.
>
> I think the all-time greatest passing coach in the history of football is Sid Gillman. He was in San Diego, and he got a good team right away. Al Davis was in Oakland, and he's a very innovative guy. The coaches were very innovative. They put in a lot of new stuff. And the two-point conversion was exciting, and they have that now in the NFL. But [the AFL] had things the NFL didn't have that were appealing to fans.

Teams like the Chargers and Bills had styles suitable to their surroundings. Balboa Stadium's claylike playing surface was baked hard by the San Diego sun. To make maximum use of the slick track, Gillman designed a speed-oriented offense with wide running plays and streaking fly patterns.

While the fast-break Chargers reflected the fast-lane lifestyle of nearby Hollywood, the Bills typified the blue-collar mentality of the rust belt. Playing their home games in War Memorial Stadium, a Depression-era structure built on a leaky reservoir, the Bills were a no-nonsense, nine-to-five troop who slogged their way through the muck of War Memorial with a power running game and punishing defense.

The differences in each AFL stadium influenced to a degree the style of play within their confines. When the Raiders moved from Frank Youell Field to the new Oakland Coliseum, they inherited a stadium built below sea level — a condition that left the turf permanently damp, if not wet. To take advantage of the slow, heavy turf, the Raiders built a power running game geared to plodding, heavy-legged backs like Hewritt Dixon and Clem Daniels.

What each of the old AFL stadiums had in common was its second-class citizen look. Houston's Jeppesen Stadium was home to both the Oilers and local high school teams, and the constant use made for sparse turf. Even a moderate rain would turn the field to mud. When the Oilers planted grass seed to build up the turf, it left a Mohawk effect down the crown from one end of the field to the other. The Houston climate was unpredictable, ranging from stifling humidity to sudden monsoons. When the heavy rains struck, the floor of Jeppesen Stadium had the same texture as slow-drying cement.

War Memorial was an old stone stadium located in one of the roughest sections of downtown Buffalo. The Polo Grounds in New York was historic, but the steel edifice was caked with rust and dirt. Oakland's Frank Youell Field, as already mentioned, was a high school structure named after an undertaker. When the Patriots played in Boston's Fenway Park, visiting teams had to take the field from behind the third base dugout where they had to stand, jammed up and hunched over, in a cramped hallway complete with leaking water pipes overhead.

Balboa Stadium in San Diego was a sunken, bowl-shaped structure whose Roman columns at one end of the stadium gave it the look of a minicoliseum and whose leaky plumbing gave it the feel and smell of an oft-used outhouse. *San Diego Tribune* sportswriter Jerry Magee, who has covered the Chargers since their move to San Diego in 1961, says:

> Balboa Stadium was an edifice that was built as a WPA project in the 1930s. It was pretty much a high school type of venue, and it adjoined a San Diego high school. They used to hold a lot of events there, and it was used hard, everything from high school football and track to midget auto racing. It was the biggest stadium we had in San Diego in 1961, but you couldn't play big league football there at first. The city finally agreed to put a second tier on it, and while it wasn't a major league facility, it was adequate for the AFL at that time.
>
> One thing about Balboa Stadium was it was a beautiful place to watch a game. The sidelines were close to the field and you got a real good view of everything. But it wasn't a luxury stadium. Seats were cement slabs, the locker room facilities were terrible, very small, and your ass got wet from the overflowing toilets.
>
> Most of the old AFL stadiums were makeshift arenas. Even the newer ones, like the Oakland Coliseum, were built on the cheap. I was there the day the Oakland Coliseum opened, and it leaked that day! Those stadiums were built on the cheap, but each one had a personality. I remember covering games in War Memorial Stadium in Buffalo, and that place was in one of the worst neighborhoods in America. I think War Memorial fans went to games with one idea in mind—steal a football.
>
> I remember being in the press box after the game, writing a story, and the wind would come through and rattle all the empty beer cans left in the stadium. You'd hear this rattle, and it was almost like the place was mocking you. And when you stood outside the stadium after the game, in the dark, you made sure you had a real good grip on your typewriter.

AFL stadiums were less than glamorous, and the fans who inhabited them less than hospitable. Magee remembers Raider fans in old Frank Youell Field "throwing beer cans, and they weren't always empty. Frank Youell Field had a personality, and it was a *riotous* personality."

Boston fans were known for sneaking up behind the opposing team's bench and stealing its footballs. Kansas City's Municipal Stadium fans were so loud they were called "the Wolfpack." Bills fans hovered near the rickety wooden staircase that led from the opposing team's locker room to the field and doused enemy teams with equal parts beer and insults. As Bills owner Ralph Wilson remembers:

> Buffalo had that old stone stadium downtown. Houston played in a high school stadium, the Raiders played in Youell Field, another high-school sized stadium. Those stadiums were typical of the early years in the AFL. But you know, we were a new league, just starting out. We didn't need to play in the Taj Mahal.
>
> Those stadiums did have a sort of charm, though. We drew big crowds in Buffalo. I remember we added something like 7,500 seats in the middle sixties. When we played home games, we'd have people standing around the field, standing in the end zones. It was pretty nostalgic.

Boston's Gino Cappelletti, one of just 19 players whose careers spanned the entire 10-year life of the AFL, has fond memories of playing in the league's original stadiums.

> They were old, dilapidated, antiquated stadiums, but they had a lot of charm, history, and tradition. At the time, it was the big leagues. It was the Big Show for us. Buffalo's War Memorial was in one of the roughest sections of town. As was the Polo Grounds [in New York], but those stadiums had a lot of history. The Raiders had Frank Youell Field that they built while waiting for something to happen there. The Chargers had Balboa Stadium, which was in Balboa Park where they had the zoo. And in Houston there was Jeppesen Stadium, where the high school teams played too, so you never knew what the condition of the field was going to be like on Sunday when you played. Each of those old stadiums had their own individual meaning.

Babe Parilli, another of the AFL's "Original 19," agrees that each of the old AFL stadiums had its own personality. But one thing they each had in common was outdated accommodations.

"The dressing rooms, the locker facilities were terrible," Parilli says. "You might have one shower working. It was really bad, and most of them were that way. But they were classic stadiums."

Also classic were the old nylon uniforms and plastic helmets, which had web-suspension padding and single-bar facemasks. AFL uniforms were distinctive from the NFL in the 1960s in that each AFL player was identified with a nameplate sewn to the back of his jersey. Initially, NFL owners scoffed at the printing of players' names on their jerseys.

"The NFL criticized us for labeling players, claiming it was 'glamour sports,'" AFL commissioner Joe Foss said. "Actually, I think they were more concerned that certain players might develop too much bargaining power if they were visible to the crowds."

The best of the AFL's early uniforms undoubtedly belonged to the Chargers, whose colors were sky blue, sunshine gold, and wedding-gown white. Jagged lightning bolts, symbolizing their quick-striking play, were located on the sides of their white helmets and pants and around the shoulder loops of their blue jerseys. When the NFL honored its 75th anniversary in 1994 by adopting "throwback" uniforms, the Chargers' 1961 uniform was among the more popular of the old styles.

Of course, the most infamous attire in the AFL belonged to the 1960–61 Denver Broncos — but as bad as Denver's uniform was, players like all-star wide receiver Lionel Taylor were just glad to be playing pro football.

"I was happy to have a pair of those socks," Taylor says with a laugh. "I just wanted to play. I think everybody was more happy to have an opportunity to go out and play than worry about the socks. But just think about all the money Jack burned [at the public bonfire]. I wish I had a pair of those socks now. They're worth some money."

AFL players weren't the only ones on the field with a distinctive uniform. League officials wore jerseys that had red and white vertical stripes, a marked contrast to the NFL's more traditional black and white striped shirt. The official AFL logo — a thin capital-A placed above a football and in front of a winged eagle — adorned the shirt and front of the cap.

The final piece of AFL equipment that was distinctive from the NFL was the ball. From its inception, the AFL adopted the Spalding J5-V, which had been the official NFL ball from 1920 to 1940, before Wilson Sporting Goods became the manufacturer of official NFL footballs in 1941 and introduced its ball, "the Duke." The nickname had first been used by the NFL during the 1930s. "The Duke" was the boyhood nickname of Wellington Mara of the New York Giants. The J5-V was thinner and longer than "the Duke," though the differences were smaller than many believed. The AFL ball measured ¼" longer (11¼" vs. 11") and was thinner in circumference (21¼" vs. 21½"). The NFL ball was larger and more rounded; the AFL ball more pointed. The lacing was also slightly different. Some football people, like Green Bay's Vince Lombardi, believed the differences made the AFL ball easier to throw and catch.

The week following the West's 21–14 win over the East in the second annual AFL All-Star game produced two announcements that in time had a profound effect on pro football. On Monday, January 15, David A. "Sonny" Werblin offered $1.3 million to buy out Harry Wismer's bankrupt New York Titans.

On Thursday of that week, January 18, the Oakland Raiders announced that former San Diego assistant coach Al Davis had accepted a three-year, $60,000 contract to become the team's new general manager and head coach.

"I'm not interested in the job," Davis told reporters. "I'm interested in whether I can *do* the job."

The son of a garment maker, Davis was born in Brockton, Massachusetts, and raised in Brooklyn. He graduated from Erasmus Hall and Syracuse University, then moved to Long Island in 1950 when he got the job as assistant football coach and head baseball coach at Adelphi University. Drafted into the army two years later, Davis was sent to Fort Belvoir, Virginia, where he helped build a strong service football team.

Following his discharge, Davis joined the Baltimore Colts as a scout, and then became line coach at the Citadel. Davis' success as a recruiter helped the Citadel to its best record in 13 seasons. He earned additional notoriety as a recruiter after moving to USC and signing some of the players that helped the Trojans win a national championship. In 1960 he was hired by Sid Gillman as the offensive backfield coach for the fledgling Los Angeles Chargers.

The success of the Chargers in the AFL's early years shed a spotlight not only on the players but on the coaches. Gillman's staff included Davis, defensive backfield coach Jack Faulkner, and defensive line coach Chuck Noll. Faulkner went on to coach the Denver Broncos and later director of administration for the Rams. Noll became defensive backfield coach for the Baltimore Colts in 1966 and helped the Colts to an NFL title in 1968 before being named head coach of the Pittsburgh Steelers. Noll remains the only head coach in NFL history to win four Super Bowls.

But in the early 1960s it was Davis who gained national attention with shrewd negotiating tactics that allowed him to sign outstanding college talent away from the rival NFL. Davis' signings in the early years of the AFL read like a Who's Who of Charger stars. In 1960, Davis signed offensive tackle Ron Mix and halfback Paul Lowe: in 1961, fullback Keith Lincoln: in 1962, defensive linemen Ernie Ladd and Earl Faison: and in 1963, flanker Lance Alworth. Each of the above earned all-pro status.

In winning just three games in two years, the Raiders had lost both an estimated million dollars in operating costs and most of their modest following. Bay area football fans laughed off the Oakland franchise. On the *Captain Satellite* kiddie TV program, the following question was asked: "What has 22 legs and lives in the cellar?" The answer was "The Oakland Raiders."

When the Raiders put up signs urging fans to follow the team, someone scrawled, "Who are the Oakland Raiders? And where are they going?"

Boston head coach Mike Holovak remembered the '62 Raiders as a "walking, screeching band of ineptitude."

The Raiders were born on January 30, 1960, the products of an eleventh-hour effort to fill the void left when the Minneapolis group pulled out. Originally, the team was going to be called the *Señors*, in honor of the Spanish influence in Oakland. In 1960 and '61, the Raiders didn't even play in Oakland, they played across the Bay in San Francisco, sharing first Kezar Stadium and then Candlestick Park with the 49ers. Raider attendance for 1961 was barely 40,000 for the entire season. Scotty Stirling, the team's public relations manager, used to drop 10-12 free passes on Charlie Zeno, then sports editor of the *Contra Costa Times*. "Charlie, give them to anybody," Zeno said, "just let them come to the Raiders."

"If I could give away two," Zeno said, "I felt successful."

The Raiders labored in anonymity during their early years. As they left the field following a game against the Titans in the Polo Grounds, the public address announcer referred to them as the *Oklahoma* Raiders. The team's practice field was located at a naval air station, next to a runway. When the jets warmed up for a takeoff, the sound drowned out quarterback Tom Flores' signals. The coaches would order the team to stop practice and run laps around a field littered with rocks and broken glass.

By 1963, Oakland ownership was determined to turn the team around. On Wednesday, January 10, Davis met with Oakland owners Wayne Valley and Ed McGah five separate times in a hotel room in San Diego, the site of the AFL All-Star game. Davis wanted the job, but had concerns about the Raiders' commitment to building a first-class organization. He asked *Oakland Tribune* sports editor George Ross and football writer Scotty Stirling if the club was going to survive financially. Because the *Tribune* had been influential in making the Raiders a reality in 1960, Davis knew Ross and Stirling had inside information.

Ross assured Davis that Raider management was prepared to turn the team around. In meeting with Valley and McGah, Davis gained a multiyear contract as head coach and an operating budget large enough to build the club into contenders. "What I want," Davis said, "is enough time and money to build the Raiders into a professional football team."

On January 29, the Oakland City Council approved plans for the construction of a new stadium. The announcement heartened Davis, who had been disconsolate after arriving in Oakland and finding the team's front office located in a small mezzanine atop the lobby of the Hotel Leamingtown in the center of the city.

"I came here from San Diego gambling on the development of a Coliseum," he said, "and emergence of the Oakland area into the sports capital of the West."

Immediately after being named head coach and general manager, Davis made sweeping changes in the Raiders' front office and coaching staff. He also remade the Raider image, throwing away the old black and gold uniforms that had been bought at cut rate prices from the University of the Pacific football team, and replacing them with a silver and black combination patterned after West Point's Black Knights of the Hudson.

The Raiders didn't have the money to sign blue-chip college players, so Davis and his staff worked the phones. By opening day of the '63 season, the Raiders had made 18 trades. The biggest addition was the signing of free-agent Art Powell, a classic deep receiver perfect for the vertical passing game Davis was installing. Flores recovered from a lung infection that had sidelined him in 1962, and he and Powell made a formidable combination. Flores threw for 20 touchdowns, and Powell led AFL receivers in yards and touchdowns.

Halfback Clem Daniels topped the league in rushing and receiving average. The Raiders' 363 points scored ranked second in the league to San Diego, and Oakland finished at 10-4, a game behind the Chargers in the West.

While Davis rebuilt the Raiders, Lamar Hunt was looking to relocate his defending league-champion Dallas Texans. In three years, the Texans had built a championship team filled with young stars, and their imaginative brand of football was superior to that being played by Tom Landry's Cowboys. But the Cowboys' ability to break even with the Texans in game attendance was largely due to the caliber of the competition; in 1962, the NFL still had a considerable advantage over the AFL in the realm of player prestige. Dallas fans were content to pay to see the NFL's elite teams perform in the Cotton Bowl, even if it meant a loss for the Cowboys. In 1962, advance tickets sales for AFL games averaged just 7,000; the NFL average was 28,000.

Realizing Dallas could not support two pro football teams, Hunt decided to move his team, and put out feelers for a city to adopt the champions of the AFL. H. Roe Bartle, the mayor of Kansas City, invited the Texans to take up residence in Missouri. Bartle told Hunt the Texans would enjoy "three times" as many season ticket sales in Kansas City as they had in Dallas. The mayor promised to enlarge the city's Municipal Stadium and rent it to the Texans for just $1 a year. Hunt, who was also considering New Orleans as a possible site for his team, agreed to visit Bartle in Kansas City. The meetings were shrouded in secrecy. When Hunt and general manager Jack Steadman arrived, Bartle called them "Mr. Lamar" and "Jack X."

Bartle's lavish promises and the mayor's persuasiveness won Hunt over. On February 8, the Texans owner announced he was moving his franchise to Kansas City.

On May 22, the Texans were renamed the "Chiefs," in deference to Mayor Bartle, who was known around Kansas City as "the chief."

The Chiefs were favored to repeat as division champions, but a fatal preseason injury to rookie Stone Johnson demoralized the team, and Kansas City fell to third place in the Western Division with a 5-7-2 record. Years later, Jerry Mays, who was the club's defensive captain, said the franchise move from Dallas to Kansas City was a factor in the team's disappointing season.

"Did I feel resentment at the move?" Mays asked. "Big time. I was born in Dallas, raised in Dallas, played high school and college football in Dallas, and then we had to move to Kansas City. At that time, we had a lot of no-shows in Kansas City [for home games]. We felt like we'd sell out every home game, and we didn't. I felt then like the people in Kansas City didn't have a clue about what football was. I think there was a lot of skepticism in Kansas City about the AFL."

The changes engulfing the AFL were felt not only in Oakland and Kansas

David A. "Sonny" Werblin saved the AFL's New York franchise from bankruptcy in 1963, and helped build the Jets into world champions. (*Photo courtesy of the New York Jets.*)

City, but in New York as well. The Titans were so bogged down in litigation that sportswriter Dan Parker said the team's theme song should be "Sweet *Sue*."

With Harry Wismer involved in bankruptcy proceedings, Joe Foss jetted around the country seeking prospective buyers for the franchise. Foss found what he was looking for in a five-man syndicate headed by David A. "Sonny" Werblin and composed of Leon Hess, Phil Iselin, Donald Lillis, and Townsend B. Martin. The group agreed in February to purchase the Titans franchise for $1 million. On March 28, the deal was concluded, and the Harry Wismer era mercifully ended.

Though Wismer was now officially out of the AFL, his leaving did not pass without lament. Said Titans publicist Murray Goodman, "Don't forget that if it weren't for Harry Wismer there mightn't have been a league. He is the guy they have to thank for their television deal."

In Wismer's place came a group of men who instantly gave the Titans and the AFL a new sense of respectability. Werblin, the organizer of the syndicate and the man who negotiated the sale of the Titans with Foss, was in 1963 the president of the Music Corporation of America. "His chief business," wrote Joe Durso of the *New York Times*, "was entertainment."

Werblin's business acumen impressed the AFL commissioner. "The minute I met him," Foss said of Werblin, "I knew he was the man for the New York franchise."

Born in Brooklyn on St. Patrick's Day in 1910, Werblin's background was pure show business. As the impresario of the Music Corporation, the balding, 5-foot-10 Werblin was a giant among men. He joined the entertainment complex at the age of 20, and over the next 35 years helped establish MCA as the largest talent agency in the world. When Werblin resigned as president of the MCA in 1965, George Rosen, a reporter for *Variety*, wrote that Werblin's resignation meant the end of an era: "For in those more than three decades, Werblin wielded more influence, made more money, made and broke more careers than perhaps any other show biz impresario in New York."

Werblin's show biz background served him well in pro football. To Sonny, sports was entertainment, and dealing with high-priced athletes was the same as dealing with major recording stars. Werblin applied business principles to the game of football; he sought players and coaches who had "star quality" and could attract paying fans to the stadium. The late Howard Cosell, who was then director of WABC Radio in New York and a friend of Werblin's, characterized Sonny as "a man who took performers nobody ever heard of and made them into stars, like Andy Williams, for instance. He would do the same with the Jets."

While Werblin was the organizer and front man of the Gotham Football Club, his partners comprised a rich and powerful conglomerate. There was oilman Leon Hess, whose career could be traced to Bayonne, New Jersey, where he sold oil off a truck in the post–World War II years; Phil Iselin was a giant in the garment industry; Don Lillis a stockbroker and president of the Bowie Race Course in Maryland; and Long Island society man Townsend B. Martin a horse breeder and investment broker. Just when the New York franchise and the AFL in a larger sense were trying to meet their payroll, the entrance of this powerful syndicate came at a critical time in AFL history.

"The turning point for the league was ... when Sonny Werblin and his group took over the New York club," Hunt says. "He brought the Titans out of their bankruptcy situation. Sonny gave us immediate believability with the press."

When the new owners took over, Werblin announced his intention to sweep the slate clean. "There will be nothing left of the old regime," he said, and to emphasize the new beginning, he changed the team's uniform colors from blue and gold to kelly green and white. To coach the Jets, Werblin picked 55-year-old Wilbur "Weeb" Ewbank, an elfin figure who was an astute judge of talent and specialized in rebuilding projects. Ewbank began his pro coaching career in 1949 as an assistant on Paul Brown's AAFC Cleveland Browns team. In 1954 Ewbank was hired to coach the Baltimore Colts, and in 1958–59, he led the Colts to consecutive NFL titles. But the team slumped from 1960 to 1962, and Rosenbloom replaced Ewbank in January of 1963 with Don Shula.

Werblin learned of Ewbank's availability in Toot Shor's, a late-night gathering place for New York's sporting public. Ewbank also had a reputation of maintaining good relations with the media, and Werblin, aware that New York had seven daily publications, saw this as another reason for hiring him.

Ewbank moved quickly to improve the Jets. He stocked his coaching staff with quality assistants: Walt Michaels, Chuck Knox, and Clive Rush all went on to become NFL head coaches. He signed ex–Colts like Winston Hill and Bake Turner to bolster his roster. "We have 65 bodies," Ewbank said, "but few players."

Werblin saw to it that Jets coaches and players had first-rate equipment. When he saw a team trainer taping a pair of cracked shoulder pads, Werblin ordered, "Throw those [pads] away. Get new ones. Everything's going to be first class around here."

New York's football fans took notice of the changes, and responded at the ticket office. Attendance for home games rose to 103,550, and the Jets finished the season with a 5–8–1 record.

While the Raiders and Jets rebuilt, San Diego head coach Sid Gillman reloaded. The Chargers had won division titles in 1960–61, and as '63 approached Gillman was building up his squad for its greatest season ever.

"We had good people," Gillman says today. "We had an aggressive organization, a real fine staff, and our scouts were on top of all the available talent."

The Chargers had superior talent at nearly every position. The backfield was comprised of the "L Boys"—Keith Lincoln and Paul Lowe. Lance Alworth was the best wide receiver in the league, and Ron Mix the top offensive tackle. The "Fearsome Foursome" defense featured all-pros Ernie Ladd and Earl Faison.

The Chargers' offense of the early 1960s ranks as one of the best in league history. Lowe and Mix were perennial all-pros, and the addition of Lincoln, Tobin Rote, and Alworth allowed Gillman to bring his elaborate blackboard X's and O's to life.

Lowe, a onetime track star and street kid from Watts, picked up his distinctive high-stepping style as a hurdler in high school and college.

"I was a track man," said Lowe, who attended Oregon State University, "a high-hurdle champion. That's where I got my style from with the high knee action. I only weighed 170 pounds, so I wasn't going to run over anybody."

Lowe skipped his senior season at Oregon State to turn pro. He went to a 49ers tryout camp, but despite a dazzling 105-yard kickoff return in an exhibition game, Lowe was cut from the team because of his slight build. When the AFL began operations in 1960, he was a 23-year-old family man working in Barron Hilton's Carte Blanche offices in Los Angeles. By the time Lowe contacted the Chargers for a tryout, he had bulked up to 180 pounds through a weight-lifting regimen that added 10 pounds of muscle to his frame.

As he had in San Francisco, Lowe returned his first kickoff with the Chargers 105 yards for a score. L.A. assistant coach Al Davis, who remembered Lowe from his Oregon State days as a player who Davis said could "get the ball in the end zone," signed Lowe to a contract that called for a $750 bonus.

Lowe sat out the first five games of the 1960 season, but inserted into the lineup in week six, he ran for a team-high 855 yards. He led the AFL with a 6.3 yards-per-carry average and nine rushing scores, and was named all-pro.

At 6-foot-1, 210 pounds, Lincoln felt he was too small to handle the job of fullback, preferring instead to play halfback. A conflict arose, as the Chargers already had Lowe tabbed for the left halfback spot. Lincoln arrived for the '63 camp prepared to duel Lowe for the starting role. Of the competition between the two men, Lincoln said at the time, "It's good for both of us. Keeps us on our toes in the game."

Gillman had other ideas. To make use of both halfbacks, Gillman persuaded Lincoln to play fullback. "[Lincoln] has the speed to go outside," Gillman told reporters, "and the power to break tackles."

Paired in the San Diego backfield, Lincoln and Lowe became the most explosive backfield combination in AFL history. They didn't particularly complement each other as running mates, as both were halfback types. But the "L Boys" did have several points of similarity in their respective backgrounds.

Like Lowe, Lincoln was a high school star who headed to the Pacific Northwest to play college ball. Recruited by Washington State as a quarterback, Lincoln broke his collarbone during his freshman season in a fraternity house wrestling match. Given the option of taking a year off as a red-shirt quarterback or joining the team immediately as a running back, Lincoln opted to play.

Drafted by the Chargers in 1961, Lincoln reported for the College All-Star game against the NFL champion Philadelphia Eagles. Told by Stars coach Otto Graham that he was not cut out for a pro offense, Lincoln began weighing his options.

"I had an opportunity to play in Canada," he says. "They were fairly aggressive. My thought process at that time was that I wasn't concerned about the new league. At that time, there was a distinct money difference in the two leagues, and I felt if I couldn't make it in the AFL, I couldn't make it in the NFL."

When he joined the Chargers, Lincoln was initially kept on defense because the club had good depth at running back. But he was switched to offense for the '61 season and carried 41 times for 150 yards. With Lowe sidelined by a broken arm, Lincoln emerged as the club's leading rusher. By 1963, Gillman was ready to pair them in his halfback-oriented offense.

"We wanted to get all the speed we could muster," Gillman said. "We didn't have patience for slow, lumbering people."

The same went for San Diego's offensive linemen, where Gillman put together a light, fast unit whose specialty was pulling out to lead sweeps. The unit's most heralded member was right tackle Ron Mix.

"When you're running behind Mix," Lowe said, "it's like you're a little kid and he's your big brother protecting you from the wolves."

Considered the greatest tackle in AFL history, the 6-foot-4, 250-pound Mix studied law and was so technically correct on the field that he was known as "the Intellectual Assassin." In his 10 years in the league, Mix was called for holding just twice.

"Ron Mix was one of the greats of all time," Gillman says. "I think he's the greatest tackle who ever lived."

Mix had what coaches call "fire out," an ability to explode off the ball from his lineman's stance with speed and force. Gillman once stopped practice so the rest of the team could watch Mix in a one-on-one blocking drill. "Oh, it was beautiful," said Al Davis, "watching real fundamentals in action."

"With a man outweighing you by anywhere from 10 to 50 or 60 pounds, you have to use a lot of technique blocks," Mix said. "You're just not going to be able to drive a man out by force and outpower him as you could do in college when you were playing against men your own weight."

The lead blocker on San Diego's celebrated toss sweeps, Mix occasionally startled Charger broadcasters. "I think I saw Ron Mix take out *three* men," they announced once. "Is that possible?"

Gillman shored up the quarterback position by acquiring the rights to 35-year-old Tobin Rote. A veteran of the NFL, Rote's pro football career began in 1950 when he was drafted by the Green Bay Packers. He was dealt to Detroit the following year, and when starter Bobby Layne suffered a broken leg late in the season, Rote took command of the offense. The Lions rallied to beat the 49ers in a Western Conference playoff game, then routed Cleveland in the NFL title game, with Rote throwing for three TDs and running for a fourth in a 59–14 win.

In 1960 Rote became embroiled in a salary dispute with Detroit management. He played out his option and joined the Canadian Football League, leading the CFL in passing in 1961–62. The Buffalo Bills obtained the negotiating rights to Rote. But after getting Jack Kemp off the Chargers' waiver wire for $100, the Bills sought to deal their rights to Rote in a trade.

In January 1963 Foss met with Gillman and Denver head coach Jack Faulkner in a San Diego hotel room. A coin flip would decide which team, the Chargers or Broncos, would gain the rights to Rote. Gillman won the toss, and Rote stabilized San Diego's quarterback position.

Rote's arrival saw Alworth emerge as the league's best receiver. Free from the injuries that hampered his rookie season, Alworth dazzled AFL audiences with his leaping catches. His large brown eyes, fawnlike grace and startling bolts off the line of scrimmage earned Alworth a nickname he despised.

"You're Bambi," fullback Charlie Flowers told Alworth at a practice in 1962. "For your big brown eyes and the way you move."

In later years, Alworth would grow his hair and dye it red, trying to dispel the Bambi image. But the nickname remained.

Settling into his three-point stance at the line of scrimmage, the fingers of his left hand twitching, Alworth launched himself forward at the snap of the ball. Outrunning the bump-and-run coverage of AFL defenses, he bounced through the secondary like a pinball. His trademark was to leap high for a pass and pull the ball to his chest.

"One reason I jump is to get my body into the ball so it can't be knocked away," Alworth once explained. "If you catch the ball only with your hands, it gets jarred loose when you get hit. When you're up in the air, you don't get hit so hard."

Gillman was instrumental in developing Alworth's talents. The Chargers collected film on all the great receivers in NFL history, and used them to make a precise study of each receiver's moves and patterns. On the practice field, Gillman took Alworth aside to sell him on his aerial axioms.

"Take a drive corner, Lance," Gillman would say, "from a good wide position. Start it right down that middle and break it off to the corner."

Gillman's game planning and Alworth's talent helped make him the game's premier deep threat. The Chargers' number-one pass play was the Curl and Fly, in which Alworth would sprint upfield, Rote would pump-fake the curl, and then throw deep and to Alworth's outside shoulder.

Much of Alworth's success can be traced to his competitive drive. Oakland Hall of Fame cornerback Willie Brown said Alworth had a "great hunger for the ball." Jets cornerback Johnny Sample, who kept a book on the AFL and NFL receivers he covered in the late '50s and '60s, had a personal rating system by which he graded receivers on speed, pass patterns, catching the ball, blocking ability, and intimidation. Sample said Alworth was the only one who had top grades in every category. "He did everything perfectly," Sample said.

Despite their awesome talent, the Chargers had lost to Houston in the 1960 and '61 AFL championship games, and dropped to third place in the West in '62. Sensing the team needed mental toughness, Gillman moved the training camp to a desolate dude ranch outside San Diego called Rough Acres.

"I felt that we needed a little toughening up," Gillman said. "We'd been training in the San Diego area, and even though you couldn't call our camps a resort area, I thought it would be a novel idea to take them to Rough Acres. What I didn't know was that the place was crawling with snakes."

Located on Highway 80, some 66 miles east of San Diego, Rough Acres sat adjacent to a desert-outpost of a town whose population in 1963 was listed at 50 people. A serpentine dirt road led from the highway to the barren, rock-covered ranch. Diamond-shaped stone duplexes bordered the football field. Few trees were on hand to provide shade from the white-hot glare of the sun, and the surrounding terrain offered an unending view of hills and sunbaked flatland.

To improve his team's physical condition, Gillman hired Alvin Roy, strength coach of the U.S. Olympic team. Roy put the Chargers on a program of weight training and isometrics. Roy's strenuous conditioning program and the bleakness of their surroundings cause ex–Chargers to cringe when they recall Rough Acres.

"Oh my God!" Ladd shrieks. "The rattlesnakes, the hundred-and-five degree weather. Rough Acres almost turned everybody against football!"

"That was a hell of a preseason," Lowe says. "It was terrible. The flies ate more than we did. It was so hot you couldn't sleep at night. There were snakes everywhere, tarantulas.... The sand was blowing everywhere, it was in our beds. It was bad."

The San Diego Chargers of the early 1960s featured the AFL's first great defensive unit. Two reasons for the Chargers' success were 6-foot-9, 320-pound defensive tackle Ernie "Big Cat" Ladd (77) and defensive end Earl Faison (86), shown here pressuring Bills quarterback Jack Kemp in the Chargers' championship season of 1963. (*Photo courtesy of Thom Vollenweider, San Diego Chargers.*)

Also bad were the biting commentaries offered by line coach Joe Madro. The Oilers had accused the Chargers' offensive line of being soft in their two previous AFL title games. "Lambsie-pies" was the printable term the Oilers defense had used. Under the glaring desert sun, Madro toughened his line with grueling drills. "I guaran-damn-tee you they won't be calling us 'lambsie-pies' this year," he shouted throughout the camp.

Rough Acres served its purpose. Spurred on by Roy's conditioning program, Madro's acerbic comments and Gillman's game planning, San Diego's star-studded offense peaked in '63. Rote led the league in passing, completing 59 percent of his passes. Lincoln averaged an AFL-record 6.5 yards per carry, and Lowe rushed for 1,010 yards. Alworth's 20 yards per catch led the league. With their offense in full gear, San Diego sprinted to an 11–3 record, the club's best of the decade. Their 399 points scored marked a team record under Gillman.

The final element to the Chargers' success in the '60s was its team togetherness. At a time when racial tension was rife around the country, Gillman encouraged his players to mix off the field. Lowe, Mix, Ladd, Faison, and John Hadl engaged in daily card games, while Sam DeLuca and Bert Coan held what Mix described as "world problem solving sessions." Lincoln and Ladd dueled daily at noon for the World Ping-Pong Championship, and Mix and receiver Don Norton got together for guitar sessions.

"We were friends," Lincoln says. "We'd go to dinner together before the game. We had some excellent talent, and we grew together."

Sportswriter Jerry Magee covered the 1963 Chargers for the *San Diego Tribune*. Like many other people who saw that team firsthand, Magee regards them as one of the AFL's all-time best clubs.

> I think that team could have arguably given the Chicago Bears, who were the NFL champions that year, a good game. Rote was a veteran quarterback with a lot of experience, and Alworth was clearly a man apart. He was perfectly defined by his nickname "Bambi." He was like a creature of the forest, extremely graceful and fast, and he could jump. Lance was like two different people. From the waist up he was very slender. But from the waist down he was built like a stevedore. He had great balance, and he was the best wet-field receiver I ever saw.
>
> Lincoln wasn't your prototype fullback, but he had tremendously strong legs and he was fast. Lowe was as good a running back as I've ever seen, and he's the best back I've ever covered. He had great ability, and if you got him outside, you'd get a touchdown. Their defense was good too. They had people like Ladd and Faison, and they set a pro football record in 1961 for most interceptions in a season. It was a great team.

For the first half of the season, it appeared the Chargers would meet the Oilers again for the AFL title. Houston led the East through the season's first eight weeks and seem destined to win their fourth straight division title. Quarterback George Blanda continued to firebomb AFL defenses, leading the league with 224 completions and 3,003 yards. But an injured back and pulled thigh muscle left halfback Billy Cannon corseted and bandaged, and limited him to 45 yards rushing for the season. The offense was further hampered when starting offensive tackle Al Jamison retired with a bad back.

Defensively, the Oilers lost end Don Floyd to a broken jaw. Without their best pass rusher, the Houston defense dissolved down the stretch. The Oilers lost five of their last six games to fall out of the playoff race.

Instability at the coaching position also contributed to the end of the Oilers' reign. Houston's first three division titles had all been won under different coaches: Lou Rymkus, Wally Lemm, and Frank "Pop" Ivy. The musical-chair trend continued through the middle of the decade as the once-proud Oilers became mired in mediocrity. Sammy Baugh was named Oilers head coach in 1964, and he was followed in '65 by Hugh "Bones" Taylor, who in turn was followed by Lemm in '66. The constant turnover prompted an Oilers executive to tell his secretary, "If the head coach calls while I'm out, be sure to get his name."

Helping to push the Oilers off their marble pedestal were the Patriots, a team that had finished second to Houston in 1961 and '62, but beat them twice in '63. The Patriots had strengthened themselves in the off-season by signing their number-one pick, Boston College receiver Art Graham. Graham was an effective receiver with excellent foot speed, but injuries interrupted his career. He spent so much time in the Patriots' whirlpool baths that the steel tubs came to be known as the "U.S.S. Graham."

The Patriots of the early '60s were a colorful organization. They made football history in 1963 by becoming the only team ever to draft the same player twice in the same draft — tackle Dave Adams of Arkansas — and the team's coaches and players had nicknames like "Swamp Fox," "Babe," "Boardhands," "the Duke," "Earthquake," and "the Wild Man."

Like the Chargers, the Patriots were a team whose diverse personalities meshed well. Afternoon practices were followed by team gatherings at the Red Boot Tavern in Taunton, or at the Bolo near Fenway Park. Boston's offense flourished under the leadership of quarterback Vito "Babe" Parilli, fullback Larry Garron, and ends Gino Cappelletti and Jim Colclough. Sideline passes to Colclough, turn-ins to tight end Tony Romeo, and halfback sweeps by Jim Crawford all helped the Patriots move the ball against AFL defenses, but the Boston attack was built on two basic plays — a fullback draw to Garron and a fly pattern to Cappelletti.

Parilli, Garron, and Cappelletti were inspirational players who had made it to pro football against long odds. After leading the University of Kentucky to the Orange Bowl, Sugar Bowl, and Cotton Bowl in successive seasons, Parilli was the top draft choice of the Green Bay Packers in 1952. In 1956, Parilli began a traveling odyssey that saw him dealt to the Cleveland Browns and then back to the Packers. In 1959, he joined the Ottawa Rough Riders of the CFL and then signed with the Oakland Raiders in 1960.

Unhappy with Oakland head coach Eddie Erdelatz's training methods — "He made us run two miles at top speed," Parilli said — Babe was traded to the Patriots. Late in the '62 season, Parilli became the permanent starter.

"Parilli was a great quarterback," Mike Holovak, the Patriots' head coach in 1963, says. To Holovak, Parilli was the perfect example of a quarterback who had to experience failure to achieve success. Parilli became an all-league performer who could throw the short hitch pass as well as the bomb, and he directed the offense in a cool, nerveless manner.

Garron's football career at Western Illinois University began when he answered head coach Lou Saban's newspaper ad for athletes. Garron rode the bench for the first half of his first game, but then came on to score three TDs in the second. He earned Saban's admiration when he won a game for him while playing with two broken ribs.

When Saban became head coach of the Patriots in 1960, Garron joined the team as a 165-pound flanker. Weakened by tonsillitis, he had trouble holding onto the ball. Teammates derided him as "Boardhands." He was cut after the fourth game of the season, but spent the next year in a local YMCA, building his body with a weight-lifting regimen. When Saban invited him to camp in '61, Garron was a sturdy 195 pounds. Garron became an inside runner who earned the hard yards, and he gained respect by learning to block the team's toughest pass-rushers.

Holovak remembers a practice scrimmage where Garron went one-on-one against 230-pound linebacker Tom Addison. His nose bloody, his hands scraped, Garron finally dropped Addison. "Atta boy, Lar," Addison said. "You're learning."

Cappelletti had all but given up on playing professionally until the AFL began in 1960. Defensive backs respected Cappelletti because he ran disciplined patterns, made the tough catch, and wasn't afraid to block downfield. The fact that Cappelletti doubled as the Patriots' placekicker allowed him to lead the league in points scored in 1961 and '63.

On a team known for its characters, Cappelletti was the ringleader. Nicknamed "the Duke" because of his expensive wardrobe — he owned 20 pairs of dress shoes — Gino and his mates once cornered team trainer Bill Bates on a road trip to San Diego. They wrapped Bates in a hotel bedsheet, taped him up like a mummy, and left him in the hallway. Bates bounced from wall to wall looking for help, and finally bumped into the hotel manager, who got over his initial scare to fine Bates $16 for the sheets.

The Boston offense played inspirational ball, but it was the defense that won league-wide acclaim. Coached by Marion Campbell, a cunning assistant known as "the Swamp Fox," the Patriots used an array of blitzes featuring middle linebacker Nick Buoniconti and safety Ron Hall. In a game against Houston, the Patriots blitzed on 75 percent of their plays. By the fourth quarter, Oilers quarterback George Blanda was panting like a marathon runner and had to be taken out.

"It really wasn't a sound type of defense," middle linebacker Nick Buoniconti said once. "But it sure was fun."

Holovak says the Patriots blitzed out of necessity. "It's a little harder to build a defense than it is an offense," he says. "[In the AFL], we spent more time on offense than defense. What we were doing then [in Boston] was a lot of blitzing. Out of four downs, we might blitz three times. Sometimes we'd blitz one guy, sometimes two, sometimes a safety. We were noted for that. But we did that to cover some weaknesses."

Boston's defensive pressure began with a strong rush, provided by ends Larry "Wild Man" Eisenhauer and Bob Dee, and tackles Houston Antwine, Jesse Richardson, and Jim Hunt.

A graduate of Prairie View A & M, Hunt was one of 19 players whose careers spanned the life of the AFL. Undrafted in 1960, Hunt joined the Patriots as a free agent. Nicknamed "Earthquake" because he once rumbled 78 yards with an intercepted pass, the 255-pound Hunt was regarded by some as the best pass rusher in the AFL.

While Hunt was a spot starter in the Patriots' lineup, Antwine was an all-pro. Known as "Twine," the 270-pound Antwine was an NAIA wrestling champion at Southern Illinois, and he used his powerful arms and quickness to neutralize blockers. Signed by the Lions as an offensive lineman, Antwine was cut by Detroit and joined the Patriots in 1960. Holovak moved Antwine to defensive tackle, and AFL coaches like Sid Gillman and Weeb Ewbank both called him the best in the game in the mid–1960s. Boston center Jon Morris worked against Antwine in practice. "Twine hits," said Morris, "and is gone before you know it."

Eisenhauer's antics — he once ran out onto a snow-strewn field in Kansas City for pregame practice wearing nothing but his Patriots helmet — earned him the nickname "Wild Man." But the 6-foot-5, 245-pound graduate of Boston College used savvy and a series of educated moves to gain all-pro honors.

"I was known as the class clown," Eisenhauer said, "but everything I did ... was to keep everybody hanging loose. I was a very emotional player and did a lot of stuff to psych myself up for the game."

Eisenhauer would hit lockers, doors — even his own teammates. He slammed locker doors until they bent on their metal hinges. Before a game in Buffalo, the "Wild Man" drove his helmeted head through a partition. He paced the sidelines before games, looking for someone to hit. He once drilled safety Ron Hall so hard in warmups that Hall was sidelined with a shoulder injury.

"I liked to run off the field right after the pregame introductions and blast one of our guys as hard as I could," Eisenhauer said. "It got so that everybody was running and ducking as soon as I was introduced because they didn't want to get hurt."

New York Jets tackle Winston Hill, who played across the line from Eisenhauer, remembered him as a clawing, screaming pass rusher who would go to any lengths to sack the quarterback. "He even bit me once," Hill said.

Richardson earned notoriety by being one of the last pro players to go *sans* facemask. "I could see better without it," Richardson said then. "I didn't wear tape either, and no pads."

Richardson suffered five broken noses in his career, which he reset each time by massaging the bone until it popped back into place. Some tackles, like Ron Mix, fought the temptation to helmet-butt Richardson in his face. "I thought he must be the toughest guy on two legs," Mix said. "I wasn't trying not to engender his anger or anything, but I just didn't have the heart to hit him in the face."

Backing up the front four was Buoniconti, the premier middle linebacker in the league. A native of nearby Springfield, Massachusetts, Buoniconti went to Notre Dame on a football scholarship and was named to several All-America teams. But Buoniconti's size — 5-foot-11, 215 pounds — discouraged pro scouts.

"I was really down," Buoniconti told sports writer John Devaney. "I had always thought I could make a pro team that needed linebackers. All I wanted was the chance to prove myself."

Buoniconti's chance arrived on the thirteenth round of the 1962 draft. At a time when AFL teams were seeking to establish ties with the community by drafting players native to the area or who played at local colleges, the Patriots took a chance with Buoniconti, signing him for $10,000. To celebrate, Buoniconti and his wife, Terry, ordered $1,000 worth of beer to their cottage house near the campus. A truck dropped off a small mountain of beer cans to his lawn, and the party lasted for two days.

After joining the Patriots, Buoniconti grew into the role of team leader. One of the smartest linebackers in the 1960s, Buoniconti was an outstanding blitzer. But his all-pro status came from his agility, which allowed him to flow from sideline to sideline to make tackles. Charger back Keith Lincoln remembered a play where he caught Buoniconti blitzing and flipped him with a block. When Lincoln turned back to look at quarterback John Hadl, he was stunned to see Buoniconti making the tackle.

The Patriots' defensive success was due to some unique adjustments in their 4-3 alignment. One scheme moved right outside linebacker Jack Rudolph into the gap between Dee and Antwine, with Dee taking a wide split and lining up on the outside shoulder of the offensive left tackle.

The move accomplished two things. It gave Dee a better angle to pass-rush, and with Rudolph in the end-tackle gap, it effectively gave the Patriots a five-man front they could shift into or out of at the snap of the ball.

The Patriots fought their way to a 7-6-1 record, then had to face the Bills in a special one-game playoff to decide the Eastern Division title. Buffalo had rebounded from a slow start to tie the Patriots for the division lead at season's end. Keying the Bills' title drive was a stingy defense and a ball-control offense sparked by 243-pound fullback Cookie Gilchrist. The highlight of the Bills' season came on December 8, when Gilchrist churned over the Jets and the weather-beaten turf at War Memorial Stadium an AFL-record 36 times for a pro-record 243 yards. He scored five touchdowns in a 45–14 Bills victory.

On December 28, the Patriots and Bills gathered at War Memorial to decide who would face the Chargers for the AFL championship. Frigid winds dropped the temperature to 10 degrees, and viewers tuning in on TV saw bulldozers shoving snow off the field. Some 33,044 packed the old stadium, and spent the pregame pelting Pinkerton guards with snowballs.

Boston took the early lead, scoring the second time they had the ball when Cappelletti kicked a 28-yard field goal. The Patriots made it 10-0 on their next series when Garron took a pass in the flat, broke two tackles, and went 59 yards for the score.

The play was a pivotal one, and resulted from two key factors: Buffalo's respect for the Patriots' deep passing game and the icy field conditions, which made for difficult footing. Seeing the Bills defenders backpedaling at the snap of the ball, Parilli pump-faked a bomb to Cappelletti and floated a screen pass to Garron, who was already 10 yards downfield.

Two second quarter field goals by Cappelletti gave the Patriots a 16-0 halftime lead. The Bills replaced Kemp with rookie Daryle Lamonica in the third quarter, and Lamonica responded by hitting Elbert Dubenion for an AFL playoff-record 94-yard TD pass. The Bills then scored on the two-point conversion to half their deficit to 16–8, but Boston put the game away in the fourth when Parilli found Garron for a 17-yard TD. Cappelletti's 36-yard field goal, his fourth of the game, closed the scoring at 26–8.

The '63 Patriots were the only Boston team to win a title in the AFL. Some 30 years later, Holovak, now a member of the Oilers' front office, remembered 1963 as "a vintage year." So, too, does team founder Billy Sullivan.

> With reference to the 1963 team, I think that this was one of the best of the Patriots in the pre-merger days. Babe Parilli was as fine a quarterback as there was in the league and Gino Cappelletti was the leading scorer in the AFL, as well as the most valuable player in the league. We had other extraordinarily capable people on the team, including 'Cowboy' Jim Crawford, who was one of the nation's leading ground gainers at the University of Wyoming, and two extraordinarily fine defensive players, Jim Lee Hunt and Houston Antwine. We also boasted people of the caliber of Larry Eisenhauer and Bob Dee, both of whom made the all-pro team.

By the end of the 1963 season, the AFL's exciting style of play, its emphasis on offense and flashy formations, and its wise off-field decisions — the AFL earned plaudits from the sporting public for suspending its games the weekend of President Kennedy's tragic assassination, something the NFL failed to do — were instrumental in increasing its fan base to more than 1.2 million. The rise in attendance marked a trend that would continue through the years.

The public's growing acceptance of the AFL was evident not only in its attendance increases, but also in the media. Commenting on the AFL's decision to cancel its weekend games following the death of President Kennedy and the NFL's decision to play its games, Chicago columnist Warren Brown wrote: "The American Football League, which has been sneered at by the NFL since its inception, was in this 'what to do?' period the BIG league of professional football."

In *The Sporting News*, Sam Blair noted the maturity of the young league and Foss' response to it. "Foss is delighted to see that the crowds are growing along with the players," Blair wrote. "This, he'll quickly tell you, could be the start of something big."

Chapter Eight

1964: The Turning Point

FOUR MINUTES, FORTY-ONE SECONDS remaining in the ballgame, the Bears lead the Giants by a score of fourteen to ten. Once again, on third down with long yardage, the Chicago Bears are digging in as the New York Giants have to come up with that big play.... Y. A. Tittle dropping straight back to pass ... he's hit just as he throws the ball! It's up in the air ... and intercepted by the Bears in the end zone!

On December 29, 1963, in the frozen sunlight of Chicago's Wrigley Field, the Bears defeated the New York Giants 14–10 to win the championship of the National Football League. Jimmy Givens' call over NBC Radio that Sunday afternoon was just one of the highlights provided by the Bears defense, which in '63 was considered one of the greatest of its era.

Coordinated by head coach George Halas and assistant George Allen, Chicago's five-man multiple fronts and intricate zones ranked number one in the NFL against the run, the pass, and in overall defense, only the third team in history to accomplish that trifecta. In the championship game, the Chicago defense battered Giants quarterback Y. A. Tittle, intercepting five of his passes and setting up the team's only two touchdowns.

Far removed from the frigid confines of Wrigley Field, San Diego head coach Sid Gillman sat down in the early days of January 1964 to devise a game plan for playing the Boston Patriots. Like the Bears, the Chargers were the standard-bearers of their league. The San Diego offense featured a stable of AFL stars: quarterbacks Tobin Rote and John Hadl, running backs Paul Lowe and Keith Lincoln, end Lance Alworth, and tackle Ron Mix. Arguably the greatest array of offensive talent in AFL history, San Diego represented the striking edge of their league.

Orchestrating the Charger offense with a touch as deft as the one he used to play Chopin was the most famous Charger of them all: "El Sid." Pacing the sidelines in bow tie and sunglasses, puffing his ever-present pipe, Gillman struck a scholarly pose. So refined was the San Diego attack, a kind of poetry in motion, that one could quote Tennyson to capture the team's swashbuckling image:

> The heavens darken 'midst the clouds
> Hear rolling thunder nigh
> White lightning's flash a bolt of power
> Its fury cracks the sky.

"We had no weaknesses," Lowe says today. "We knew we were as good as anybody in the league. We were solid. We had a helluva passing game, we had good defense, we had the running backs with me and Lincoln. Rote was a good quarterback, and Lance made him look even better than he was. Kocourek was a good tight end, and our line, with Mix and Ernie Wright at tackles, Walt Sweeney at guard, was just great. It was a hell of a line to run behind."

The Chargers had fielded similarly talented teams in 1960–62, only to fall flat in the championship game. Their title-game opponents in January 1964, the Boston Patriots, made it to the championship game with a heralded defense and scrappy offense. In their two previous meetings in '63, the Chargers had won both games, but only by a combined margin of five points. If there was one thing Gillman wasn't concerned about leading up to the AFL title game, it was overconfidence on the part of his players. Gillman recalled:

> We had missed our goal of gaining the title twice in the previous three years, and each time we had felt that our team had been good enough to go all the way.
>
> I did not have to say anything special to the squad in order to get them "up" for Boston. Most of the players had been in our two other championship games and were just as disappointed as I had been in our failure to win either one. Now, we had another chance, and the players did not have to be reminded about the importance of being able to go all the way this time.

Boston's "Ban the Bomb" defense was a concern to Gillman. The Patriots prided themselves on delivering the big play — the sack, the loss, the turnover. Under defensive coordinator Marion Campbell and assistant Fred Bruney, Boston used linebacker and safety blitzes to foil blocking schemes and confuse quarterbacks. The Patriots expected their mobile linebackers — middle man Nick Buoniconti in particular — to chase down wide running plays.

Throughout the '63 season, Boston's defense had allowed averages of just 79 yards rushing per game, and 265 yards of total offense. Though they had lost twice to the Chargers during the regular season, both games were close — 17–13 and 7–6. The latter was the lowest-scoring game in league history. The Patriots' defense had held San Diego's offense, which in '63 averaged 28 points per game, to a total of 24 points in two games. Lowe, San Diego's 1,000-yard rusher, had been shut down in both games, gaining six yards in the first game and *zero* in the second. Boston's blitz tactics were key to their defense. The Patriots blitzed 70 percent of the time.

"I don't think that I ever saw a team that could blitz as much as they did and get away with it," Gillman said. "They used a combination of different linebackers and were one of the first teams to use safety blitzes effectively."

Gillman figured he had two courses of action to follow in approaching Boston's unconventional defense. He could employ a safe approach aimed at preventing big losses and maintaining ball control by grinding out short gains. Or he could gamble on taking the occasional big loss but countering that with the long gain. Gillman opted for the latter.

First, he changed his team's strongside-weakside alignment, shifting tight end Dave Kocourek into the backfield and motioning him to one side or the other. To further counter Boston's blitzes, the Chargers decided to put Lincoln and Lowe in motion to force Boston's linebackers out of position and open up the trapping game. Gillman also lined his team up in the "East Formation," with Kocourek lined up as a weakside tight end, and Alworth and Don Norton on the opposite side of the field. The formation forced the safety, who was used to covering plodding tight ends, into man-on-man coverage on Norton or Alworth, neither of whom was slow. Finally, to give Rote time to throw against the blitz, offensive line coach Joe Madro gave his linemen a "double read" to pick up blitzing linebackers.

Defensively, the Chargers moved middle linebacker Chuck Allen and an outside linebacker — either Emil Karras or Paul Maguire — to the weakside, where they could stunt and blitz.

As game day approached, Gillman was confident. But intricate planning could blow up if the Boston blitzers caught Lincoln and Lowe in the backfield. If they got free, the Chargers had the speed to break big plays.

"It was feast or famine," said Gillman, who in those days liked to title each of his game plans. As he put his strategy down on the large play charts he carried on the sidelines, Gillman settled on a name for his scheme. Appropriately enough, his three-page plan was called "Feast or Famine."

To this day, Lowe remembers the meticulous planning the Chargers engaged in for the Patriots. "We had been in the championship game twice before and lost," he says, "and we didn't want it to happen again. We studied their game films, we knew when we could go out into the patterns and when we had to block. We knew what they were going to do. They were a blitzing team and we decided to trap them. It was a super game plan."

Balmy, 71-degree temperatures greeted game day; by kickoff, some 30,127 sat in sun-bleached Balboa Stadium. It took just two plays from scrimmage to put the fans on their feet.

On the Chargers' opening play, Rote, whose throwing arm was inflamed with a late-season case of bursitis, dropped deep, faked a bomb, and found Lincoln for a 12-yard gain on a screen. On the second play, Rote read a Patriot blitz, faked a quick toss to Lowe, turned, and issued an inside handoff to Lincoln on a trap play. With Buoniconti out of position, Lincoln burst through the line and sped 56 yards to the Boston 4 before Dick Felt brought him down. Lincoln, who later admitted he was too keyed up at game time, trotted off to the sideline and threw up.

Two plays later, Rote carried it in from the 2 for a 7–0 San Diego lead. On the Chargers' next series, Rote crossed up the Boston defense again. Having just been sacked for an 8-yard loss on the previous play and reading another blitz, Rote faked inside to Lowe and pitched to Lincoln on a quick toss. Lincoln broke one tackle, hurdled a second defender, and raced 67 yards for a touchdown.

Boston countered when Patriot quarterback Babe Parilli found Gino Cappelletti for a 49-yard gain and Larry Garron followed with a 7-yard scoring run. But the Chargers closed out the first quarter with another big play, Rote faking an inside handoff to Lincoln and pitching out to Lowe, who swept right behind a great block by right tackle Ron Mix and then cut back en route to a 58-yard TD run.

Ahead 21–7, the Chargers' first quarter statistics were staggering. In quick succession, San Diego had scored touchdowns on its fourth, sixth, and tenth plays from scrimmage. On his first two carries of the game, Lincoln had rushed for 123 yards. An exchange of field goals in the second quarter gave San Diego a 24–10 lead. Before the half, the Chargers made it 31–10 when Rote hit Norton with a flanker screen for a 14-yard TD.

On the Boston sideline, head coach Mike Holovak couldn't believe what he was seeing. "We were all fouled up," he understated.

In the third quarter, Rote used a play-action fake to freeze the Patriot secondary long enough for Alworth to sprint deep for a 48-yard TD and a 38–10 Charger lead. In the fourth, Charger backup quarterback John Hadl hit Lincoln on a circle pass out of the backfield and the fullback churned 25 yards for the score and a 44–10 lead. Hadl himself capped the scoring with a 1-yard TD dive that made the final score 51–10. The San Diego sideline was so relaxed that Alworth spent the final minutes filming the action with a hand-held movie camera.

Rote was an old friend of Holovak's, and as bad as the Patriot boss felt, he respected the aging Rote's performance.

"I could only stand there and think, 'Well, at least I made it to the finals,'" he said. "Darn that Tobin. I gotta respect that — for what he did."

More than 30 years have done little to dim Holovak's memory of the '63 Chargers.

"They had some great players," Holovak said. "They read our blitzes and picked us apart. That was a great team."

One aspect of the '63 title game that isn't always remembered is that the Chargers had two weeks to prepare for the game, since Boston had to play Buffalo in a special playoff game to decide the Eastern Division title. As Parilli says,

> That hurt us. We had to play a playoff game and San Diego had a chance to rest. We were a blitzing team, and they had a chance to prepare for us. They were quick, and they turned the game into a footrace to the goal line.

> Defensively, they were a pretty decent team. They were probably ahead of their time with their physical size. They were the biggest team in the AFL. Ernie Ladd was so big he just overpowered everybody. He was charging hard that day.

Cappelletti says the Patriots were emotionally spent following the playoff with Buffalo.

> The Chargers had two weeks to get ready for us. We were so high after that playoff game we didn't have time to get back up for San Diego. I think we might have been a little surprised with the win at Buffalo.
>
> San Diego outsmarted us and outplayed us. They started going up and down the field in big chunks, and it was no contest after that. It was quite obvious the Chargers were the cream of the crop that year. Their defense complemented their offense, and they had been knocking on the door for three years. That was their year to put it all together.

It was an enormous victory for the Chargers. San Diego set AFL records that day by gaining 610 yards of total offense and averaging 10.2 yards per play. Lincoln accounted for 349 all-purpose yards, including 206 rushing against the Eastern Division's best run defense.

Gillman strode off the field with the game ball in one hand and a cigarette in the other. After the game, he deflected some of the praise for his planning. "No game plan works *that* well," he said. "I think it was just one of those days more than anything else. The big play was the fake toss and the trap to Lincoln. That's what sort of broke the whole thing open."

Lowe, who rushed for 94 yards and one TD on 12 carries, says the Chargers peaked in the '63 title game.

> We came out fast and never let up. We didn't do anything wrong. We were really confident that whole year. We were a close-knit bunch of guys. We always talked football. We'd go into games that season and we *knew* we were going to win. It was just a question of by how much.
>
> Lincoln had a great game, and we just didn't have enough footballs for everyone that day. I wanted the ball, Keith wanted the ball, Lance wanted the ball. We knew we could run the sweeps. That was our bread and butter play. We wanted to get outside.

Lincoln's memory of that game is how unexpectedly easy the victory was.

> We had a lot of respect for Boston, particularly their defense. But we jumped on them early, and the game was a runaway. It was a shock to us how easy it was.
>
> It all goes back to Sid and his staff. They put some bullshit to the Patriots, showing them motion and everything. We had a good football team and we executed.

Walt Sweeney, a rookie guard with the Chargers in '63, calls the win a testament to Gillman. "I don't think anyone was ever any smarter than Sid in making up a game plan," says Sweeney. "He was a great coach, and he's still a great man."

Chargers defensive tackle Ernie Ladd knew the Patriots were in trouble early on. "We had some problems when we played them in Boston that year because we were playing in snow and ice," Ladd says. "But [in the title game], Lincoln hit two long runs and we were up by 14, 21 points real quick. They had to change their game plan after that, and we just put our ears back and went after them."

After the game, the inevitable comparisons were drawn between the NFL and AFL champions. "The Bears may be champions of the world," San Diego defensive end Earl Faison said, "but we're champions of the un-i-verse."

"We're the champions of the world," Gillman said. "If anyone wants to debate it, let them play us."

Otto Graham, who quarterbacked the Cleveland Browns to "Team of the Decade" status in the 1950s, called the Chargers pro football's premier team in 1963.

"If the Chargers could play the best in the NFL, I'd have to pick the Chargers," Graham said. "They have the linemen and everything to go with them."

To this day, members of the '63 Chargers remain confident they could have beaten the Bears if there had been a Super Bowl.

"I thought we could play with anybody," Ladd says. "We had the horses on offense, and we were great defensively. I remember one time when we held Buffalo on eight downs on first-and-goal."

"We billed ourselves as the world champions that year," Sweeney says. "We had a great team, everything seemed to fit. I think we could have beaten anyone in 1963."

"Of course we would've won," Lowe says. "With our offense, defense, and depth, we had no weaknesses. We knew we had a better team than the Bears."

"I think the '63 Chargers are one of the great teams in history," Gillman says. "I think we would have done well against the Bears."

That the Chargers were able to inspire talk of being on par with the NFL's best was a step forward for the AFL. Billy Sullivan, president of the Boston Patriots, told reporters that the Chargers' win was good for the league, even if it had to come at the expense of his team.

"It almost killed me to have to watch it," Sullivan said. "But when you think about it from the standpoint of our league, well then you'd have to say that San Diego did us all a favor. They're good for our league, and that is now more important to all of us than anything else."

The Chargers' rise was critical to the AFL because the league still suffered from an inferiority complex. Bears boss George Halas referred to the AFL as "that damn Mickey Mouse league." Giants coach Allie Sherman said AFL football was an "inferior" product, and offenses like San Diego looked good because no one bothered to play defense.

"They just throw the ball up and down the field," Sherman said, "and don't bother to play any defense. What is the thrill to the fan of having a good offense, when in reality it is just that there is no defense?"

Baltimore quarterback John Unitas agreed. "From a quality standpoint, I don't think too much of the AFL yet," Unitas told writer Ed Fitzgerald at the time. "It seems to me they play strictly offensive football, and almost all passing at that. They have no defense at all. I know it has been said that some of their better clubs could beat some of our clubs. But I can't see it. I don't think they would stand a chance, principally because they don't have any defense. They aren't really complete football teams yet."

The AFL's prestige was on the rise, but the growing pains that sometimes accompanied the young league's emergence are legendary.

The Boston Patriots were leading the visiting Dallas Texans 28–21 when the Texans attempted a desperation flea-flicker play in the game's final seconds. The pass went 70 yards in the air and was caught by Dallas end Chris Burford at the three-yard line. Thinking time had elapsed, thousands of Patriot fans stormed the field to celebrate an apparent victory. Announcing there was enough time for one more play, the referees ushered the fans off the field but allowed them to stand at the back of the Patriots' end zone.

One Boston fan however, stood undetected in the Patriot secondary. When Dallas quarterback Cotton Davidson dropped back to pass and threw to Burford in the end zone, the fan-defender leaped in front of Burford and knocked the ball away as the gun sounded. The fan then disappeared into the delirious crowd.

During a nationally televised regular-season game between the New York Titans and the Dallas Texans, executives of ABC Sports sat slack-jawed during an interminable volley of long, arcing passes, few of which made it into the intended receiver's hands. What made the situation worse was the sight of the officials trying to chase down the incompletions and throw the ball back to the line of scrimmage on less than ten bounces.

With 7 P.M. approaching, ABC programming chief Edgar Scherick called network president Tom Moore and said, "We've got trouble." Moore's reply was to wait an additional ten minutes, but after watching the referees attempting to *kick* the ball back to the line of scrimmage, even Moore had enough.

In a line that would become timeless, an exasperated Moore cried, "Who could be watching this piece of shit?"

With that, Moore and Scherick pulled the plug on the AFL. The time was 6:58:30, Eastern Standard Time. As if in answer to Moore's question, thousands of calls flooded ABC switchboards.

Following the '63 title game, league executives went to work on a major television deal that would guarantee the AFL's survival. The five-year television contract with ABC that had been signed on June 9, 1960, was nearing its conclusion. Though Foss and the league's owners may have fully expected the pact to be renewed, ABC was involved in bidding rights with CBS and NBC for broadcasting rights to TV games of the rival NFL.

At precisely 11 A.M. on Friday, January 29, 1964, at a televised press conference, Pete Rozelle smiled into the lenses of a CBS camera crew and revealed the sealed bids that had been proffered by the three major networks. Rozelle's announcement that he would accept the bids to televise the NFL's 1964–65 regular-season games was a brilliant manipulation of the media. CBS had telecast the NFL's title games for both the 1961 and '62 seasons, and NBC had paid just under a million dollars to broadcast the '63 championship. Since ABC still had a contract with the AFL, the network wasn't considered a serious contender in the NFL bidding war.

What wasn't known except to a few was that Ed Scherick and Tom Moore had studied the legal papers the NFL had sent to all three major networks and found a loophole worth investigating. Scherick was the first to discover the absence of any prohibitions against televising Sunday doubleheaders. The idea was that ABC could televise an Eastern-based game at 1 P.M. and then switch to the West Coast for a 4 P.M. start.

Excited, Scherick gave the NFL booklet to Moore, with the instructions to "read this damn thing and see if we can't do doubleheaders."

Moore read it through, and came to the same conclusion; doubleheaders were doable — and affordable. With rumors abound that both CBS and NBC were preparing bids in the neighborhood of $18 to $20 million for the two-year contract, Scherick and Moore came in with a bid for $26 million over two years.

A meeting was convened at ABC to discuss the financial aspects of the situation. Board members discussed the situation all day and on into the next morning. By mid-afternoon of the following day, Moore was given the go-ahead to further explore the situation with Rozelle. In the NFL offices in New York's Rockefeller Plaza, Moore met with Rozelle.

"Pete, we're ready to bid on this thing, and it's a very big item," Moore said. "If we read this right, we can have doubleheaders."

If Rozelle had failed to realize the open-ended nature of the TV contracts, it didn't take the commissioner of the NFL long to comprehend the impact a steady spate of doubleheader Sunday afternoon games would have on the rival AFL. Behind the scenes, Rozelle was maintaining a keen vigilance on the AFL's progress, both on and off the field.

"AFL games were scheduled so they could be seen in many cities after the NL home games went off the air," wrote Wells Twombly in his book *200 Years of Sport in America*. "In an attempt to deprive the new league of its television underpinnings, CBS began to schedule doubleheaders, following up a home game with a nationally significant match."

Upon his return to ABC, Moore told board members the NFL was ready to allow televised doubleheaders. Moore's proposed offer of $26 million was approved by the board. What the ABC executives couldn't have known was that CBS knew of the availability of doubleheaders, and was preparing a significant bid. When Rozelle read the bids at his press conference, CBS had come in first at $28.2 million, followed by ABC at $26.1 million. Ignorant of the doubleheader deals, NBC came in a distant and humiliating third in the televised bidding with an offer of $20.6 million. Embarrassed, Carl Lindemann, NBC's head of sports, left the press conference and returned to his office. Waiting for him was a note to return a phone call. When Lindemann read the words "Call Joe Foss," his spirits soared.

Meeting with Foss and Sonny Werblin of the New York Jets, Lindemann rapidly came to terms on a massive $36-million, five-year pact that would commence with the 1965 season. At Lindemann's request, the deal was pushed through quickly to prevent any TV spies of sending word of the deal to ABC.

Foss, however, had reservations about going behind the back of ABC, the network which had given the AFL its first exposure to the sporting public and helped sustain it in the early years. While Lindemann and Werblin were locked with their respective lawyers in the final stages of negotiations, Foss picked up a copy of the contract, walked out of the room, headed for the nearest on-street telephone and called Tom Moore. Within the hour, Foss and Moore were meeting over a cup of coffee in a Fifth Avenue drugstore, right across from the Time-Life Building.

Moore was stunned as he studied the contract. The NBC deal was worth close to five times what ABC was paying to televise AFL games. ABC's contract had called for each AFL team to be paid $261,000 of TV revenue; under NBC, each club was to receive $900,000. With expenditures running about $800,000 per team, NBC helped legitimize the AFL.

On January 29, 1964, the same day of the Rozelle news conference, Joe Foss signed the AFL's TV rights over to NBC.

"The AFL's lucrative television contract brought new prestige to the league, as well as over twenty new requests for franchises and several offers to buy existing teams," Foss said. "That year, I estimated that the weakest team in our league would sell for at least $9,000,000."

Billy Sullivan called January 29, 1964, "the greatest day in our history." Foss called it a turning point. "After I signed that contract," he said, "people stopped asking me if we were going to make it. Everyone knew we were."

Some 30 years have passed since the NBC deal was struck, but Lamar Hunt still recalls its impact upon the AFL. "The television contract," Hunt says, "gave the league the stability and financial ability to compete for players."

The AFL's steady climb from ridicule to respectability was evident by the fact that for the first time in its brief history, the league succeeded in signing its number-one draft pick. Ohio State's Matt Snell, a punishing 6-foot-2, 220-pound fullback, was the number-one pick in the 1964 AFL draft, and Jets owner Sonny Werblin signed him away from the New York Giants.

Snell's signing, plus the addition of talented new rookies like linebacker Ralph Baker and defensive end Gerry Philbin, brought the Jets respect from the influential New York media. So did the Jets' move from the Polo Grounds to the newly constructed William A. Shea Stadium. Opened by the New York Mets baseball team in the spring of 1964, "Big Shea," as the stadium was called, offered an attendance capacity of 60,000, making it at the time the largest stadium in the AFL.

Werblin outfitted all stadium personnel — the ground crew, ticket takers, and ushers — in Jet colors, and home games saw a scale-model Jet plane buzzing along the sidelines and a 110-piece Jetliner Band. Promotions were targeted at every age group. Children visiting the Jets' training camp in Peekskill, New York, were given free T-shirts that read "I'm a Jet Fan." The Jets' schedule was posted on buses across the city. "Jet-Set Janie" continued her nasally, Brooklynese-tainted radio spot commercials.

Werblin, who had been hospitalized for minor surgery, crawled out of his sickbed to attend the regular-season home opener. An AFL-record 45,497 fans took advantage of the warm evening weather and poured into Shea Stadium to see the Jets host the Denver Broncos. New York quarterback Dick Wood threw touchdown passes in a 30–6, win but the real star was newly obtained Jets middle linebacker Wahoo McDaniel, a Choctaw Indian and off-season wrestler.

McDaniel set the tone for the evening by making the Jets' first tackle of the game, and the public address announcer sent a shiver of laughter through the crowd with the declaration, "Tackle by Wahoo McDaniel." As McDaniel began to dominate the game, the P.A. announcer shortened his description to "Tackle by Wahoo." In the second half, as the Jets took control and the crowd began to relax, the announcer would wait for a McDaniel tackle and ask the crowd, "Tackle by who?" to which Jet fans would clap and shout back, "Wahoo!"

The Jets' new linebacker became such a hit with the fans that Werblin changed the nameplate on his jersey from "McDaniel" to "Wahoo." McDaniel didn't mind. "The name 'McDaniel,'" he said, "never made me five cents." Wahoo might also have noted that "McDaniel" was misspelled on the back of his jersey.

"I guess we've sold AFL ball to New York," a beaming Werblin said after the Jets' home opener. New York went on to set subsequent attendance records, drawing 47,746 against the Chargers and 60,300 for a November meeting with the Bills.

While the Jets made strides towards respectability, the Buffalo Bills were building a championship team that reflected its city's attitudes. With an offense geared to the big back tandem of 250-pound fullback Carlton "Cookie" Gilchrist and 220-pound halfback Wray Carlton, and a defense as harsh and punishing as Buffalo winters, the Bills were the embodiment of their swing-shift, blue-collar fans — as was their head coach and acting foreman, Lou Saban.

"You go with the guns you got," Saban says now, reflecting on those Bills championship teams. "For us, that was running the ball and playing defense."

Larry Felser, who has covered the Bills for *The Buffalo Evening News* since 1960, says the style of the '64 team was not customary. "That team was out of sync with the rest of the AFL," Felser says. "They had the big backs and 'Elephant Backfield' and they had a great defense."

Under the direction of coordinator Joe Collier, Buffalo's defense dominated the AFL in 1964. The Bills set a pro football record by yielding just 913 yards rushing, an average of 65 per game, and set or tied league marks for fewest rushing TDs allowed and QB sacks in a season. The Bills also led the AFL in interceptions and points allowed.

Fronting the unit was a large, mobile line that listed Ron McDole and Tom Day at defensive end and Jim Dunaway and Tom Sestak at tackle. The combination of the 276-pound Dunaway and the 270-pound Sestak gave the Bills one of the biggest tackle tandems in pro football.

Selected in the seventeenth round of the '62 draft, Sestak developed into an all-star right defensive tackle and captained the Bills unit. Known as "Big Ses," Sestak used his great strength to full advantage on a straight-ahead power rush, and his one-arm tackles became his trademark. Though he had the mobility to work outside stunts, Sestak excelled at the interior pass rush, where he sometimes had to fight off double- and triple-team blocking.

Sestak's partner at tackle, Jim Dunaway, had been the number-one draft choice of the NFL's Minnesota Vikings in 1962, but opted to play for the Bills. A great run stopper, Dunaway developed into a strong pass rusher as well.

At left end was McDole, a 270-pound free-agent tackle out of Nebraska. Nicknamed the "Dancing Bear," McDole's mobility and quickness allowed him to pursue plays away from him, and he made more opposite-field tackles than any other end in the league.

Like McDole, who broke into pro football as an offensive tackle with the St. Louis Cardinals, Tom Day was a guard with the Cards in 1960 before joining the Bills as a defensive tackle. Tall and rangy, Day was the focal point of a unique 3-4 alignment that moved him from his right defensive end position to a standup linebacker spot in the middle of the line. Day talked constantly to opposing players. During a win over the Jets in 1966, in which Day blitzed quarterback Joe Namath into the turf, he asked Namath how he was doing. "Bad day, Day," Namath said. "Bad day."

The quarterback of the Bills' defense was middle linebacker Harry Jacobs. A taxi-squad member of the Detroit Lions and St. Louis Cardinals, Jacobs joined the Patriots in 1960 and played middle linebacker for Saban despite just three days of preparation. Saban became head coach of the Bills in '62, and Jacobs rejoined him there one year later.

Flanking Jacobs was Mike Stratton and John Tracey, both of whom had converted to corner linebacker. Stratton had the ability to elude pass-blocking backs on blitzes from his right linebacker spot, and both he and Tracey were tremendous hitters. From 1963 to 1966, Jacobs, Stratton, and Tracey played a pro-record 62 straight games together at linebacker. The secondary was led by cornerback George "Butch" Byrd, who led the team with seven interceptions, and heady George Saimes, an all-pro at free safety.

"They were a good, smart defense," recalls Patriots wide receiver Gino Cappelletti. "They were systemized. They always had their people in the right positions. They were one of the first AFL teams to play zone, and their linebackers always positioned themselves nicely and took nice drops [in zone coverage]."

Cappelletti's teammate, quarterback Babe Parilli, remembers the Bills being strong on every line of defense. "Their front always gave them a pretty good rush, their linebackers worked well as a unit, and their secondary, with Byrd and Saimes, was pretty good."

Felser says the Bills' defense excelled because Saban was a coach ahead of his time. "He wanted athletic guys on defense," Felser says. "Guys who could drop back and cover."

One of the keys to the Bills' defense was Mike Stratton, whose career paralleled the Bills' emergence as the AFL's dominant team. Stratton says:

> I can remember at our first training camp [in 1962], there were so many players there we had to dress in shifts. We had 120, 130 players there that first day. We had to swap equipment just to practice. So many of them were weeded out of there, I didn't know what to think. When you see so many players come out for practice the first day, and then see so many of them leave, your anxiety goes up a little bit.
>
> We won as a team, but control of the game depended on the defense. If the defense didn't control the game, we didn't have much chance of winning.

The Bills opened with nine straight wins and wrapped up a 12–2 record and the Eastern Division title with a 24–14 win over the Patriots in frozen Fenway Park in the season finale. The backbone of the Bills' offense was its relentless rushing attack. Buffalo's league-leading 400 points came as the result of a ground game that led the AFL in yards and touchdowns. Gilchrist led the AFL with 981 yards rushing. He averaged 4.3 yards per carry, much of it coming on off-tackle power plays.

Gilchrist played fullback with the mentality of a linebacker, a position in which he starred with the Canadian Football League, when he played both ways. Described as "an army of one," Gilchrist stood 6-foot-3, weighed 250 pounds, and had a 20-inch neck. He used his size to good advantage, intimidating defenses with his pile-driving power. He ran with shoulders squared and sprinter's speed. Not shifty, Gilchrist rarely attempted to sidestep a tackler, preferring instead to turn his body just enough to absorb the hit from the side, then slide off and slip away. When defenses jammed the inside, Gilchrist's speed allowed him to break outside, where he ran over cornerbacks.

"I like to run at tacklers," Gilchrist said at the time. "I'm bigger than most guys who play in the secondary. So I figure if I give them a harder jolt than they give me, they'll be worried the next time."

When he wasn't running over defenders, Gilchrist was laying them out with vicious pass blocks. Fox sportscaster John Madden, whose coaching career with the Raiders began in the AFL, called Gilchrist the best blocking back he's ever seen. Madden was so impressed by Gilchrist's pass blocking that he spliced together a film of Cookie's techniques. But when Raider defenders got queasy over seeing a linebacker go into convulsions after being flipped by Gilchrist on a blitz, Madden edited the hit out of the film.

Gilchrist's off-field behavior was as legendary as his on-field performances. His ideas ranged from a clothing store called "Cookie's Closet" to the manufacturing of some 15,000 Cookie Gilchrist earmuffs to be sold at Bills home games.

Despite Gilchrist's sometimes erratic behavior, his teammates drew inspiration from his personality and bruising performances.

Wray Carlton remembers Gilchrist's intimidating presence on the field:

> I've seen guys hit him and just bounce off. He'd hurt 'em. You could tell by the way they would try to tackle him after he hit 'em. They didn't want to hit him head on. They'd go around and try to jump on his back and ride him. They just did not want to face up to him.
>
> When he ran for 240 yards against the Jets [in '63], I know, in the fourth quarter of that game, they did not want to tackle him. Nobody would hit him head on. I've seen collisions made when people tried to tackle him. Ross O'Hanley, a guy who played safety with Boston, was a tough Irish kid, hard as nails. He came running up and hit Cookie one time, and happened to catch him head on. [O'Hanley] was out cold, and there was a crack in his helmet.

Kansas City free-safety Johnny Robinson said at the time that Gilchrist "likes to run over people, not around them." Patriots middle linebacker Nick Buoniconti could attest to the force of Gilchrist's runs. "Even when you stopped Cookie, "Buoniconti said, "you felt it in your bones a week later." Jets linebacker Wahoo McDaniel incurred a gnarled left ear thanks to Gilchrist's ferocious blocking. McDaniel said Gilchrist hit him so hard he cracked the big Indian's helmet and damaged his hearing.

Felser remembers Gilchrist's punishing use of his forearms on would-be tacklers. When a defender closed on him, Gilchrist thrust his forearm into the defender's stomach or chest. "It caused an awful thump," Felser recalled.

Felser said it was Gilchrist who set the tone for the Bills' division-clinching win over the Patriots in a Buffalo snowstorm late in 1964. The Bills' first play from scrimmage was a sweep left with Gilchrist carrying. A hole opened wide, but Gilchrist cut inside, where he was on a collision course with Boston cornerback Chuck Shonta. Gilchrist knocked Shonta out with a forearm shiver.

Gilchrist could have gained a few more yards by running wide, Felser noted, but "Cookie had delivered his message to the Pats. He was ready."

Despite Gilchrist's shadowy off-field reputation — it was said he brawled with policemen, a charge Gilchrist always refuted — Cookie never backed off from the controversial. In a time when black athletes, and athletes in general, were supposed to adopt a quiet, unassuming public persona, Gilchrist chose to speak his mind.

> There have been numerous stories about me over the years that are untrue. Well, I haven't been the run-of-the-mill Negro athlete who accepts the crumbs offered. I felt that I produced better than the white athlete and I wanted to get paid better. Some people have been shocked at my extreme individuality and outspokenness.
>
> Canadian football gave me a chance to exercise my individualism, which I think this country was founded on. America was built on individualism. America needs more individuals like me. I was selling my body for X number of dollars and when I negotiated a contract I was negotiating my future.

Lacking in education, Gilchrist also lacked money skills. He was forever investing in exotic money schemes — mining copper in Zambia, or heading to the frozen north in search of oil wells. Gilchrist's investments left him cash poor, and he badgered management to renegotiate his contract. Unsurprisingly, Gilchrist wore out his welcome at each stop, bouncing from three CFL teams to the AFL, where he played for three teams — Buffalo, Denver, and Miami — in a span of six years.

Gilchrist, who had been benched late in the season after a publicized flare-up with coach Lou Saban, turned in an all-pro season in 1964, thanks largely to an outstanding offensive line. The strength of the unit was its left side, where all-pros Billy Shaw and Stew Barber started at guard and tackle, respectively. The 260-pound Al Bemiller wore the center's towel, while 272-pound Dick Hudson started at right tackle.

Shaw, a perennial all-pro who was named to the All-AFL team in 1970, was arguably the best run blocker in league history. A greyhound guard at 248 pounds, Shaw excelled at escorting Buffalo's backs around end. On one play against the Oilers, Shaw pulled to his right on a Bills sweep and ran step-for-step with halfback Wray Carlton down the sideline on an 80-yard TD. When the pair crossed the goal line, Shaw was a step ahead.

A graduate of Georgia Tech, Shaw joined the Bills in 1961. Some AFL people thought the best one-on-one show in pro football in the mid–60s was Buffalo's weekly scrimmages when Shaw squared off against Sestak. Bills coaches said Shaw had no weaknesses in his game; he was equally efficient blocking for the pass and run, firing out or pulling and leading. AFL coaches and players usually made Shaw the top vote-getter in the annual All-AFL ratings. Shaw says today:

Our offensive line started coming together in 1961, but our success really started with the arrival of Jack Kemp [in 1962]. I was surprised we got him, especially for the waiver wire price of a hundred dollars. He could really throw the football. Dick Hudson and [right guard] Joe O'Donnell joined us the same time as Kemp and [wideout] Ernie Warlick. So the nucleus of that team started to come together in 1963.

We were not a big line but we had good foot speed. Because of Cookie's brute strength and ability, we were geared to running the football. Our offense centered around Cookie's abilities. We were so basic it was boring. Defensively, we were doing things that were probably more exciting than what we did on offense. We didn't score a lot of points, but our defense was able to hold teams to point totals within our range.

Our best running play was a "42" or "43" to either side of the center. Basically, it was a straight handoff to Cookie. He read the offensive line's blocks and picked the hole. The only bad thing about blocking for Cookie was that if my man held me to a stalemate, Cookie would run up my back, and that hurt.

"I guess," Shaw says, laughing, "that gave me added incentive to make my block."

The passing game consisted of slant patterns to Glenn Bass, deep posts to Elbert "Golden Wheels" Dubenion, sideline passes to tight end Ernie Warlick, and swing passes to Gilchrist. The final weapon in Buffalo's arsenal was rookie Pete Gogolak, pro football's first soccer-style kicker, who scored 102 points as the Bills won the first division title in team history.

In the Western Division, the San Diego Chargers won their second straight title and their fourth in five years. Plagued by nagging injuries to Tobin Rote, Lance Alworth, Keith Lincoln, and Paul Lowe, and lacking a reliable field-goal kicker, San Diego finished the season with an 8-5-1 record. Their postseason chances were dealt a damaging blow in a loss to Oakland in the regular season finale, when Alworth went out with a knee injury.

To avoid direct confrontation with the Baltimore–Cleveland NFL championship set for Sunday, the AFL scheduled its title game for Saturday, December 26. The day after Christmas found a frigid but festive championship-game-record crowd of 40,242 huddled into fog-shrouded War Memorial Stadium. The setting was positively polar: gray-flannel skies overhead and freezing temperatures that turned the players' breath into clouds of smoke. Workers spent the pregame hours pouring bags of sand on top of the ice-slicked field to provide traction for the players.

"The Rockpile," Bills linebacker Mike Stratton says, recalling War Memorial with a laugh. "It was built on a dump, and it was wet and smelly all the time. You hated to fall on that kind of surface."

To Buffalo football fans, creaky old War Memorial Stadium was like a twelfth man for their beloved Bills. The concrete structure, with its entrances that bore bison logos reminiscent of old buffalo nickels, was a $3 million Depression-era project built in 1937 under President Franklin Roosevelt's

War Memorial Stadium in Buffalo was typical of the early AFL stadiums. Built during the Depression, War Memorial was known as "the Rockpile" and played host to two AFL championship games. (*Photo courtesy of the Buffalo Bills.*)

Works Progress Administration. Because of its dreary, gray appearance, War Memorial was known as "the Rockpile."

Because it was situated on top of an old reservoir, portions of the playing surface were continually damp and wet from excess drainage, particularly the baseball infield. In December, when the sun set early on late afternoon games, half the field would freeze in the dark shadows. The Rockpile's locker rooms were cramped and dark, and it was a good day when the plumbing was working.

Pigeons circled continuously overhead, littering players and fans with their droppings. The Rockpile was especially tough on opposing teams. Visiting players had to descend a rotting wooden staircase to get to the field, then run a gauntlet of boozy, boisterous Bills fans, who weren't above spilling a beer or two on enemy players.

Brock Yates captured the aura of War Memorial Stadium in a *Sports Illustrated* article in 1960. "It is an arena," Yates wrote, "that looks as if whatever war it memorializes was fought within its confines."

"I loved War Memorial Field," Billy Shaw says. "It had a closeness that made me feel at home. The locker rooms were terrible, but once we started winning, the fans really made us feel at home. It held about 40,000 people, and most of those seats were taken. You didn't see any empty seats. The field always seemed spongy, and when we played in December, it was like playing on a sheet of ice. Late in the season, the field had no grass; we had worn it out because we practiced there. But I loved that field. It was a good ol' stadium."

Wray Carlton recalls the distinct home-field advantages War Memorial Stadium gave the Bills over their opponents.

> They all hated to come in there, and part of it was the weather. If you had a late season game [in Buffalo], you never knew what you were going to get into. And the atmosphere there was kind of drab. You had the old concrete and the rickety showers, and visiting teams did not like coming in. They knew that with the fans and our players, they were going to have a tough time. Late in the year, when the weather got bad and the field was crummy, it was always either half snowing or snowing, and the field was like muck. You could tell when [opponents] ran on the field, they hated it. They just wanted to get it over with. And that was an advantage to us.

On game day, the Chargers grimaced as they tested their footing on the weatherworn turf. San Diego was a team built on speed and quickness, and Lowe was one of many Chargers uncomfortable with the conditions in Buffalo.

"I hated that ol' raggedy town," Lowe says now. "The locker rooms were wet and cold, and there was no hot water. I think they probably did that on purpose. I hated playing there. I remember that '64 game. The weather was cold and the field was bad. We were thinking more about the weather than the Bills."

The Rockpile was the perfect proving ground for Buffalo's rock-ribbed style of play. And even though the oddsmakers favored the defending champion Chargers, the Bills were confident, having defeated San Diego twice in '64.

"We were underdogs," Saban says, "but we were still a pretty good football team. We just didn't get a lot of attention."

"We enjoyed a lot of success in '64," says Shaw. "We had offensive and defensive linemen who had played together for a number of years. We had tasted the playoffs in '63, and Cookie had one of his better years in '64. Lamonica came on in '63, and he brought us the long ball. He gave us a different attitude. He was cocky, boisterous, and he could throw the ball a mile. He took more chances than Jack. Jack was more methodical. He didn't take a lot of chances."

Kemp said the reason the Bills were made underdogs in their home stadium was because pro football experts considered them a team that couldn't win the big game. The Bills had lost their only previous postseason game — the division playoff to Boston the year before in Buffalo. But what the oddsmakers forgot, Kemp said, was that the Bills had just beaten the Patriots 24–14 in a Boston snowstorm in the season-closing showdown December 20, a game that decided the Eastern Division title.

"We wanted to prove a few people wrong," Kemp said.

So did Kemp, who had quarterbacked the Chargers to the AFL title game in 1960 and '61 before being put on the waiver wire by Gillman.

"The Chargers tried to recall Jack off the waiver wire," says Van Miller, the Bills' longtime radio announcer, "and Joe Foss said, 'Sorry boys, it's too late now.' Jack's a skier, and he wanted to go to Denver and play for the Broncos. He hated the thought of coming to Buffalo. He was in the pits when he joined the Bills in Houston. But he came to Buffalo and made some good stock investments, made millions and then got into politics. That probably wouldn't have happened if he hadn't been in Buffalo."

As the Bills and Chargers assembled next to each other for the pregame introductions, Carlton found himself standing next to the Chargers' Ernie Ladd. Carlton was a big man, standing 6-foot-2 and weighing 216 pounds. But he was stunned by the huge mass of the 6-foot-9, 321-pound Ladd.

"I remember before the game," Carlton says, "we were waiting in the tunnel to be introduced, and their defense was being introduced with our offense. I was standing there in the tunnel next to Ernie Ladd, and I was looking at eye level with his bicep. And I was saying, 'Oh my God.' They called him 'the Big Cat,' and he was what — 6-foot-9, 330 pounds? He was a monster."

The Chargers opened the game as if they would defend their AFL championship in runaway fashion. On San Diego's first play from scrimmage, Lincoln bolted up the middle on a draw for a 39-yard gain. Lincoln carried again for four more yards, and then took a pass from Rote for 11 yards and another Charger first down. At the Buffalo, Rote faked a handoff to Lowe, sidestepped Sestak and found tight end Dave Kocourek open in the end zone on a post pattern for the score. San Diego had made it look easy, and the sell-out crowd was stunned. Only 2:11 was gone from the stadium clock and already the Chargers led, 7–0.

On San Diego's next series, Lowe ripped off a 16-yard gain, and Rote followed by running for six more. What followed became the game's pivotal play, and remains the most famous tackle in league history.

In the Charger playbook, it was known as "Delayed Double Flare Action." Its design was to spread the weakside of the defense by spending the split end, Don Norton, on a medium range curl pattern and the fullback, Lincoln, into the flat. Rote keyed the weakside linebacker, in this case, Mike Stratton. If Stratton dropped into a hook zone to double cover Norton, Rote would dump a pass to Lincoln in the flat. If Stratton came up to cover Lincoln, Rote would throw to Norton.

Taking the snap, Rote dropped back, pump faked, turned to his left, and flipped a short flare pass over a leaping Sestak to Lincoln. As Lincoln extended his arms to catch the ball, Stratton, who had taken a short drop, came charging on a dead run from his right linebacker position. Stratton buried his helmet in Lincoln's midsection, and game tapes show Lincoln being lifted off his feet and dropped heavily to the frozen ground, where he lay writhing in pain.

"We started off fairly good in that game," Lincoln recalls, "and on that play, I ran a circle pattern. Well, here comes ol' Stratton. Rote hesitated for a second, and then threw that damned thing like he was throwing a snowball into a chimney. Stratton had a twenty-yard head of steam, and he really hit me."

Stratton says:

San Diego ran a pass route, where they sent a back on a flare and the split end on a curl. If I backtracked to cover the curl, they passed to the back on the flare. If I came up, they hit the flanker.

What I was hoping for was an interception. I just kept running as hard as I could. Fortunately for me, and unfortunately for Keith, I arrived the same time as the ball. They hung him out to dry on that play.

Everyone expected Keith to come back into the game, and not having him took the wind out of their sails. What I recall about that game is that the Chargers would get something going on offense, but they couldn't keep it going.

Before he was a Congressman, Jack Kemp quarterbacked the Buffalo Bills to consecutive AFL championships in 1964–65. (*Photo courtesy of the Buffalo Bills.*)

Helped off the field by his teammates, Lincoln was diagnosed with a clean break of his tenth rib. Stratton's hit ignited half-frozen Bills fans, who stood as one at War Memorial Stadium. To this day, Lowe still vividly remembers the details of Stratton's hit on Lincoln.

"I was close to that play," Lowe says, "and I just went '*Oooh.*' I could hear the ribs breaking. I remember thinking, 'I'm glad it was him and not me.' It was like that the whole game. Saimes, Stratton and Sestak, it seemed like their helmets were in my numbers all day long."

"Stratton's hit," Saban says, "electrified us." Kemp said the Bills could feel their intensity and confidence increase after Stratton's hit.

"That hit turned the game around," Shaw says. "It did two things. It took Keith out of the game, and he was a major threat for them, and it showed our offense that the defense came to play. That turned the whole flavor of the game around. It was the hit heard 'round the world."

Or at least it was heard as far as the San Diego sideline. "Rote's arm was gone," says Ladd, who saw the play from the Chargers bench, "and he just floated that ball out there. It was a brutal lick."

With Alworth and Lincoln sidelined, the San Diego offense sputtered, and the Bills took charge. A 12-yard field goal by Pete Gogolak cut the Chargers' advantage to 7-3 in the first quarter, and Buffalo took the lead in the second on a 4-yard touchdown run by Carlton. Before the half, a 17-yard Gogolak field goal gave the Bills a 13-7 lead.

With the Chargers' running game hampered — Lowe was held to 34 yards — the Bills pressured Rote and John Hadl into three interceptions. Hadl had to be helped off the field, and Lowe was limping at game's end as well. "Buffalo played well," Lowe says. "They blocked and tackled and just knocked the hell out of us."

On offense, the Bills stuck to their conservative ground, game. Through a scoreless third quarter and on into the fourth, the Bills pounded the Charger defense with their big back attack, sending Gilchrist and Carlton on alternate smashes into the line. Buffalo ran the ball 41 times for 219 yards and averaged more than 5 yards per rush. The Bills' ball-control tactics kept the Charger offense idling on the sidelines, trying to stave off the cold in their dark blue warmup jackets.

"The Chargers had weapons out the wazoo," Carlton says. "Sid Gillman still says that was the most explosive offensive team he ever had. We knew they were good. Defensively, they were big up front and their linebackers were quick. Our game plan was to help our defense as much as we could. We were a methodical, lunch-pail group, and we were just going to grind them down no matter what."

In the trenches, Shaw and Ladd engaged in an intriguing matchup of all-pros. "Ladd was huge," Shaw says, "and unfortunately I had to match up with him. If he had a little more quickness, no one could have handled him. Someone my size, if I didn't get to him quick, I couldn't move him."

"Billy Shaw was a great guard," Ladd remembers. "He and Bob Talamini (of the Oilers and Jets) could play with anybody back then. Shaw to me was one of the all-time great finesse guards. We had a competition going. I would hit Shaw and knock him flat, and he would leg-whip me and trip me up."

In the fourth quarter, with the ball on the Chargers' 49-yard line, Kemp fired a quick slant to end Glenn Bass, who carried to the 1 before being brought down. From there, Kemp ran it in to give the Bills a 20-7 victory.

The win offered personal redemption for Kemp, who bristled over the fact that Gillman and the Chargers had put him on waivers in 1962. Calling a masterful game, Kemp rid himself of the reputation that he could not win the big one. He completed 10 passes for 168 yards, and rode off the field on the shoulders of Bills fans.

The game was also a matter of redemption for Gilchrist. After a season in which he had feuded openly with club management, his coaches, and teammates, Gilchrist responded in the biggest game of his life. Carrying the ball 16 times for 122 yards, he averaged 7.6 yards per run and had one run for 43 yards. Carlton added an additional 70 yards on 18 carries.

As the stadium clock wound down and darkness settled over the stadium, Buffalo fans celebrated the city's first-ever major sports championship with a hail of cannon shots and confetti. Chargers coach Sid Gillman watched the final seconds tick away from beneath the brim of his fedora. Says *San Diego Tribune* sportswriter Jerry McGee:

> Sid had a lot to do with the AFL's survival. He taught the new league how to operate, how to perform. The other teams in the league knew they had to compete with Sid or they would be consumed by him, which he tried to do.
>
> The 1963 Chargers was definitely the best team Sid ever had. With guys like Rote, Alworth, Lincoln, and Lowe, that team could have competed in the NFL. But in 1964, Rote didn't have much left, his arm was shot. Alworth was out, and then Stratton put that thunderous hit on Keith Lincoln. Lincoln was exposed, and Stratton ripped him. The Bills were good. They had guys on defense like Sestak and Day that could play today.

With the Colts expected to beat the Browns in the NFL title game the next day, a sign was unfurled inside War Memorial Stadium: *Bring on the Colts*.

Inside their steamy locker room, the Bills were ready to take on the NFL. Ignoring a *Sports Illustrated* article in which its NFL writer, Tex Maule, predicted the Colts would beat the Bills 48-7 in a dream game, Buffalo players believed they could match up with the NFL's best.

"We could hold our own," Gilchrist said, "against the NFL."

Saban suggested that the only difference between the two leagues could be found in one man—Colts quarterback John Unitas. "No, we don't have Johnny Unitas," Saban told assembled writers, "but there are 13 teams in the National Football League that don't have him, either."

Foss, who had predicted in 1960 that the AFL would be as strong as the NFL in three seasons, openly campaigned for head-on championship. Says Foss:

> To me, accomplishing that would signal the fulfillment of my professional goals as commissioner. My suggestion of a playoff between the leagues ... had tremendous appeal for fans and sportswriters alike.
>
> Rozelle and the NFL ridiculed the notion—not based on projections that the public would not respond enthusiastically to a real championship contest,

but on the fact that their acceptance of a showdown with the AFL would acknowledge recognition of the league itself. Rozelle regularly dismissed questions about an interleague playoff, implying that the new league couldn't field a team good enough to make it an interesting game.

All this did was create a backlash that worked in our favor.

Ever mindful of the lawsuits Foss and the AFL had brought against the NFL, Rozelle answered the question of an interleague title game thusly: "We don't play with people who sue us."

The euphoria of the Buffalo faithful was felt throughout the organization. At a luncheon the day before the game, a friend of Bills owner Ralph Wilson had given Wilson's wife a football wrapped in mink. When Wilson saw the ball, he had to laugh.

"Five years ago this league didn't even have a football," Wilson said, a reference to remarks made in 1960 by Chicago Bears owner George Halas. "Now we have one made out of mink. That shows how far we've come."

Chapter Nine

1965: From Buffalo to Broadway

ON NEW YEAR'S NIGHT in 1965, in the Miami Orange Bowl, number-one-ranked and undefeated Alabama met once-beaten and fifth-ranked Texas with college football's national title at stake. Quarterbacking the Crimson Tide was a stoop-shouldered senior named Joe Namath. With his rocket right arm, quick release, and sleepy good looks, Namath gained national attention as he led the Crimson Tide to a 27–3 record as a three-year starter.

As a senior in 1964, Namath completed a career-high 64 percent of his passes. But his right knee buckled and collapsed in an October game against North Carolina State, and Namath was forced to undergo treatments for his injured leg. He watched as backup quarterback Steve Sloan led the Tide to a 10–0 finish.

In the Orange Bowl against Texas, Alabama was trailing 14–0 when Tide head coach Paul "Bear" Bryant sent Namath into the game in the second quarter. What followed was a performance that captivated the 72,000 in attendance and a national television audience. His right knee heavily taped, Namath threw two scoring passes as 'Bama cut Texas' lead to 21–17. With time running out in the game, Namath moved the Tide to the Longhorns' 6-yard line. On fourth-and-goal, with seven seconds left, Namath called his own number on a quarterback sneak. For a moment it appeared Namath had scored, but no signal was given, and 'Bama's bid for a perfect season ended on the Texas goal line.

Having completed what was then an Orange Bowl record 18 passes for 255 yards and two touchdowns, Namath was named the game's most valuable player. In bringing 'Bama back, he had shown talent and tenacity, and, as New York Jets owner Sonny Werblin noted, star quality and charisma. Werblin told associates:

> He's exciting to watch when he steps back in those white shoes and tosses those long passes. He could bring people into the park to watch the Jets and the entire American Football League. He'd have people watching the American Football League on television.
>
> This Joe Namath can be great. He can be as important as Red Grange was to the NFL when it got started. A star. Someone people will knock down gates to see. And he's always been a winner. He can make winners of the Jets.

The New York Jets' record-setting 1965 signing of blue-chip quarterback Joe Namath was not only the most expensive in pro football history at the time, it also helped hasten the AFL–NFL merger. (*Photo courtesy of the New York Jets.*)

To sign Namath, Werblin had to first move up in the AFL draft and then outbid the rival NFL. The Houston Oilers had originally drafted Namath, and the Jets traded quarterback Jerry Rhome to Houston in exchange for the rights to Namath. On November 28, 1964, the Jets made Namath the top selection in the draft.

"Quarterbacks are the stars," Werblin told reporters. "I know box office from my 33 years with MCA, and I know you have to have stars on the stage."

The St. Louis Cardinals also selected Namath number one, and in the weeks leading up to the 1965 Orange Bowl, Namath's lawyer, Mike Bite, took turns talking contract with Werblin and Bill Bidwill of the Cardinals. Namath surprised Werblin when he said he preferred the NFL.

"I have always been an NFL fan," Namath shrugged. "I just think I would like to try myself against the better league."

Werblin blinked behind his circular, dark-rimmed glasses. The Jets, he said, would match any offer the NFL made. Then he addressed Namath's remark about the quality of the leagues.

"You," Werblin said, "will make the AFL a better league."

As the dollar figures escalated, Cardinal officials offered the son of a western Pennsylvania steel-mill worker a final package deal of $389,000 — an extraordinary amount at the time. But the Cardinals also indicated to Namath that their offer required him to host a radio show. Namath balked at the idea, telling a Cardinal official, "Man, I'm just a football player, and what I make will be for football only."

With that, St. Louis dropped out of the bidding. "There is no question that Namath is a great quarterback," one Cardinal official told the press. "We have offered him $389,000 to sign with us. But he wants to play in New York."

Namath made that official when he told Werblin he would accept the Jets' offer of a three-year, $427,000 contract. As Namath walked slowly off the Orange Bowl field on New Year's Day night, Werblin was waiting by the Tide's bench. Namath sat down, and Werblin pulled a contract and pen out of his inside pocket. Namath took the pen and scrawled his name on the contract.

The next morning, in a press conference at the Miami Harbor Inn Hotel, the Jets announced the signing of Joe Namath. The details of the contract shocked the football world:

- Salary (4 seasons at $25,000) $100,000
- Signing bonus $200,000
- Scouting positions for
  Namath's three brothers and brother-in-law at $ 10,000
  per year each $120,000
- Jet Green Lincoln Continental $ 7,000

Reactions to the Namath signing were varied. Frank Ryan, who quarterbacked Cleveland to an NFL title the week before, told a reporter, "If that kid is worth $400,000, then I'm worth a million."

In Baltimore, John Unitas' wife, Dorothy, picked up a newspaper the day after the Namath signing. The headline on the article read "Ewbank Says $400,000 Quarterback Another Unitas."

Dorothy Unitas smiled. "Yeah," she said, "only richer."

In Kansas City, Chiefs quarterback Lenny Dawson felt the enormous publicity surrounding Namath could only help the AFL.

"Four hundred thousand dollars to play football," Dawson said. "Well, that's ridiculous. Football players said it was ridiculous, everybody said it was ridiculous for somebody to pay that kind of money. But what it did accomplish looking back now is that it got everybody to look at the American Football League, and finally they said 'Well, I'm going to watch this.'"

Talk of the contract was not limited to the inner circles of pro football. Comedian Bob Hope incorporated Namath jokes into his routine. "Joe Namath," Hope quipped, "is the only quarterback in history who'll play in a business suit."

Werblin welcomed the enormous publicity surrounding Namath's contract. Namath had enough flair and style to draw fans to Jets games in every AFL city. Namath's signing sold New York football fans on the team's legitimacy in its battle with the New York Giants. Jets fans responded at the box office, where season-ticket sales increased by 25,000.

"Sonny Werblin did a great job of selling the Jets to the people of New York," linebacker Larry Grantham says now. "He brought us out of bankruptcy, and drafted players like Snell and Namath. I think the league would have survived with or without Joe. But he helped give the young people of New York an identity. He really helped younger people to identify with us."

Like Grantham, wide receiver Don Maynard had been with the Jets beginning with their lean years in 1960. He remembers the profound impact Werblin had in making the franchise respectable.

"Sonny Werblin was a great marketing man," Maynard says. "Whatever he did, he got publicity. And he got a lot of publicity when he signed Namath. I thought Joe's contract brought up the salary level, both on the Jets and around the league. I always thought, 'If Joe makes this amount, then I'll be able to make a little more too.'"

The Namath signing was the biggest story that emerged from the 1965 draft war, but the two leagues hustled to sign great college players. AFL and NFL teams were both engaged full-time in the "baby-sitting" business, sending scouts and coaches to watch over college players they had drafted and hoped to sign.

To meet the competition provided by the AFL, the NFL put together a 72-page book called *The NFL and You*, aimed at convincing college players there was just one *real* pro football league. The book was one more indication of how high the stakes were in 1965, when the draft included such future stars as Namath, Gale Sayers, Dick Butkus, Bob Hayes, Dan Reeves, Craig Morton, Ken Willard, Jack Snow, Jim Nance, Fred Biletnikoff, and Otis Taylor.

But for the NFL's Buddy Young, the AFL might have signed Gale Sayers as well. Sayers was drafted by both the Chiefs and the Bears, and when Kansas City general manager Don Klosterman told Sayers the Chiefs were prepared to pay $23,500 a year for three years, with a signing bonus of $45,000, Sayers was seriously considering signing with the AFL. He might have, had it not been for Young, the coordinator of the NFL commissioner's office, whose appearance on the scene could not have been more timely — for Sayers, the Bears, and the NFL. A onetime halfback for the Baltimore Colts in the mid–'50s, it was

Young's job in 1965 to represent the NFL in its signing war with the AFL. Young talked to Sayers about pro football, telling him the NFL offered better opportunities for black players.

"The choice you make ought to have to do with markets," Young said. "That's the important thing, especially for a Negro back of your caliber. We know the AFL wants you ... I just want to open your eyes to the situation."

Several factors helped Sayers make up his mind, the most important being his desire to measure himself against the top players in the game.

"The best was in the NFL at the time," Sayers said. "I really felt that way."

With Sayers gone to the Bears, the Chiefs turned their attention to a Prairie View A & M pass catcher named Otis Taylor. More than any other incident, the Taylor signing highlights the intrigue that marked the height of the AFL-NFL draft war.

Selected on the fourth round of the AFL draft by the Chiefs and the fifteenth round of the NFL draft by the Philadelphia Eagles, Taylor was closely guarded by Chiefs scout Lloyd Wells. Wells was close to Taylor's family in Houston — so close, in fact, that Wells took for granted that Taylor would sign with Kansas City and left the area to scout other players.

With Wells out of town, NFL scouts arrived, put Taylor in a car and quietly spirited him from Prairie View to Houston to Dallas, from motel room to motel room. At one stop, NFL scouts took Taylor and a host of college players through the front door of a motel, into the lobby, and out a side door, where a motorcade was waiting. Armed with information provided by one of Taylor's girlfriends, Wells tracked the players' trek through the Southwest, where they eventually stopped at a motel north of Dallas and registered under assumed names.

Enlisting the aid of some of the motel's bellboys, cooks, and kitchen help, Wells found out the group was lodged in suites 101–105. Draping an unloaded camera around his neck, Wells told NFL scouts he was a newspaperman. Wells met privately with Taylor, and the pair agreed to sneak out at midnight, taking Taylor's teammate Seth Cartwright along with them.

What Wells didn't realize was that one of the NFL scouts had spotted him in the dining room that night, recognized who he was, and called police to report a prowler. Confronted by the authorities and threatened with jail if he went near the motel again, Wells returned to Dallas. At 3:30 A.M. the next morning, Wells received a phone call from Taylor, begging to be picked up. Wells immediately returned to the motel, tapped on Taylor's window, and he, Taylor, and Cartwright — who were waiting with bags packed — drove straight to the airport at Love Field in Dallas. Wells drove Taylor and Cartwright to the Fort Worth airport, where at 7:40 A.M., they caught a plane to Kansas City. As Taylor remembers:

> I was talked into signing with the Chiefs by Lloyd Wells. Mr. Wells was a pretty shrewd person, as far as making things happen. I was put in a "baby-sitting"

situation, where I was put up in a motel, and they had someone sitting outside the door. But they made you feel comfortable, it wasn't like being in a hostage situation.

Mr. Wells had been searching through town, trying to find me, and he almost gave up trying to find me. I didn't have a real preference for the AFL or NFL, but I had a relationship with Mr. Wells. He had known me since junior high. I wasn't obligated to him, but I felt I owed him something.

Wells was one of the major reasons the AFL was able to sign a number of outstanding athletes from black college campuses. He explains:

> I was the sports editor of the *Houston Informer* from 1953 to 1963, and I promoted black college and high school football games in Texas. I formed a black high school all-star game in Beaumont, Texas, and we had players like Bubba Smith and Jim Kearney in it. We moved the game to Houston in 1963, and I invited Lamar Hunt to that game. He was impressed with the way the promotion ran, and in January of 1966 I signed as the first full-time black scout.
>
> I delivered Robert Holmes, Gloster Richardson, Warren McVea, Andy Rice, Mack Lee Hill, Willie Lanier, Mike Garrett, Jim Kearney, Aaron Brown, Frank Pitts, and Otis Taylor. I also brought in Warren Wells to Kansas City, but Mr. Hunt traded him to Oakland.
>
> Most of the players I brought in were from the SWAC, the Southwestern Athletic Conference. The success of the Otis Taylor [signing] really opened up the eyes of other scouts as to small black colleges.

The race to sign college football's best players was so hotly contested between the two leagues that long-standing rivalries were put aside for the time being. Partisanship and individual interests yielded to what was best for the advancement of the league. NFL coaches and scouts steered certain players to other teams in their league; "baby-sitters" were used to hide out prospects until they could be signed. Some NFL scouts went so far as to present college seniors with "open" contracts, where players were allowed to sign on with any team of their choosing, so long as it was in the NFL.

The AFL also engaged in baby-sitting. Raiders general manager and head coach Al Davis hid college players in Hawaii until they were signed. Since the AFL was at a disadvantage in its scouting abilities, team reps sometimes went to extra lengths to help one another out.

"The NFL had players stashed away," Wells says. "They started the baby-sitting. But Al Davis was the king of it. He brought the NFL to its knees."

Davis outhustled the Detroit Lions and signed Florida State flanker Fred Biletnikoff, an All-America, in the aftermath of the Seminoles' 36–19 win over Oklahoma in the Gator Bowl. Afterward, he quickly telephoned another AFL owner. "We've got *ours*," Davis said into the phone. "Now you get *yours*."

"In those days of the [draft] war," Sayers remembered, "the NFL teams worked pretty closely together.... Same in the AFL, which allowed Kansas City to draft me without competition."

"We helped each other," Sid Gillman says. "We shared ideas, information. We worked together. Looking back, it was a beautiful thing. If one club had the rights to a player who might be more useful, say, might draw better in another area, we shifted them around. That's how Boston let us have Ron Mix in San Diego."

In the aftermath of the draft, the AFL was stunned by a player walkout five days before the January 15 league All-Star game in New Orleans. Charges of discrimination were voiced by black representatives in New Orleans, and the site of the game was moved to Houston's Jeppesen Stadium.

AFL commissioner Joe Foss, in Chicago at the time of the strike, came under fire from league owners for not moving fast enough to resolve the issue. Foss ordered the game switched from New Orleans to Houston, but he was criticized for not doing enough to prevent the walkout before the game.

With a financial guarantee from NBC of $36 million over five years, the AFL upped the ante in its war to win over the football public. At a June meeting in Monmouth Park, New Jersey, the league's executive committee voted for expansion, declaring their intentions to add two teams for the 1966 season. Two months later, on August 16, the city of Miami was given the AFL's first expansion franchise. Joe Robbie, a Minneapolis attorney, and entertainer Danny Thomas were announced as the club's joint partners.

Robbie, a classmate of Foss when the two were at the University of South Dakota, initially acted as an intermediary between Foss and a friend who was seeking to establish an AFL franchise in Philadelphia. Citing the Eagles' exclusive rights to Franklin Field, Foss dismissed Philadelphia as a possible AFL outpost, suggesting instead the city of Miami.

"With the population growth and climate," Foss told Robbie, "it'll be the best franchise in the league."

Since he owned a home in Miami, Robbie decided to sound out potential financial backers. He found one in Danny Thomas, who was a co-worker with Robbie on the board of St. Jude's Hospital. Thomas had been frustrated in his attempt to buy the Chicago White Sox, and he agreed to become a partner.

Robbie also enlisted the help of an old friend from Minnesota, then U.S. vice president Hubert Humphrey. With Humphrey exerting considerable influence, Miami Mayor Robert King High opened the door for AFL expansion into his city. The mayor assured Robbie use of the Orange Bowl stadium for home games. The price tag for entry into the AFL was now $7.5 million.

On June 8, one day after having awarded an AFL franchise to Miami, the league voted to grant approval to the city of Atlanta as well. J. Leonard Reinsch of the Cox Broadcasting Corporation headed the Atlanta group, but plans for an AFL team in Atlanta suffered a humiliating public defeat at the hands of NFL commissioner Pete Rozelle.

Rozelle, who earlier in the year had said that NFL expansion would not be undertaken until 1967, was taken aback by the AFL's aggressive behavior.

He sent public opinion pollster Lou Harris to Atlanta to conduct a poll among citizens of the city. The question was asked, "Which would you prefer to have in Atlanta, an AFL or NFL team?" The Harris poll concluded that an overwhelming number of Atlanta's football fans preferred the NFL.

On June 30, Rankin M. Smith, a 41-year-old executive vice president of the Life of Georgia Insurance Company, was granted an NFL franchise for the approximate sum of $8.5 million. Once again, Foss came under criticism from league owners, who felt the commissioner was not aggressive enough in dealing with the NFL.

The biggest news of the AFL off-season came from the defending league-champion Buffalo Bills, who dealt fullback Cookie Gilchrist to Denver. Long a problem child with the Bills, Gilchrist stirred up further dissent in the wake of the team's 1964 AFL championship game win over the Chargers.

Feeling unfairly compensated for his play, Gilchrist went to head coach Lou Saban in the off-season and demanded a $3,000 bonus. Saban promised to talk with team owner Ralph Wilson about Gilchrist's demand, but Cookie went him one better. Boarding a plane, Gilchrist flew to Detroit to speak with Wilson himself. Wilson turned down Gilchrist's request. Knowing Gilchrist's tendency to sulk and disrupt the team when his demands weren't met, Saban contacted Denver head coach Mac Speedie, and Gilchrist was dealt to Denver for fullback Billy Joe.

Bills players knew they'd feel the loss of Gilchrist's power running, but they also knew Gilchrist's behavior had forced Buffalo management to trade him. All-pro guard Billy Shaw remembers having mixed emotions about the Gilchrist trade.

"Tom Sestak and I were the captains of those Bills teams, and we had some dealings with Cookie," Shaw says. "You know, Cookie was Cookie. In a way the trade surprised me, but in a way it didn't. I thought it would hurt us, but Wray Carlton came on and did an excellent job. We weren't as dominant as we had been in '64, but we did the job."

Linebacker Mike Stratton feels the Gilchrist trade helped solidify the Bills' team unity. "We hated to lose what he could do for you, but it showed no one is indispensable," Stratton says. "That trade showed that football is still a team sport."

With Gilchrist gone, and with Joe lacking the ferocious running style of his former fullback, Saban switched gears in 1965. At times the Bills used a double-tight end, one-back set. The alignment featured 240-pound Paul Costa and 235-pound Ernie Warlick at tight end, and 220-pound halfback Wray Carlton as the lone back. The alignment proved to be a forerunner of the Ace formation popularized by Washington Redskins coach Joe Gibbs in the 1980s.

"We felt we could still control the ball," Saban says of the double-tight end alignment, "but we were going to go to a more wide-open passing game."

Heading the new-style attack was veteran quarterback Jack Kemp. Even with the passing game hindered by injuries to ends "Golden Wheels" Dubenion and Glenn Bass, Kemp's leadership abilities and bullet passing led the Bills to a 10-3-1 record and a second straight Eastern Division title.

"Jack threw the ball accurate and hard," Shaw says. "Our passing game was basically a lot of slants by our wide receivers, because they had such a lot of speed. The backs caught the ball a lot in our scheme, a lot of safety valves and screens. Our tight ends ran curl pattern after curl pattern."

Stratton, who sometimes caught Kemp's passes in pregame warmups, says Kemp's throwing style made it difficult for defenses to adjust to the Buffalo passing game.

"Anybody who can drop back seven yards and throw the ball from one sideline to the other like he did, there wasn't anything a defensive back could do about it," Stratton says. "Jack could whistle that ball. When you were catching him warming up on the sidelines, he would release it at eye level and it would reach you at eye level. It really stung your hands."

By 1965, Kemp's long, slow maturation process was complete. He not only owned what was arguably the strongest throwing arm in pro football, he had also developed into one of the game's better quarterbacks at reading defenses. His long and difficult career, which began in 1957 with the Pittsburgh Steelers and included three years with the Chargers before joining the Bills, helped make him a leader, and the images that remain are of a confident, championship quarterback.

After the Bills broke from the huddle, Kemp would approach the line of scrimmage, head up, in a slow and deliberate manner. Standing behind center Al Bemiller, he would pause and read the defense, looking first right then left, studying the feet and movement of the defense for any tip-offs that would indicate what defense they were in. Cupping his hands to his mouth, Kemp would shout out the play.

"I think what Jack brought to the table was character," Shaw says. "Jack gave us an example of how football players should act. He was a confident person and gracious person. People looked up to him. He wasn't a rah-rah person, but he was physically tough. He led by example."

Kemp was the forerunner of Joe Kapp and Jim McMahon as a quarterback who had a lineman's mentality. Charlie Flowers, who was Kemp's teammate with the Chargers, said Kemp was always challenging his linemen to arm wrestling matches. "And," Flowers said of Kemp, "he hardly ever lost."

Kemp's right arm was two inches bigger around than his left, the result of squeezing a rubber ball and lifting dumbbells. For sheer strength, Kemp had one of the best arms in football in the '60s. He had a shotgun delivery. Lee Grosscup, who played quarterback in both the NFL and AFL, said Kemp could throw a football "60 yards falling backward."

Even opposing coaches admired Kemp's style. "He was beautiful to watch in action," said Mike Holovak, then head coach of the Boston Patriots. "He [had] a beautiful style."

Platooning less with backup Daryle Lamonica than he had the previous year, Kemp earned all-pro honors in 1965, completing 46 percent of his passes for 2,368 yards and 10 touchdowns. The ground game, keyed to the inside running of Carlton and Joe, led the AFL with 16 rushing touchdowns. When the offense stalled in enemy territory, Saban went to kicker Pete Gogolak, whose 28 field goals led the league in 1965.

As it had in 1964, the Bills' defense keyed the championship run. The unit featured all-pros on every line of defense. Right tackle Tom Sestak, left end Ron McDole, and right outside linebacker Mike Stratton headed a front seven that was the league's best against the run. The Bills allowed 3.1 yards per run and just five rushing touchdowns. During the '64–'65 seasons, the Bills put together an amazing streak of not allowing a rushing touchdown for 17 consecutive games.

For the third straight year, Sestak was named to the all–AFL team. Saban called him one of the best defensive tackles he's ever seen. Patriots head coach Mike Holovak agreed. "I don't think there was ever a better tackle than Sestak," Holovak said. "He was great."

Saban admired Sestak's willingness to play hurt. Injuries to Sestak's left knee forced him to undergo two operations to have cartilage removed, and after games, his knee would swell to volleyball size and have to be drained.

Discovered at McNeese State College in Lake Charles, Louisiana, by Bills talent bird-dog Harvey Johnson, Sestak proved his talent from his first day at the Bills' camp. When the Bills drafted him, Saban initially planned to use him at tight end or linebacker. But one look at the 245-pound Sestak convinced Saban the rookie would grow into a defensive tackle. As he matured physically, reaching 270 pounds, Sestak also matured talentwise.

"He grabs you by the shoulders," one AFL guard said of Sestak, "and he throws you someplace."

Buffalo's success against the rush forced offenses to put the ball in the air, where the secondary was waiting. Cornerbacks Booker Edgerson and Butch Byrd and safeties George Saimes and Hagood Clarke led a defense that led the league with 32 interceptions.

"There were some good defenses then, but from 1963 to 1968, we were the most consistently dominating defense," Stratton says. "We had a fine group of people, and we played together. We had it all, good defensive backs, linebackers, and a line strong enough to put the rush on and agile enough to play the run. By playing defense like we did, we put a lot of pressure on the quarterback. That was the key. If we had pressure, we could play games with blitzes and change coverage responsibilities."

The strength of the secondary was found in all-pros Saimes and Byrd. An intelligent player who rarely made a mental mistake, Saimes was a voracious reader of both books and opposing quarterbacks. Called "Camus in Shoulder Pads" and the "Existentialist Pass Defender," Saimes was an All-America halfback at Michigan State who switched to safety when he joined the Bills as a rookie in 1963. Because he was just 5-foot-10, 185 pounds, Saimes played free safety with speed and savvy. His ability to dissect offenses made him particularly effective on the safety blitz, and he was an effective open-field tackler. During the Bills' 17-game streak of not allowing a rushing TD, Saimes was a key factor, making 160 tackles and missing just six.

While Saimes was a crafty player who relied on his cunning, Byrd played cornerback with an aggressive, hard-hitting style. He used the AFL's trademark bump-and-run style, and was equally effective forcing the run. At 6 foot, 211 pounds, Byrd was like a fourth linebacker, and he gained a reputation for cutting down sweeps. Byrd's hobby was driving fast cars, but he seemed better suited to a demolition derby. When Boston receiver Charley Frazier beat Byrd for a touchdown, Byrd exacted revenge by leveling Frazier on his next pattern.

Hagood Clarke, who played left corner, benefited from Byrd's reputation. Unwilling to throw at Byrd, AFL quarterbacks looked to pick on Clarke, a second-year man. But Clarke responded to the challenge and led the Bills with seven interceptions.

One of Buffalo's three defeats in 1965 came at home against the Jets, a 14–12 loss to rookie quarterback Joe Namath. Namath helped lead New York to a 5–8–1 record and a second-place finish behind the Bills. After throwing for 18 touchdowns and directing the Jets to five wins in their last eight games, Namath was named AFL Rookie of the Year in both wire service polls.

For the second straight year, the Bills' opponents in the AFL championship game were the San Diego Chargers, who won the West with a 9–2–3 record. Sid Gillman's team went undefeated in their first seven games and beat their chief challenger, the Oakland Raiders, twice, including a 24–14 win in San Diego on the season's final weekend. The win over Oakland gave the Chargers their third straight division title and fifth in six years.

The most notable absentee from the Chargers was Tobin Rote. Persistent arm problems forced the old quarterback to retire after the '64 title game. The Chargers turned to John Hadl, who had backed up Rote in 1963–64. By 1965, Hadl had assumed the role of triggerman in the most potent offense in pro football. When he walked to the line of scrimmage and flipped the towel that hung from center Sam Gruneisen's pants, Hadl was flipping the switch that produced the electricity in the Lightning Bolt's attack.

"With Tobin gone I have more responsibility," Hadl told writer Bill Gutman. "It's a difficult job, but I like it."

Connecting with all-pro end Lance Alworth on passes like "Split End Delay," Hadl finished the season as the AFL's second-ranked quarterback. He completed 50 percent of his passes, throwing for 20 touchdowns and an AFL-high 2,798 yards.

Hadl's task was made easier by a strong supporting cast. Halfback Paul Lowe led the league in rushing yards and average per carry and was named Player of the Year. Alworth's acrobatic catches allowed him to lead the AFL with 1,602 yards receiving, a 23-yards-per-catch average, and 14 touchdowns. Lowe, Alworth, and tackle Ron Mix were all-pros on a unit that ranked first in points scored, rushing, passing, and first downs.

San Diego's high-octane offense overshadowed a defense that has never had its just due. After intercepting 49 passes in 1961, a pro record that still stands, the Charges in '65 became the first AFL team — and just the fourth club in pro football history — to rank number one against the run, pass, and in overall defense. The strength of the San Diego defense remained its front four. The charge of the AFL's "Fearsome Foursome" was led by end Earl Faison and tackle Ernie Ladd, all-pros known for sacking quarterbacks but equally successful in stuffing the run. In one game, the Chargers held their opponents eight straight downs in a first-and-goal situation.

On a sunny, balmy day after Christmas in San Diego, the Bills and Chargers met for the second straight year to decide the AFL championship. Oddsmakers favored the Chargers, who in their two previous meetings with Buffalo in 1965 outscored the Bills 54–23 and outgained them 816–381 in total yardage. San Diego newspapers played up the Chargers' statistical dominance. On Christmas Day, the *San Diego Evening Tribune* ran a cartoon on its sports pages that depicted huge Ernie Ladd hovering over the tiny, frightened figure of Bills quarterback Jack Kemp.

"We were supposed to kill Buffalo," says Walt Sweeney, who started at right guard for the Chargers. "I remember one story said that Buffalo playing San Diego was like a box kite going against a missile."

The Bills read those stories too, and used them to help stoke their inner fires. "Our motivation for that game came from the San Diego newspapers, and all the talk coming out of San Diego's camp," Billy Shaw says. "But we had confidence going in that we could win. We figured if the defense could hold them, we'd win."

Kemp, who took offense at his cartoon caricature, said many people felt the Bills had won the year before only because Alworth and Keith Lincoln were injured. The Bills went into the '65 championship feeling they had something to prove. Bills defensive coordinator Joe Collier said his players were fired up so high before the game that he was "talking to their kneecaps."

To give the Chargers some new looks, Saban and Collier drew up different offensive and defensive alignments. Defensively, Collier added to the Bills' base 4-3 alignment with a five-man line that had middle linebacker Harry Jacobs among the front four, and added a three-man line with end Tom Day dropping back into coverage. Collier also assigned double-coverage to Alworth, and made plans to blitz free-safety George Saimes.

"We felt we could control the Chargers offense by giving them some different looks," Saban says.

"Everyone said the San Diego offense was too good," Stratton says, "and that Buffalo couldn't handle them. They were favored by two TDs, but I remember we played Tom Day as a linebacker in that game and went with four linebackers and three linemen. That was totally unexpected from San Diego's point of view. It flustered them. They had to call timeout two or three times. That was one game where our coaching won it for us more than anything else. They couldn't find a way around it."

Alworth presented a special problem for defenses, but the Bills countered with shifting coverage. "We ran long and short coverage on Lance," Stratton says, "either with two defensive backs or with a back and a linebacker."

Alworth managed four catches for 82 yards, but had to run through a thicket of elbows and shoulders. "One guy was always knocking me off line," Alworth said later.

Saban's strategy moves on offense were more by necessity than design. The Bills were hampered by the absence of receivers Bass and Dubenion to knee injuries, Kemp had a sore knee and shoulder, and center Dave Behrman was out with a bad back. To replace Behrman, Saban switched right guard Al Bemiller to center, a position he hadn't played in two years, and put second-year man Joe O'Donnell at guard. Buffalo's offense suffered another loss when all-pro left guard Billy Shaw was injured on the opening kickoff and had to be replaced by George Flint. Saban teamed Ernie Warlick with Paul Costa in a double-tight end alignment and kept fullback Billy Joe — who at 250 pounds was like a third guard — in the backfield for maximum pass protection.

"Warlick was an excellent blocker," Shaw says. "When he was in the game it was like having another tackle. But the unsung hero of that game was George Flint. He only weighed 225, 230 pounds at the most, and during weigh-ins, George used to put weights under his arms to get to 240. He got thrown in against Ernie Ladd, who was huge, and George did a good job. But that was the character of our team. If someone got hurt, someone else was there to step in."

The Bills got on the board late in the second quarter on an 18-yard touchdown pass from Kemp to Warlick that gave Buffalo a 7–0 lead with five minutes left in the half. The Bills' defense forced a punt on the Chargers' next possession, and Butch Byrd stunned the crowd by streaking 74 yards for the score.

Buffalo carried its 14–0 lead into halftime, and a pair of Gogolak field goals gave the Bills an insurmountable 20–0 lead heading into the fourth quarter. Kemp, who earned game MVP honors, kept the Chargers off balance with his play calling, and Gogolak concluded the scoring with a 32-yarder in the final period to make it a 23–0 final, the Chargers' first shutout in four years. In the game's final minutes, Bills linebacker John Tracey did the twist and taunted the Charger offense. "Come out," Tracey called as the Chargers huddled, "and we'll show you some defense."

In the Charger locker room, Hadl said, "They stopped our running and our passing. There was nothing left."

Billy Shaw was an all-pro guard for the Bills during their playoff seasons of 1963–66 and was voted to the AFL's all-time team. (*Photo courtesy of the Buffalo Bills.*)

Hadl completed just 11 passes in 23 attempts, and was hurried into two interceptions. Despite Hadl's scrambling ability, the Bills totaled 45 yards in sacks. Charger backs Lowe and Lincoln were held to a total of 73 yards rushing, 47 of which came on one long run by Lowe.

"We were a little overconfident," Lowe says. "We felt like we could go out there and say, 'We're the Chargers.' But they played well, and Kemp had a great game. He lifted his team up."

Hall of Fame receiver Lance Alworth, left, and quarterback John Hadl keyed the San Diego Chargers' passing attack, which came to symbolize the AFL's wide-open style of play. (*Photo courtesy of Thom Vollenweider, San Diego Chargers.*)

So dominant was the Buffalo defense that the Chargers never advanced past the Bills' 24-yard line. San Diego did mount a second quarter drive, moving from their own 11 to the Buffalo 28, but Dunaway got a hand up to block Herb Travenio's field-goal attempt. The Bills took advantage of matchups along the line of scrimmage, especially along the right side, where Day and tackle Tom Sestak gave San Diego's Ernie Wright and Ernest Park fits. The Bills' intensity was best demonstrated by Sestak, who on one play collapsed the pocket, dove over a downed Park, and reaching out with his right hand, pulled Hadl down.

"We whipped them in the trenches," Saban stated afterwards.

With the victory, the Bills joined the 1960–61 Oilers as the only teams in AFL history to repeat as league champions, and earned the right to be ranked among the elite times of the decade.

"For us to win the title back-to-back," Shaw says, "that was more than you ever dream about.

Chapter Ten

1966: A Negotiated Peace

WHEN THE NEW YEAR BEGAN, the Buffalo Bills reigned as the American Football League's most dominating team. Circumstances beyond the team's control were weakening the Bills' hold on the rest of the AFL. The loss of 250-pound fullback Cookie Gilchrist hurt Buffalo's power rushing game in 1965. The 1966 season saw a still greater loss. One week to the day after the Bills shut out the San Diego Chargers to capture their second consecutive league title, Buffalo head coach Lou Saban shocked the football world by announcing his resignation on January 2 to become head coach at the University of Maryland.

There were a number of reasons for Saban's decision to leave Buffalo. Though he had just been named AFL Coach of the Year for the second straight year and offered a lucrative, two-year contract by Bill's owner Ralph Wilson, Saban was disappointed by the short-term nature of the pact.

Disgruntled with his contract, and with the excessive deals given to unproved rookies — "How do you discipline a big-bonus boy with a no-cut contract?" he asked — Saban sought new challenges. He accepted a four-year contract at the University of Maryland.

To replace Saban as head coach, Wilson tabbed Bills defensive coordinator Joe Collier. The guru of Buffalo's great defensive teams, Collier had enjoyed a long apprenticeship under Saban. They had been together nine years — at Western Illinois, in Boston with the Patriots, and finally with the Bills.

Saban's resignation set in motion what many pro football historians consider to be the most eventful year the sport has seen since 1920. The AFL–NFL draft war heated up considerably as the two leagues spent a combined total of $7 million to sign 1966 draft choices. Green Bay Packers head coach and general manager Vince Lombardi shocked the sports world by signing rookie running backs Donny Anderson of Texas Tech and Jim Grabowski of Illinois for a combined $1 million. Lombardi saw the signings as necessary to prevent the AFL from challenging the Packers in the Milwaukee area, where the Packers played some games at County Stadium. Since the AFL challenged NFL teams in cities like New York, Los Angeles, and Dallas, Lombardi was concerned the AFL might put a team in Milwaukee to challenge the Packers. To further strengthen his team, Lombardi signed Anderson away from the Oilers and Grabowski away from the Miami Dolphins.

Having lost their 1965 top choice, Donny Anderson, to the Packers, the Oilers sought to sign their number-one pick in 1966 — Texas All-America linebacker and Outland Trophy winner Tommy Nobis. Both the Oilers and the NFL's expansion Atlanta Falcons drafted Nobis on the first round. The Oilers were thought to have the edge when astronaut Frank Borman, who was orbiting the earth in his Gemini 7 space capsule, sent a radio message to the Manned Space Center in Houston: "Tell Tommy Nobis to sign with Houston."

Despite Borman's plea, Nobis signed a reported $600,000 pact with the Falcons. The '66 draft yielded a number of players who would become staples of the AFL–AFC in years to come. Emerson Boozer and Pete Lammons were signed by the New York Jets; Pete Banaszak and Rodger Bird by the Oakland Raiders; Howard Twilley by the Miami Dolphins; Hoyle Granger by the Houston Oilers; and Mike Garrett and Aaron Brown by the Kansas City Chiefs.

But the loss of Anderson, Grabowski, and Nobis to the NFL left AFL owners bitter, and they directed their anger at commissioner Joe Foss. One owner, speaking on condition of anonymity, said the commissioner was poorly organized. "This should be one of the commissioner's prime functions," the owner said, "to see that we're prepared to wage an all-out fight for players."

The acrimony between the commissioner's office and embattled owners came to a head in the spring. On Monday, April 7, Foss officially resigned as commissioner of the AFL. Among the more impressive accomplishments of his tenure were the AFL's newfound financial stability, its signing of star players, and its ever-growing popularity. In 1965, the *average* game attendance of 31,000 represented a mark higher than any single game had drawn in the entire league schedule in 1960. In his letter of resignation, Foss called for the NFL and AFL to emulate major-league baseball. "Professional football should be operated with one commissioner and two league presidents as is major league baseball," Foss wrote. "Those in pro football owe it to the general public to present it with an annual world series and an all-star classic."

Recalling the difficulties that sometimes marked his tenure, Foss also had some advice for his still-unnamed successor. "Wear a thick skin," Foss said, "a soft smile, and carry a sense of humor and determination to do the job as you see best."

Foss had shepherded the AFL through its formative years, had played a major role in the television contracts that had underwritten the league's success, and was a factor in helping cities like Oakland and Miami field AFL teams. But his clashes with the owners had taken their toll through the years. The man who had startled New Yorkers by running the city's sidewalks in business clothes had grown tired of what he called "the carping in the sports pages."

On February 16, 1965, Foss told a gathering at the Lynchburg Sports Club that the leagues would soon merge under one commissioner, and that the long-awaited interleague championship game would "take place in 1967 or at the end of the 1966 season."

Rather than deal with further dissension in the owners' ranks, Foss decided to step down. "Our relationship had been good," he said, "and I didn't want to destroy that. Also, I didn't want to battle them. So I figured it was time for me to move on."

History has been kind to Foss' reign as commissioner of the AFL's early years, and original league owners, like Buffalo's Ralph Wilson, recall Foss fondly.

"Joe Foss gave the AFL credibility," Wilson says. "He had been the governor of San Diego, he was a World War II hero in the marine corps, and [had] won a Congressional Medal of Honor. He didn't know much about football at the start, but he learned."

To fill the commissioner's position, AFL owners turned their sights westward. At a league meeting in Houston on March 31, Raiders owner Wayne Valley asked his colleagues to consider his GM and head coach, Al Davis, for the commissioner's job. The choice of Davis split the eight-man group almost evenly. On the one side, Valley and Buffalo's Ralph Wilson, a silent partner in the Raider organization, pushed hard for Davis. The opposition was headed by Boston's Billy Sullivan, who knew Davis from their days together growing up in Brooklyn. In the end, the owners hired Davis by a margin of one vote. At first, Davis seemed unsure of his new opportunity. "I'm a football coach first," he said. Persuaded by Lamar Hunt, Sid Gillman, and Wilson, Davis accepted the position.

"I guess they thought I'd be a catalyst," Davis said. "It was a situation that called for some constant pressure to be put on the other side."

On Tuesday, April 8, Davis was formally named AFL commissioner. For his new responsibilities, he was granted a five-year contract at $60,000 annually, a private limousine, and an expanded budget to operate the league. In choosing Davis as league commissioner, AFL owners were getting a man who was diametrically opposite from his predecessor. Where Foss was warm and engaging, Davis was cold and calculating; where Foss could charm with homespun yarns and "good ol' boy" talk, Davis was withdrawn. What league owners did have in the person of Davis was an energetic young executive who had blazed a trail for himself from obscurity to the highest office in the AFL.

Davis' inaugural speech was to the point. "My job," he said, "is to make the AFL the best league in pro football. I'll work at this job night and day and do the best I can."

From the start, one thing seemed certain. Davis would be a much more aggressive and hands-on commissioner than Foss had been. Mel Durslag, writing in the *Los Angeles Herald Examiner*, stated that Davis' appointment to the commissioner's post would strengthen the AFL's hand in the draft war.

"When the time comes for the two leagues to sign players again," Durslag wrote, "the AFL won't be standing behind the door with Al, who knows a few things about recruiting."

The differences between pro football's two top executives, Davis and the NFL's Pete Rozelle, made for some intriguing comparisons. Rozelle was clean-shaven, suave and sophisticated, a 39-year-old Wall Street type who could charm with an easy smile and well-modulated tones.

Though just three years younger than Rozelle, Davis cut a vastly different image. With the hair receding from his slicked-back pompadour, with his long sideburns and pin-striped suits, Davis looked and acted the part of an aging rebel. His words carried the unmistakable accent of Brooklyn's city streets.

Ed Levitt of the *Oakland Tribune* focused on the inherent differences between the two men. "The skirmishes that are bound to pop up between Davis and ... Rozelle should make things lively in the football front for some time."

While Davis was planning to take the NFL on at every turn, Hunt was seeking détente in a Dallas meeting with Cowboys general manager Tex Schramm. Preliminary meetings were held near the towering statue of a Texas Ranger at Love Field on Sunday, April 6, two days before Davis was officially named league commissioner. Peace talks between representatives of the two leagues were nothing new; they had been going on informally since 1960. Colts owner Carroll Rosenbloom had talked with the Jets' Sonny Werblin and the Bills' Ralph Wilson.

Schramm, who was convinced the framework of pro football was being destroyed by the draft war, felt he had a plan the AFL might accept. Earlier negotiations failed because the NFL had insisted upon a merger that would allow only the AFL's strongest teams in, while disbanding weaker clubs like the Denver Broncos. Schramm's plan called for an inclusive merger.

With that idea in mind, he phoned Los Angeles Rams owner Dan Reeves and outlined the details of his plan. Reeves felt it was workable, and advised Schramm to contact Rozelle. When Schramm asked if he should pursue it further, Rozelle told him, "Go ahead, give it a try." But the NFL commissioner cautioned Schramm to keep negotiations confidential. Schramm agreed, and his planning involved only two NFL cub owners — Wellington Mara of the New York Giants and Lou Spadia of the San Francisco 49ers. The reasoning for involving Mara and Spadia was obvious — both had teams that were in direct competition with the AFL.

"We felt," Schramm said, "that if the NFL could come up with an acceptable plan that was good for the sport, it could then be presented to the American Football League. If they liked it, fine. If not, we could settle down to an all-out war."

With Rozelle's backing, Schramm placed a phone call to the Chiefs' owner early in 1966. Apart from owning a house three blocks from Hunt's family residence in Dallas, Schramm felt he could deal successfully with Hunt.

"He *was* the league," Schramm said. "He started it. I also thought he was the guy who would see a way to get it done."

Hunt was cautiously optimistic about Schramm's proposal to talk, and while en route to Houston for the AFL meetings, he stopped at Love Field to see Schramm. The two men shook hands under the giant Texas Ranger statue outside the terminal, and headed to the parking lot to Schramm's 1966 Oldsmobile.

For half an hour, the 33-year-old AFL boss and 45-year-old NFL representative talked of a merger that would end football's cold war. Hunt wanted to see the AFL survive, even if it meant under the banner of the NFL.

"We needed stability," Hunt said. "We needed for the public to know that our teams were going to succeed in the cities where they were located."

On that note, the initial meeting ended, and Hunt headed to Houston for the AFL meetings. Not until early May did Hunt inform his fellow owners of the talks he had with Schramm. Though doubts were expressed as to the viability of the negotiations, Hunt was adamant. The talks would continue, he said, and he appointed Wilson and Sullivan as partners in the upcoming discussions.

In the first days of May, Hunt and Schramm held two meetings at Hunt's home. On Tuesday, May 3, the two men convened at 9 A.M. to discuss the problems inherent in New York and San Francisco, where the AFL and NFL fielded teams in direct competition with one another. For the first time, Schramm brought up the fact that Mara and Spadia would expect millions of dollars in indemnity payments—paybacks for the financial damage done to their teams from the loss of revenue in the competition with AFL clubs.

Hunt studied the proposal, and asked for a week to think it over. He called Schramm on Monday, May 9, and arranged for a second meeting the next day. In earlier talks, Hunt had always maintained an air of aloofness, staying noncommittal on the issues separating the two leagues. But on May 10, Hunt expressed optimism that any problems confronting them could be solved, and gave Schramm the okay to continue talks within the NFL.

On Friday, May 13, three days before the NFL meetings were to start at the Plaza Hotel in New York, Schramm, Rozelle, Mara, and Spadia met to discuss the progress of the peace talks. Mara and Spadia continued to voice their reservations about a merger. From this meeting, in which they faced a united front, Schramm and Rozelle concluded that it was not yet time to present the idea at a league meeting, and instead formulated a strategy to talk with NFL owners separately.

The early planning between Schramm and Hunt nearly blew up on Tuesday, May 17, at a meeting of NFL owners, when Mara announced the Giants' signing of Buffalo placekicker Pete Gogolak, who had played out his option with the AFL champion Bills. The Gogolak signing broke a verbal agreement between the AFL and NFL that neither would recruit a player from the opposing league. To some, Mara's stunning move was borne out of desperation.

"The Giants were in disarray," Howard Cosell said. "Their old grandeur was dissipated. They had become losers. Wellington Mara was desperate. He did something nobody else in the National Football League would even think of doing. He turned a bidding war into open piracy."

Mara's announcement set both sides aflame with anger and anxiety. Schramm recalled NFL owners at the league meeting as "absolutely irate." In the AFL, the Gogolak signing fueled the antimerger arguments of the league's hawks, who told Hunt the NFL couldn't be trusted. Davis declared open warfare on the NFL. He mobilized a staff that saw Mickey Herskowitz, Irv Kaze, and Val Pinchbeck serving as publicists and former New York Giants great Mel Hein as director of officials. Hunt, Sullivan, and the doves of the AFL leadership were stunned at the sudden escalation of hostilities. Davis had turned the tables on the league bosses; he was the AFL's hawk, and he moved quickly to line up allies and solidify his power base. Schramm said Gogolak's signing had given Davis "an open door" to sign NFL players. Syndicated columnist Larry Merchant sized up the two principal leaders and stated his belief that the NFL had begun a battle it couldn't hope to win.

"Davis versus Rozelle, despite the NFL's prestige, is a mismatch," Merchant wrote. "The Giants, Rozelle, and the NFL have played right into Davis' strength. By signing Pete Gogolak, they have brought the level of the war down to a level that Davis can't be beaten at."

Davis and the AFL reacted swiftly to the Gogolak signing. Expert negotiators like Kansas City's Don Klosterman were given a free hand to sign established NFL stars. Quarterbacks were a prime target. The Raiders' Scotty Stirling signed Los Angeles Rams quarterback Roman Gabriel to a four-year, $400,000 contract. San Francisco's John Brodie signed with Bud Adams and the Houston Oilers. The Oilers also reached contract agreement with Chicago Bears all-pro tight end Mike Ditka by offering him a $50,000 signing bonus. The New York Jets sought out Packers halfback Paul Hornung. Davis, acting on behalf of the Jets, contacted Green Bay stars Willie Davis and Herb Adderley. The Packers, in turn, talked with Oakland's all-pro center Jim Otto. Davis later claimed that of the 14 starting quarterbacks in the NFL, half of them had agreed to exercise their options and sign with AFL teams.

Raiders executive Al LoCasale, who started his pro career as a member of Sid Gillman's organization in San Diego, recalls the meeting where he first learned that open hostilities existed.

> We were told to bring our phonebooks to our Saturday meeting and keep quiet about it. We went into the office and sat quietly, and Sid came in and said the NFL had signed Pete Gogolak. Al Davis said later that he wanted to know which people had contact with NFL players that we might be able to sign. The NFL had struck a blow and we reacted to it. It was a case of action-reaction. They had taken a shot using a revolver, and Al shot back using a machine gun.

1966: A Negotiated Peace

I remember in one meeting Billy Sullivan, the owner of the Patriots, said, 'Why don't we get out of the way and let Davis, LoCasale, and Klosterman do the job?' One of the strengths of the AFL was that the owners and commissioner knew enough to get out of the way and let the football people make the decisions.

In the end, it was the owners who made the right decisions. On June 8, the AFL and NFL announced they would merge for the 1970 season. To Davis' credit, his aggressive action as commissioner undoubtedly quickened the pace of negotiations. Hunt believes that while the merger was going to happen sooner or later, the fact that the signings were taking place helped speed the process up. But the popular history that says Davis forced the merger is hotly disputed by Bills owner Ralph Wilson. Wilson says:

> Al was not heavily involved in the merger at all. After we got the NBC television contract in 1964, the NFL knew we were here to stay and that they were in for a big fight for players. Carroll Rosenbloom, the owner of the Baltimore Colts, was appointed by the NFL to speak to us about a merger. Barron Hilton, who was president of the league at the time, appointed myself and Sonny Werblin to talk to Carroll.
>
> Carroll visited with me in 1965, and told me he had a plan set out. He said "There's no love lost between the leagues, so it's going to be difficult to merge your cities into ours." So he said, "You play your league games and we'll play ours, but take all the TV money and save it. We won't play regular season games between the two leagues for four years, and then we'll have a complete realignment." Carroll wanted to go into the realignment gradually so tempers could subside. Carroll saw it as a cooling off period.
>
> But Sonny was against the merger. So was Wayne Valley in Oakland. Wayne wanted to fight the 49ers. But I was in favor of it, and the reason was that we had small cities and they had big cities. Denver, San Diego, and Oakland were small cities at the time. Buffalo was one of the largest cities in the AFL. It was a matter of economics, and economics always win out.
>
> So in 1966, Lamar met with Tex Schramm and they worked out the merger. The merger committee was Lamar, Wayne Valley, Billy Sullivan, and myself. We approved the merger, and we had to talk Wayne into going for it. But Al Davis had nothing to do with the merger. What Al did was that when war broke out between the leagues, Al moved in and signed some quarterbacks. And that helped speed up the merger. But Davis did not force the merger. That's not true at all. The genesis of the merger was created long before that, and Al was not in on the original merger talks.

With events moving rapidly, Hunt, Sullivan, and Wilson joined together to hammer out the final details of the merger. The trio invited Davis to a meeting at Werblin's Manhattan apartment. Davis was informed of the merger terms that had been agreed to. The plan surprised Davis because he assumed the merger would set pro football up in the fashion of major-league baseball, in which the American and National Leagues maintained separate regular-season schedules, league presidents, and identities but operated under one commissioner. It was Davis' belief that he would be president of the AFL, while Rozelle headed the NFL. When informed that would not be the case, Davis grew bitter. He accused AFL owners of "selling out" to the NFL, and called the merger football's version of Yalta.

"Al felt at the time," LoCasale says, "that we had won the war but lost the peace."

Despite Davis' objections, AFL owners ratified the merger by a 7–2 vote. "It was the intelligent thing to do," Hunt says today. "We were heading for financial ruin."

"I think when all was said and done, most of the AFL teams were glad to see the merger," Adams says. "There was a lot of camaraderie with the old AFL members, and I think that was an important stepping stone for getting the merger with the NFL. Salaries were really sky-rocketing. Everyone had to be losing money. There were quite a few teams on the ropes. We had to stop the blood bath we were going through."

Just as importantly, the merger helped legitimize the seven-year-old AFL, giving it equal partnership with the 47-year-old NFL. Pittsburgh Steelers owner Art Rooney summed up the junior status the AFL had before the merger when he said the young league would "no longer have to address us as 'mister.'"

A press conference was announced for 6 P.M. Wednesday, June 8, at the Hotel Warwick in New York. Snarled traffic on Sixth Avenue caused Hunt and Schramm to arrive at the press conference 15 minutes late. Schramm saw an ironic symbolism in their late arrival. "Maybe," he mused, "we were a long time coming to this peace, too."

Dressed in dark suits, white shirts, and dark ties, Rozelle, Schramm, and Hunt took their seats on a stiff-backed, powder-blue couch at the Hotel Warwick. Rozelle, flanked by Schramm and Hunt, smiled broadly through the proceedings.

The major points of the unification announced at the press conference were as follows:

- the AFL and NFL to realign under the NFL banner and be renamed the American Football Conference and National Football Conference, with Pete Rozelle the commissioner of the leagues;
- no relocation of existing clubs;
- two expansion franchises to be added by 1968, one for each league;
- a common draft, scheduled to begin in January 1967;
- preseason interleague play to start in 1967;
- a world championship game between the two leagues, with the first to follow the 1966 season;
- the AFL to pay the NFL an $18 million indemnity over 20 years.

The last point was galling to Hunt and the AFL owners, who had assumed that all NFL teams would share in the payout. It wasn't until a month had passed after the merger agreement that a breakdown of how the money was to be spent was fully spelled out. It was then that Hunt realized that of the $18 million, the New York Giants would get $10 million and the San Francisco 49ers $8 million as reparations for damages caused by competing AFL teams in their areas. Each AFL team would pay $50,000 a year, with interest, for 20 years. "We just considered it a long, slow note," Hunt said.

Art Daley of the *New York Times* saw nothing wrong with the AFL paying compensation to the NFL. Though Daley admitted that a multimillion-dollar settlement may have appeared harsh, the AFL had reaped the rewards of decades of ground breaking by the NFL. The AFL, he wrote, "moved into pro football at a time when the cream had come to the top of the bottle and it merely had to ladle it off. However, it had been churned there by decades of painful and profitless stirring by the NFL."

Whatever their private feelings, AFL and NFL owners publicly endorsed the agreement when it was announced. Hunt said the AFL got what it wanted the most: a world championship game between the two leagues and preseason contests.

"When you look at all the aspects of this championship game," Hunt said, "personally, I think it will be one of the biggest sporting events of the year, *every year*, in America."

AFL owners went public in their support of the merger. Werblin told the media that the merger would improve the Jets' season ticket sales, which in 1966 had stood at 43,000. Valley called it "desirable and necessary." Sullivan went a step further, saying the merger was "the Great Sports Marriage." Adams said it would "end the financial strain on pro teams." The Broncos' Gerald Phipps called the merger a "great thing." Said Wilson, "We had to do something. The players had taken over the game."

Gillman makes it plain that the Chargers voted for the merger. "We wanted it," he says now. "We were ready to go broke. We were running out of money. I remember when we would get ready for the draft, we would have two boards with names on them. One of the boards had the names of players we wanted, the other had the names of players we could afford to sign."

Sports Illustrated editorialized that the pro football "war" was less a conflict than the practice of free enterprise. The merger was forced, first and foremost, by finances. "Ostensibly, what dictated the peace," *SI* stated, "were the terrific bonuses that certain college seniors commanded and the prospect of established pro stars jumping from one league to the other for immoderate sums."

The *New York Times* agreed. "The peace pact is welcome," Daley wrote in a *Times* editorial. "If the cost is high, a continuation of the warfare would have been costlier."

One of the AFL's original owners, San Diego's Barron Hilton, had already found the cost of pro football too high. The Chargers lost $910,000 in 1960, and despite the team's on-field success, averaged losses of $645,000 a year through 1964. When Fidel Castro nationalized the Havana Hilton, Barron remarked, "Given a choice, we would have preferred he take the Chargers instead."

By 1966, Hilton was anxious to sell the team. His father Conrad wanted to name his son president and chief executive officer of the Hilton Hotel empire. Before he could be appointed, however, Barron was told by his father he had to be free of pro football. Millionaire Eugene Klein learned at a Beverly Hills cocktail party in 1966 of Hilton's desire to sell the Chargers, and on August 25, Klein and Beverly Hills' Sam Schulman headed a group of 21 investors who put up $10 million to buy the Chargers.

With the politicking finished, the AFL got down to the business of playing the 1966 season. The Bills opened the season as solid favorites to win their third straight Eastern Division title. Their defense was the best the AFL had seen to that point; from 1964 to 1966, six of its 11 starters were named to AFL all-pro teams. The front four of Tom Sestak, Jim Dunaway, Ron McDole, and Tom Day comprised one of the great defensive lines of the '60s. The offense included stars like Jack Kemp, Elbert Dubenion, and Billy Shaw and added a flashy rookie halfback named Bobby Burnett, whose 766 yards rushing earned him Rookie of the Year honors.

Under Joe Collier, who at 34 was the youngest head coach in pro football, the Bills started slowly, losing their first two games of the season. Collier was well aware of the difficulties the Bills would encounter in seeking a third straight league title. In the Bills' 1966 highlight film, Collier pointed out the problems facing his club.

"Taking over a championship club like the Bills is a tremendous challenge," Collier said. "I feel fortunate in that I know the players in having been assistant coach. Sure, we have a problem in that no team has even won three consecutive titles in either the AFL or NFL."

With Kemp struggling to overcome arm injuries and the offense lacking a deep passing game, the Buffalo defense led the team to seven wins in their final eight games. Individual heroes included safety Hagood Clarke, whose last-minute 66-yard interception return was the difference in a 27–20 win over Houston; Dunaway, who ran 72 yards with a blocked field goal in a 14–3 win over the Jets; and cornerback Butch Byrd, who in a span of five plays turned in a 60-yard interception and 72-yard punt return to down the Dolphins.

The Bills won the East with a 9–4–1 record and joined the 1960–62 Oilers, 1963–65 Chargers, and 1967–69 Raiders as the only teams in AFL history to win three consecutive division titles.

Finishing second to the Bills in the East were the Boston Patriots, who featured one of the dominant runners in the game in 235-pound, 23-year-old fullback Jim Nance. In his rookie season of 1965, an overweight Nance had struggled to gain 321 yards on 111 carries, a mere 2.9 average. But under threats of being turned into an offensive lineman, Nance shed 15 pounds, reported to camp at 235, and went on to set AFL records for carries (299) and rushing yards

Tom Sestak anchored the Bills' great defensive fronts, which dominated AFL offenses in the mid–1960s and produced two league titles. (*Photo courtesy of the Buffalo Bills.*)

(1,458). He ran for a league-high 11 touchdowns and averaged 4.9 yards per carry.

Nicknamed "Odd Job" by his teammates after the rugged character in the James Bond movie *Goldfinger*, Nance gained more yards in 1966 than any other back in pro football. He was named AFL Player of the Year. Patriots owner Billy Sullivan called Nance "the biggest thing to hit Boston since Ted Williams."

Boston Patriots fullback Jim Nance earned all-pro status in 1966 after leading the league in rushing with an AFL-record 1,458 yards. (*Photo courtesy of the New England Patriots.*)

Head coach Mike Holovak's system of optional blocking, in which the offensive linemen drive their opponents in the direction the defense initially charges, was perfectly suited to Nance. Reading the blocks of his line, which featured all-pro center Jon Morris, Nance picked the path of least resistance.

"They can't stop me going up the middle with our system," Nance told a reporter in the midst of his great season. "No matter what they do to defense us, they can't stop me from finding a hole. With our system of optional blocking, optional running, there are so many things I can do when I go up the middle. If there's a hole where there's supposed to be, I take it. If there's not, I find my own hole."

The expansion Miami Dolphins played their first regular-season game under the lights of the Orange Bowl against the Oakland Raiders. The first official play in Dolphin team history saw Joe Auer take the opening kickoff and streak 95 yards for a touchdown. Auer's run brought the Orange Bowl audience of 26,776 to its feet, but the Raiders won 23–14. The Dolphins lost their first five games, finally beating Denver 24–7 in week six to earn their first official victory. They finished with a 3–11 record.

The Kansas City Chiefs cruised to the Western Division title with an AFL-best 11–2–1 record. The addition of a big-play wide receiver in Otis Taylor and breakaway back Mike Garrett gave the Chiefs the most explosive offense in the AFL, and the maturing of defensive stars Bobby Bell and Buck Buchanan gave them a second generation of stars to go along with the stars of the 1962 championship club.

The presence of Taylor and Garrett allowed ebullient head coach Hank Stram to fine-tune his innovative offense. Stram, whose language was as colorful as his team's strategies, said the 1966 season would feature a "souped-up" offense.

"In the past, we ground out yardage, inch by inch," Stram said in the preseason. "We moved by bus; now we travel by jet."

The Chiefs' signing of Garrett, who won the Heisman Trophy in 1965 as the featured back in USC's offense, came as something of a surprise to many in pro football. Though just 5-foot-9, 185 pounds, Garrett was a Trojan workhorse under head coach John McKay. His senior season Garrett led the nation in carries, rushing yards, and yards per carry.

Despite the fact that he had averaged 20 carries a game during his career at USC, including 26 his senior season, Garrett's size caused concern among pro scouts. Overlooked, however, was his quickness — Garrett's low center of gravity, sense of balance, and powerful legs gave him a distinct running style — and his innate toughness. Few knew that on mornings following games, Garrett literally dragged himself from bed to bathroom, his body so sore he couldn't even walk.

Because he was raised in the Los Angeles area and had played college football at nearby USC, most AFL insiders felt Garrett would sign with the Los Angeles Rams, who had made him their number-two pick in the 1966 NFL draft. The Chiefs took a chance and selected Garrett on the twentieth round of the AFL draft. Garrett quickly made it plain to representatives of both teams that he would sign with the team that offered him the best deal. As Garrett recalls:

The Rams made a pretty good effort to get me. They were equal with the Chiefs at one time in the bidding. Naturally, I was leaning toward the Rams because it was a local team and all that, but after it progressed and I talked to both teams ... I picked Kansas City.

But the Rams were very close to signing me. They wanted to know if I'd sign with them if they drafted me number one. I turned it down because I didn't want to sacrifice my bargaining chances. Kansas City gave me the better deal, so I went there.

Utilizing a flashy I-formation offense and assortment of defenses, the Chiefs hit their stride in midseason, just in time to impress Rozelle, who flew to Kansas City to watch the divisional showdown with the Chargers. It was the first AFL game Rozelle had seen in person. The Chiefs beat the Chargers 24–14 and won the division with an 11–2–1 record.

Nine Chiefs players were named to the AFL all-pro team. Len Dawson was the AFL's top-ranked quarterback, and Taylor led the league with a 22-yards-per-catch average. Dawson and Taylor were particularly effective in Kansas City's "Flanker Square-Out," a play that utilized the Chiefs' moving pocket and Dawson's sprint-out ability. Running an off-tackle play that featured double-team blocking, Garrett led the Chiefs in rushing with 801 yards, second most in the league, and led the AFL in average yards per carry (5.5).

The Kansas City defense, which led the league in interceptions with 33, featured all-pros in defensive linemen Buck Buchanan and Jerry Mays, linebacker Bobby Bell, and safety Johnny Robinson, who tied with teammate Bobby Hunt for the league lead in interceptions (10).

The title game between the two-time defending AFL champion Bills and the multitalented Chiefs matched a great defense against an explosive offense. Experts favored the Bills. Buffalo had the AFL's best defense, quarterback Jack Kemp was 9–1 against the Chiefs, and from 1964 to 1966, the Bills were the winningest team in pro football. They also had a considerable home-field advantage, playing in War Memorial Stadium in the frigid cold.

Some of the Chiefs, however, didn't mind playing at War Memorial at all. "The field was muddy," Garrett says, "but that stadium was very old, very nostalgic. The place had a lot of character. I loved playing there."

"We had confidence in ourselves," Taylor says. "The thing I remember most about that game was the cold. It was dreadful cold, and we didn't have any gloves, or any heaters. Buffalo was the coldest place to play; unbelievably cold. Just talking about it, I get cold."

Because of the impending world championship game with the NFL, the 1966 AFL title game meant more than any in league history to that point. If that wasn't enough motivation, there was the extra money each player would receive for playing in the Super Bowl. To make sure no one forgot that latter fact, Kemp had a 4-foot by 2-foot facsimile of a check posted on the wall of the Bills' dressing room. It was made out to "John Q. Buffalo Bill."

Game day brought gray-flannel skies and icy weather to Buffalo. New Year's Day saw the city whipped by 45-mile-an-hour winds. The Chiefs entered the game with an elaborate offensive game plan that called for 12 different formations of the I-set alone. The worth of head coach Hank Stram's planning was proven immediately. Kansas City's kickoff to start the game was high but short, and the Bills' Dudley Meredith fumbled on the Buffalo 31. Jerrell Wilson recovered the ball for Kansas City. From the Buffalo 29, Dawson hit a wide-open Fred Arbanas for a 7–0 lead.

"The Bills were a great team," Stram says now, "but they were a lot like NFL teams at that time. They used a 4-3 defense, and they didn't do a lot of different things. In our preparation for them, we went with a lot of variety. I can still see that Arbanas touchdown. He was so wide open, it looked like he had run out of the bleachers."

The Bills tied it four minutes later. With the ball at the Buffalo 31, Kemp read a Kansas City blitz and buggy-whipped a pass to Elbert "Golden Wheels" Dubenion. Dubenion made the catch at midfield and outran the Chiefs' secondary for a 69-yard TD.

Among the 42,000 standing, cheering fans in War Memorial Stadium that afternoon was a seven-year-old Little League football player named Jim Burt. The future two-time Super Bowl champion with the New York Giants and San Francisco 49ers huddled next to his dad, Don Burt. The Burts were Bills fans, and young Jim was, as he recalls, "a pretty happy kid" when Kemp hit Dubenion to tie the score.

"We were on our way," Burt recalled. "My Bills were going to the Super Bowl!"

As the Chiefs gradually took over the game, Jim Burt's enthusiasm waned. But the competitive fire that marked his career had been lit. "Dad, I can go down there and play. I can do that," Jim recalls telling his father. It was the beginning of a dream that exactly 20 years later carried Burt and his Giants to Super Bowl XXI and a win over the Denver Broncos.

In the second quarter, Dawson directed the Chiefs to the 29 and found Taylor open at the Buffalo 10. Cornerback Tom Janik hit Taylor high, but bounced off and sank to the ground. Taylor spun around and was blasted by Byrd, one of the AFL's hardest-hitting defenders. Both men recoiled at the force of the collision, but Taylor recovered and scored.

"Heck, if it had been a warm day in Buffalo I'd have been knocked out," Taylor said of his collision with Byrd. "It was so cold that I stayed conscious."

The Chiefs avoided disaster minutes later when Dawson, looking to hit Garrett on a swing pass, misread the Bills' coverage. Janik had his hands on the ball at the Chiefs' 20 and could have scored easily. But the slush-covered ball slipped through Janik's grasp. Just before the half, Kemp moved the Bills to the Chiefs' 10-yard line and then looked for his primary receiver, split end Bobby Crockett, who was angling toward the end zone on a post pattern. Willie

Mitchell, Kansas City's left corner, slipped and fell on the play and Crockett was open. But safety Johnny Robinson made a fingertip interception in the end zone and returned the ball 72 yards to the Bills' 28. Mike Mercer's field goal gave the Chiefs a 17–7 lead at halftime.

"It was a big play," Robinson says today. "I was fortunate to be in the right place. That's what you're there for, to make a difference."

As the game wore on, playing conditions worsened. The field was half frost and half mud, temperatures were in the low 30s, and a steady, cold rain pelted War Memorial Stadium. Through the scoreless third quarter, the intensity of the game heightened. Buck Buchanan, the Chiefs' defensive tackle, and Billy Shaw, the Bill's guard, waged a terrific battle of all-pros.

"Buck Buchanan and Ernie Ladd were two of the best defensive tackles I played against," Shaw says. "But Buck was entirely different than Ernie. He wasn't as physically strong as Ernie, but he had some quickness. As time went on, Ernie's wheels weren't what they used to be."

Buchanan recalled a play in the second half where Shaw surprised him on an inside rush and nearly knocked Buchanan unconscious. "I had been going outside on Billy Shaw all day without much luck," he said. "I did well on the running plays, but not the pass plays. I was getting close, but not close enough. Finally there came a time in the ballgame when I decided to go inside. Shaw's been thinking outside, outside, outside! So here I go inside and he's still waiting on me. He drops his head and he hits me. Bam! Just like that. And it stunned me right then, but I had momentum and I kept going. I got the quarterback and shoved him down on the ground, but Shaw's blow had stunned me. I was almost knocked out of the ball game."

The Chiefs put the game away in the final quarter on two touchdown runs by Garrett in a span of two minutes. The first came courtesy of a 45-yard pass from Dawson to Burford. On fourth-and-goal from the 1-foot line, Garrett slipped out of defensive end Ron McDole's tackle at the line of scrimmage and scored to give the Chiefs a 24–7 lead.

"I remember going into Buffalo on the team bus the day of that championship game," Garrett says today. "We knew they had the premier defense in the league. We started the game conservatively, feeling them out. By the second quarter though, we were pretty confident we could move the ball."

Kemp began the next Bills series with a 19-yard completion to Glenn Bass. But Fred Williamson drilled Bass to the sodden turf, knocking the ball loose, and safety Bobby Hunt recovered. Three plays later, Garrett took Dawson's handoff at the 18, started left, reversed his field, and ran it in to the end zone.

Kansas City's 31–7 win ended the Bills' hopes of an AFL "three-peat" and the chance to play the NFL in Super Bowl I. It also ended the Buffalo dynasty.

"I don't know how we lost that game to the Chiefs," Bills all–AFL linebacker Mike Stratton says. "I think had we been fortunate enough to win against Kansas City, and gone on to play Green Bay, we wouldn't have been intimidated by the Packers. We wanted that [first Super Bowl] game so badly we could taste it. I remember when I was watching the Chiefs play the Packers, I kept wondering how the game would have gone if there had been buffaloes on those helmets instead of arrowheads."

Billy Shaw wonders, too. "At that point in time, I feel like we would have represented ourselves well," he says. "The philosophies of our teams — Green Bay and ours — were similar. The matchups in a Bills–Packers game would have been different than they were in the Chiefs–Packers game. Whether we could have controlled the football on them, I don't know. But I would've liked the opportunity."

Despite the pain of their defeat, the Bills left no question as to where their loyalties lay for the upcoming meeting with the NFL. As Dawson left the field that day, Bills center Al Bemiller caught up with him.

"Now," Bemiller said in a classy gesture, "show those other guys how tough *our* league is."

Chapter Eleven

Super Bowl I: "Max"-imum Effort

CREDIT LAMAR HUNT not only for creating the league that forced the AFL-NFL merger and the showdown between the champions of the two leagues, but for naming the game the "Super Bowl."

During merger talks with Cowboys general manager Tex Schramm, Hunt had insisted upon a season-ending title game that would finally allow fans to see the champions of the two leagues on the same field. Since the AFL's inception in 1960, the younger league had put forth feelers toward the NFL for an interleague championship game similar to baseball's World Series that matched the champions of the National and American Leagues.

At the time, the game was simply referred to as "the AFL–NFL World Championship Game." The official press guide for the game does not carry the term "Super Bowl." Chiefs owner Lamar Hunt was a member of the merger committee, along with the AFL's Billy Sullivan and Ralph Wilson and the NFL's Art Modell, Tex Schramm, and Dan Reeves. The group had meetings every three or four weeks to discuss details of the game, and they kept referring to it as "the final game" or the "championship game."

During one of the meetings, Hunt was talking about the impending January 15, 1967, AFL–NFL showdown at the Los Angeles Memorial Coliseum when he blurted out, "When we get to the final game, the last game, the *Super Bowl*..."

According to Hunt, the term "Super Bowl" stemmed from a children's toy that was popular at the time called a "super ball."

"My daughter Sharon had a toy, a rubber ball, that was called a Super Ball," Hunt says. "You could bounce it off the concrete and it would literally bounce as high as a house. During the meetings we were talking about the game, and I referred to it as the 'final game,' the 'last game,' the 'Super Bowl.' It just came out of my mouth that way."

Three days after their New Year's Day victory over the Buffalo Bills in the 1966 AFL championship game, the Kansas City Chiefs boarded a chartered 727 and headed for Los Angeles. It seemed entirely fitting to AFL owners that their league representative was the Chiefs, owned and operated as they were by Hunt, the league's founding father.

"Poetic justice," Patriots owner Billy Sullivan told reporters at the site of the game. "Lamar's team had to be here. I can't tell you what Lamar has meant to us all, how many times he has voted to help the league even when it hurt his own team, how many times he has bailed other people out."

"It was an exciting time," Hunt says now. "It was exciting to be involved in that first Super Bowl game. We felt positive we were going to be a good representative of our league."

Despite the fact that Green Bay was installed as the 14-point favorite, some pro football observers shared Hunt's confidence. Joe King of *Sporting News* wrote that the Chiefs were the only AFL team that could match up with the Packers. "The AFL is lucky to have [the Chiefs] stand for the circuit," King wrote. "No other club would be ranked as highly."

The Chiefs and the AFL had come a long way since 1960; how far would be determined by the Packers on January 15 at the Los Angeles Coliseum. Having won four NFL championships in six years, including two straight in 1965–66, the Packers were the measuring stick of pro football. "You never know how good you are," Dallas Cowboys head coach Tom Landry said at the time, "until the Packers test you."

Of the five championship teams Green Bay head coach Vince Lombardi fielded during the 1960s, pro football historians consider the 1962 and '66 squads his two best. For Hall of Fame quarterback Bart Starr, who directed Green Bay to five NFL championships and victories in the first two Super Bowls, 1966 represented his peak year professionally. The NFL's top-ranked quarterback that season, Starr led the league in completion percentage (62.2) and fewest interceptions (three). Though considered to be a percentage passer, Starr led NFL quarterbacks in yards attempted per pass, and five of his 14 touchdown passes covered 40 yards or more.

In a *Sports Illustrated* article that season, NFL writer Tex Maule explained the emergence of Starr as a great quarterback. "Part of the trouble ... was that Starr had a powerful running game in support, and frequently gave the ball to Hornung or Taylor. He passed enough, however, to keep the Packers' opponents honest and to improve his own skills. This year, for the first time, these skills are being recognized as of classic quality."

With halfback Paul Hornung sidelined by a pinched nerve in his neck and fullback Jim Taylor wearing down physically, the Green Bay ground game was not the unstoppable force it had been in 1961–62. It was left to Starr and his receivers to pick up the slack, and they did. In the NFL title game on New Year's Day in the Cotton Bowl, Starr shredded the Dallas "Doomsday" defense by completing 68 percent of his passes for 304 yards and four touchdowns in a 34–28 win.

Sealing the championship game win was the Green Bay defense, which led the league in seven different categories, including fewest points allowed (163).

Confused for three quarters by the Cowboys' computer-complex offense, the Packer defense made a goal-line stand in the final minute to prevent Dallas from scoring a touchdown and forcing sudden-death overtime.

The Packers entered Super Bowl I with a 13–2 record and had come within four points of a perfect season. Green Bay was a team of great stars, its roster listing future Hall of Famers like Starr, Taylor, Hornung, Forrest Gregg, Ray Nitschke, Willie Davis, Henry Jordan, Willie Wood, and Herb Adderley. To date, a record 11 members of the Lombardi Packers have been named to the NFL Hall of Fame.

Kansas City head coach Hank Stram calls the 1960s Packers one of the great "glamour" teams of sports. One Chief who was not impressed was Fred Williamson, Kansas City's all-pro left cornerback. Upon arriving at Long Beach, Williamson began a daily monologue aimed at intimidating the Packers. Known as "the Hammer" because he liked to blindside receivers with a forearm to the facemask, Williamson was a handsome, flamboyant type who wore white shoes on the field and made "B" movies off of it.

"The Packers, sheeit, Taylor, sheeit, Lombardi, sheeit," Williamson said. "We're going to whip their asses, all of them, and if Boyd Dowler or Carroll Dale or any of those other guys have the nerve to catch a pass in my territory they're going to pay the price. I'm going to lay a few hammers on 'em and they're going to go back into the huddle with their heads ringing like they're hearing chimes and their eyes full of stars and dots and their legs twanging like rubber bands."

As a team, the Chiefs held mixed views on Williamson's downgrading of the Packers. The late Buck Buchanan, the Chiefs' Hall of Fame defensive tackle, said in a 1990 interview that Williamson's words had no impact on him.

"Fred didn't affect me," Buchanan said. "Some players were upset with him, because they thought he was going to make the Packers mad. I know Hank Stram wanted to kill the Packers with kindness and then kick the crap out of them when the game started."

Rookie wide receiver Otis Taylor was one of those upset with Williamson. "I don't mind a guy talking," Taylor says, "but he's got to back it up on the field. A lot of guys didn't like what Fred was doing."

The Packers arrived in Santa Barbara on January 8, and those who wondered what effect Williamson's words had on the champions of the NFL might have been surprised. Several Packer players drew hammers on their white practice jerseys, and when a hard tackle was made, the practice field would reverberate with chants of "the Hammer just got ya."

"You accept people for what they are," Starr says, looking back at Williamson's bravado. "We took it in stride. We were more amused than anything else."

Headquartered on the University of California campus, the Packers' coaching staff spent long hours studying Kansas City game films. The late Phil Bengston, Green Bay's defensive coordinator and assistant head coach, said in a 1992 interview that the Packers' preparation for Super Bowl I was routine.

"We had an exchange of films with the Chiefs and we went about our normal preparation," Bengston said. "The Chiefs had some fine personnel and they were well prepared, but preparing for their style of offense wasn't that difficult. Dallas used more formations than the Chiefs did."

Starr says the Packers came away from film study of the Chiefs impressed by what they had seen, and recalls his team's preparation for Super Bowl I as very businesslike.

"The Chiefs were very strong and physical," Starr says. "The media thought we were just hyping the game, but players and coaches recognize talent. The Chiefs had a good team, and we knew it."

The Packers' defense shared Starr's feelings. Middle linebacker Ray Nitschke says getting ready for Kansas City presented numerous problems.

"It was real difficult," Nitschke says. "We didn't know how good their opponents were, so it was pretty hard to judge [the Chiefs]. I know that was a big concern for Coach Lombardi."

At Long Beach, Stram and his team watched the Green Bay game films and looked for weaknesses in Lombardi's team. What the Chiefs saw was a team that ran just a few formations offensively and defensively, a team that relied on discipline and execution.

"They were pure vanilla," Stram says. "No nuts, no chocolate, just plain vanilla. Preparing for that game was so simple it was amazing. We saw everything in the AFL, and here we were, preparing for a team that defensively used just one alignment and one coverage. It was unbelievable. But they were good enough to get by with it."

Chiefs quarterback Len Dawson recalls being impressed with Green Bay's teamwork. "They were a solid football team defensively," Dawson says today. "Our approach going into that game was that we couldn't afford turnovers, we couldn't afford to make mistakes."

Kansas City linebacker Bobby Bell says the Packers' offense emphasized the same no-nonsense approach. "They were a basic team," Bell says. "They ran a ball-control offense; they only had about ten plays."

The magnitude of Super Bowl I is evident by the fact that it remains the only game in pro football history to be broadcast by two major networks—NBC and CBS. NBC was the official TV network of the AFL; CBS carried NFL games. The CBS-TV crew at Super Bowl I listed Ray Scott as the play-by-play commentator, with Jack Whitaker, Frank Gifford, and Pat Summerall supplying color commentary. The NBC crew included Curt Gowdy as the play-by-play commentator, with Paul Christman and Charlie Jones providing color commentary. Gowdy says today:

> Christman and I could have done that game from Billings, Montana. We took the CBS feed, and what we saw on the screen was covered by CBS. They produced it, and we just supplied the voice.

> I really looked forward to that first Super Bowl game, because I was curious to see if the AFL could play against the NFL.

The first Super Sunday dawned sunny and bright over greater Los Angeles. By the time Kansas City rookie Fletcher Smith, a 22-year-old defensive back, approached the ball on the opening kickoff, a hazy smog hung over the L.A. Coliseum. League officials on both sides were surprised the game was not a sellout; only 61,946 of the vast stadium's 93,000 seats had been sold.

League allegiances were in evidence throughout the Coliseum that day. Not only was each team represented by its league's TV network, but the Packers and Chiefs used their own game balls as well. When Green Bay was on offense, the Packers used the Rawlings-made NFL ball, "the Duke." The Chiefs used the AFL's J5-V, made by Spalding.

Both the Packers and Chiefs spent the early minutes of the game probing one another for weaknesses. Each team registered one first down on its initial series before turning the ball over. The clock showed 6:04 left in the first quarter when Starr read a blitz on third-and-three from the Chiefs' 37 and hit wide receiver Max McGee on a pass play known as "Fullback Slant X Post." The Chiefs blitzed their weakside linebacker E. J. Holub on the play, and Starr, given time by a good block from Taylor, threw to McGee in the vacated area. The 34-year-old McGee stuck his right hand out, made a one-handed circus catch behind diving cornerback Willie Mitchell, and loped into the painted end zone untouched.

Kansas City's all-pro free-safety Johnny Robinson was skeptical of the Chiefs' decision to blitz Starr. "We ran a blitz that took me out of the middle of the field," Robinson says. "It was something we rarely did, but we felt we needed a stronger pass rush on that side of the field. So we blitzed our weakside linebacker [Holub]. I had to come out of the free-safety position to cover the halfback, and they hit McGee on the post. It changed the complexion of the game."

The Chiefs tied the game early in the second quarter with a 66-yard scoring drive highlighted by play-action passes off their "floating pocket." Dawson's 31-yard pass to Otis Taylor put the Chiefs on the Packers' 7, and K.C. tied the game one play later when Dawson found fullback Curtis McClinton wide open in the left side of the end zone.

Green Bay responded with a drive that Bengston said looked like "a scene out of a 1962 newsreel." Starr methodically moved his team 73 yards in 13 plays, taking more than six minutes off the clock. The canny Green Bay quarterback kept the drive going with four key third-down completions to four different receivers. On third-and-five, Starr hit McGee for 10 yards. On third-and-10, he hit Carroll Dale for 15. On third-and-five, Starr found Marv Fleming for 11. On third-and-seven he connected with Elijah Pitts for 10 yards. On the next play, Taylor took Starr's handoff on a weakside sweep, McGee wiped out three Chiefs with a chain-reaction block, and Taylor scored from 14 yards out.

Green Bay wide receiver Max McGee carries Kansas City cornerback Willie Mitchell on his back after hauling in a Bart Starr pass for a 37-yard gain in Super Bowl I. McGee caught seven passes and scored two touchdowns in the Packers' 35-10 win over the Chiefs. (*Photo courtesy of Vernon J. Biever.*)

Kansas City countered with a seven-play drive capped by Mike Mercer's 31-yard field goal, and the half ended less than a minute later with the Packers nursing a slight 14–10 lead.

"We had gone into that game apprehensive," Dawson says. "But we had moved the ball on the Packers, and by halftime we believed we could win."

Some of the Chiefs weren't so sure. Halfback Mike Garrett remembered feeling extremely tired during the game. Garrett attributed his fatigue to what he believes were overzealous practices leading up to the game.

"I think we practiced too hard and too long for that first Super Bowl," Garrett says. "We were on dead legs going into that game."

In the press box high above the stadium floor, members of the media were surprised at the Chiefs' strong showing. Jerry Magee, who covered the AFL for the *San Diego Tribune*, remembers Maule being so upset he couldn't sit still. "Tex was very worried," Magee says with a laugh. "He kept stalking up and down the press box."

Lee Remmel, who covered the Packers for the *Green Bay Press-Gazette*, was also concerned. "The major element to that first Super Bowl," Remmel says, "was the unknown. You had two leagues meeting for the first time in a showcase game. There was no question the Packers had the mystique, but the Chiefs were coming on strong, they had outplayed the Packers in the second quarter. I was very concerned at halftime."

So, too, was Lombardi. A blackboard in the Green Bay dressing room carried the words *Know Thyself*. Lombardi stood in front of his team and asked, "Are you the world champion Green Bay Packers? Go out on that field and give me your answer."

It took five plays for the Packers to respond. On third-and-five from the Chiefs' 49, Dawson dropped back and tried to hit tight end Fred Arbanas with a short pass over the middle. But the Packers, who had blitzed just 5 percent of the time in third-down situations during the season, crossed up Dawson. Bengston called for a double blitz, sending outside linebackers Lee Roy Caffey and Dave Robinson in on Dawson. Green Bay defensive tackle Henry Jordan hit Dawson's elbow as the Chiefs' quarterback released the ball, and the result was a weak floater that free-safety Willie Wood intercepted at the Packers' 45. Wood returned the ball to the Chiefs' 5. One play later, Pitts slashed in for the score, and Green Bay led 21–10.

Stram said later that Wood's interception changed the personality of the game by forcing the Chiefs out of their offense. K.C. did have one more chance, but when Caffey stuffed back Bert Coan for a 4-yard loss on a third-and-one play at midfield, the Chiefs were done.

Starr used two more time-consuming drives to wear down the Chiefs. He capped the first march with a 13-yard scoring pass to McGee — who made a juggling catch in the middle of the Chiefs' end zone — and capped the scoring by sending Pitts over the left side from the one-yard line with 6:35 left in the game.

The late Jerry Mays, then the Chiefs' defensive captain, recalled the Packers in a 1990 interview as a team without peer.

"The thing that got me about the Packers was that they didn't have a weakness," Mays said. "Every team has a weakness where you have to compensate, but they didn't. And history has shown that, too."

With their lead now at 35–10, the Packers had one more bit of business to take care of. With less than four minutes left in the game, Williamson was knocked cold courtesy of a Green Bay power sweep.

The Packers won by exploiting the right side of the Kansas City defense both on the ground and through the air. All three of the Packers' rushing touchdowns were scored on runs off their left, and both of Starr's TD passes came on plays where the Chiefs blitzed weakside linebacker E. J. Holub. Though few realized it at the time, Green Bay's success stemmed in part from a stomach ailment afflicting K.C. right defensive end Chuck Hurston.

Though he was listed in the media guide as weighing 240, Hurston's actual weight on game day was only 204. Weakened by his ailment, Hurston was no match for the Packers' 250-pound left tackle Bob Skoronski. On running plays, Hurston was overpowered at the point of attack. The Chiefs tried to beef up their pass rush by blitzing Holub, but Starr usually caught them in it, and hit McGee in the vacated zone for substantial gains.

Green Bay's 35–10 victory did much to justify the NFL's aura of superiority over the AFL. "People thought the NFL was better than the AFL," Remmel says, "and 35–10 is pretty decisive."

Not all of the Chiefs were ready to concede superiority to the Packers or the NFL. "The Packers were a great team," Garrett says. "They had much more balance than we did. But I felt like if we played them 10 times, it might not be a five-five split, but we would win a couple of them."

To their credit, the Packers spoke highly of the Chiefs after the game, and still do to this day. "We came away from that game with a lot of respect for Kansas City," Nitschke says. "They were a quality team with a lot of talent."

The day after the game, the *New York Times* ran a banner headline proclaiming, "Packers Rout Chiefs with 21-Point 2d Half and Win Super Bowl Game, 35–10."

Times writer William N. Wallace ended his story of Super Bowl I on a prophetic note:

> The Super Bowl games will now go on year after year, but it may be some time before an American League team will be good enough to win one, especially if the National League champion comes from Green Bay.

In the Green Bay locker room, McGee accepted praise from his teammates. Having caught just four passes in the NFL season, the aging McGee had devastated the Chiefs with seven receptions and two touchdowns. Making the rounds after the game, Lombardi stopped at each of his players' locker stalls and gave each man a wide grin and a fierce handshake. When he congratulated McGee, Max grinned.

"Any end could've done the same," McGee said, trying to be modest.

"Yeah, you're right," Lombardi answered.

"You sure took the edge off that," McGee laughed.

For the moment, the edge was off the NFL–AFL rivalry as well. Green Bay's one-sided victory had taken care of that.

Chapter Twelve

1967: Oakland's Angry Eleven

THE DAY AFTER Super Bowl I, Green Bay Packers head coach Vince Lombardi walked into an NFL owner's meeting and received a standing ovation. To a man, the owners were still glowing over Green Bay's performance the day before. "We prided in this proof of our superiority," Chicago Bears owner George Halas said years later.

AFL owners took the stance that their league was not inferior to the NFL, only to the Green Bay Packers. "They were clearly the superior team," Kansas City owner Lamar Hunt said of the Packers following Super Bowl I. The AFL absorbed the blow dealt by the Packers, and then continued to move forward. On May 24, the city of Cincinnati became the second expansion franchise in AFL history. Cincinnati's City Council, concerned the Reds baseball team would leave town and pressured from within by business owners who longed for a pro football team to bring added revenue to local merchants, had agreed the previous December 15 to start construction of a new stadium. The site was a 48-acre downtown plot that bordered Second Street and the Ohio River. Appropriately enough, the new stadium, built for both baseball and football and owning a capacity of 56,200, was titled "Riverfront Stadium."

On September 27, Paul Brown, founder and former head coach of the Cleveland Browns, returned from five years' forced retirement when his group was awarded the 10th and final AFL franchise. In 1963, Brown had been called into the office of Browns owner Art Modell and, despite having six years left on his contract, was relieved of his duties as general manager and head coach. The abrupt firing shocked pro football and sent into early retirement one of the game's foremost legends.

The NFL's loss, however, was the AFL's gain. Brown set himself up as part owner, general manager, and head coach of the new Cincinnati franchise. The principal architect of the Cleveland Browns' dynasty in the 1950s, Paul Brown's presence in the AFL added class and respect. Brown continued the exodus of former NFL coaches to the AFL, joining Sid Gillman, Wally Lemm, Weeb Ewbank, and George Wilson.

"I feel as if I'm breathing again," Brown said upon his return. Drawing upon the city's historical connection with pro football, Brown named his new team the Bengals after the 1937 Cincinnati franchise that had played in the second of the three early AFLs. Orange and black were the colors selected for the Bengals' helmets and uniforms.

For football fans, the highlight of the preseason was the matchup of AFL and NFL teams in exhibition games. On August 5, at Bears Stadium in Denver, the Broncos made pro football history by becoming the first AFL team to beat an NFL team. The Broncos' 13–7 victory over the Detroit Lions embarrassed the Lions, particularly all-pro defensive tackle Alex Karras. Karras had vowed he would walk home to Detroit if the Lions lost to Denver.

"We all felt like fools," said Karras, who was thrown out of the game in the second half for kicking Broncos fullback Cookie Gilchrist in the stomach during a pileup.

Throughout the summer, AFL teams surprised NFL fans with their strong showing. Ironically, it was the Chiefs, who had been humiliated by the Packers in the Super Bowl, who dealt the biggest blow to NFL pride. Four games into the preseason, the Chiefs hosted the Chicago Bears on a muggy night at Kansas City's Municipal Stadium.

For the Chiefs, the game against the Bears was their first opportunity to play against an NFL team since their loss to the Packers in January. Chicago was one of the NFL's flagship franchises. Coached by the legendary George Halas, the Bears featured two of the NFL's greatest stars, halfback Gale Sayers and middle linebacker Dick Butkus. In preparing for the Bears, Chiefs head coach Hank Stram made sure his players remembered the loss to Green Bay by showing them the NFL's highlight film of Super Bowl I.

"We got a copy of the Super Bowl film that week," Stram said. "They belittled our team. Before we left our last practice for that Bears game, I told the team we were going to have a short meeting. We watched the Super Bowl film, and then we stormed out of there. You know, I was always a great Bears fan, but we were ticked off."

"It was payback time," said defensive tackle Buck Buchanan. "We dedicated ourselves to putting everything together for that effort. I remember Otis Taylor was very emotional before that game. He was hollering at the Bears, we had to hold him back. That game was more emotional for us than it was for them."

"The Super Bowl loss was a big letdown," says linebacker Bobby Bell. "I remember thinking that the next NFL team out of the chute was going to catch it."

Unveiling his vast arsenal of offensive formations, Len Dawson threw four touchdown passes in the first half and led the Chiefs to 32 points in the second quarter. The Bears had trouble coping with Kansas City's multiple offense; the Chiefs' shifting I, moving pocket, and double-tight end formations confused the Chicago defense. In the second half, Kansas City added another touchdown in the third quarter and three more TD's in the fourth to beat the Bears 66–24.

With each Chiefs score, it was customary for the team mascot, a horse named "War Paint," to thunder up and down the sidelines in celebration. At game's end, War Paint and his rider were nearing exhaustion.

"After that game," Johnny Robinson says, "[Bears safety] Richie Petitbon came up to me and said, 'We didn't touch you guys on the field, but we almost killed your horse.'"

In the Bears' locker room after the game, Halas was asked if the Chiefs compared favorably to NFL teams. "Yes, you've got to say that they do compare with other NFL teams in every way," Halas said. "They certainly played a spirited game. They've been pointing toward this since the end of January."

Will McDonough, who covered the AFL for the *Boston Globe*, returned to the office following a Red Sox game and saw the score of the Chiefs' win come over the wire. McDonough smiled. He recalled Green Bay coach Vince Lombardi's comments in the locker room following the Super Bowl.

"Well, they can't play with the best teams in our league," Lombardi said of the Chiefs. "They can't play with the Lions or Bears."

When Lombardi's comments were passed on to Stram, the Chiefs' coach was surprised. Stram was in a press room in the Los Angeles Coliseum, talking about the loss with McDonough and some NFL writers. But Stram stopped every few minutes to ask, "Did Vince really say that we weren't that good? That we couldn't play at that level? Vince is a friend. Did he really say that?"

Now, seeing the 66-24 final, McDonough said to himself, "I'm sure that was for you, Vince."

The Chiefs were unable to maintain their emotional peak over the course of the season, however, and slipped to 9-5. Replacing Kansas City as the dominant force in the West was a team built on power and intimidation — the Oakland Raiders. The Raiders won the division with a 13-1 record, the best regular-season mark in league history. General manager Al Davis, who in his own words was in "a relentless fight to be Number One," engineered a daring trade in March of 1967 that shaped the style and future of the Raider organization over the next decade. Looking to add more octane to the long-ball, "vertical" passing game he desired, Davis sent quarterback Tom Flores and wide receiver Art Powell to the Buffalo Bills. In exchange, the Raiders got Daryle Lamonica, a strong-armed backup quarterback. The addition of Lamonica and a speedy young receiver named Warren Wells, who had been cut by the Chiefs, gave the Raiders the deep passing game Davis wanted.

The makeup of the 1967 Raiders was a tribute to Davis' skills and eye for football talent. Lamonica, tight end Bill Miller, and defensive tackle Tom Keating had all been pried loose from the Bills; fullback Hewritt Dixon and cornerback Willie Brown came courtesy of the Denver Broncos. Safety Howie Williams and defensive end Ben Davidson were free-agent pickups who had played for the 1962 NFL champion Packers. From the Oilers came Billy Cannon and George Blanda. Dave Grayson and Warren Wells had both been with

Oakland Raiders quarterback Daryle Lamonica, whose deep passing ability earned him the nickname "the Mad Bomber," launches a pass over Tom Day of the San Diego Chargers. (*Photo courtesy of the Oakland Raiders.*)

the Chiefs. Mined from the college draft was a host of talented players: center Jim Otto, guard Gene Upshaw, tackle Harry Schuh, wide receiver Fred Biletnikoff, defensive tackle Dan Birdwell, and linebacker Dan Conners — all of whom were all-pros in their AFL careers.

Head coach John Rauch molded his talent to fit Davis' philosophy. On offense, the Raiders combined Sid Gillman's high-tech aerial concepts with classic power running. Lamonica led the AFL with 30 touchdown passes and was named league MVP. Balancing the deep passing game was a ground attack built on power sweeps and off-tackle slants. Tackles Harry Schuh and Bob Svihus were power blockers who had crafted their art in the mud-bowl atmosphere of the Raiders' old home, Frank Youell Field. Buttressed by Schuh, who weighed 260, and the 255-pound Upshaw, the Raiders excelled in straight-ahead football. At 240 pounds, tight end Dave Kocourek blocked like a sixth lineman. Behind an offensive line that averaged 248 pounds per man were Clem Daniels, a 218-pound halfback, and 220-pound Hewritt Dixon, a tight end converted to fullback.

Daniels was a Raiders reclamation project, a misplaced player who found a home with the Silver-and-Black. Thick-legged with a tapered waist and sprinter's speed, Daniels played high school football in Dallas and then enrolled at Prairie View A & M. Slowed by injuries in college, Daniels graduated and was coaching high school ball in Dallas when the AFL began in 1960. Daniels signed with the Texans as a free agent — "for a couple of peanut shells," Daniels said — and spent most of the season on the bench as a reserve defensive back. The Texans released him the following year, and Daniels joined the Hamilton Tiger Cats of the CFL. Daniels was contacted by Raiders coach Eddie Erdelatz, who invited Clem to Oakland for a tryout. The same day Daniels arrived, Erdelatz was fired and replaced by Marty Feldman.

Initially assigned to the Raiders' taxi squad, Daniels eventually got a chance to play. He started the team's final three games of '61 and averaged 5.1 yards per carry. Daniels established himself as one of the league's top backs the following year, gaining 187 yards rushing in a game against the powerful Oilers and finishing as the league's fourth-leading rusher.

A combination of speed and power, the 220-pound Daniels ran the 100 in 9.8 seconds. Davis called him "one of the quickest big men I've ever seen," and Daniels combined quickness with balance, the latter the result of ballet courses he took in college.

Daniels led the Raiders in rushing in '67 with 575 yards, and he became the first back in league history to rush for more than 5,000 yards in his career. Daniels benefited greatly from the Raiders' system of option blocking. "I don't have to crash an opening where a hole is supposed to be," Daniels said. "If I see there's no opening, I have an option of sliding along the line and finding my own way through."

Otto, who had been with the Raiders since the team's inception in 1960, captained the offensive line. Oakland linemen had four different methods of blocking, and it was up to Otto to make the call at the line of scrimmage before each play. It was a Raider custom to run their sweeps the first series of the game, sending guards Gene Upshaw and Wayne thundering around end to soften up the cornerbacks and open the airways for Lamonica.

Oakland's number-one running play was Fullback to the Weakside Power, or "69 Boom Man" in team terminology. Run from Oakland's "East Formation Right," which saw the tight end lined up on the left side and the two wide receivers spread wide to the right, 69 Boom Man sent the fullback carrying the ball behind Svihus and Upshaw. The backs were in a pro-set formation, split behind the quarterback. "Boom" was the team's code word for the halfback's block and "Man" signaled the man-to-man blocking the offensive line used on the play.

Running the play from the East Formation created problems for opposing defenses. The placement of two wide receivers to the right side forced the strong safety to move that way as well, effectively removing him from the flow of the play, which was to the left. If the right defensive tackle closed tight on the play, Upshaw simply body-blocked him. If the defense adjusted by sending the right defensive end wide on the initial charge, Upshaw responded by pulling and hooking the defensive end.

Just as the Raiders borrowed from Gillman and the Chargers in developing their passing game they also utilized some of Stram's strategies in shaping their defense. As early as 1962, Stram's Texans were confusing enemy offenses with a variety of defensive looks, notably the 3-4 — a three-linemen, four-linebacker set — and the odd-man front, where a defensive tackle lined up on the center. When Davis joined the Raiders in 1963, he highlighted Dan Birdwell, a mobile, 250-pound defensive lineman who had once played linebacker. What made the Raiders' defense unique was not the 3-4 look they presented to opponents, but their innovative use of Birdwell as a "rover"—a defensive player who lined up at various positions during a game.

In the Raiders' "Over-30-Lou" defense — a 5-1 overshifted line to the strong side — Birdwell's position was opposite the tight end. If the defense called a "Special Under 40-L" formation — a 5-1 under — Birdwell lined up against the weakside tackle. Oakland also had an "Orange" formation, where Birdwell played a fourth linebacker, alternately blitzing and dropping back into coverage.

The Raiders' multiple defenses took advantage of the quickness of defensive tackle Tom Keating. In Oakland's 5-1 under and over defenses, Keating lined head-up on the center and the defensive line shifted to the weakside. The 5-1 under allowed for a strongside run, but the Raiders counted on Keating to penetrate quickly and close down the run. In the 5-1 over, the Raiders allowed for a weakside run, but again, Keating was called on to elude the center's charge and disrupt the blocking scheme.

The Raiders' front line featured powerful ends in 6-foot-8, 265-pound Ben Davidson and 6-foot-5, 270-pound Ike Lassiter, as well as mobile tackles in the 247-pound Keating and the 250-pound Birdwell. Raider linemen flowed to the football, sliding their alignments into even and odd shifts and then slanting past bewildered blockers. The linebackers — Dan Conners, Gus Otto, and Bill Laskey — shifted too, and were never far behind in getting to the ball carrier.

The Raiders' most revolutionary technique on defense was their style of pass coverage. The bump-and-run had been used by NFL defensive backs like Tom Brookshier of the Eagles and Dick Lynch of the Giants in the 1950s, but their style consisted mainly of playing receivers to the outside and bumping them to the inside where the safeties could help out in coverage.

The bump-and-run was brought to the AFL by Jack Faulkner, who, along with Al Davis, worked under Sid Gillman with the Chargers in 1960–61. When Faulkner became head coach at Denver in '62, he taught the bump-and-run to free-agent Willie Brown. Davis in turn took the style to Oakland.

The origins of the bump-and-run can be traced to the Los Angeles Rams' 1950 training camp. K. C. Jones, who had played basketball at the University of San Francisco and would eventually gain fame as a defensive specialist for the Boston Celtics, had a brief tryout with the Rams. Despite the fact that Jones had played basketball only in college, the Rams liked his size (6-foot-1, 200) and athleticism and drafted him on final round in '55. In one-on-one drills, Jones lined up head-to-head with Ram receivers and hand-checked them throughout their route. Though frustrated Ram receivers insisted the move was illegal, Faulkner, who was the team's defensive backs coach, scoured the NFL rules book and found no mention of it.

"That's where I learned [the bump-and-run]," Faulkner said. "I was so impressed I took it with me when I went to the AFL."

In Oakland, cornerbacks Willie Brown and Kent McCloughan were fast and physical, perfect types to play the bump-and-run. The Raiders' bump-and-run technique was to place Brown and McCloughan directly in line with the receiver, jam them at the line of scrimmage, and then run step-for-step in coverage. By maintaining contact with the receiver until the ball was actually in the air, Raider defensive backs pushed receivers around and destroyed timing patterns. Because Oakland's bump-and-run was as revolutionary for its time as the safety blitz, offenses had difficulties dealing with it.

The Oakland pass defense benefited from having two all-time all-AFL players; right cornerback Willie Brown and free-safety Dave Grayson. A star running back at Oregon, Grayson broke into the AFL with Dallas in 1960 and started for the Texans' '62 AFL championship team. He intercepted 26 passes his first six years in the league and was named all-pro four times.

"At free safety you're responsible for plays on each side of the field," Grayson said at the time. "I like the challenge of being active in every play."

At 5-foot-10 and 187 pounds, Grayson wasn't the classic bump-and-run type. Willie Brown was. A graduate of Grambling, Brown tried out with the Oilers as a free agent and was cut before the '63 season began. Picked up by the Broncos, Brown learned the bump-and-run under Denver head coach Jack Faulkner. He picked off nine passes in '63 and an AFL-record four in one day in '64, the first of three consecutive years he was named all-pro. Brown was dealt to the Raiders in 1967 and became the team's starter at right cornerback, a position he held through 1976.

"Nobody has a tougher job in football than the cornerback," said Brown, who was named to the Pro Football Hall of Fame in his first year of eligibility. "Football depends on the pass, and football also depends on stopping the pass."

Lance Alworth, the Chargers' Hall of Fame receiver, was instrumental in Oakland's obtaining Brown in 1967. "Al Davis called me up ... asked me about Willie, said he had a chance to trade for him," said Alworth. "I said, 'Al, he's the best, no one's close.' I can't forget the guy. I still think about the trouble he gave me."

Oversized at 215 pounds, Brown had exceptional speed and reflexes. His reaction time was so fast Brown could afford to play off the ball if he wanted to. He rarely did. Brown preferred to take his shots at the line of scrimmage, take away the short route and force offenses to beat him deep. "That's all I wanted," Brown said, "one shot at the line of scrimmage."

Pro football historian Joe Horrigan said Brown frustrated receivers because he never gave an inch. "He was on wide receivers like glue," said Horrigan. "He hit 'em at the line and stayed with them stride for stride."

John Madden, who coached the Raider linebackers in 1967 and became Oakland's head coach in 1969, said Brown never let up in coverage, not even in practice. The Raiders acquired Denver's great receiver Lionel Taylor in '67, but released him. The reason, Madden said, was because Brown shut Taylor down in camp.

The Oakland secondary was further bolstered by Kent McCloughan, Oakland's left cornerback, who was acquired from the Oilers in his 1965 rookie season. Madden said that when McCloughan lined up in tight coverage, receivers couldn't get away from him. McCloughan used hand checks to feel which way the receiver was going.

McCloughan was one of three Raider defenders to earn all-pro honors in '67, joining Davidson and Keating. Nicknamed "Tree," Davidson was signed as a free agent by the Raiders in 1964 after spending time with Green Bay and Washington in the NFL. He had unusual agility for a man his size, and his great strength made him difficult to handle one-on-one. More than anyone else, it was Davidson who established the image of the Raiders. He was a free spirit who liked to decorate his helmet with flowers before practices, and his handlebar mustache, motorcycle, and journeyman past gave him the look of a renegade.

What people didn't know about Davidson was that he was a gentleman off the field. He routinely gave his 20 free tickets to Raider games to patients at a local veterans hospital, and he appeared at numerous charity functions.

While Davidson relied on strength to get to the ball carrier, Keating emphasized quickness. Because of his size and agility, Keating was compared to Green Bay great Henry Jordan — so much so that Keating was called "the Henry Jordan of the American League." Al Davis said Keating set the Raiders' attitude in the old days, and Keating's quick wit helped make him a team leader. Of linemate Dan Birdwell, Keating said, "He'd give you the shirt off your back, but who'd want it?"

Birdwell had huge ears and hands — his fingers were size 17 — and Keating remarked, "You can put a quarter through his wedding band." Teammates nicknamed Birdwell "Herman Munster" after the TV monster. "The thing about Birdwell's face," Elinor Kaine wrote in her book *Pro Football Broadside*, "is that he doesn't have any lips. His face is like a skin farm."

A graduate of the University of Houston, Birdwell's off-field outfit included string tie, silver belt buckle, and 10-gallon hat. An ornery Texan, Birdwell was frustrated in a game against the Oilers because he couldn't get to quarterback George Blanda. So Birdwell pulled the towel out of the Houston center's belt and threw it at Blanda to force an incompletion.

Lassiter was the quiet man of the Raider defense. But his strength and quickness made him arguably the team's best defensive lineman. In a 1967 game against the Jets, Lassiter broke quarterback Joe Namath's jaw with a blow to the head.

The Raiders set the attitude for their '67 season with a 51–0 win at home against Denver. The offensive output was highlighted by Blanda's 50-yard touchdown pass to Wells, but the day belonged to the defense. Nicknamed "the Angry Eleven" by *New York Post* sportswriter Paul Zimmerman, the Raiders limited the Broncos to a net of *five* yards on offense.

"If there's one thing we can do," Davis boasted, "it's play defense."

The AFL's Eastern Division was supposed to belong to Buffalo for a fourth straight season, but a series of injuries slowed the offense. Quarterback Jack Kemp had an off-season, throwing nearly twice as many interceptions as touchdowns, and the Bills scored just 237 points, second lowest in the league. Buffalo averaged just 16 points a game and finished with a disappointing 4–10 record.

After a four-year absence from contention, the Houston Oilers returned to capture their fourth division title in franchise history. A 3–11 team in 1966, the Oilers became the first club in AFL history to go from last place to first in one season. Houston's startling turnaround was attributed to several factors. Don Klosterman, who had helped build the Kansas City Chiefs organization, had joined the Oilers in 1966 as the club's new executive vice president and general manager. Klosterman and club owner Bud Adams decided to bring back Wally Lemm, the defensive architect of the Oilers' 1960–61 title teams. Klosterman and Lemm drafted for defense in 1967, making Michigan State linebacker George Webster their number-one pick and finding a sleeper in the ninth round in the person of Prairie View A & M defensive back Ken Houston.

At 6-foot-4, 223 pounds, Webster was a prototype of the new-style outside linebacker. Lemm built his defense around Webster, devising a double-blitz specifically for Webster. Kenny Houston took over at strong safety and contributed four interceptions and three touchdowns in his rookie campaign. Miller Farr, obtained from the Chargers in a trade, was inserted at left cornerback and led the AFL with 10 interceptions.

With Webster and Farr turning in all-pro seasons and Lemm confusing enemy offenses with his blitzing schemes, the Oilers' defense was the best in the AFL. Houston led the league in fewest touchdowns allowed, rushing, passing, and set a then-league record for fewest points allowed (199) in a season.

The Oiler offense was tailored to second-year fullback Hoyle Granger. Big enough to break tackles at the line of scrimmage, the 6-foot-1, 225-pound Granger was also quick enough to break off long-gainers. Particularly effective on the fullback draw, Granger led the Oilers in rushing, receiving, and touchdowns scored.

An 18–7 loss to Boston in week eight gave Houston an unimpressive 4–3–1 record, but the Oilers went on to win five of their last six games. Houston clinched the division on the season's final weekend by beating the Dolphins, 41–10.

The Oilers' late run allowed them to slip past the New York Jets, who had led the Eastern Division through the first half of the season and dealt the Raiders their lone loss of the late season. Halfback Emerson Boozer's knee injury, suffered in a November 5 game against Kansas City, slowed the Jets' attack, which more and more had to rely on quarterback Joe Namath and receivers George Sauer and Don Maynard, who finished first and second in the league in receiving.

The Jets clinched their first winning season in franchise history with a win over Boston November 19, but were eliminated from the title race when the Raiders beat them in a get-even game in Oakland. Namath was roughed up in the game, suffering a broken jaw from Lassiter and several hard hits from Davidson, one of which sent Namath's helmet flying off his head. Namath recovered to play in the season finale in San Diego, where, equipped with a new half-cage facemask to protect his jaw, he became the first pro quarterback to throw for over 4,000 yards in a season.

The AFL championship game, played on New Year's Eve, 1967, was billed as a showdown between Houston's league-leading defense and Oakland's big-play offense. Individual matchups included a pair of all-pros — Oiler left guard Bob Talamini and Raider defensive tackle Tom Keating — going head-to-head in the trenches. On the outside, Houston cornerback Miller Farr, an all-pro and AFL interception leader, was matched against the Raider passing combination of all-pro quarterback Daryle Lamonica and his number-one receiver, Fred Biletnikoff.

Before a raucous silver-and-black clad crowd of 53,330 in the Oakland Coliseum, the Raiders struck first on Blanda's 37-yard field goal. In the second quarter, fullback Hewritt Dixon veered left on the Raiders' signature play, the weakside power sweep, and ran 69 yards for the score. Ahead 10–0 with 18 seconds left in the half, the Raiders lined up for an apparent field-goal attempt. But Lamonica, who was holding for Blanda, crossed up the Houston defense with a 17-yard touchdown pass to Dave Kocourek.

The score deflated the Oilers. Houston's Zeke Mowatt fumbled the second half kickoff, and the Raiders recovered. Seven plays later, Lamonica carried it in from the 1, giving Oakland a 24–0 lead. The Raiders got three more field goals from Blanda and a 12-yard TD pass from Lamonica to Bill Miller for an overwhelming 40–7 win.

Having earned a date with the Green Bay Packers in Super Bowl II, Al Davis' "relentless fight to be Number One" was only one game from being fully realized. What came to be known in Raider circles as the "great snow job" was about to begin. And Davis, the street kid from Brooklyn, was ready.

"Imagine," Davis said in bemused tones, "the li'l ol' Raiders on the same field with the Green Bay Packers. *Imagine....*"

Chapter Thirteen

Super Bowl II: Oakland Gets "Starr"-struck

IN THE HOURS BEFORE the Oakland Raiders hosted the Houston Oilers for the AFL championship on New Year's Eve, 1967, the NFL title game was being waged in Green Bay, Wisconsin.

For the second year in a row, the Packers and Dallas Cowboys met to decide the NFL's representative to the Super Bowl, and like the year before, the game was a classic. The drama of the 1967 NFL championship, however, has made it a game for the ages. An overnight cold front plummeted temperatures in Green Bay to a record low of minus 16 degrees, with windchill readings of minus 50. Historic Lambeau Field froze solid; the stadium floor, made hard and slick by ice, was later likened by players on both sides to a marble surface.

Frank Gifford, who was a member of the CBS-TV broadcast team that day along with Jack Buck and Ray Scott, remembered dressing in the heaviest socks, sweater, coat, and gloves. "But," Gifford said, "everything was bitingly cold, the chairs, the booth, the microphones, the monitors."

Gifford turned the broadcast over to Jack Buck for the start of the game and motioned for one of the young runners in the press box to get him a cup of coffee. The young runner poured out a cup of steaming coffee and placed it on the ledge in front of Gifford. When Gifford reached for the cup just a couple of minutes later, the coffee inside had frozen solid.

The Packers won the game by a score of 21–17, driving 68 yards in the final five minutes before quarterback Bart Starr tunneled in from the 1-yard line behind blocks by Jerry Kramer and Ken Bowman with 13 seconds left.

In many ways, the '67 championship was a microcosm of Green Bay's season. Under the whip of headmaster Vince Lombardi, the aging Packers regrouped from the loss of star running backs Jim Taylor and Paul Hornung to win an unprecedented third straight league championship. Injuries took a toll on the team, wiping out Green Bay's starting backfield and limiting Starr's playing time, and the Packers won the realigned NFL's new Central Division title with a 9–4–1 record.

Unimpressive at times during the regular season, Green Bay turned the intensity up a notch for the money games. They opened the playoffs at home against the Los Angeles Rams, a team generally considered to be the finest in football. But on a dark December afternoon in Milwaukee, the Green Bay line pried gaping holes in the celebrated "Fearsome Foursome" defense and Packer runners galloped through them en route to a 28–7 victory.

One week later, Green Bay rallied from a 17–14 deficit to beat the Cowboys, fighting the bitter cold and the Dallas "Doomsday" defense for the title and the right to advance to the Super Bowl.

From both a defensive and offensive standpoint, the Raiders presented the Packers with a strategic picture unlike anything Green Bay had faced in the NFL. Having scored 49 points in the playoffs against two of the best defenses in the NFL, the Packers headed south to Miami to face a Raiders defense that ranked among the best in AFL history.

Oakland's "Angry Eleven" defense had succeeded in confusing AFL offenses in 1967. The Raiders stunted and blitzed, switched from 4-3 to 3-4 alignments, and shut down enemy passing games with their revolutionary "bump-and-run" coverage tactics.

Oakland was just as aggressive offensively. Their huge offensive line was perfectly suited to both the power running and deep passing the Raiders relied on, and the Raiders confused defenses with their "East" Formation.

Their talent and tactics, their silver-and-black uniforms, and their Blackbeard the Pirate image had all helped the Raiders intimidate the AFL en route to a 13-1 regular-season record and a 40-7 romp over Houston in the league title game.

The Packers however, were unimpressed. Years of NFL warfare and Lombardi's tough-minded influence had pushed them beyond the point of intimidation. Middle linebacker Ray Nitschke told reporters, "I don't care if they come blowing Chinese bugles, riding horses, and waving sabers."

Despite Nitschke's words, the Packers had trouble rallying themselves for Super Bowl II. The strain of the long 23-game season, the string of injuries, and the physical demands of the "Ice Bowl" had left the Packers mentally and emotionally drained.

"The Raiders had a good team, and they were excellent representatives of their league, just as the Chiefs had been the year before," Starr says. "But preparing for Super Bowl II was very difficult for us. We had a very emotional season, and we were coming off the Ice Bowl win. We did not have a good week of practice before the game, and I remember by Thursday were still not ready to play."

Like many of the Packers, Nitschke was hurting physically. But one of Lombardi's favorite sayings had always been that "hurt is in the mind." That credo, which had helped Green Bay take the tough road to the top of the NFL in the 1960s, was called upon one final time.

"I had lost 10, 15 pounds from the flu," says Nitschke, who also had frostbitten feet from the Ice Bowl. "But I was going to be there [against Oakland] if I had to be there on a stretcher. The character of the Packers came through that year. We played every game for 60 minutes, we let it all hang out. There was no tomorrow for us. We got the adrenaline flowing, and we let it go, man."

What also got the Packers going was the realization that Lombardi was going to retire following the Super Bowl. Though their head coach had not yet announced his plans, there was an unspoken recognition among the Packers' players and staff that the game against the Raiders would be his last as head coach.

"Knowing that Lombardi was going to retire gave us an edge," Nitschke says. "That was extra motivation for us. We weren't going to get beaten by anybody."

The Raiders, like the Chiefs the year before, were well aware of the Packers' reputation for winning big games. Oakland quarterback Daryle Lamonica had been drafted by both the Packers and the Bills in 1963, but had opted to play in the AFL. Lamonica knew that facing the veteran Packers in the Super Bowl was going to be difficult for a Raider team that, while talented, was still maturing.

"We were a very young ballclub," Lamonica says, "and we were facing some old warhorses who could really put the leather to you. Nitschke, Dave Robinson ... those guys were solid. We weren't in awe of the Packers, but they had that mystique, and we respected that."

All-pro center Jim Otto was one of several Oakland players who had ties to the Green Bay area. Otto had grown up in Wausau, Wisconsin, and being an original Raider and a member of the AFL since its inception in 1960 made playing against his hometown team something special.

"I grew up in the Wisconsin area," Otto says, "and going up against a team from the great Vince Lombardi era was very exciting for me."

At approximately 3 P.M. on January 14, 1968, the Packers and Raiders took the decorated field of the Miami Orange Bowl under partly sunny skies and before a festive crowd of 75,546 and a national television audience. Unlike the year before, when the Packers seemed caught up in the event and did not settle down until halftime, Green Bay took control of the game from the outset.

Throughout the '67 season, the Raiders had run weakside sweeps with great success. It was a formula they believed would work against Green Bay too, and on the game's first play from scrimmage, Lamonica sent 230-pound fullback Hewritt Dixon around left end. Nitschke, who was to frustrate the Raiders all day, flipped Dixon heels-over-helmet for no gain. The Packers' defense had set the tone for the day.

On the Packers' first series of the game, Starr coolly directed his team on a nine-play, 34-yard march that resulted in Don Chandler's 39-yard field goal. When Green Bay got the ball back four minutes later, Starr continued to dissect the "Angry Eleven." With his almost instant recognition of Oakland's shifting defenses, Starr mixed his plays expertly, marching the Packers 80 yards in 16 plays from his own 3 to the Raiders' 13. From there, Chandler kicked his second field goal, a 20-yarder, and Green Bay's lead increased to 6–0.

"We had seen teams that played the Raiders' style of defense before," says Starr, explaining Green Bay's success in Super Bowl II. "Their alignments really didn't cause any problems for us."

Having consumed time and Oakland energy with two long drives, Starr crossed the Raiders up by striking quickly on Green Bay's next series. On first down from his own 32, Starr faked a handoff to halfback Travis Williams, turned, and threw to flanker Boyd Dowler, who was all alone at the Oakland 44. Dowler gathered in Starr's pass in stride, and the 62-yard TD gave the Packers a comfortable 13–0 lead.

On the verge of being blown out, the Raiders regrouped. For the first and only time in the game, Oakland's offense resembled the unit that had scored 468 points during the AFL season. Alternating between handoffs to his backs Dixon and Pete Banaszak and short passes to end Fred Biletnikoff and tight end Bill Miller, Lamonica drove his team 78 yards. On the Packers' 23, Oakland shifted into a double-wing formation whose intent was to flood the left side of the Packer defense. Miller slipped in between linebacker Dave Robinson and strong safety Tom Brown, caught Lamonica's pass at the 5, and just beat Brown to the flag.

The touchdown cut Green Bay's lead to 13–7, and the fired-up Oakland defense sacked Starr on Green Bay's next series and forced a punt. But just when it appeared the Raiders had climbed back into the game and would carry the momentum into halftime, an Oakland error gave control of the game back to Green Bay. Rodger Bird fumbled Donny Anderson's punt with 23 seconds left in the half, and Dick Capp, a former Boston Patriot, recovered it for the Packers at the Oakland 45. Starr hit Dowler with a 9-yard sideline pass at the Raiders' 36, and Chandler followed with his third field of the first half for a 16–7 Green Bay lead.

Just as they had against the Chiefs, the Packers put the Super Bowl away in the third quarter. Again, it was the Starr-to-Max McGee combination that did in the AFL. On third and one at the Green Bay 40, McGee slipped away from three Raider defenders to catch a 35-yard pass from Starr in the middle of the field. The first down kept alive Green Bay's 11-play, 82-yard drive. Starr moved the Packers to the Raiders' 1 when he rolled right and fired a comeback pass to Anderson. Two plays later, Anderson veered right and followed Jerry Kramer and Forrest Gregg into the end zone for a 23–7 advantage.

"We were a very basic team from the standpoint of fundamentals," Starr says. "I think that's a tribute to Coach Lombardi and his philosophy."

By the end of the quarter, Chandler, who retired after the game, kicked his fourth field goal, this a 31-yarder, and the Packers led by 19, 26–7. Midway through the fourth quarter, AFL fans began booing the Packers every time they broke the huddle. All-pro cornerback Herb Adderley put the exclamation point on the Packers' performance by stepping in front of Biletnikoff, intercepting Lamonica's pass, and returning it 60 yards for a touchdown.

To their credit, the outclassed Raiders never quit. Lamonica and Miller hooked up for one more score, a 23-yard pass down the middle, but all it did was close the scoring at 33–14.

Almost to a man, the Raiders looked upon their encounter with the Packers as a learning experience that would serve them well later on. This was true for Lamonica in particular, who kept a book in his locker entitled *Quarterbacking by Bart Starr*.

"After the game, I talked to Bart Starr at midfield," Lamonica says. "We shook hands, and he said, 'Daryle, you guys have a great team. You'll be back.' I think we probably should have tried some more things in that game. But I think we got just outfoxed in some areas."

In the aftermath of the Packers' overwhelming victory, the question of NFL superiority was raised again by fans and media alike. Raiders general manager Al Davis captured the true essence of the first two Super Bowls when he said the difference wasn't between the two leagues, it was between the Packers and everybody else.

With the impending retirement of Vince Lombardi and some of the Packers' key players, the balance of power between the leagues was shifting — ever so subtly.

Chapter Fourteen

1968: The Jet Age

IT WAS THE AGE OF AQUARIUS, and the psychedelic '60s were peaking. Throughout the decade, the forces of protest and Establishment had been on a collision course. In 1968, they vectored in a storm of violence across the United States and around the world.

In Chicago, 10,000 antiwar protesters clashed with police and national Guardsmen at the Democratic National Convention.

In Memphis, Tennessee, civil rights leader Martin Luther King Jr. was struck down by a sniper's bullet. In Los Angeles, Senator Robert F. Kennedy was assassinated.

In Watts, in Newark, in Washington, D.C., in some 125 U.S. cities in all, race riots erupted.

At Harvard, at Berkeley, at Columbia, and on numerous other college campuses across the country, students protested against U.S. involvement in the Vietnam War, burned their draft cards and often took control of office buildings to stage their stands. Unisex clothing and gold-chain necklaces were among the year's newest fads. By 1968, the term *Black Is Beautiful* was no longer a militant slogan. The Afro hairstyle was among the growing forms that many black people took to express pride in their culture. Artists like Peter Max and Isaac Abrams captured the essence of the pop generation with psychedelic creations.

As turbulent as 1968 was, the year closed on an up note. On December 21, a Saturn V booster carried U.S. astronauts William Anders, Frank Borman, and James Lovell into space, and the three men rocketed toward the moon aboard Apollo 8. The flight was history in the making, the first manned orbit of the moon. On Christmas Eve, the three men took turns reading from the Bible. On Christmas Day, with their eighth lunar orbit completed, they began their return trip home. Upon the successful completion of their voyage, a friend excitedly telegraphed Mission Commander Borman: "You have bailed out 1968!"

Following a second straight one-sided Super Bowl loss to the rival NFL, the AFL needed bailing out as well. In the week of Green Bay's domination of Oakland, Hamilton "Tex" Maule, the nation's premier football writer in the 1960s, laughed off the notion of the Super Bowl as a legitimate championship game.

"They can play for ten years," Maule wrote, "but the American League will never whip the NFL in a Super Bowl. The really big game of the year is the National Football League playoff. This is just anticlimax and it will be years before the Super Bowl is real competition."

Others followed suit. Marty Ralbovsky of the *New York Times* wrote: "There was little to justify the wasting of three hours to watch this Super Bowl game either in person or in front of television picture tubes.... Like the year before, it was a matchup of a good football team and a condescending one. It was questionable whether the American Football League would ever win one of these games. The Raiders, like the Chiefs before them, were not disgraced; on the other hand, neither were they overly combative. For two straight years, the Packers merely showed up and took the title home with them."

Jerry Izenberg, sports columnist for the *Newark Star-Ledger*, pointed out that in two years, the AFL had lost the Super Bowl by scores of 35–10 and 33–14. "The American League, therefore, over a span of two seasons, has cut the margin by six points," wrote Izenberg. "At their current rate of progress, the Americans should manage to get a tie somewhere around 1971."

The media's lack of respect and disparaging remarks about the quality of AFL football did not go unnoticed by AFL coaches and players. A growing resentment toward what AFL players like Kansas City quarterback Len Dawson regarded as the media's pro–NFL "propaganda" was felt throughout the American League. New York Jets cornerback Johnny Sample carried in his wallet a wadded bit of faded newspaper headline. It was dated January 16, 1967, the day after Super Bowl I, and read, in block letters, "LOMBARDI SAYS AFL INFERIOR."

"Probably all the publicity has been favorable to the National Football League," Dawson told an interviewer in response to a question about AFL inferiority. "I think that we're on an equal basis with the National Football League today, and I think that as soon as the American Football League wins a Super Bowl game, there isn't going to be this question."

Dawson's statement was issued in the summer of '68, when the AFL was laboring under the brand of an inferior league. Even the fact that AFL teams finished the 1968 preseason with a 13–10 edge over the NFL in interleague competition did little to dispel the notion among many that the AFL was a second-class league.

But the AFL's exciting brand of football and the ongoing emergence of star players and personalities continued to win over a new generation of football fans. By the end of the 1968 regular season, the AFL's regular-season attendance climbed to a league-record 2,635,004, a 14.8 percent increase over the 1967 figures.

One of those stars was New York Jets quarterback Joe Namath. Since he had burst upon the pro football scene with a megacontract in 1965, Namath had excited thousands of fans with his strong and accurate passing arm, and infuriated thousands more with his swinging lifestyle.

New York Jets quarterback Joe Namath hands off to halfback Emerson Boozer in a game against the Miami Dolphins. (*Photo courtesy of the New York Jets.*)

Namath opened 1968 in dramatic fashion, throwing two touchdown passes and then plunging 1 yard with 58 seconds left in the game to lead the East to a 25–24 win over the West in the AFL All-Star game. The game was played the week after Super Bowl II, and drew a record crowd of 40,103 in the Gator Bowl in Jacksonville, Florida.

With Vince Lombardi's retirement as head coach of the world champion Green Bay Packers, Namath became the dominant figure in pro football. In an era of black high-top cleats and crew cuts, Namath wore low-cut white shoes, long hair, and a drooping Fu Manchu mustache. Photos of him adorned in sun glasses and a $5,000 double-breasted mink coat contributed to Namath's rebel image. So, too, did his everyday dress. Namath was known to show up for Jets practices wearing violet-colored bell-bottoms, white sockless loafers, and flowered print shirts.

Consciously cultivating his "Broadway Joe" persona, Namath was the first white athlete to attack the stereotypes of his sport. Just as Muhammad Ali refused to be the modest, unassuming heavyweight champion that Joe Louis, Rocky Marciano, and Floyd Patterson had been, Namath shunned the noncontroversial public lifestyles that Johnny Unitas and Bart Starr led. Broadway Joe owned a gold cadillac and a Kelly green Lincoln, and his Manhattan apartment was famous for its leather bar, llama rug, and lovely young ladies. He was the subject of numerous Leroy Neiman sketches and paintings and appeared in ads featuring everything from boots to pantyhose. One ad in particular was memorable. Namath, in his Jets uniform, sat on a bench in front of his locker. The locker door, flung wide open, revealed a naked woman and a cooler of champagne.

In the generation gap that was the 1960s, Namath's honesty and unflinching candor made him pro football's rebel. He dressed in leather, starred in a movie with Ann-Margret, and owned a controlling share in an East Side bar called Bachelors III. Namath talked openly about his drinking and dating, and wrote a book that included a chapter entitled *I Like My Girls Blond and My Johnnie Walker Red.*

On the field, Namath's white shoes and strong arm set him apart from other quarterbacks. Stoop-shouldered and with oversized braces visibly supporting both knees, Namath was a picture of courage as he stood deep in the pocket, seemingly oblivious to the swirl of combat that surrounded him. His crystal-fragile knees prevented him from scrambling away from huge defenders, and he seemed to be in mortal danger every time he took the field. AFL audiences held their collective breath whenever Namath started back in one of his patented deep drops. His courage brought admiration from the game's old guard, and his quick release, which saw him spin tight spirals to streaking receivers downfield, was enough to excite even the purists. "Joe Namath," Vince Lombardi opined, "is an almost perfect passer."

Jets fans and the New York media succeeded in turning Namath into a cult figure. He became many things to many people. Though he hailed from western Pennsylvania, Namath made like a native New Yorker and became "Broadway Joe." To identify closer with some of his southern teammates, Namath drew on his college days at Alabama and called himself "Joe Willie."

Namath confounded his critics. Writer James Reston noted Namath's duality when he said that Namath represented both the Establishment and the counterculture. "He defies both the people who hate playboys and the people who hate bullyboys," said Reston. "He is something special: a long-haired hardhat, the anti-hero of the sports world."

Many football players felt the same as Reston. Jerry Kramer, an all-pro guard for the Green Bay Packers, said Namath at first seemed to be more style than substance. "When Namath first came into pro football, a lot of us didn't quite know what to make of him," Kramer said. "You have to understand, of course, that we lived under Lombardi and his Spartan concept for a long time. With that kind of a background, it was hard to accept Namath as a pro quarterback. You know, he went the Fu Manchu bit, the nightclub scenes, the chicks, the white llama rug. He seemed more of a showboat to us than he did an athlete. Of course, we never realized at the time that you could be both."

While the public wrestled with Namath's seeming duality, members of the AFL realized full well Namath's impact upon their product. "Namath made us," Oakland Raiders owner Al Davis said. Jets owner Sonny Werblin agreed. "Joe Namath was the most important man in football during the 1960s."

To a large part, the Jets followed Namath's lead. Teammates grew long hair, sideburns, and mustaches. The Jets' unshorn look became a symbol of the team's determination to make 1968 a championship season at Shea Stadium. Players vowed not to shave or cut their hair until the Eastern Division flag had been won.

Response to Namath and the Jets' decision to go unshorn was swift. AFL commissioner Milt Woodard wrote a letter to the Jets stating it was bad for football players to be identified with society's extremist elements. Lombardi told an interviewer that Namath "set back the image of football twenty years." Even FBI director J. Edgar Hoover became alerted to the situation. "You won't find long hair or sideburns à la Joe Namath here," Hoover said. "There are no hippies in the FBI."

The Jets organization reflected a number of changes in the 1968 off-season. On May 20, Werblin—whose show-business flair had not only helped make the Jets the number one team in New York but in so doing had saved the AFL—was bought out by his partners, Leon Hess, Phil Iselin, Don Lillis, and Townsend Martin for $1.6 million. The buyout was the end result of a bitter dispute Werblin had with his partners. Werblin had strongly opposed the 1966 merger with the NFL and flew into a rage when told of the $18 million in "territorial rights" the AFL would have to pay the NFL, $10 million would go to the Giants.

"Ten million dollars?" Werblin screamed at the time. "To the Giants? What for? I'm like Macy's, in competition with Gimbel's."

Jets ownership was also at odds over Namath. Werblin and Namath had cultivated a close relationship, but there were reports that Iselin and Martin resented Namath's longterm, high-salary contract. With Werblin's departure, Lillis assumed the presidency of the club. Lillis died on July 23, and Iselin was named team president August 6. Namath underwent surgery to repair a small tear in the tendon of his left knee. The Jets' late-season collapses in 1966 and 1967 caused many pro football experts to write the team off as title contenders. Some even suggested that Namath be traded, and that his reported run-ins with head coach Weeb Ewbank were tearing the team apart.

But many pro football observers, like Berry Stainback, the managing editor of *Sport* magazine, picked New York to win the AFL East. The Jets were coming off a solid 1967 season. Namath had become the first pro quarterback to throw for more than 4,000 yards in a season, and in George Sauer and Don Maynard he had the AFL's two leading receivers. Despite the loss of running backs Matt Snell and Emerson Boozer to injuries, the Jets had finished second in the East with an 8–5–1 record, their first winning season in franchise history. Setting records off the field as well as on, New York sold out all of their home games at Shea Stadium and set an AFL attendance record with 437,036 tickets sold for seven games.

The Jets opened their 1968 regular season in Kansas City, a game that proved to be one of the turning points in the Jets' greatest season. The game against the Chiefs was an early test for Boozer and Snell. The previous November, Boozer was enjoying his best campaign when a knee injury suffered in Kansas City's Municipal Stadium ended his season and started the Jets on a downward spiral that cost them the division title. Municipal Stadium was also an important testing ground for fullback Matt Snell. Like Boozer, Snell had ripped up a knee in the '67 season. If the Jets were to have a balanced offense in 1968, the health of Snell and Boozer was paramount.

On a sun-drenched afternoon, a record Kansas City sports crowd of 48,871—2,833 of whom paid $5 each to watch the game from a corner terrace—crammed Municipal Stadium. The Jets struck early when Namath took a deep drop and buggy-whipped a tight spiral that hit Maynard in stride on a deep crossing pattern.

The Jets led 17-3 at the half, but the Chiefs closed to within a point, 20-19, late in the fourth quarter. Following a Kansas City punt, the Jets took control at their own 5-yard line, in the shadows of their own goal post. Just over five minutes remained, and if the Chiefs' great defense could force the Jets to punt from their own territory, they would take over in field-goal range. Instead, Namath mixed his plays expertly, running off 15 plays and running out the clock. The key call was a third down slant-in from Namath to Maynard that carried for 16 yards and a critical first down. Over the game's final five minutes, Namath drove the Jets 72 yards in 15 plays, converting four third-down situations in a masterpiece exhibition of ball control.

"There was no way in the world I thought the Jets could go from the 5-yard line and maintain possession until the end of the game," Chiefs coach Hank Stram said.

For Namath, who had been named offensive team captain the day before the game, the victory over the Chiefs marked his emergence as a team leader. He connected on 17 of 29 passes for 302 yards and two touchdowns, and his command of the game was equally impressive. Namath's play calling on the Jets' final drive of the game was evidence of his transformation from a great passer to a great quarterback. Throughout the '68 season, Namath's deft play calling and strategic passing made him a shrewd diagnostician, and his evolution as a quarterback was evident when Namath went seven games without throwing a touchdown pass—and the Jets won all but one of those games.

Namath's maturation process depended heavily on the pass protection afforded by his offensive line, and in 1968 the Jets yielded the fewest sacks in pro football. Much of the success for the Jets' pass blocking can be traced to Chuck Knox, who served as an assistant to Ewbank from 1963 to 1967. Knox taught the Jets the technique of "spear blocking," in which linemen targeted an area on an opponent's body, took aim with their helmet, and then drove their opponent in the direction of the defender's momentum.

The most successful practitioner of Knox's methods was tackle Dave Herman. "My head is my number-one weapon," Herman said at the time. "That's where my strength is." Herman's neck measured 18½ inches, and his helmet — sized at 7⅞ inches — was the largest on the Jets. Herman used his head like a battering ram, and he developed a calcium ridge in the middle of his forehead. Namath once described Herman's pass-blocking method as "a machine gun going off into [a defender's] chest," and it was common for Herman to use up two to three helmets a year.

With his blockers forming a formidable shield, Namath coolly picked enemy defenses apart. Running off-tackle slants and sweeps, Snell and Boozer combined for over 1,000 yards rushing, and the Jets led the league in rushing touchdowns. Wide receivers Don Maynard and George Sauer and tight end Pete Lammons comprised one of the top receiving units in the game. On this trio of Texans, Maynard was the deep threat, a lanky end who used his speed to beat defenders on the Jets' most dangerous pass play, the deep post.

Maynard, along with Larry Grantham and Bill Mathis, was one of three Jets who were with the team when it started in 1960 as the Titans. Maynard had been a backup flanker with the New York Giants in 1958, but was cut the following year. Some said the reason the Giants cut Maynard was because they didn't approve of his sideburns, which were almost as long as his thoroughbred strides. But when Maynard passed Colts great Raymond Berry in 1968 as the all-time leader in receiving yards, Jets radio announcer Merle Harmon quipped, "I don't think Weeb cares how long [Maynard's] sideburns are."

Maynard played one year in the Canadian Football League, then joined the Titans. He was also contacted by Vince Lombardi, his former offensive coordinator on the Giants, who had become the head coach of the Green Bay Packers. But Maynard decided to go with the AFL.

"We had a lot of former NFL players in the AFL at that time," says Maynard, who was elected to the NFL Hall of Fame. "Most of the guys were former NFL players, and we had some outstanding guys just out of college. We had a lot of quality ballplayers. When we started in 1960, it was just like opening up a new business. We were going up against guys who had been in the business for 40 years. But I'll tell you what the AFL did. It gave 400 jobs to players, it gave 50 jobs to coaches, it gave 50 or 60 jobs to personnel people in the front office, and it gave teams to cities who couldn't get NFL teams."

While Maynard was the Jets' big-play man, Sauer was a great possession receiver who usually came up with the clutch catch. At 228 pounds, Lammons was a strong blocker, and his soft hands and good speed allowed him to run a clearing pattern underneath that freed Maynard and Sauer to work the outside and prevent double coverage from the safeties.

Defensively, the Jets were an undersized unit that relied on quickness and intelligence. Lou Michaels had played outside linebacker with the Cleveland Browns under Paul Brown, and he drilled the Jets in the importance of reading plays and filling gaps. Because of the Jets' relative lack of size up front, New York played an unconventional style of defense, a 4-4 stack and a pure 4-4. The Jets' 4-4 stack shifted to the strong side of the offensive formation, with middle linebacker Al Atkinson and the weakside outside 'backer, Larry Grantham or Ralph Baker, lining up behind the tackles. Though it was really a 4-3 alignment, the Jets gave enemy offenses a 4-4 look by walking a safety, usually the 210-pound Jim Hudson, directly behind the strongside linebacker.

"We use [the stack] because of the type of personnel we have," Michaels said at the time. "If I had some powerhouse 270-pounders at the defensive tackles, I might go with the 4-3."

The Jets' front four was led by left end Gerry Philbin. At 6-foot-2, 245 pounds, Philbin was New York's best pass rusher and one of the AFL's premier defensive linemen. He led the Jets with 19 quarterback sacks in 1968, the first of two straight all-pro seasons. He's also a member of the all-time AFL team. Intelligent, and with great instinct and determination, Philbin frustrated offensive linemen with an assortment of spins and fakes that left them out of position.

The rush of the front four, which finished third in the league in sacks, allowed Jet linebackers to drop deep into pass coverage. The elder statesman of the New York defense was Larry Grantham, one of the original Titans. Grantham was just 6-foot-0, 210 pounds, but he was such a student of the game that it was like having a coach on the field.

"I realized that because of my smaller size I had to be a little smarter, a little sharper," Grantham says now. "I studied films every night at home. I would try to see why the good linebackers were successful, how they were handling certain situations and certain players. I would also study the quarterbacks and their inclinations."

The Jets' secondary was an unlikely collection of four free agents who became starters. The glue that held the unit together was defensive captain and cornerback Johnny Sample. It was Sample who was responsible for signaling Jet coverages: a clenched fist was a blitz; two upraised fingers meant zone coverage to the weak side; three fingers meant a regular zone. Four fingers upraised meant the New York secondary would play a weakside "double-it," and five fingers called for a strongside "double-it." In Jets terminology, "double-it" called for a linebacker, defensive end, or cornerback to cover short on a flanking back or end.

Behind a high-powered offense and opportunistic defense, the Jets won seven of their first nine games to take a comfortable lead in the Eastern Division. In the West, the Oakland Raiders, Kansas City Chiefs, and San Diego Chargers engaged in a fierce race for a division title. On November 17, the Jets

1968: The Jet Age

headed to Oakland for a regular-season game that became the most famous in league history, and one that changed forever network television's policy toward pro football.

Because of the preponderance of good teams, the AFL's Western Division had built up intense rivalries, all of them involving the Raiders. "Everyone wanted to beat the Raiders," Oakland center Jim Otto recalls, "because everyone wanted to beat Al Davis."

Yet while the Raiders had rivalries with their Western Division neighbors, they had also developed a special rivalry with the Jets. The year before, the Jets had spoiled Oakland's perfect regular-season record by handing the Raiders their only loss of the season. Oakland responded later in the season by punishing Broadway Joe at the Coliseum; Ben Davidson sent Namath spinning to the turf, separating him from his helmet, and Ike Lassiter fractured Namath's jaw.

The Jets–Raiders regular-season showdown in November was considered the AFL's marquee matchup of the weekend. NBC, which owned exclusive rights to AFL games, considered the game such a ratings draw that it planned to cut away from the first game of the afternoon doubleheader, San Diego at Buffalo, so that a nationwide TV audience could view the Jets–Raiders game in its entirety. NBC executives also figured that since the Jets versus Raiders would make such good theater, it was a natural lead-in to the network's special presentation of Johanna Spyri's children's classic, *Heidi*, which was set to air promptly at 7 P.M. (EST). The show was preempting *Walt Disney's Wonderful World of Color* that Sunday evening.

A playoff atmosphere prevailed at the Oakland Coliseum as 53,318 raucous Raider fans stormed through the turnstiles. From the start, the game crackled with excitement and intensity. The hitting was savage. Namath was sacked six times, and once jackknifed in pain after being punched in the groin by Raider Dan Birdwell. New York fullback Billy Joe blew out a knee; Grantham had to be helped off the field after falling hard on his neck. Tempers flared and emotions reached the breaking point. Jet safety Jim Hudson was ejected from the game in the third quarter for unsportsmanlike conduct after screaming at field judge Frank Kirkland, who called Hudson for face-masking Hewritt Dixon. As Hudson left the field, he brought Raider fans to their feet by giving them the finger — on national TV. The Jets set team records by being penalized 13 times for 145 yards. *Five* of those New York penalties were for face-masking. In all, there were 19 penalties for 238 yards.

A 9-yard touchdown pass from Lamonica to Warren Wells gave the Raiders a 7-6 first quarter lead, and Oakland made it 14-6 in the second when Lamonica bombed the Jets defense with a 49-yard scoring pass to tight end Billy Cannon. New York countered on Namath's 1-yard touchdown run, but the missed extra point left the Raiders leading 14–12 at the half.

The teams traded scoring runs in the third; Bill Mathis carried it in from 4 yards out to give the Jets a 19-14 lead, but the Raiders regained the lead on a 3-yard run by Charlie Smith and a two-point conversion pass from Lamonica to Hewritt Dixon.

Ahead 22–19, the Raiders were driving for another score when the New York defense produced a big play. With the ball at the Jets' 3, linebacker Paul Crane, Grantham's replacement, forced a fumble from Charlie Smith and Philbin recovered.

With New York 97 yards from a score, Namath got them there in two plays. On first down, Namath dropped deep into his own end zone and hit Maynard for a 47-yard gain to midfield. One play later, Namath dropped back again and connected with Maynard for a 50-yard touchdown play. Jim Turner's third field goal of the game gave the Jets a 29–22 lead with 8:49 remaining. Lamonica rallied the Raiders again, finding Biletnikoff on a 22-yard touchdown to tie the score.

With Namath calmly controlling the clock, the Jets moved into position to win the game. Turner's fourth field goal, a 26-yarder, put New York ahead 32–29 with just 1:05 to go.

In New York, Julian Goldman, the president of NBC, glanced at his wristwatch; 7 P.M. was fast approaching. In the past, the TV coverage of regular-season football games had routinely been cut off if games ran over their allotted three hours. NBC had done it that very afternoon with the Chargers–Bills broadcast. Also, even though it was the Jets versus the Raiders, it was still AFL football, and NBC executives weren't sure just how many people would really be watching the game. *Heidi* was being sponsored totally by Timex, which had paid for the entire three-hour prime-time slot, so NBC's plans for the Jets–Raiders game called for a 7 P.M. cut-off, regardless of the situation.

Starting at 6:45 P.M., when it became clear that the game was going to run long, calls to the switchboard exchange at NBC Broadcast Operations Control were flooding in from viewers who were arguing either for or against the game staying on the air. Dick Cline, who was NBC Broadcast Control Supervisor in 1968, was on duty in New York that Sunday night. It was Cline's job to make sure each program got on the air as scheduled. NBC executives in New York tried to contact Cline but couldn't get through because the switchboard was jammed. Instead, they contacted the mobile unit in Oakland, and asked them to call Broadcast Operations directly. The call was placed and the message relayed, but Broadcast Operations countered that they needed direct orders from the NBC brass in order to rearrange the scheduled programming.

Cline, sitting in the NBC control center in New York's Rockefeller Center, was in the eye of a storm. Normally, a football game with a kickoff time of 4 P.M. on the East Coast would be over by 7 P.M. But Namath and Lamonica were locked in an aerial war that saw a combined 71 passes and a fourth quarter that in itself took 45 minutes to play.

From 6:45 to 7 P.M., more than 13,000 calls came in to the switchboard exchange concerning the game's long running time. The overload caused the switchboard to jam, and 26 fuses were blown in all. The game was being fed on telephone lines and not satellites, and Cline had no monitor to see what was happening in the final minute. With no official word from Goodman or any other exec, a beleaguered Cline stayed with the original plan and gave the order to change the programming. At 7 P.M. EST, in an NBC studio in Burbank, California, where the TV feed was being controlled, the switch was thrown.

Lamonica had just completed a 20-yard pass to Smith and the Jets had just picked up their fifth facemasking foul. The Raiders were at the New York 43, and 50 seconds remained in the game. There was a commercial interruption, and then the millions of viewers east of Denver who had been watching the Jets and Raiders were suddenly staring at Jennifer Edwards, the little girl who was starring in the title role of *Heidi*, yodeling to a herd of goats.

Outraged callers phoned NBC, other TV stations, newspapers, even the New York City Police Department's emergency number, trying to find out what was happening in Oakland. Those who flicked their radios on and tuned to WABC listened to the Jets' broadcasting team of Merle Harmon and Sam DeLuca describe the incredible action:

Fifty seconds remaining. Lamonica goes back to throw. Lamonica looking, Lamonica throwing.... He's got Charlie Smith on the twenty, down to the fifteen, the ten, five, touchdown!

Mike Eischied to kick off, and downfield comes the football.... He boots it on the ground, it's going to be fielded by Christy at the ten. He bobbles it and goes back to pick it up on the twelve. Christy ... is ... shaken, fumbles the ball! It is recovered ... by Oakland for a touchdown! The ball bounced into the end zone. It was recovered by Preston Ridlehuber for a touchdown!... Oakland has scored two touchdowns in nine seconds.... Thirty-three seconds left, the score Oakland 43, New York 32. An unbelievable finish.

Meanwhile, *Heidi* rolled on. As Klara, the paralyzed cousin, struggled to take her first, halting steps, the Raiders' 43–32 win over the Jets was displayed at the bottom of the screen. Amid the furor surrounding NBC's decision to cut away from the game, Goodman issued a public apology the next day. He called it "a forgivable error ... committed by humans concerned about the children.... I missed the end of the game as much as anyone else."

The lasting effect of the *Heidi* game was that it forever changed NBC's policy toward pro football. In 1975, the network put out a small fortune to promote another children's movie, *Willie Wonka and the Chocolate Factory*. But as the scheduled time for the movie to begin drew closer, the network's coverage of a game between the Raiders and Washington Redskins ran into overtime. Rather than risk another *Heidi* affair, NBC stayed with the game to the end.

The Raiders' dramatic win over the Jets came in the midst of an eight-game winning streak that allowed Oakland to end the regular season at 12–2 and tied with the Chiefs atop the West. Injuries prevented the Raiders from reaching the same level of excellence they had achieved the year before. Hit hardest was the defensive unit, where all-pros Tom Keating and Kent McCloughan were sidelined for sizable portions of the season.

With the defense in transition, the Oakland offense scored more points (453) than any other team in pro football. Leading the Raider attack was quarterback Daryle Lamonica. By 1968 Lamonica, like Namath, had matured into one of the top quarterbacks in pro football. A graduate of Notre Dame, Lamonica was chosen by both Green Bay and Buffalo in the 1963 draft. He recalls:

> I always was a Green Bay fan. Even at Notre Dame I sort of idolized that club, their style and their spirit. In some ways, they were a lot like Notre Dame.
> But when they drafted me, I started to think twice. After all, the Packers had Bart Starr at quarterback. He was already a top passer and was going to be around for a good few years. I figured Lombardi would put me on the bench and that would be it.
> Buffalo, on the other hand, seemed like an up-and-coming team, but one unsettled at quarterback. Jack Kemp had already joined the team, and he had experience. But I thought I'd have a better chance of playing behind him as opposed to Starr.

The decision to join the AFL is one Lamonica looks back on today with no regrets.

> I was drafted by Green Bay and Buffalo, and Green Bay called and told me, "We'll get back to you." But weeks went by and they never called. But the AFL people were calling me every day, talking about the pluses and minuses of the NFL and the upstart AFL.
> You know, I talked to Vince Lombardi at a Touchdown Club years later, and he said, "How come you didn't sign with Green Bay? Bart was hurt this year and you would've been my starter." I said, "You never got back to me." But what Vince told me about being a starter for him was the highest compliment I could have.
> I remember the first game I started in the AFL. We played the Boston Patriots, and they were bringing corner blitzes, safety blitzes. They were beating me before I could even set up.

Lamonica played sparingly in 1963, attempting just 71 passes, but the following year relieved Kemp in nine games and helped the Bills to a 12–2 record and an AFL title. Lamonica threw for 1,337 yards and six touchdowns in 1964, and Buffalo head coach Lou Saban didn't hesitate to use him whenever the offense appeared sluggish under Kemp. As Bills fans at War Memorial Stadium chanted, "We Want Lamonica," Daryle, who paced the sidelines restlessly when he wasn't playing, would stride in from the sideline like a relief pitcher coming in from the bullpen, and immediately begin fire-bombing enemy secondaries. Lamonica says:

Buffalo's an outstanding town, and the Bills fans at Memorial Stadium knew their football. I learned from Jack as his backup. Jack and I were always very close — he was my tutor. I'll tell you, Jack Kemp had one of the strongest throwing arms in history. He was a great influence on me.

Looking back, it was a benefit playing under Lou Saban. Lou was demanding, but he treated everybody on his team like men. Our philosophy under Lou was to win and lose as a team. Lou and Jack taught me how to win. And when I left Buffalo, I took that attitude to Oakland.

Among those who noticed Lamonica's contribution to the Bills' championships was Raider general manager Al Davis. Davis believed in a long-ball offense, and he liked Lamonica's deep, 9-yard set in the pocket, strong arm, and long strides when he threw. Davis often told confidants, "If we could just get that big kid away from Buffalo...."

Lamonica earned championship rings with the Bills in 1964–65, and following the '66 season was dealt to Oakland for quarterback Tom Flores and all-pro end Art Powell. Lamonica, who had been increasingly unhappy with his role as a backup, was hunting bobcat in the mountains near his Fresno home when he was told by a friend he had been traded to Oakland.

"I'm grateful to Lou Saban," Lamonica said. "He didn't throw me to the wolves. He brought me along slowly. I developed during my four-year education in Buffalo. But I'm also grateful to Al Davis for having the faith to trade for me and to John Rauch for having the faith to use me.... I always had confidence in myself and always felt that all I needed was the opportunity to prove myself."

Reaction to the trade was mixed. While some questioned trading an established starter like Flores for a backup like Lamonica, Kemp graciously told reporters Lamonica would "rise to the occasion" in Oakland. "As a matter of fact, Kemp said, "I think he'll lead the Raiders to a division title."

Lamonica proved the worth of Kemp's words in 1967, leading the Raiders to the best regular-season record in AFL history, a league championship, and a berth in Super Bowl II. He did it with an aggressive, go-for-broke attitude that had the Oakland offense always on the attack.

"I'm thinking end zone all the time," Lamonica said. "I think there's less risk in passing once for fifteen yards than three times for five yards each. I like to throw for the end zone. That's where the touchdowns are made. I throw to score. I only make one of three like that, but that one will beat you."

"Daryle gave our offense the confidence it needed," Raiders head coach John Rauch said. "Even when we were getting bad breaks, he kept his head and the offense moving."

Oakland coach John Madden agreed. "Daryle Lamonica was the perfect quarterback for the Raiders at that time," Madden told Dave Anderson. "He wasn't intruding on a team that was set. Instead he eased into a team that was being built, a team that went to Super Bowl II that season, a team that was starting a tradition of success. In those years, most teams used man-to-man defenses against the pass, not the zone defenses they went to later. With his strong arm, Daryle could throw against a man-to-man as well as anyone.... Daryle loved to throw deep."

One of Lamonica's teammates said the young quarterback threw deep too much. "He thinks he can throw a TD on every play. He's bomb crazy." ABC sportscaster Howard Cosell called Lamonica "The Mad Bomber," a nickname Lamonica learned to use to his advantage.

In his six seasons as a starter in Oakland, Lamonica threw 32 touchdown passes of 40 or more yards, and he twice threw more than 30 TDs in a 14-game season. It was his love of the long ball that made Cosell nickname him "the Mad Bomber." At first, Lamonica disliked the nickname because of its connotation of schoolyard ball. But the more he thought about it, the more Lamonica realized he could use his "Mad Bomber" title as a psychological weapon against defenses.

Lamonica would approach the line of scrimmage, look over the defense, and then lock eyes with a particular cornerback. If the cornerback started backpedaling, Lamonica knew he had him. Lamonica says:

> It was an exciting time. We were innovative in the AFL. We tried formations where you had both wide receivers on the same side of the field, we used spread formations. We brought the passing game more into play than the NFL did. AFL fans wanted to see the ball in the air, and we did throw the ball.
>
> Our long passing game on the Raiders came from Al Davis. He convinced me that the vertical game would work. He wanted to throw the ball downfield. Al was always looking for three, four big plays a game.

The downside to the deep passing game was that Lamonica had to hold onto the ball for that extra split second in the face of the defensive rush. On an average, quarterbacks had from 3 to 3.4 seconds to get rid of the ball. But Oakland's vertical passing game meant a later break for receivers, meaning Lamonica had to have the discipline to wait until the last possible moment before throwing. To compensate, he took a deep, 10-yard drop to give him clearance in the pocket to stride forward to throw.

"Al felt I was tough enough to stand back there and take it," Lamonica says. "And he thought I had the talent. That's why he traded for me."

Even today, the "Mad Bomber" can still throw a scare into old opponents. "I saw [Chiefs linebacker] Bobby Bell recently," Lamonica laughs, "and Bell said to me, 'You son-of-a-gun, you cost me a lot of sleepless nights.'"

Lamonica showed off his strong arm to the Chiefs in a special divisional playoff game December 22 in Oakland. Kansas City entered the game with a defense that set an all-time AFL record in 1968 by yielding the fewest points in a season—170. Their 18 touchdowns allowed tied the league record set the year before by the Oilers, and their four rushing touchdowns allowed tied the

Raiders quarterback Daryle Lamonica sets to throw despite pressure from New Jork Jets defensive end Gerry Philbin. (*Photo courtesy of the Oakland Raiders.*)

league record set by the 1964 Bills. The Chiefs held seven of their 14 opponents to single digits in scoring.

With a crowd of 53,605 on hand at the Oakland Coliseum, Lamonica stunned the Chiefs by throwing five touchdown passes — three in the first quarter — in a stunning 41-6 rout.

"The 'Mad Bomber,'" Chiefs quarterback Len Dawson said. "They named him right. He was going after it. He went back and unloaded that ball. He was going for broke on *every* play."

Lamonica and the Raiders were favored to repeat as AFL champions in 1968, and as game day for the league championship game with the rival Jets drew near, angry rumblings emerged from both sides.

"We felt like we didn't get a fair shake at Oakland," Jets linebacker Larry Grantham says. "It was a tough loss for us. But the thing was, Al Davis had been commissioner of the league, and a lot of the refs thought they owed their jobs to Davis. I think that game gave us a lot of initiative for when they came to New York. All we wanted to do was get the Raiders on *our* home turf."

The verbal sparring between the clubs intensified by midweek, when Davidson told reporters that Namath could expect more rough treatment. "He gets paid enough to get hit, doesn't he?" Davidson said. "On Sunday, we'll hit him again hard enough to let him know he's earning his money."

Ewbank knew the tough talk was aimed at getting the Jets to lose their poise, as they had in Oakland. As kickoff neared, the Jets' head coach urged his team to keep calm. "We have to keep our poise," Ewbank said. "Losing control is what the Raiders try to get you to do."

In their loss to the Raiders in Oakland earlier in the season, the Jets had been exploited at two key areas. On offense, rookie right tackle Sam Walton had a long day against Oakland defensive end Ike Lassiter. On defense, Jets cornerback Johnny Sample had been victimized for big plays by Fred Biletnikoff.

Ewbank and offensive line coach Joe Spencer decided to bench Walton and replace him with Dave Herman, whose normal position was guard. Randy Rasmussen, who had lost his left guard position to Bob Talamini, was inserted at right tackle. Defensively, Ewbank decided to stay with Sample, but he gave his cornerback a warning. "We want you to take the post pattern away from Biletnikoff," Ewbank said. "The first time he runs one against you, out you go."

Game day in New York was overcast and cold. Sunday, December 29, saw strong gusts from nearby Flushing Bay slash through Shea Stadium at a rate of 30–35 miles per hour, causing dirt and dust from the baseball infield to swirl upward in small tornado-like funnels and making it feel much colder than the 37 degrees that showed on the thermometer. Larry Fox, a sportswriter for the *New York Daily News*, said Shea Stadium felt like "a snowless version of the Russian front."

Ewbank, wearing a white and green baseball-style cap and a green vinyl jacket buttoned to the chin, studied the field during the pregame warmups. The baseball infield was slick with mud, and the area around home plate, which dipped at a slight angle and sat three feet lower than the rest of the field, offered uncertain footing.

Even more uncertain was the howling wind at Shea Stadium. Various nearby bodies of water and open spaces in the stadium caused the wind to blow in various directions down onto the field. The pregame warmups saw both Namath and Lamonica testing the unpredictable winds swirling through Shea. Off to one side, Don Maynard sprinted onto the field, helmet in hand, his trademark cutoff sleeves flapping in the wind. The Jets' deep threat had pulled a hamstring in his leg in the penultimate regular-season game against the Bengals. But with a trip to the Super Bowl just four quarters away, Maynard's focus was on the Raiders.

"That was the biggest game of my career," Maynard says. "We always had a tough time with Oakland, and that was a 'must-win' game. We had to win to get to the Super Bowl."

In order not to clash with the CBS telecast of the NFL championship game between the Baltimore Colts and Cleveland Browns in Cleveland, NBC scheduled the AFL title game to begin one hour earlier. With a packed house of 62,627 roaring their approval, Namath revealed New York's strategy on his first three passes of the game. Maynard had burned rookie cornerback George Atkinson in Oakland earlier in the year, catching 10 passes for 228 yards and one touchdown. The Jets began the championship game by testing the Raider rookie again; two of Namath's first three passes went in Atkinson's direction.

With 3:39 gone in the opening quarter, Namath put the Jets up first as Merle Harmon and Sam DeLuca called the action on WABC Radio in New York:

HARMON: *Namath back to pass on second down, throws for the end zone ... touchdown to Maynard!*

Later in the quarter, Namath led the Jets on another drive, culminating in a 33-yard field goal by Jim Turner that gave New York a 10–0 lead. With their long passes buffeted by the wind — Namath and Lamonica were a combined 6-for-27 passing in a first quarter that lasted 45 minutes — Lamonica switched to a short passing game. Forty-eight seconds into the second quarter, he found Biletnikoff on "91 Comeback," a short post pattern over the middle. Biletnikoff shook free from Sample at the 11 and outran Randy Beverley to the end zone. When Sample went to the sideline, Ewbank replaced him with Cornell Gordon. It was the first benching of Sample's career.

The remainder of the second quarter saw the Jets and Raiders trade field goals, giving New York a 13–10 halftime lead. In the New York locker room, Dr. James Nicholas, the Jets' team physician, examined Namath closely. On the series following his touchdown pass to Maynard, Namath dislocated the ring finger on his left hand after a collision with a Raider lineman. As Namath picked himself up off the sodden turf, Ike Lassiter stared at the Jet quarterback's left hand. "Look at your finger!" he shouted at Namath. Namath looked down and saw his ring finger bent in three different directions. On the sideline, team trainer Jeff Sneeker popped the disjointed finger back into place and taped it to the index finger. Namath's physical problems did not end there. In the second quarter, he suffered a jammed thumb on his throwing hand, and was left dizzy following hits by Lassiter and Davidson.

That Namath was not himself was evident on the Jets' first play of the third quarter. Taking the center snap, Namath stumbled backwards and fell for a 4-yard loss. While Namath regrouped, Lamonica went deep, connecting on a 37-yard completion to Biletnikoff and a 40-yarder to Warren Wells. With the Raiders at the New York 6, the Jet defense stiffened. Safety Jim Hudson keyed a great goal-line stand with three straight tackles, and the Raiders settled for a 9-yard Blanda field goal.

The Jets countered with an 80-yard, 14-play drive. With the ball at the Oakland 20 and the Raider defense standing in the mud of the baseball infield, Ewbank recalled the poor footing and uneven surface at that end of the field.

"How about a 'Q'?" he said to an assistant. "Run a guy into that soft stuff," Ewbank said, pointing to the field, "and then go go go to the sidelines."

Less than a minute remained in the third quarter when Namath, on third-and-10, rolled left from the Raider 20. He faked a handoff to Bill Mathis, and with Davidson in his face, spiraled a pass to tight end Pete Lammons at the 10.

HARMON: *Third-and-ten for New York.... Fake handoff to Mathis, Namath in trouble, throwing ... caught by Lammons at the ten, five, touchdown!*

Early in the fourth quarter, Lamonica found Biletnikoff deep for a 57-yard gain, highlighting a six-play drive that ended with Blanda's 20-yard field goal. With their lead cut to 20–16, the Jets went to the air on their next series. On first down, Namath aimed a pass at Maynard, who took eight steps up and cut for the sideline.

HARMON: *Namath throwing for Don Maynard ... it is intercepted by Atkinson at the thirty! Don to the twenty, he's down to the ten, the five, and he is knocked out of bounds.*

Namath shoved Atkinson out of bounds at the 4. One play later, Pete Banaszak's touchdown run gave the Raiders the lead for the first time at 23–20. On the Raiders' sideline, linebacker coach John Madden looked at the scoreboard, saw his team leading by three with 8:18 to play, and felt the sting of the icy winds inside Shea. He watched as Namath trotted onto the field, head bowed against the swirling dirt. "He can't throw against that wind," Madden thought.

With a first down at the New York 32, Namath stood at the line of scrimmage and saw Raider cornerbacks Atkinson and Willie Brown, playing seven yards off George Sauer and Maynard. Taking advantage of the Raiders' soft coverage, Namath threw a sideline pass to Sauer for a 9-yard gain. With a second-and-one, Namath called two plays in the Jets huddle. Earlier in the game, Maynard had told Namath, "I've got a long one when you need it." Namath figured the time was right.

"If they climb up to the line," Namath said in the huddle, "I'm gonna check off and I want maximum protection. Don's gonna get a step so be alert for the audible."

HARMON: *Namath dropping back to pass, he is looking, he is gonna throw long for Don Maynard and ... Maynard makes the catch down on the ten! He is dumped out of bounds on the eight-yard line. A great over-the-shoulder catch, Don Maynard against George Atkinson.... It is first and goal-to-go.*

Maynard's 52-yard catch down the right sideline was made despite near-perfect coverage from Atkinson, who ran parallel to Maynard on his left side. With Atkinson on Maynard's outside shoulder, Namath tried to lay the pass inside. But the ball had moved cross-wind as it came down, and Maynard found himself craning his neck and looking to his right to make the grab.

Larry Fox wrote later that Maynard and Atkinson "battled stride for stride like thoroughbreds down the stretch and Maynard had to make a great over-the-head baseball catch."

With a first down at the Oakland 6, Namath opted for a play-action pass. The Jets had been successful all afternoon with Snell running left on a weakside power play called "19 Option." Namath expected the Raiders to key on Snell, so he called "Nine Option," a play that began with a fake to Snell and was supposed to end with a pass to halfback Bill Mathis in the left flat.

The Raiders read the play, however, and only a great block by Snell on Oakland linebacker Gus Otto prevented a sack. What followed was a tribute to the Jets' line blocking and Namath's coolness under pressure.

Namath rolled left, looked for Mathis, but saw that Raider safety Dave Grayson had picked him up out of the backfield. Namath searched for Sauer, who was cutting across the middle from his left split end position, but Willie Brown was with him. Namath then looked to Lammons, who was running from right to left across the middle. But Lammons was covered as well.

Finally, Namath went to his *fourth* receiver on the play, Maynard. After being bumped by Atkinson off the line, Maynard pulled a little spin move, and drifted toward the goal line. When he saw Namath in trouble, Maynard sprinted for the back of the end zone. Namath set himself to throw, but suddenly felt his left leg give way underneath him. Namath recovered, and threw what he later called one of the hardest passes of his life. It was a bullet, a low line drive that Atkinson had no chance to react to. Maynard cradled it as he went to his knees in the end zone.

HARMON: *Here's a fake handoff to Matt Snell, Namath looking for the end zone, throwing ... touchdown to Maynard! Joe Namath throwing to Don Maynard ... he was not the intended original receiver.*

In just 31 seconds, Namath had moved the Jets 68 yards in three plays to the go-ahead score. "Joe Namath didn't worry about the wind at Shea any day," Madden said. "Joe threw the ball right through the wind. It didn't matter whether the wind was with him or against him. Joe just threw the ball."

The Jets now led 27–23, but Lamonica directed the Raiders on an immediate countering drive. The march stalled at the New York 26, and with a fourth-and-10, circumstances dictated that the Raiders try for a field goal, which would have cut the Jets' lead to one point with plenty of time remaining. John Rauch instead went for the first down.

HARMON: Almost 63,000 fans standing as Oakland is going to go for it. Fourth and ten on the 26 ... Lamonica calling the play, goes back to pass, he looks ... he is hit by Biggs and brought down at the 34!

"It was a key play," Grantham says, "when their coach decided not to take the field goal. It showed how much respect they had for Namath, because they must have figured they needed the points. Joe had proved Rauch right earlier by showing how quickly he could get the ball into the end zone."

Needing a touchdown to win, the Raiders rallied one final time. Lamonica, who threw for 401 yards on the afternoon, hit Biletnikoff and Wells with deep passes that cut through the gathering darkness. The ball was at the New York 13, with 2:20 left, when the Jet defense made the play of the season.

HARMON: Lamonica back to pass, throwing a swing pass ... he threw the ball behind Charlie Smith! It's covered by the Jets! Picking up the ball is Ralph Baker!

"I did not know it was a live ball," Smith said later. "It all happened so fast. You either react or you don't. I didn't."

"We wasted a play to get to that one," Lamonica says today. "We just didn't execute."

The fumble finished the Raiders. When the final gun sounded, Ewbank was hoisted onto the shoulders of players Steve Thompson and Mike D'Amato. The coach's right leg was wrenched by a young fan, and Ewbank's tears after the game were a mix of joy and pain. In the Jets' locker room, talk show host Johnny Carson got a champagne bath.

Jets offensive left tackle Winston Hill wore a broad grin following the game. Hill had battled "the Mustache," Oakland's defensive end Ben Davidson, throughout the long, cold afternoon, and had kept Davidson away from Namath. It was a performance that Hill, an all-pro, still relished 25 years later. In a 1993 interview, Hill said:

> I enjoyed pass protection. I would stay after practice and work with [defensive end] Verlon Biggs. When you're going against all-pros every day in practice, it's got to help you. My philosophy has always been that you have to *want* to be the best. The will to win is an individual thing. Chuck Knox, who had been my line coach with the Jets, destroyed a myth I grew up with, and that was "Practice makes perfect." Chuck said practice doesn't make perfect, you can practice something wrong for fifty years. He said perfect practice makes perfect.
>
> Pass protection was something we prided ourselves on. We had a quarterback in Joe Namath who couldn't run. So we had to be the best when it came to pass blocking.
>
> When we played Oakland, Ben Davidson always complained a lot. He gave a hundred percent, but he did some things that were questionable. He would grab my facemask and kick me at the same time. Then he would complain that I was holding him.

That AFL title game in '68 was the critical game for us. It was the scariest game I ever played in. We almost blew it. After that, the Super Bowl was almost anti-climactic.

It's not remembered now, but Hill, not Namath, was the first Jet to publicly guarantee a victory in Super Bowl III. Moments after the AFL title game, Hill was interviewed by Sam DeLuca in the Jets' lathery locker room.

"Are the Jets going to win that Super Bowl?" DeLuca asked Hill.

"Yes, we are."

On a dais in front of the TV cameras, Ewbank cradled the game ball as he stood answering questions from NBC color commentator Charlie Jones. "Right now," Jones said, "Baltimore is leading in the NFL."

Namath asked a reporter, "What's the score now?"

"17–0."

Namath smiled. "I guess it'll be Baltimore."

Chapter Fifteen

Super Bowl III: Joe Guarantees It

TO MOST PRO FOOTBALL FANS, Super Bowl III shaped up as a mismatch. Although the NFL no longer had Vince Lombardi's magnificent Green Bay Packers lining up for them, the Baltimore Colts were being considered by some experts as one of the great teams of all time.

Despite the loss of legendary quarterback John Unitas to arm problems, the Colts had cruised through the regular season with a 13-1 record, their only loss a 30-20 decision at home against the Cleveland Browns. In the NFL playoffs, the Colts had left Joe Kapp and the upset-minded Minnesota Vikings in the sleet and mud of Memorial Stadium, then rematched with the Browns in the NFL championship game. On a cold, dark December afternoon in Cleveland, the Colts played a nearly flawless game, holding NFL rushing leader Leroy Kelly to 28 yards and routing the Browns 34-0.

The shutout was the fourth of the season for the Baltimore defense, which tied an NFL record by allowing just 144 points all season. On the team's season highlight tape, Colts announcer Chuck Thompson described the Baltimore defense as "invincible, flawless, and superb ... the main reason for bringing an NFL championship back to Baltimore."

Head coach Don Shula and defensive assistants Bill Arnsparger and Chuck Noll fashioned a fearsome unit that featured all-pro caliber players Bubba Smith, Mike Curtis, and Rick Volk in shifting alignments. The Colts confused NFL offenses with a rotating zone and an eight-man maximum blitz and paved the way to a Western Division title.

With Unitas sidelined, the Colts relied on Earl Morrall, a journeyman quarterback who enjoyed a Horatio Alger season in 1968. Morrall summoned up every ounce of his poise and skill to post an MVP season. Morrall presided over a strong supporting cast that included tough inside runners Tom Matte and Jerry Hill, veteran receivers Jimmy Orr and Willie Richardson, and a solid offensive line.

As a unit, the Baltimore offense, coached by Don McCafferty, was solid but unspectacular. Baltimore's only true game-breaker was at tight end, in the person of all-pro John Mackey. At 6-foot-1, 250 pounds, Mackey combined lineman's size with wide receiver's speed. The Colts' highlight film shows Mackey taking short passes from Morrall and running over linebackers and defensive backs alike on long runs to the end zone.

Baltimore's great defense and the outstanding numbers put up by Morrall and Mackey led Las Vegas oddsmaker Jimmy "The Greek" Snyder to list the Colts as 18-point favorites, the largest spread in Super Bowl history. According to Glenn Ressler, Baltimore's starting left guard, the Colts felt the oddsmakers were right on target.

"I certainly think we underestimated a lot of the talent on that Jets team," Ressler says. "They had a good team, and we took them too lightly. We felt the AFL wasn't on par with us. Green Bay had handled their teams pretty easily in the first two Super Bowls, and we had scrimmaged AFL teams in the preseason. We felt like they weren't on our level."

The Colts' training camp in Boca Raton, the same site the Oakland Raiders had used the year before in Super Bowl II, reflected the relaxed attitude of the Baltimore players. During the 1968 season, the Colts had dispatched the NFL's strongest teams — the Rams and Vikings twice each, the Packers, and the Browns — and it was hard to convince Baltimore's veterans that the AFL Jets could succeed where the NFL's best had failed.

Earl Morrall told reporters that a close win by the Colts would represent a moral victory for the Jets. Defensive tackle Billy Ray Smith, a 12-year veteran whose quick moves earned him the nickname "Rabbit," said while Baltimore's defense respected Joe Namath, the Colts' sophisticated alignments — which featured 20 variations of blitzes and five different fronts — would give the Jets' young quarterback problems.

"The man can throw a football into a teacup at fifty yards," Smith said of Namath. "But he hasn't seen defenses like ours in his league. Our defenses are as complicated as some team's offenses.... I think reading our defenses will be a new experience for the man."

After gunning down the Raiders in the AFL title game, Namath took aim on the Colts. In a maneuver that some writers likened to Kansas City cornerback Fred "the Hammer" Williamson's carnival-barking before Super Bowl I against the Packers, Namath took some public potshots at the Colts. He told *New York Times* sportswriter Dave Anderson there were four or five quarterbacks in the AFL who were better than Morrall — including his backup, Babe Parilli.

"I said it and I meant it," Namath said. "You put Babe Parilli with Baltimore instead of Morrall and Baltimore might be better. Babe throws better than Morrall."

Namath's comments, naturally, were relayed to the Colts' camp. While Morrall shrugged them off — "Joe's getting his newspaper space," he said — Shula did not.

With his face reddening and the veins in his neck protruding, Shula said, "I don't know how Namath can rap Earl.... Anyone who doesn't give him the credit he deserves is wrong. But I guess Namath can say whatever the hell he wants."

On the Thursday before the game, Namath headed to a banquet at the Miami Springs Villa, where he was to receive the Miami Touchdown Club award as the "Outstanding Football Player of 1968."

As Namath made a few remarks, a voice from the back of the room yelled, "Siddown!" Namath brought a laugh from the crowd when he remarked, "Must be a Colts fan."

The fan retaliated with a comment about what the Colts would do to Namath Sunday, and for a brief moment, Namath's mood darkened. Tired of being run down by NFL partisans, Namath shot back, "We're going to win Sunday. I *guarantee* it!"

The next morning, the *Miami Herald* ran a banner headline in its sports section that read, "Namath Guarantees Jet Victory."

"I could've shot him," says Weeb Ewbank, the Jets' head coach in Super Bowl III. "Some people were talking like the Colts were going to have a dynasty, but with Joe's quick release and our two great receivers, George Sauer and Don Maynard, we thought we could lick their defense. But we didn't want to say anything before the game."

Jets linebacker Larry Grantham had been a member of the New York franchise since their Titan days in 1960. Grantham was one of the Jet players unhappy with Namath's prediction.

"I don't like Doberman dogs," Grantham says today, "but I'm not going to walk into the room and kick the son of a gun in the mouth. And that's what I felt Joe had done. I know Weeb was really upset about it."

Throughout the Jets' preparations, Ewbank stressed the need for his team to keep its poise. The Jets boss felt Kansas City and Oakland had allowed Green Bay's mystique to rattle them in the first two Super Bowls. It was a situation Ewbank wanted to avoid against the Colts.

"Green Bay was head and shoulders above everybody else in the National League," Grantham says. "They were the dominant team of their time, but I went to those first two Super Bowl games, and I didn't think that Kansas City or Oakland played up to their potential. I think they felt the pressure of those games."

The differences between the team personalities of the Jets and Colts, the differences in the leagues they were representing, and the differences in the individual players caused some people to draw sociological lines around the Orange Bowl on Super Sunday, January 12. The '60s marked the Age of Aquarius, a time when the country was divided into young and old, black and white, the Establishment and the counterculture.

Those differences crystallized on Super Sunday. Simplistic as it was, many felt that the Colts represented the NFL, the 49-year old Establishment. The Jets were the upstarts, representatives of the new order, the nine-year old AFL.

Game day in Miami was overcast and cool, and the threat of rain hung in the air as the two teams assembled on the field before a crowd of 75,377. With NBC providing exclusive television coverage of the event, legendary sportscaster Curt Gowdy, the Oklahoma cowboy, was on hand to provide the play-by-play, with assistance from Al DeRogatis and Kyle Rote.

"Super Bowl Three is still the most memorable sports event I've ever done," Gowdy says today. "Not the best one or the most exciting, but the one that had a real impact on America. I remember I saw Howard Cosell in the press box before the game, and he says to me, 'Cowboy, the Colts are going to break Joe Namath's legs.'"

Gowdy wasn't so sure. He knew the Jets had a strong passing attack and solid defense. So, too, did Vince Lombardi. The former Packers coach confided to reporters that the Jets' offense was good enough to give the vaunted Colt defense some problems.

The Jets knew it, too.

"When Joe sat down and analyzed Baltimore's films, he knew he was going to get us some points," Grantham says. "The Colts beat people because their defense caused a lot of breaks. But I thought Joe would get us 21 or 30 points. That's how confident we were."

The Jets took the opening kickoff, and it took just two plays for New York to do something no NFL team had done all season — establish a running game against the Colts' great defense. On first down at his own 23, Namath went to an unbalanced line and sent fullback Matt Snell off left tackle for 3 yards. On the next play, Snell headed left for 9 more yards and knocked Colt safety Rick Volk out of the game with a mild concussion. The Jets' running game, which had received little recognition before the game, had earned the respect of the Colts.

The Jets' first drive stalled at their own 43, and following Curley Johnson's punt, the Colts took over at their own 27.

Baltimore's opening drive was their most impressive of the day. On first down, Morrall hit Mackey on a screen, and the big tight end ran over two Jets en route to a 19-yard gain. Matte swept right for 10 yards, and Hill headed left for 7 more. The Jets were cursing themselves in their defensive huddle. Morrall's 15-yard pass to backup tight end Tom Mitchell put the Colts at the New York 19.

But Baltimore's placekicker, left-footed Lou Michaels, missed a 27-yard attempt. It was the first of several scoring opportunities the Colts failed to capitalize on in the game.

Near the end of the first quarter, Namath found Sauer with a short pass, but Colts veteran cornerback Lenny Lyles forced a fumble, and linebacker Ron Porter recovered at the Jets' 12. At the start of the second quarter, Matte picked up 7 yards. One play later, Morrall dropped back, but his quick pass to Mitchell was tipped by linebacker Al Atkinson, bounced off Mitchell's pads, and was intercepted by cornerback Randy Beverly.

Though he failed to record a catch in Super Bowl III, New York Jets Hall of Fame wide receiver Don Maynard, shown here catching a pass out of bounds against Baltimore Colts safety Rick Volk, was instrumental in the Jets' 16-7 upset win. (*Photo courtesy of the New York Jets.*)

The turnover, Baltimore's second of the game, sparked the Jets' offense. Starting at his own 20, Namath revealed New York's disciplined game plan. Contrary to what the experts had predicted, the Jets planned a weakside attack, running and throwing against the Colts' left side. Snell started the drive with four consecutive weakside runs totaling 26 yards. Namath followed with consecutive passes to Sauer for 25 yards. A 12-yard pass to Snell moved the ball to the Baltimore 9.

On the Jets' sideline, Ewbank looked on with satisfaction. "Our game plan was beginning to take shape," he said. "Joe was mixing his plays beautifully."

Snell ran left on first down for 5 yards, then left again on "19 Option" for the Jets' touchdown. The score climaxed an 80-yard, 12-play drive that consumed more than five minutes off the clock. Jim Turner's extra point gave the Jets a 7–0 lead—the first time in Super Bowl history an AFL team was ahead.

On New York's WABC Radio, Jets broadcaster Merle Harmon called the action for his listeners:

Second down and goal-to-go for New York ... Namath on a handoff to Matt Snell. Snell at the five, Snell at the three, Snell touchdown! Matt Snell in the end zone on a wide sweep to the left! He shook Rick Volk at the five-yard line and banged into the end zone where Lenny Lyles hit him, and this crowd is up and standing and yelling as the Jets have drawn first blood!

The Colts countered immediately. Morrall and Matte connected on a 30-yard pass play, but Baltimore missed another scoring opportunity when Michaels' 46-yard field goal was no good. On the Colts' next series, Matte ran through a tackle by Jet safety Jim Hudson and bolted 58 yards down the sideline to put Baltimore in scoring position again, this time at the New York 16. But two plays later, Morrall was intercepted a second time when his pass to Willie Richardson was picked off by John Sample at the Jets' 2.

Forty-three seconds remained in the first half when the Colts got the ball back again. The Baltimore defense, which had allowed only seven touchdowns in the previous 10 games, was doing its part. The high-powered Jet offense had been held to just seven points in the first half, despite two Colt turnovers. But the Baltimore offense, which had scored 61 points in its two previous playoff games, continued to drown in two feet of water.

From the New York 41, the Colts went to the flea-flicker play. Morrall handed to Matte who headed right, stopped, and tossed the ball back to Morrall. The play was designed specifically for split end Jimmy Orr, and had worked earlier in the year for an easy touchdown against the Atlanta Falcons.

Game films show Morrall taking a quick look downfield for Orr, who was so all alone at the Jets' 10 he was waving his arms. But Morrall instead turned and threw to fullback Jerry Hill, who was slanting over the middle. Hudson leaped in front of Hill at the 12, intercepting the ball and returning it to the 21 as time expired.

Shula, dressed in a Colt blue windbreaker, couldn't believe his team's first-half performance. Baltimore's precision offense, which had looked so devastating in the icy climes of Cleveland just two weeks before, looked snakebitten against the Jets. Poor play, bad breaks, and New York's opportunistic defense all combined to frustrate the Colts in the first half of Super Bowl III.

"Dammit," Shula hissed to an assistant. "The flea-flicker is designed for Orr. What in hell is happening?"

Ewbank had little trouble understanding the first half. The Jets were playing solidly on both sides of the ball. Their offensive game plan, ironically, had an NFL look to it. The Jets were emphasizing the simplest of running plays — the off-tackle fullback slant. Namath was beating the Baltimore blitz with his quick release, and he took advantage of the Colts' double-teaming of speedy Don Maynard by throwing basic hook and turn-in passes that punctured the Colts' rotating zone.

"We had been able to run and pass well during the first half," Ewbank said, "and I felt no need to change our game plan for the final 30 minutes. Baltimore's vaunted blitzes had been negated by Joe's quick wrists and the favorable reactions of our receivers. Furthermore, if the Colts continued to double-team Maynard, Joe could go to other targets as he did so successfully in the first two periods. I was proud of our defense. If they could just match their first half performance, Baltimore would not be able to beat us."

The game's turning point came on the Colts' first series of the second half. Shula's fiery pep talk had stirred the Colts, and Baltimore came out ready to exact revenge for their first-half humiliations. But on Baltimore's first play from scrimmage, Matte fumbled after being hit by defensive end Verlon Biggs, and linebacker Ralph Baker recovered for New York on the Colts' 33. Turner followed with a 32-yard field goal and a 10-0 lead. From that point on, the game belonged to New York.

On the Jets' next drive, Namath marched his team 45 yards in 10 plays, and Turner kicked his second field goal, a 30-yarder, for a 13-0 lead.

The Colts were shaking their horseshoed helmets in disbelief. Namath was becoming the dragon slayer just as he had guaranteed. He strode to the line of scrimmage in his white uniform and white shoes, read the Colts' shifting defenses, and time and again picked them apart with weakside handoffs to Snell or precision passes to Sauer. Through it all, Merle Harmon continued to describe the unbelievable upset as it unfolded:

Namath, back to pass, Joe looking, throwing ... and it's completed on the 47-yard line to Sauer....

Namath calling signals, goes back to pass, he throws over the middle to Lammons, slant-in, he's got the ball at the 40-yard line....

Namath, back to pass on third down, throwing up the middle to Sauer ... leaping catch at the 25! And it's another first down for the New York Jets.

As dusk settled over Miami, the huge Orange Bowl crowd erupted as Baltimore's familiar Number 19 trotted out to the Colts' huddle. Though his famous passing arm was little more than a memory, John Unitas still owned a fighting spirit and a champion's heart.

"I knew I couldn't throw a long pass," Unitas said, "but I figured we could still score if I could get a short one in the right place."

Unitas' first two passes both fell incomplete, and the third quarter ended with the Jets in control and their confidence growing.

"I saw [Unitas' wobbly passes]," Grantham said, "and I figured it was over. We had stopped Unitas. What else did they have?"

Two minutes into the fourth quarter, Turner kicked his third field goal of the game, a 9-yarder, and the Jets' margin was 16 points. Unitas responded by moving the Colts to the New York 25, but his end zone pass to Orr was a weak floater that ended up in the arms of Beverly, the Jets' fourth interception of the game.

Midway through the final quarter, Unitas finally recaptured the magic that had made him football's all-time quarterback. Suddenly it was 1958 again, and Unitas drove his team across the darkening field of the Miami Orange Bowl to the Jets' 1-yard line. Hill cracked the end zone, and the Colts had cut their deficit to 16-7 with 3:15 remaining.

When Tom Mitchell recovered Lou Michaels' onside kickoff at the Jets' 44, the Orange Bowl crowd stirred. Unitas was back on the field, and memories of Unitas engineering Colt comebacks in past years shimmered into the minds of many, including Unitas' ex-coach.

"With Unitas," said Ewbank, "even an ailing Unitas, anything could happen."

Anything almost did. Unitas fired three straight completions to move the Colts to the New York 19. Three incompletions followed, and the Colts faced a fourth-and-five situation that meant the game. Shula opted for the first down rather than the field goal, and Harmon called the decisive play of Super Bowl III:

Fourth down for Baltimore. Unitas back to pass, the rush is on, Johnny U. throws ... it is tipped and knocked away by Larry Grantham! Intended for Jimmy Orr, and the Jets take over. Two minutes and twenty-one seconds left to play in this ballgame as Larry Grantham takes off his helmet and throws it high into the air.

"We had won the ballgame," Grantham said. "Nobody could take it from us. Nobody. Not even the great Johnny Unitas."

Namath was named game MVP for his masterful play calling and precise passing. The Jets quarterback completed 17 of 28 passes for 206 yards, and he kept the Colts' defense off balance and the Colts' offense off the field with time-consuming drives.

After the game, Namath was approached by NBC announcer Kyle Rote, the former New York Giants star.

Toweling off his face, Namath smiled at Rote. "Welcome," the Jets quarterback said, "to the AFL."

Few games have a profound and lasting effect on their sport, but Super Bowl III is one of the benchmarks of pro football history. Because it helped legitimize the American Football League in the eyes of many fans, the game has been recognized as one of the most important ever played.

At the time of their victory, however, few of the Jets realized what they had accomplished.

"The long-range effect of that game, the historical aspect of the impact it had on the game of football, we didn't realize any of that at the time," said Jets offensive tackle Winston Hill, who opened the holes that helped Snell gain a then-record 121 yards rushing on the day. What I remember most about that Jets team was what a great group of guys we had. We were always together, and that's what I enjoyed. Being with friends."

Chapter Sixteen

1969: A Wild West Show

THE IMPACT OF SUPER BOWL III on pro football was immediate. The New York Jets' startling win over the 18-point favorite Baltimore Colts is generally regarded as the greatest upset in sports history. But as pro football historian Robert Smith wrote in *The Illustrated History of Pro Football*, the Jets' win was more than just an upset.

"It altered the whole aspect of professional football," Smith wrote. "Now it was clear that the leagues were at last on a par."

To this day, NFL Commissioner Pete Rozelle refers to Super Bowl III as the "Magic Game." After overwhelming victories by the Green Bay Packers in the first two AFL–NFL championship games, the Super Bowl had not been recognized as a legitimate title game; the NFL championship game was considered to be the *real* championship. But the Jets' win in Super Bowl III legitimized both the AFL and the Super Bowl. Rozelle believes it made the Super Bowl game a permanent part of the American sports and entertainment consciousness.

"It didn't take a brain surgeon to figure out that the Jets' victory was going to mushroom interest in our game," Rozelle said. "At that point, the merger that would be implemented after the next season was all set. By winning, the Jets proved the AFL teams belonged."

In the spring of 1969, AFL and NFL owners began a series of marathon meetings that stretched from Palm Springs to New York to decide on realignment for the 1970 season. Because the NFL had 16 teams and the AFL only 10, it was necessary for three of the NFL teams to join the new American Football Conference in 1970. The NFL owners' attitude toward the realignment was summed up by Minnesota Vikings owner Max Winter.

"I'm going to do everything possible to stay with my NFL friends," Winter said. "This is the biggest fight of my career."

Throughout the first two meetings, not a single NFL owner volunteered to move his club to the AFC. Dallas Cowboys president Tex Schramm said the gridlock was due to the polarization that occurred when all 26 owners were together in one room. "That makes agreement almost impossible," Schramm said.

To break the deadlock, Rozelle met privately with various NFL owners. The third owners' meeting began Wednesday morning, May 7, in the National Football League offices at 410 Park Avenue. Frustrated by the lack of progress on the realignment issue, Rozelle opened the meeting with a declaration:

"This," he stated, "is going to be the final meeting on realignment. We're going to stay here until we get it done."

Rozelle ordered pillows and blankets to be delivered to NFL offices. Only the NFL's elderly owners — George Halas of the Bears and Art Rooney of the Steelers — were allowed to return to their rooms. The rest of pro football's owners slept on couches, desks, and floors in the NFL offices. Negotiations dragged on. The final sessions required owners and general managers to go 35 hours and 45 minutes without sleep to reach an accord. Finally, an agreement was reached in which the Colts, Browns, and Steelers would move to the AFC in 1970.

Sixteen days after the realignment was announced, ABC signed a contract with the NFL to do *Monday Night Football,* scheduled to begin in 1970. The deal marked pro sports' invasion of prime time. For the first time ever, a regularly scheduled series of sports events would be available to viewers during prime network hours.

The merger agreement reached between the AFL and NFL in 1966 allowed for separate TV schedules through 1969. CBS continued to broadcast NFL games; NBC remained the standard-bearer for the AFL. The NFL offered *Monday Night Football* to ABC because it was the lone major network that had no contract for pro football. ABC had been the AFL's original network from 1960 to 1964. By 1969, ABC was in the midst of one of its worst years ever, having lost $20 million due to a combination of programming problems and an economic crunch. The NFL and ABC reached agreement, and ABC's first Monday night game matched the Jets and Cleveland Browns on September 21, 1970, in Cleveland's Municipal Stadium.

On June 6, nearly six months after leading the Jets to a Super Bowl title, Joe Namath stood before a battery of microphones in his Bachelors III restaurant-bar on Lexington Avenue in New York City and told reporters he was quitting football rather than sell his interest in the bar.

Bachelors III was a small bistro located in the heart of Manhattan. Originally known as "the Margin Call," the bar was purchased in the spring of 1968 by Namath and friend Ray Abruzze. Because Namath, Abruzze, and restaurant manager Bobby Van were all single, they decided to name the establishment "Bachelors III."

As Namath's popularity and celebrity increased, Bachelor's III became one of the city's "in" places to go. Frank Sinatra and Johnny Carson were among the celebrities who frequented Bachelors III. The year before, Rozelle began receiving reports from the NFL's security police that alleged gamblers were frequenting Bachelors III. On Tuesday, June 3, 1969, Namath was at the New York Football Writers' dinner at the Waldorf-Astoria when he was approached

The 1969 season marked the AFL's final year of existence. In this AFL–NFL exhibition game, Boston Patriots defensive linemen Jim Hunt (79) and Larry Eisenhauer (72), who played together from 1961 to 1969, rush Atlanta Falcons quarterback Randy Johnson. (*Photo courtesy of the New England Patriots.*)

by Phil Iselin, one of the Jet owners, head coach and general manager Weeb Ewbank, NFL security agent Jack Danahy, and an unidentified FBI agent. Namath was told that New York City police were going to raid Bachelors III and close it down.

The next day, Namath and his two attorneys, Jimmy Walsh and Mike Bite, met with Rozelle in Rozelle's Manhattan apartment. The meeting lasted from

2 P.M. to 7 P.M. "We got to know each other," Rozelle said. "We talked about everything, not just professional football."

"Rozelle and I respect each other," Namath replied. "He thinks I'm a helluva passer and I think he's the best commissioner in pro football."

To friends, Namath said Rozelle had ordered him to sell his share in the bar in two days or be suspended from football. Walsh and Bite immediately argued that Namath couldn't possibly sell his share in just two days; the approval of the sale by the State Liquor Authority would take longer than two days. Rozelle said that Namath had to take the first step toward selling the bar within the next two days.

Though he felt compelled to resist Rozelle's ultimatum as a matter of principle, Namath knew that suspension from football could cost him up to $5 million — from his Jets contract, which still had two years remaining on it, as well as from endorsements and commercial possibilities. "Sell, man," Abruzze told Namath. "It's the only smart thing to do."

That night, as he attended the grand opening of teammate Gerry Philbin's restaurant in Long Island, Namath had changed his mind. He told some of his teammates at Philbin's restaurant he would retire rather than sell his bar. Namath called a press conference for 9:30 A.M. the next morning at Bachelors III. Making his way to the back of the restaurant, Namath sat down at a table and was flanked by Frank Gifford and Kyle Rote. On the opposite side of the table sat Howard Cosell.

"I'm not selling," Namath said tearfully. "I quit. They said I'm innocent but I have to sell. I can't go along with that."

Sportswriter Murray Olderman called Namath's action a rebellion against authority. "It's really the biggest sports story of the summer in its pervasiveness," Olderman wrote, "with rangier social implications."

Namath's retirement lasted just over a month. On July 18, a compromise was announced that allowed Namath to return to the Jets and still retain the right to invest in other restaurants around the country. He also gained the right to sell Bachelors III to anyone approved by the State Liquor Authority.

Namath's return to pro football all but insured the Jets of a second straight Eastern Division championship. With its explosive passing attack keying one of pro football's best offenses, New York was easily the best team in its division.

The Jets' offense in 1969 continued to be based on a three-pronged attack: the weakside running game, short outs to George Sauer, and deep posts to Don Maynard. The quality of New York's attack was evident by the fact that four of its stars, Namath, Maynard, Matt Snell, and Winston Hill, were named to the AFL's all-pro team in 1969.

The Jets clinched their second straight Eastern Division title by beating the rival Oilers 34–26 in Houston on Saturday, December 6. New York's defense established a club record with six interceptions, and Namath led the offense to an early lead with touchdown passes to Sauer and Bill Mathis.

New York's 10–4 record was easily the best in the East, but it was clear throughout the season that the Jets were not the same team that had beaten Baltimore back in January. Most of the team's problems were on the defense. The secondary was weakened by the retirement of Johnny Sample, the defensive captain and starting left cornerback. Strong safety Jim Hudson was slowed by injury, and the Jets had problems against high-scoring offenses, losing to Oakland, Kansas City, and San Diego.

The Houston Oilers finished second to the Jets in the East with a 6–6–2 record, yet the Oilers made the playoffs for the second time in three years thanks to the AFL's new expanded playoff format. The strength of the Oilers remained their defense. End Elvin Bethea, linebackers George Webster and Garland Boyette, and the secondary of Miller Farr, Zeke Moore, Ken Houston, and W. K. Hicks ranked among the league's best.

While the Jets and Oilers earned playoff berths, the Buffalo Bills built for the future, making USC tailback Orenthal James Simpson their top pick in the draft. One of a long line of Trojan horses that included Mike Garrett, Anthony Davis, Ricky Bell, and Charles White, Simpson was a record-setting Heisman Trophy winner in 1968.

As the deep back in USC's I-formation offense, Simpson established himself as one of the great running backs in college football history. Trojan head coach John McKay called Simpson the best broken-field runner in USC history. At the time of his graduation in 1969, Simpson owned NCAA career records for carries and yards rushing, had averaged more than 5 yards per carry, scored 36 touchdowns, and set nearly a dozen USC rushing marks. Nicknamed "the Juice," Simpson helped the Trojans to an 18–2–1 record in the 1968–69 seasons and three consecutive Pac-10 Conference championships. In the Trojans' 1968 Rose Bowl win over Indiana, Simpson rushed for both touchdowns in a 14–3 victory and was named game MVP.

Because the Bills had the worst record in pro football in 1968, winning just once in 14 games, Buffalo owned the number-one pick in the draft. There was speculation among some football people that the rebuilding Bills might trade Simpson in return for two or three quality players.

But one veteran NFL coach and general manager scoffed at that idea. "The team lucky enough to get him will keep O. J. Simpson," Vince Lombardi said. "You don't get many chances at a super player like him. He'll be another Jim Brown."

Four months of rigorous negotiations between the Bills and Simpson followed the college draft. Deals with General Motors, Royal Crown Cola, and ABC-TV guaranteed Simpson an annual income of $950,000 outside of football. Simpson's agent, Chuck Barnes, told the Bills O. J.'s signing price was $650,000 over five years, plus a $500,000 loan. Bills owner Ralph Wilson was taken aback at the demands; most college stars were signing for $50,000 a year. Simpson, aware that he was not just another rookie, told reporters if the Bills

New York linebacker Larry Grantham helped lead the Jets to a second straight division title in 1969. Grantham is one of just 10 players who played their entire AFL career with the same team. (*Photo courtesy of the New York Jets.*)

didn't come up with the right offer, he was prepared to sit out the season. One month after the start of training camp, Simpson and the Bills finally agreed to terms. Featured on a strongside sweep, Simpson gained a team-high 697 yards rushing, but the Bills still struggled to a 4–10 finish.

The AFL West featured an exciting race that saw the Chiefs and Raiders duel for two playoff berths. The San Diego Chargers threatened to make it a three-team race, but a four-game midseason losing streak knocked the

Chargers out of the playoff picture and forced head coach Sid Gillman into early retirement with an ulcer.

The Chargers finished with an 8–6 record, but they did have reason to celebrate in their season finale at home against old rival Buffalo. Playing before a sun-drenched crowd in Jack Murphy Stadium in the final regular-season game in AFL history, Charger flanker Lance Alworth used his trademark leap to haul in a short slant pass from quarterback John Hadl. The first-quarter catch allowed Alworth to topple Green Bay great Don Hutson's towering record of at least one reception in 95 straight games. Alworth finished the game with seven catches for 122 yards, giving him 1,003 receiving yards for the year, and a pro-record seventh straight thousand-yard season.

Though the Chargers fell off the pace, the Chiefs and Raiders continued on a collision course that wasn't decided until the final game of the regular season. Under rookie head coach John Madden, the Raiders rolled through the first seven weeks of the season, the only blemish on their record a tie with Miami. In Week Six, Oakland routed Buffalo, 50–21, with quarterback Daryle Lamonica bombing his old team with six touchdown passes. One week later, he led the Raiders past San Diego, allowing Oakland to tie the league record for consecutive unbeaten games at 15. The streak ended in Week Eight, when Oakland was ambushed by Cincinnati 31–17, the Raiders' only defeat of the season.

As he had since arriving in Oakland in 1967, Lamonica led the Raider attack. His 34 touchdown passes led the league, and Lamonica was named the AFL's MVP for the second time in three years. Raider receivers Warren Wells and Fred Biletnikoff used speed and savvy, respectively, to combine for 101 receptions, more than 2,000 yards receiving, and 26 touchdowns. Wells led the league with 14 TD catches and a 27-yards-per-catch average.

Protecting Lamonica was an offensive line that featured all-pro-caliber players in center Jim Otto and guard Gene Upshaw. Otto wore jersey number 00 to coincide with the first and last letters in his name. He was the only all-pro center in league history, and he was known as "Mr. AFL" because of the fierce pride he had in his league. It's a pride he carries to this day.

"I think the AFL was a very big key to what the NFL is today," Otto says. "I think the AFL opened the eyes of the public to more football, and it was the beginning of marketing exposure for TV."

Oakland's high-octane offense led the Raiders to an 11–1–1 record and a season-ending showdown with their archrivals, Hank Stram's Kansas City Chiefs. Stram's offense featured multiple looks. In the tight-I, tight end Fred Arbanas was lined up in the I-formation along with backs Mike Garrett and Wendell Hayes. In the "Camouflage Slot," wide receiver Otis Taylor was positioned in the backfield slot between guard and tackle. The Chiefs opened the season outscoring San Diego and Boston by a combined margin of 58–9. But Kansas City quarterback Len Dawson suffered a knee injury against the

Patriots, and was out of action for six games. Dawson was replaced by backup Jacky Lee, who suffered a cracked bone in his ankle the following week in an upset loss to the Bengals.

Mike Livingston became the third Kansas City quarterback in as many games, and with his quarterback situation unsettled, Stram stuck to his ground game. Running behind a massive line that included all-pros Jim Tyrer and Ed Budde, the Chiefs' "mini backs"—Mike Garrett, Warren McVea, and Robert Holmes—each averaged more than 4 yards per carry and combined for more than 1,800 yards and 15 touchdowns.

Dawson returned for the season's stretch run and combined with ends Otis Taylor and Frank Pitts to open up the Chiefs' passing game. Throughout the '69 season, Dawson was a model of courage. Called "Ajax" by his teammates because he hated to get his uniform dirty, Dawson not only played with a bad knee in '69 but had to overcome the untimely death of his father in the days leading up to the Chiefs' key game in New York against the Jets in Week 10. Both teams were on six-game winning streaks, but Dawson threw three TD passes to Taylor and the Chiefs' defense kept Namath under wraps in an impressive 34–16 win over the world champions in wind-swept Shea Stadium.

Throughout the '69 campaign, the Kansas City defense outfought and outthought its opponents with a blend of strength and strategy. A big factor in the success of the unit was its ability to stay healthy; not one member of the Chiefs' starting 11 missed a game in '69. The front four listed all-pro caliber players in Jerry Mays, Buck Buchanan, and Curley Culp, and the linebacking corps of Bobby Bell, Willie Lanier, and Jim Lynch was football's best. Safety Johnny Robinson and cornerback Emmitt Thomas led the secondary by combining for 17 interceptions. The Chiefs led the league in fewest points allowed (177) and became just the second team in league history to achieve the difficult triple crown, leading the league against the run, pass, and in overall defense.

Buchanan and Bell were perennial all-pros who were both products of the Chiefs' great 1962 draft, the most successful in franchise history. Buchanan graduated from a Birmingham, Alabama, high school in 1958 and was headed for a job in the steel mills alongside his father when one of Buck's uncles contacted Grambling head football coach Eddie Robinson by letter. After receiving the letter, Robinson placed a phone call to the Buchanan home. When Robinson learned of Buchanan's size — 6-foot-7, 211 pounds — Robinson offered him a football grant-in-aid.

Despite his success on the football field, basketball remained Buchanan's first love. It was the sport, along with football, in which he had excelled in high school.

Buchanan died in July of 1992 from cancer, but in a phone interview conducted earlier that year, he spoke candidly about his early days at Grambling.

"I didn't care for football in high school," Buchanan said. "The only reason I played football during my junior and senior years was because the basketball coach wanted me to stay in shape."

At the time of Buchanan's arrival at Grambling in 1960, Robinson, college football's all-time winningest coach, was developing a powerhouse team. Robinson's team at that time included future all-pros in Buchanan, Ernie Ladd, and Willie Brown. Grambling went undefeated in 1960, and the team was so dominant that Robinson later remarked he found the team's intrasquad scrimmages more interesting than the games on Saturday afternoon.

In 1962, Buchanan became the first Grambling player to be a number-one draft choice in pro football. Drafted by the Dallas Texans of the AFL and the NFL's New York Giants, Buchanan said he chose the AFL because of the young league's attitude.

"[The NFL] made it sound as if they'd be doing me a favor by drafting me," Buchanan said. "Everything was National Football League this and National Football League that. I knew Emlen Tunnell well and I knew Buddy Young, too. But the attitude of the NFL angered me. I liked Don Klosterman very much, and Ernie Ladd helped me make my decision, too."

To hide Buchanan from NFL "baby-sitters," Klosterman, the Texans' GM, hid Buchanan for four days in a secret Dallas apartment. In private, Klosterman told Buchanan, "We're going to make you our number-one draft choice."

Buchanan instantly recognized the historical significance of what Klosterman had told him.

"No player from an all-black college had ever been drafted number one," Buchanan said. "That meant a lot to me."

When Klosterman arrived in Dallas to meet with Buchanan, he had with him a sculpted young linebacker from the University of Minnesota, Bobby Bell.

At the time, Klosterman called Bell "the best all-around athlete in America. Bobby Bell is a professional prospect at almost any position you can name — and a good one."

Bell's football career began in Shelby, North Carolina, where his team had played six-man football. It wasn't until Bell's senior year that he played 11-man football, and even then his squad numbered just 18 players total. Still, with Bell at quarterback, his team won a state championship for head coach Jim Tatum. Recruited by, among others, Notre Dame, Michigan, and Illinois, Bell chose the University of Minnesota, and in 1960, was part of head coach Murray Warmath's national championship team.

In 1962, Bell was drafted by both the Vikings and the Texans. Klosterman met with Bell in Minneapolis, and after 10 hours of negotiations signed Bell to a five-year deal that Dallas team officials called "one of the most fabulous offers ever proposed to a collegiate player."

The move stunned the Vikings, who had assumed they had the inside track on Bell because he played his college ball at nearby University of Minnesota. Lamar Hunt thought as much, which explains why the Texans waited until the seventh round of the AFL draft before selecting Bell. Bell says today:

Lamar didn't think he'd be able to get me. He thought I was going to sign with the Vikings. But then he thought about it and said, "I'm going to go after this guy." Lamar, more than anybody, was the guy who recruited me, and he sent Don Klosterman to talk to me.

I signed with the Chiefs — they were the Dallas Texans then — because they offered me a better deal. The Vikings offered a three-year contract and the Chiefs offered a five-year *guaranteed* contract. So I ended up with the Chiefs because I knew what I'd be doing for the next five years.

The AFL was something different then. It was just getting started, and I was 21 years old and just coming out of college. The thing about the Vikings was I didn't like how [head coach Norm] Van Brocklin treated his players at the time. I heard he used to cut guys at halftime.

You know, I just wanted to play football. I'd have gone to Nigeria to play if I had to. Some people told me I was too small to play, but my attitude was, "Before you start judging me, look at me when I play. Don't just look at my size." All I wanted was an opportunity to perform.

Buchanan and Bell became the prototypes for their respective positions. A six-time all-pro, Buchanan played in 181 of 182 games from 1963 to 1975. Buchanan was huge — 6-foot-7, 267 pounds — but it was his strength, quickness, and agility that set him apart from other big men.

Buchanan revolutionized his position by being the first tall defensive tackle. Defensive linemen with his height usually lined up at defensive end; Buchanan, along with San Diego's Ernie Ladd, became one of the first tall defensive tackles. Buchanan's size and speed allowed him to collapse the pocket with just a couple of steps inside, and when he wasn't sacking quarterbacks he was altering the trajectory of their passes with his long arms.

Buchanan became such a problem for opposing linemen that Raiders owner Al Davis sought to neutralize him by making 6-foot-5, 255-pound guard Gene Upshaw his number-one pick in the 1967 AFL draft.

"I figured if Buchanan was going to play for the Chiefs for the next ten years, we better get some big guy who can handle him," Davis said. "So we got Upshaw. Those two guys put on some stirring battles over the years."

Raiders–Chiefs games featured the game-within-the-game between Upshaw, who started at left guard, and Buchanan, who lined up at defensive right tackle. It was a matchup of two future Hall of Famers, and Upshaw recalled those battles with a sense of awe for Buchanan's ability.

"I was big, but Buck was bigger and stronger and turned me every which way but loose," Upshaw said. "When you played Buck, you couldn't sleep the night before a game. You don't imagine a guy 6-foot-8, 300 pounds being so quick. You'd go to hit him, and it was like hitting a ghost."

Bell was just as elusive. Cat-quick, the 6-foot-4, 225-pound Bell was also a great hand-fighter. Green Bay Packers all-pro Dave Robinson, who like Bell lined up at left outside linebacker in the 1960s, saw Bell first-hand in Super Bowl I. Robinson said Bell used his hands better than any linebacker he'd seen.

Chiefs coach Hank Stram called Bell the best athlete on his team, and the best in pro football at the time. "There isn't a job Bell couldn't do," Stram said, "and do well."

Oakland quarterback Daryle Lamonica agrees. "Bobby Bell," Lamonica says, "is one of the best linebackers ever to put on a uniform."

Raiders boss Al Davis said Bell's forte was the big play. "He's always intercepting a pass," Davis said, "and going sixty yards or something like that."

On the Chiefs' 1969 highlight film, narrator Bill Grigsby called Bell "a collision waiting for a place to happen."

A testimony to Bell's athleticism is the fact that Stram allowed his outside 'backer to go man-on-man with outstanding athletes like Oakland back Clem Daniels and San Diego's Lance Alworth, the AFL's best at the time. Bell says:

> We had some great players in the AFL. When we played against the Raiders, Clem Daniels was catching like 12 passes a game. Coach Stram said to me, "Wherever Daniels goes, I want you to go with him. If he goes to the bench, I want you to go with him." So after this one play, Daniels started heading towards the sideline, and I went with him. He said, "What're you doing?" I said, "Wherever you go, I'm going."
>
> When we played the Chargers, we used the bump-and-run to cover Alworth. Coach Stram told me, "Alworth's so quick, we've got to slow him down." So we decide to double up on Lance, and the first play, I go over and line up right over him. Lance looked up at me and said, "What are you doing, Bell?" I said, "I'm just here to play you, man."
>
> So the play starts and I hit Lance as soon as he comes off the line, and he goes down, flat on his back. Lance said, "Hey, man, you trying to kill me?" I said, "Hey no, man, I'm just playing the game."

The Chiefs and Raiders entered the season finale in Oakland separated by a half-game in the standings. The first-place Raiders, who defeated Kansas City 27-24 in Week 11, owned an 11-1-1 record; the Chiefs followed with an 11-2 mark. In a physical and emotional game that Kansas City radio announcer Bill Grigsby described as a "prehistoric, primeval slugging match," the Raiders beat the Chiefs 10-6 in the Oakland Coliseum to clinch their third straight division title.

The end of the '69 regular season brought to a near close the story of the AFL. The league that had fought to survive against the NFL and the fans' and media's prejudices for 10 seasons was about to be incorporated into the senior league. While the majority of AFL owners welcomed the move from a financial standpoint — it assured the survival of their teams — some coaches, players, and fans mourned the loss of the young league existing as a separate entity.

Through the second half of the 1960s, the AFL's growth had been tremendous. New stadiums were built in New York, Oakland, San Diego, and Houston, with the Oilers becoming the first pro team to play its home games inside a dome. Attendance at AFL games increased steadily. After averaging under

20,000 fans pe game its first two seasons, the AFL in 1969 was drawing twice that many, averaging 40,619 per game and a total of more than 2.8 million fans its final season.

The AFL's distinct style of play, its star performers, and its championship teams provided memorable moments and captured the imagination of millions of fans. AFL stratagems advanced from the simplistic early years, when offenses played pitch-and-catch and defensive strategy, as related by Patriots lineman Houston Antwine, was "beat the man opposite you to a pulp." The AFL graduated to multiple formations and popularized new offensive and defensive strategies, among them the use of backs and tight ends in deep patterns, shifting offensive formations, and the 3–4 defense. In so doing, the AFL served to influence a generation of head coaches, notably Chuck Noll, John Madden, and Bill Walsh, all of whom had their first pro coaching jobs in the AFL.

For AFL players, 1969 marked the end of an era. For 20 of those men, the AFL's passing meant a little extra. George Blanda, Billy Cannon, Gino Cappelletti, Tom Flores, Wayne Hawkins, Jim Hunt, Harry Jacobs, Jack Kemp, Paul Maguire, Billy Mathis, Don Maynard, Ron Mix, Jim Otto, Babe Parilli, Johnny Robinson, Paul Rochester, and Ernie Wright are the only players who started with the AFL in 1960 and were still on active rosters in 1969.

Cappelletti, who holds various AFL records, including most points scored lifetime (1,100) and — along with Blanda and Otto — most consecutive games played lifetime (140), remembers the AFL as a league of opportunity.

> Blanda, Otto, and myself were the only three guys to play in *every* AFL game over the ten years. It's an interesting mark.
>
> How did I hear of the AFL? I was tending bar in Minneapolis in my brother's place. He and a former teammate of mine at Minnesota, Bob McNamara, had bought this little bar not too far from the university and I was working in there tending bar. We were playing touch football. We had a league in Minneapolis, and we were playing a game of touch with other teams, and we were using so many old, ex–Minnesota players.
>
> Mac, who was an All-America at Minnesota, started talking about this new league. There was a little scuttlebutt going on, a little talk about it from time to time. Sure enough, we heard through the media there was this plan for a new professional football league. Mac got a call that Lou Saban was coming into town to talk to a bunch of former Minnesota players about going to the Patriots, who Lou had just signed with to coach.
>
> The reason he came to Minnesota was that he had an assistant coach with him at Northern Michigan where Saban was coaching, and he was one of our coaches at Minnesota, and he had told Saban about some players who didn't go to the pros but who he might be interested in talking to.
>
> Lou took it upon himself to fly to Minnesota; he went to the Raddison Hotel, and had a list of guys to come by and talk to him. I wasn't on that list, so I didn't get an invite to go. I was tending bar, so I told Bob, "While you're there, I'd appreciate it if you mention my name. I'd be interested in playing, too."

So Bob came back and said, "Geez, Gino, it was such a madhouse up there in that suite, I never got a chance to talk to Lou Saban, but I did get his home phone number. Or else you might try calling him at the hotel."

So I got right on the phone and called him at the hotel, and they said, "He just checked out." So then I called the airport and had him paged. I was kind of aggressive; I couldn't believe myself. He never answered the page, so I said, "Ah, that's fate. It wasn't meant to be."

So I let things go. But I had his home phone number, and I looked at it from time to time. A couple weeks later I got the nerve to pick up the phone and dial it, and I was lucky enough to catch him at home. If I hadn't, who knows when I would have gotten the nerve to call him again?

I told him who I was, and there was a lot of silence on the other end. Then he said, "Well, let me check you out and I'll get back to you." Well, two months went by and I didn't hear anything. Then, sure enough, I was home one day and the phone rang. And I hear, "Gino Cappelletti. This is Lou Saban. Look, I'm sending you a minimum contract and you have as good a chance as anybody of making this team."

Man, I was twenty feet in the air. He sent me a minimum contract—for $7,500. So I signed it and returned it. And that's where it all started.

That first training camp was about the wildest thing you could imagine. There were about 125 guys there, a lot of wannabees, guys who wanted to make it in pro football.

There was a constant turnstile scenario. One group was staying, one group was coming in, and one group was going. They were cutting guys every day. After every practice, you would go have your meal and then run back to the dorm and there'd be a list up on the dorm. And boy, you just hoped your name wasn't on that list. If it wasn't, you lived another day. And you lived from day to day like that.

Otto, the Raiders' all-time greatest center, recalls how he originally had been a member of the Oilers organization.

I was not drafted by the National Football League. I was drafted in a special round—but it was like the 27th round, very late. I was drafted by Minneapolis in the American Football League. After Minneapolis gave up its American Football League franchise to join the National Football League, the other [AFL] teams put those [Minneapolis] players in a pool, and I went to the Houston Oilers. So I got a call from the Oilers, and they said, "You are now our property. We would like to send you a contract."

So they sent me a contract and I signed it. But about a week later, a group in Oakland took the franchise of the Minneapolis group. And the AFL gave all the Minneapolis players to Oakland, and that's how I became a Raider.

The early camps were third-rate. The owners who bought the Raiders knew nothing about football. The people they hired to run it were not well versed in how to run a pro team. So the training camps were kind of crude.

On Saturday, December 20, the Chiefs and Jets took the field before 62,977 freezing fans at Shea Stadium. Game day in New York saw temperatures drop to a frigid 33 degrees, with winds gusting over 25 miles an hour. On the Kansas

City sideline, Len Dawson tried to throw light warmup passes to Arbanas, only to have the ball caught up in the wind and blown off target. Arbanas, who could only see out of one eye, was cursing his quarterback because the passes weren't on target. "It was the worst kind of wind I had ever seen," Dawson said.

With Namath having moderate success passing against the wind and the Chiefs' defense, the Jets took an early 3–0 lead on Jim Turner's 27-yard field goal. Kansas City tied the game in the second quarter on a 23-yard field goal by Jan Stenerud. Through the first two quarters, Kansas City had trouble with New York's 4-4 defense. With eight men bunched near the line of scrimmage, the Jets were able to handle the K.C. ground game. New York also double-teamed Taylor, and the combination of the double-coverage and the tricky winds effectively shackled the Chiefs' passing attack.

With the swirling winds playing havoc with long passes — Dawson missed a wide-open Taylor on a long pass late in the second quarter when the wind carried the ball over Taylor's head — the Chiefs revised their game plan for the second half. Kansas City countered both the wind and the Jets' pass rush with a short passing game — screens and play-actions. In the third quarter, Dawson exploited the Jets' blown coverage on the tight end with a short pass to Fred Arbanas, who carried the ball deep into New York territory. Stenerud's field goal from 25 yards out gave Kansas City a 6–3 lead heading into the fourth quarter.

Early in the fourth, Namath began to move the Jets. Mixing the run and the pass, he guided the Jets into Chiefs territory. On an end zone pass to George Sauer, Thomas was called for interference, and the Shea Stadium crowd roared its approval. The Jets had a first-and-goal at the Kansas City one.

On the Chiefs' sideline, Dawson turned his head from the field and covered his eyes. On the field, Kansas City linebacker Willie Lanier was cursing and crying as the Chiefs broke from their defensive huddle.

"I went crazy," Lanier said later.

"C'mon, Red," Lanier shrieked at his teammates, tears streaming down his face. "They're not going to score ... no way."

On the Chiefs' front line, tackle Buck Buchanan and end Jerry Mays turned and looked at Lanier, saw the tears, and instantly felt recharged.

"We were aroused," Buchanan said. "We *knew* they weren't going to make it. We all looked around at each other and we said that this could be our whole season right on the 1-yard line. We all dug in and gave a little extra effort. We didn't let them get that last touchdown. I think I was the proudest guy on that field, especially proud of our defensive unit that we hung in there like we did on that one-yard line for four downs and stopped the New York Jets."

"Willie Lanier got us," Mays said. "He fired me up. It was the way he did it — tears in his eyes, teeth gnashing."

"He was crying and screaming," cornerback Emmitt Thomas said. "He started running up and down the defensive line begging us to stop the Jets.

There were tears running down his face. When the Jets came up to the line, Willie yelled, 'Dammit, they're not going to score on us!' Next thing we knew, we were all saying it and we just kept saying it over and over."

Chiefs radio announcer Bill Grigsby called the most famous goal-line stand in AFL history:

> *There's a running play to Matt Snell behind right guard ... he's hit at the goal line by Johnny Robinson and tackled a yard shy of that goal line. Good tackle by John, he had to make that play along with Lanier and Jerry Mays....*
>
> *The ball is only six inches shy of the goal line.... Running play to Mathis behind left guard, he is stopped at the goal line! Lanier hits him, and gets help by Buck Buchanan, Curley Culp, and John Robinson....*
>
> *Third down and one.... A seat-squirmer here at Shea Stadium. Good goal line defense by Kansas City but now the pressure's really on. Joe Namath awaits the snap from center, Joe Willie rolling to his right, he's scrambling, dumps the ball, he is tackled near the seven yard line. What pressure put on by Bobby Bell!*

The Jets' third-down call was designed to counter the aggressive rush of the Chiefs' defense by forcing left linebacker Bobby Bell into going for the fake handoff. But when Namath looked in Snell's direction, he was startled to see Bell there. Namath tried to double-clutch and look for another receiver, but the rush forced him to hurry a pass in Snell's direction. The pass landed at Snell's feet.

"He was out there with Snell, and he had no right being there," Namath said of Bell. "If he hadn't been there, it would have been a touchdown."

Turner's field goal tied the game, but while the score stood at 6–6, the momentum was all in Kansas City's favor.

"I couldn't believe the defense had done such a tremendous job," Dawson said. "It gave me new life and it lifted the spirits of the offensive unit."

The Kansas City offense, stymied by the weather and the Jets' defense throughout the long bitter afternoon, struck back in two big plays. On first down at their own 20, the Chiefs lined up in a slot formation that had Taylor and Frank Pitts on the same side of the field. Since the Jets were using just three defensive backs, the Chiefs figured the slot would force New York into single coverage on either Taylor or Pitts. Dawson, Pitts, and Taylor traced the patterns into the dirt along the sidelines.

With the ball resting on the right hashmark, Taylor and Pitts lined up to the right side, with Pitts in the slot. Both receivers had the whole left side of the field, the wide side, in which to run their patterns. Pitts was to run a deep out; Taylor was to fake an out pattern and run a deep post. Taylor got a step on Jet safety Bill Baird, gathered in Dawson's long pass, and carried it to the New York 19, where linebacker Al Atkinson finally dragged him down after a 61-yard gain.

It was a lightning bolt of a play and rocked the Jets back on their heels. On the next play, Dawson called for a play-action pass to Garrett. Dawson faked the handoff to fullback Wendell Hayes and looked in Garrett's direction. But with Garrett covered, Dawson looked off his primary receiver and saw tight end Gloster Richardson streaking across the middle on a deep crossing pattern. Dawson's pass cut through the wind, and Richardson made a clutch catch in the end zone for a 13–6 lead.

Namath, who directed New York to 19 first downs, twice took the Jets deep into Kansas City territory, advancing as far as the Chiefs' 16- and 13-yard lines. Each time, however, the Chiefs' defense and the fickle winds frustrated the Jets quarterback. Hampered by the increasing difficulties his receivers had hanging onto the ball — at least 10 of his passes were dropped — Namath ended the day with just 14 completions in 40 attempts. After a late end zone interception by Jim Marsalis, Namath bounced his helmet off the frozen turf in frustration.

"You can make excuses all day long," said Namath, who was intercepted three times, "but the main factor out there was the wind. You just couldn't throw the ball with that wind."

Sauer, who led the Jets with five catches for 61 yards, recalled the pain in making even routine catches that day. "The ball was like an icicle," Sauer said, "wrapped in sandpaper."

The AFL playoff game the following day between the Oilers and Raiders in Oakland was not as dramatic. Before a Coliseum crowd of 53,539, the Raiders scored four touchdowns in a span of 4:22 in the first quarter and cruised to a 56–7 win over the Oilers. Lamonica threw six touchdown passes, and safety George Atkinson returned a Pete Beathard pass 57 yards for a score.

The AFL championship game was held the following Sunday, January 4, in Oakland. By 1969, the Oakland–Kansas City series had become one of the most intense in pro football. The two teams had dominated the Western Division since 1966, in the process creating a rivalry that Stram described as "bitter." Chiefs linebacker Willie Lanier said each Raiders–Chiefs game was monumental, since whichever team won the season series usually won the division. Oakland receiver Rod Sherman said he always knew when the Chiefs were next on the schedule, because that was when general managing partner Al Davis showed up to coach the Raiders. Oakland center Jim Otto compared the Raiders and Chiefs to partners of an unhappy marriage — each knew where to kick and scratch the other to cause the most anguish.

The intensity of K.C.–Oakland series was heightened by the anticipated individual matchups: Lamonica vs. Dawson; Gene Upshaw vs. Buck Buchanan; Hewritt Dixon vs. Willie Lanier. Fans took part in the rivalry as well. When the Raiders traveled to Kansas City's Municipal Stadium, Chiefs fans known as "the Wolfpack" were known to throw things at Oakland players. When the Chiefs played at the Oakland Coliseum, Raider fans turned especially hostile;

the noise of their air horns penetrated the stadium's concrete caverns and could be heard in the Kansas City dressing room. Oakland crowds were so loud they drowned out Chiefs quarterback Len Dawson's signal calls at the line of scrimmage and made audibles impossible. Kansas City's offensive linemen had to ask Dawson to shout the calls to each side of the line, and repeat them at least twice.

Both clubs dreaded playing in the opposing team's stadium. In Kansas City's Municipal Stadium, both team's benches were on the same side of the field. A man who was said to be a friend of one of the Chiefs' assistant coaches roamed the sidelines with a camera and press credentials, but he was accused of never having film in his camera. Raiders coach John Madden remembers a situation where the supposed cameraman heard the opposing team's pass play and alerted the Chiefs' coaching staff, which immediately made the correct defensive adjustments.

Sideline spies made it difficult to play in Municipal Stadium; locker room rats were part of the problem of playing in the Oakland Coliseum. Madden made it a point to tell Stram just before game time that rats had been seen in the locker rooms. "Some *rats* have been found in this locker room," Madden said, just loud enough for all the Chiefs to hear. "Just to be safe, Hank, you better warn your players about the rats."

Willie Lanier said later his teammates squirmed when they heard Madden tell Stram about rats; K.C. players checked their shoes, shoulder pads, and helmets before putting them on. Opposing players also had to contend with the Coliseum itself—the walk to the visiting team's locker room was through a damp, dirty hallway, and the locker room was partitioned into several small rooms, all of which prevented the opposition from the feeling of being together. To get to the field, the opposition had to thread their way through another damp tunnel before heading onto the field, where they were greeted by deafening air horns and loud boos.

The field itself presented another distraction. Since the Coliseum is located below sea level, the turf is always damp, presenting footing problems for quick teams like the Chiefs.

The Raiders were listed as favorites for various reasons: the game was in Oakland; the Raiders had beaten the Chiefs four straight times, and six of seven dating back to 1966; and the '69 Raider team was considered by some people close to the Oakland organization as the greatest in team history.

The Raiders' comments leading up to the game reflected their confidence. "I played my first exhibition game against K.C.," Lamonica said, "I scored my first TD pass against K.C. in my rookie year. I feel—I *know* I can beat them. I know I can score on them, on the ground and in the air. Just watch us Sunday. We are ready."

Madden said he expected the usual tough Oakland-Kansas City game, but "I think we'll win. Daryle threw six TDs against Houston so there's no question about him being ready physically."

What concerned Madden the most was the Chiefs' defense, in particular the combination of tackles Buchanan and Culp and linebacker Willie Lanier in the middle of that defense. Madden said that combination was as formidable as the Joe Greene-Ernie Holmes-Jack Lambert trio that formed the heart of Pittsburgh's "Steel Curtain" defense in the 1970s.

Madden got as little as two hours' sleep on a given day preparing for the Chiefs' defense. The Raiders' coaching staff would study Kansas City's films, then put plays on the blackboard they thought would work.

"No," Madden would say after studying the play for a minute, "that won't work." That went on for hours. The Raiders knew they couldn't move Buchanan, Culp, and Lanier for substantial yardage. At 4 A.M., Madden and his coaches would go home, get two hours' sleep, then be back at the Raiders offices at 6 A.M. to try again to solve the riddle of the Chiefs' defense.

While the Raiders wrestled with their game plan, Chiefs head coach Hank Stram headquartered his team in sunny Santa Barbara, barely beating a snowstorm that blanketed Kansas City. Stram dispelled notions of Raider superiority. "We are thinking positive," he said. "The only game that counts is the next one."

Defensive end Jerry Mays agreed. "In the past, we talked too much about getting ready for the Raiders. This time we're concentrating on getting ready for a football game."

Since the Raiders used multiple looks on defense, Stram ordered special black and silver jerseys for team practice. The idea was to give his team instant recognition of Oakland formations. Stram's offensive game plan for the championship differed from previous ones he had drawn up for the Raiders. In the Chiefs' two previous losses to the Raiders in 1969, Stram had underestimated the strength and quickness of Oakland's defense. For the championship game, Stram went all out in devising a new strategy. Rather than trying to beat the entire Oakland defense, Stram concentrated on three key players: defensive tackle Tom Keating, middle linebacker Dan Connors, and weak safety Dave Grayson. The Chiefs' offensive game plan called for double-team blocking on Keating and Connors, while isolating Grayson in man-on-man pass coverage.

Defensively, the Chiefs wanted to pressure Lamonica with an inside rush. Lamonica was a classic drop-back quarterback, and the Chiefs wanted to force him out of the pocket. Kansas City's front four, and in particular ends Jerry Mays and Aaron Brown, planned to run loops and stunts in an effort to get a strong push up the middle. To give the front four additional time to get to Lamonica, Chiefs cornerbacks Emmitt Thomas and Jimmy Marsalis were brought up closer to the line of scrimmage to bump-and-run Oakland receivers Fred Biletnikoff and Warren Wells, neither of whom was as big or strong as the K.C. cornerbacks.

The Chiefs' plan was a calculated risk. Inside rushes by their defensive ends would leave them open to Raider sweeps, but Stram, perhaps recalling Lamonica's huge performance in the '68 playoff game, decided to chance it.

On Sunday, January 4, a silver-and-black crowd of 54,444 crammed the Coliseum. Game-time weather conditions saw clear, sunny skies and a temperature of 52 degrees. Throughout the first quarter, the Raiders lived up to their role as favorites. The Raiders had eight first downs to the Chiefs' one, outrushed Kansas City 38–7, and had 63 yards passing to Kansas City's 13. Lamonica was 7-for-10 passing; Dawson 1-for-5.

With 3:31 left in the opening quarter, Lamonica marched the Raiders 66 yards in 10 plays. Halfback Charlie Smith capped the drive with a 3-yard TD run off the left side for a 7–0 lead.

Late in the second quarter, Dawson hit the big play he was looking for. With 3:24 left in the half, Dawson connected on two big plays that finally got the Chiefs on the board. With a second-and-nine at the Kansas City 26, Dawson dropped back, ducked under a blitz by linebacker Chip Oliver, and hit Taylor for a first down at the Chiefs' 40.

Two minutes remained in the first half when Dawson decided to test the Raiders deep. K.C. wide receiver Frank Pitts ran what the Chiefs called "a flat and up," Pitts faking to the sideline and then taking cornerback Nemiah Wilson deep. Dawson's pass was behind Pitts, but the Chiefs' receiver adjusted to the ball, made the catch, and carried to the 1 before Wilson dragged him down.

GRIGSBY: *Back to throw [is] Lenny Dawson. He has time to throw ... firing one deep ... wide open [is] Frank Pitts, he makes the catch! He is run out of bounds at the one-yard line!*

On the next play, fullback Wendell Hayes followed right tackle Dave Hill into the end zone. With 1:53 left in the first half, Jan Stenerud's point after tied the score at 7–7, where it stood until halftime. In the Kansas City locker room, Stram told his team, "We are 30 minutes away from the AFL championship. We have it in our grasp. All we have to do now is squeeze it."

Early in the second half, Lamonica threw deep and incomplete to halfback Larry Todd. Lamonica immediately reached for his right hand. On the follow-through of his pass to Todd, Lamonica had jammed his fingers on the helmet of Chiefs defensive end Aaron Brown, who had slipped past tackle Bob Svihus and crashed up the middle on a loop.

GRIGSBY: *Lamonica back to throw, and he's throwing that ball deep and it's broken up at the five-yard line.... Lamonica's hurt ... and out comes Lamonica.*

With his hand swelling and becoming discolored, the AFL's MVP left the field, shaking his head in despair. "I had no feel for the ball," he said. For the next eight minutes, Lamonica watched from the sidelines as 41-year-old George Blanda took over at quarterback for the Raiders.

On Oakland's next series, Blanda moved the Raiders to the Kansas City 24. For a moment, Wells was open in the end zone, but he slipped and fell as Blanda threw. The pass was intercepted by Thomas, who elected to run the ball out instead of downing it and was tackled by Billy Cannon at the Chiefs' 6. Backed up in the shadows of their own goalposts, the Chiefs lost four yards when fullback Robert Holmes was pinned at the 2 by Oliver and Lassiter. Dawson called for a pass play that flooded the Oakland secondary with five receivers.

Operating out of their "Model T" formation, the Chiefs had receivers Gloster Richardson and Otis Taylor lined up to Dawson's left, with Taylor in the gap between guard and tackle. Arbanas was lined up at right end, and Holmes was in the guard-tackle gap to Dawson's right side.

Dawson dropped deep into his own end zone, his feet nearly touching the end line. Holmes was the primary receiver, and Dawson looked his way, but the Raiders jammed Holmes at the line of scrimmage. Aware he had to get rid of the ball, Dawson saw Taylor, who was angling toward the right sideline, a half-step ahead of Wilson and reserve defensive back Howie Williams. Taylor was dangerously close to the sideline when Dawson fired his pass.

GRIGSBY: *Lenny ... back in the end zone, he throws a wobbler intended for Taylor and Otis makes a remarkable catch at the 37-yard line....*

"I let the ball go and just prayed," Dawson said. "I threw it so that it would go out of bounds if he couldn't get it."

Taylor made the catch, pulling the ball in at the Chiefs' 37. There was question later whether or not Taylor came down in bounds. It didn't matter, since the officials ruled he was shoved out by the Raiders. The 35-yard gain stood. "It was one of the greatest clutch catches of [Taylor's] career," Dawson said.

Three plays later, Dawson sent Taylor on a deep corner route. Wilson grabbed Taylor as the ball was in the air, and the pass interference call gave the Chiefs first down at the seven. One play later, Holmes followed a great block by guard Ed Budde on Carleton Oats and scored standing up for a 14–7 lead.

On the Oakland sideline, Lamonica's passing hand was swollen and discolored. The Raiders' quarterback had been physically beaten up by the Chiefs' front four. The ferocious hitting between the two teams marked the fierceness of the AFL's most heated rivalry. Raider fullback Hewitt Dixon, a bruising 230-pound power back, and Chiefs middle linebacker Willie Lanier, who weighed 245 and was nicknamed "Contact" for his hard hits, waged their own private war.

"He was a combination of halfback, fullback, and nastiness," Lanier said of Dixon. "Just a real mean sonofabitch."

Dixon recalled one collision with Lanier that left the Raider fullback head-over-heels and symbolized the intensity of the hitting that went on that afternoon. "Half of me landed in one place," Dixon said, "and the rest of me in another place."

Lamonica returned to the game and drove the Raiders to the Chiefs' 39, but his long pass to Sherman was intercepted by Jim Kearney at the 18 and returned to the Kansas City 35. But the Raiders got the ball right back when Oats fell on a Holmes' fumble at the Kansas City 24. Lamonica went for it all on first down, but his long pass to Sherman was picked off by Jim Marsalis at the Chiefs' 10.

Two plays later, Holmes fumbled again, and Conners recovered it at the Kansas City 31. But Lamonica was intercepted again, this time by Thomas at the Chiefs' 24.

GRIGSBY: *Lamonica is throwing one deep for Warren Wells ... it is intercepted at the twenty by Emmitt Thomas! Back to the thirty, the forty, he may break it. He's at midfield, at the forty, the thirty, the twenty, Emmitt Thomas is finally stopped at Oakland's 18-yard line! That is the biggest play to date.*

Stenerud's 22-yard field goal gave the Chiefs a 17–7 lead, with 4:48 left. The Raiders had one more chance to rally. With just over two minutes remaining in the game, Dawson fumbled at the Chiefs' 13 and Ike Lassiter recovered for the Raiders. The fumble was the Chiefs' third of the quarter. On the Kansas City sideline, safety Johnny Robinson, who was playing in pain with bruised ribs, exploded in anger.

"What the hell is going on out there?" he yelled. "Don't we have anybody who can hold onto that ball?"

Lamonica fired three straight incomplete passes into the Kansas City end zone. The game clock showed just 1:46 remaining. On fourth down, Lamonica dropped back and was dumped by Brown for a 7-yard loss. Dawson remembered looking up at the scoreboard as the final second ticked off and seeing what he described as one of the most beautiful sights in his life: "Kansas City 17, Oakland 7."

The postgame talk focused on Kansas City's great defensive effort in holding the high-powered Raiders to seven points. "We thought that outside pressure didn't affect Daryle Lamonica very much," Mays said. "So we concentrated on getting a little bit more of an inside rush and try to disturb his timing. We noticed a lot of their pass patterns depended on timing, and we figured if we could destroy the timing on their passes, we could destroy their passing game."

For the third time in franchise history, Lamar Hunt's team was champion of the American Football League. "We have a lot to be proud of," Hunt said. "Looking back over the years we've spent in the AFL, we've won three league championships. That is more than any other team. Buffalo and Houston each won two. Oakland won one, San Diego won one, and New York won one. That makes us the all-time AFL champions."

Mays agreed. "This was our biggest victory ever," he said in the Chiefs' crowded dressing room. "This was also the last AFL game that will ever be played. This will be the last Super Bowl in a strict sense. These two things make winning something special."

Chapter Seventeen

Super Bowl IV: Hail to the Chiefs

WHEN KANSAS CITY CHIEFS head coach Hank Stram awoke the morning of January 11, 1970, his eyes were burning, the result of a week's worth of watching game films of the NFL champion Minnesota Vikings. But the burning sensation in Stram's eyes was nothing compared to the burning desire deep within the Chiefs' boss.

To Stram and every member of his team, Super Bowl IV — the final Super Sunday showdown between the soon-to-be-merged National and American Football Leagues — represented a day of redemption. Three years earlier, Stram and the Chiefs had represented the AFL in the first-ever championship between the warring leagues, and had gotten NFL comeuppance at the hands of Vince Lombardi and the Green Bay Packers. Super Bowl IV offered Kansas City and the AFL one final chance to even the score. If the Chiefs could defeat the Vikings, then the NFL–AFL Super Bowl matchups would stand even — at two victories apiece — for time immemorial.

By a delicious bit of irony, the Vikings of the late 1960s bore a striking resemblance to the Packers of the mid–'60s. Both teams hailed from the frigid Midwest, and both disdained fancy formations for fundamentals and execution. Like the Lombardi Packers, the Vikings of Bud Grant believed in the theorem that the team that hits is the team that wins.

"Defense wins football games," Grant said. "Offense sells tickets.... Since our defense is strong, our offense doesn't have to be fancy. We just line up in the basic formations and come right at you."

In the week that he had to prepare for the Vikings, Stram was struck by the similarities between the Vikings and Packers. The '69 Vikings, Stram said, were like the '66 Packers. "In essence, they said, 'Here's what we do, try to stop us.' If they executed, they won. If they didn't...."

Stram had been unable to solve the puzzle of the Packers in Super Bowl I. He had less difficulty with the Vikings in Super Bowl IV. Stram planned to match his self-ordained "Offense of the Seventies" with its multiple formations,

Super Bowl IV: Hail to the Chiefs

Kansas City defensive tackles Curley Culp (61) and Buck Buchanan (86) sandwich Minnesota quarterback Joe Kapp during Super Bowl IV. The Chiefs beat the Vikings 23-7 in the final game ever played by an AFL team. (*Photo courtesy of Vernon J. Biever.*)

end reverses, and high-percentage passes to neutralize the "Defense of the Sixties," Minnesota's heralded "Purple Gang."

The Chiefs would double-team Viking ends Carl Eller and Jim Marshall, occupying them to open up the lanes for K.C. quarterback Len Dawson's short passes. To negate the Vikings' great defensive pursuit, Stram planned to run mini-backs Mike Garrett, Warren McVea, and Robert Holmes right at Minnesota's front four. Stram figured the Vikings could be kept off-balance with quick counts and tackle traps, and the Chiefs' small, quick backs could slither through the line for short but important gains.

The Minnesota offense relied on inside running by strong but slow backs Dave Osborn and Bill Brown, and rollout pass-run options by charismatic quarterback Joe Kapp. Half-Mexican and half-Indian, "Injun' Joe" had been brought from the frozen climes of the Canadian Football League by Grant in 1967. In three years together, Grant and Kapp had fought their way to two NFL Central Division crowns and one league title.

To contain the Viking offense, Stram planned to match power with power. Under Stram, the Chiefs owned a split personality. The K.C. offense featured deft brush blocking and fancy formations. The Chiefs' defense, by contrast, relied on crunching, brute force. Junius "Buck" Buchanan, a 285-pound defensive tackle, and Curley Culp, a 265-pound former collegiate wrestling champion, anchored the front four. Behind them stood Willie Lanier, the AFL's best-ever middle linebacker. Nicknamed "Contact" because of the force of his collisions with ball carriers, Lanier wore a specially constructed helmet with a padded strip down the middle to protect himself from his own hard hits.

Stram felt his "stack" defenses, which alternated in lining up either Buchanan or Culp head-on with the center, would stuff the Vikings' power running game. He also felt his defensive line, in particular ends Jerry Mays and Aaron Brown, could pinch Kapp in the pocket and not let him outside. Finally, the Chiefs' linebackers, Lanier, all-pro Bobby Bell, and Jim Lynch and the physical play secondary cornerbacks Emmitt Thomas and Jim Marsalis and safeties Johnny Robinson and Jim Kearney could stop the Vikings' limited passing game.

Having won 14 of their 16 games that season, the Vikings were regarded by some as one of the NFL's best teams ever. Their defense set a league record by allowing just 133 points during the season, and the Minnesota offense, conservative as it was, had scored more than 50 points in a game three times and led the league in scoring. In the NFL playoffs that year, Minnesota had fought from behind to beat an excellent Los Angeles Rams team 23–20, and then dispatched the powerful Cleveland Browns 27–7 in eight-degree weather in Minnesota to win the NFL title.

Kapp had keyed the two playoff wins with his daring play. Against the Rams, he scored the deciding touchdown when he rolled left on a bootleg and hurdled a defender en route to the end zone. One week later against the Browns, Kapp ran headlong into Cleveland linebacker Jim Houston, and knocked Houston colder than the weather.

Kapp coined a phrase that perfectly fit the '69 Vikings: "Forty for Sixty." The phrase, according to Kapp, meant 40 men playing together for 60 minutes. The Vikings took it to heart. After winning the NFL championship, Minnesota defensive end Carl Eller wrapped an arm around Kapp's shoulders and said, "Joe, you're my brother."

That a black man would call him brother was particularly moving to Kapp. The tough quarterback had tears in his eyes as he stood with Eller.

Despite the New York Jets' victory over the heavily favored Baltimore Colts the year before, most pro football experts still regarded the NFL as the superior league. For Super Bowl IV, Vegas oddsmakers installed the Vikings as 13½-point favorites over the Chiefs.

"They're doing it again," Oakland Raiders kicker George Blanda said when he heard the odds. "They're underestimating the AFL again."

Stram too, was puzzled by his team's underdog status. "As a coach, you don't pay much attention to the odds listed in the newspapers, although you can't help but be aware of them," he said. "I thought it was peculiar that even before the oddsmakers had known the opposing teams in the 1970 Super Bowl, the NFL was made a 13- or 14-point favorite, which meant to me that they were still basing their judgments on leagues instead of peoples."

The late Tex Maule, who covered the NFL for *Sports Illustrated*, agreed with Stram. Maule felt the Jets' win the year before had "shattered for all time the myth of NFL superiority." The difference between the two leagues in 1969,

Maule said, was in teams, not leagues. In his discussions with key members of the Chiefs and Vikings, before Super Bowl IV, Maule found that the underdog Chiefs, many of whom had played in Super Bowl I, were relaxed and adjusting to the big-game atmosphere. The favored Vikings on the other hand, appeared nervous and edgy.

Not even the startling report that K.C. quarterback Len Dawson had been implicated in a gambling investigation could ruffle the Chiefs. Dawson was later cleared of any wrongdoing, but the stress and strain he endured the week of Super Bowl IV drained him emotionally and left him pale and nervous.

Despite the emotional rollercoaster he was forced to undergo that week, Dawson believes now that the controversy might have helped the Chiefs. "I think it might have had a pretty good effect, looking back," he said. "My teammates were definitely on my side, and it might have given me an extra spark."

Still, as game day drew near, forces beyond the Chiefs' control seemed to be conspiring against them. Not only were they besieged by the unfounded reports concerned Dawson, the weather in New Orleans, the sight of the game, also seemed to favor the Vikings. Not only was it unseasonably cold and rainy, record low temperatures gripped the area, freezing the water fountain outside the Chiefs' team hotel.

"Viking weather," someone said, and Stram smiled grimly at the remark.

Game day was more of the same. The two teams awoke to overcast skies and intermittent rain, and Stram worried privately that field conditions could favor the straight-ahead attack of the Vikings. But any edge the Vikings might have incurred from the intangibles surrounding the game quickly evaporated as the teams arrived at Tulane Stadium.

Since the AFL was playing its final Super Bowl, Stram and team owner Lamar Hunt ordered special patches to be sewn on the shoulders of the Chiefs' red uniform jerseys. The patch bore the AFL logo, and its effect on Kansas City's players was uplifting.

"It lit us up," Lanier said. "We all knew what it meant."

As the Chiefs dressed for the game, Stram was being wired for sound by NFL Films. Ed Sabol, executive producer of NFL Films, had approached Stram in the days leading up the game and asked him if he would consent to be wired. At first Stram refused.

"Why don't you ask Grant?"

"Because," Sabol answered, "you're more colorful. Besides, you don't use language."

"Damn right I don't," Stram replied.

As kickoff drew near, omens began to favor the Chiefs. The cold front that had promised "Viking weather" for the Super Bowl gave way to a warming front. In the pregame ceremonies, two balloons, one marked AFL and the other NFL, were supposed to lift off from the soggy stadium floor and float out of the stadium. But only the AFL balloon made it — the NFL balloon crashed into the stands and was shredded by angry fans.

"We should've known," Eller mused, "something bad was about to happen."

The Vikings moved well on their opening drive, but stalled at the Chiefs' 39 when Kapp's pass to John Beasley bounced off the tight end's fingertips. On the K.C. sideline, Stram was relieved. The Chiefs' defensive game plan was focused on taking away Minnesota's wide receivers, Gene Washington and John Henderson.

"We felt that Minnesota's tight end would hurt us more than their outside receivers," Stram said, "since we [were] a zone defense team."

Following Minnesota's miscue, the Chiefs responded with an eight-play, 42-yard drive that ended in Jan Stenerud's Super Bowl-record 48-yard field goal and a 3–0 lead.

"Jan was awesome," Chiefs halfback Mike Garrett says today. "We knew if we could get the ball to midfield, we could score."

From the start, the Chiefs confused Minnesota's defense with their shifting formations and well-conceived plays.

"We had a perfect game plan," says Garrett. "We did a lot things they weren't used to seeing in the NFL."

After stopping the Vikings again, the Chiefs made it 6–0 with an eight-play, 55-yard drive that Stenerud capped with his second field goal of the game — this time from 32 yards out. Again, Dawson kept the Vikings off-balance with his shrewd play calling and crisp, short passing game.

Defensively, K.C.'s stack defense was creating problems for the Vikings' offense.

"I think the stack confused them," Buchanan said. "(Center Mick) Tingelhoff was not used to playing with someone on his nose."

Stenerud's third field goal of the game, a 25-yarder midway through the second quarter, gave K.C. a 9–0 lead. The key play in the Chiefs' drive was a reverse to split end Frank Pitts. In Stram's playbook, the call was "52 G-O Reverse." It was a play that would plague the Vikings all afternoon — and, as Stram explained, one the Chiefs had rarely used all season.

"We used a variety of end-around plays from different formations during the regular season," Stram said, "but the ones we used successfully plays we hadn't used too much before."

Safety Johnny Robinson, who played the game with injured ribs but still contributed an interception and fumble recovery, said the Chiefs matched up well with Minnesota's offense.

"The type of team that could beat us then would be a fast, quick team," Robinson says today. "We were better suited to play a physical team, and that's what the Vikings were."

Trailing 9–0, the Vikings were getting jittery. Charlie West tried to return Stenerud's ensuing kickoff on the run, but fumbled the ball. Remi Prudhomme recovered for K.C. at the Minnesota 19. Following an 8-yard loss after a sack by Marshall, the Chiefs picked up two big plays on a 13-yard draw by Wendell Hayes and a 10-yard pass to Otis Taylor.

With a third-and-goal at the Minnesota 5, Stram called for some misdirection.

"Sixty-five Toss Power Trap," Stram said to an assistant. "Look for Sixty-five Toss Power Trap and see what it looks like. They might pop it wide open."

"Sixty-five Toss Power Trap" called for left guard Mo Moorman to trap Minnesota defensive right end Jim Marshall, with Garrett following. The play worked to perfection, with Garrett scoring standing up.

"It was a toss and inside trap," Garrett recalls. "Alan Page ran himself out of the play."

Bill Grigsby called the action on the Chiefs' radio network.

Third down and five ... Running play coming to Garrett on a trap. Touchdown! Garrett scores from the five. With 5:34 remaining here before the half, the Chiefs have just driven 19 yards in six plays on a trap block. Garrett took it in and you just saw outstanding line blocking up front. The pulling guard made that play — Mo Moorman.

Kansas City carried its surprising 16–0 lead into halftime. The Chiefs had dominated the favored Vikings in every phase of the game, and Stram spurred his team on by reminding them, "Thirty more minutes and we're world champions!"

But it was the Vikings who came out for the second half determined and aggressive. Minnesota's "Purple People Eaters" punished the Chiefs' offense on their series, and Kapp took it to the K.C. defense with a 10-play, 69-yard drive that ended with fullback Dave Osborn lunging in over right tackle from four yards out.

For the first time in the game the Vikings resembled the spirited "Purple Gang" that had taken the NFL by storm in 1969, winning 14 of its 16 games.

The momentum was clearly Minnesota's, and Stram knew it.

"C'mon Leonard," he told Dawson. "Let's put out that fire."

Dawson did. The Chiefs moved from their own 18 to the 32, then called on Pitts on a key third-and-seven for another end reverse. Pitts barely made the first, keeping the drive alive.

Two plays later, Dawson read a Minnesota safety blitz and hit Otis Taylor with a short square out. The play was designed to gain 6 yards, but Taylor spun away from cornerback Earsell Mackbee, whose arm went numb from a pinched nerve when he tried to make the tackle. Taylor ran through Karl Kassulke's tackle and high-stepped his way into the end zone. The score came with 1:22 left in the third quarter and gave the Chiefs an insurmountable 23–7 lead.

GRIGSBY: *Otis Taylor, great move! He was hit at the 35, pulled loose, went down the sideline, pulled a great move, went in for the touchdown!*

"It was truly a great individual effort typical of Otis," Stram said.

"The play was called 'Red Right X, Four Pattern Hitch,'" Taylor says today. "Basically, I was just supposed to plant, turn around, and catch the ball. I liked to run with the football. I didn't like to catch it and fall down with it like you see some guys doing now. I liked to make people tackle me."

Leading by 16 points, the Chiefs' front four began to tee off on Kapp. The Vikings' quarterback was hurried into two more interceptions — one by Lanier and one by Robinson — and a fumble before being knocked from the game with a sore shoulder following a tremendous sack by right defensive end Aaron Brown with five minutes left.

GRIGSBY: *Washington to the right, Henderson to the left. The Chiefs dug in defensively. Kapp with the ball, he'll fade back, the blitz is on ... fumble on the play! The Vikings get the ball on the 17, and Kapp is hurt. Aaron Brown almost tore the head off of Joe Kapp.*

Linebacker Bobby Bell, who was voted to the all-time AFL team, says today that the Chiefs were confident they could handle the Vikings, but they also knew they had to get to Kapp to win the game.

"There was no way we were going to lose that game," Bell says. "No way. Kapp was a big, rough quarterback, and we knew we had to shut him down right off the bat."

Kapp says today that K.C.'s stack defense, which was rarely used in the NFL, confused the Vikings. The Chiefs' strategy and physical size simply overwhelmed Minnesota.

"The Kansas City defensive line resembled a redwood forest," Kapp said. "I don't remember that one individual stood out, they were all very active."

"We made a batch of mistakes," Kassulke said, "more mistakes than we made in 23 other games."

Kansas City ended the game the same way they began it, hitting off tackle with backs Holmes and McVea.

Grigsby counted the final seconds for Chiefs fans.

Twenty seconds, nineteen, eighteen, the game is going to be over.... That's it! The Chiefs are the world champions of professional football!

Stram was hoisted on the shoulders of his players and rode off the field waving his rolled-up game plan. In the Chiefs' locker room, Stram held court for the media. The architect of the "Offense of the Seventies" looked resplendent in his black blazer, red vest, and gray checked trousers.

"We didn't put in any new wrinkles for this game," he said. "The end-around surprised them, but it wasn't a new play. It might have been new to them, but we've used it before. Fortunately, it wasn't in the game films the Vikings had seen of us. Defensively, we had to keep Kapp in the pocket and prevent him from rolling out. We got a great effort from our front four in doing that."

Dawson, the game's MVP, stood in front of his locker wearing a heavy, longsleeved undershirt. He was sweating under the hot lights, but he was smiling.

"I don't think the victory vindicated anything," he said. "Unfortunately, the gambling report put a lot of stress and strain on me, and more so on my family. But I asked the Good Lord to give me the strength and courage to play my best."

While the Chiefs exulted, the Vikings were subdued in their locker room. "We played a great team today, and they beat us," Grant said. "I can't say that Kansas City is the toughest team we've played all year, but point-wise and production-wise, they outplayed us the toughest."

Kapp, who had to be helped getting showered and dressed after the game, praised the Chiefs' defense. "They took the running game away from us," he said, "and we couldn't come up with the big play when we needed it.... They just played too well defensively."

Page said Minnesota made a mistake by abandoning its reckless defensive style in an effort to cope with Stram's heralded multiple offense. Page said the Vikings tinkered with their defensive schemes the week before the game, trying to adapt to the Chiefs' offense.

"It was a waste of time," Page said, "and it didn't work."

Dawson, in contrast, remembers the Chiefs' game plan as a thing of beauty.

> I thought Hank Stram put together a heck of a game plan. The strength of the Vikings' defense was their front seven. The quickness those guys had made it tough to block them. We knew we had to slow them down, and keep Eller's hands down, so we double-teamed them. We felt we could work on their corners and play-pass their linebackers.
>
> Defensively, we were a heck of a lot stronger in Super Bowl IV than we had been in Super Bowl I. We were just going to keep banging away at Joe Kapp.

Today, Stram looks back at Super Bowl IV and points to Kansas City's dominance along the lines of scrimmage as the keys to victory.

"We double-teamed Eller and Marshall," Stram says, "and that gave us great blocking angles and allowed us to run our reverses. Defensively, we used the triple stack. People said it was goofy, but it's hard to block for the run."

A jubilant Stram proclaimed his offense to be the "Offense of the Seventies," and many observers agreed with him. In *The Illustrated History of Pro Football*, published in 1970, author Robert Smith compared Stram to Paul Brown as an innovative coach whose ideas were certain to catch on.

"Stram seemed to be doing to professional football what Paul Brown had done a quarter century before," Smith wrote, "shifting it to a higher intellectual plane, or at least developing it in the direction of an academic discipline. There was far more to learn, to practice, and to remember in Hank Stram's football than there ever had been in Curly Lambeau's, or in Jim Thorpe's."

Kansas City's decisive victory convinced even the staunchest NFL supporters that there was little difference any more between the two leagues. Tex Maule, who covered the NFL for *Sports Illustrated*, acknowledged as much after the game.

"I must admit that for a long time, I was an NFL adherent," Maule wrote. "I was raised in the NFL; I didn't think that the upstarts could match NFL teams. I don't like to say it, but I was wrong.... There is no difference now between the two leagues."

Dawson says the Chiefs' victory helped solidify the AFL and NFL as one, a fact that would become reality with the merger the following season and the creation of the National and American Football Conferences. In a 1992 interview, Chiefs defensive tackle Jerry Mays agreed with Dawson's statement, and pointed to a postgame team party as evidence.

"After Super Bowl IV, one of the first people I saw at the postgame party was Vince Lombardi," Mays said. "He stuck his hand out and said, 'Way to go, Jerry. Offensively and defensively, you had the better team.'"

Lombardi later wrote that the Chiefs' defensive execution and determination against the Vikings was something football fans would remember. "The front four — Mays, Buchanan, Culp, and Brown — were especially spectacular," Lombardi wrote.

After 10 years, the AFL had come of age. The "Foolish Club" had defied the odds and won. For the Chiefs, playing in the final AFL game offered a bittersweet moment. As *Detroit News* columnist Jerry Green stood in a knot of reporters interviewing Dawson, he looked across the room and noticed Jerry Mays. Kansas City's defensive captain was grimy but grinning, still wearing the Chiefs' jersey with its AFL patch on the shoulder.

"It was kind of like we had our own little argument with the NFL," Mays remembered. "It was like a minority against the majority. Proving parity with the NFL was important because of all the junk we went through."

As Lamar Hunt celebrated the Chiefs' victory with his players, a reporter asked him if there was any special significance to the moment, since it was Hunt who founded the AFL 10 years earlier.

Hunt smiled.

"It's been a lot of fun," he said. "I don't even care who started it. But it's nice to know that the Chiefs finished it."

Epilogue

THE OLD STADIUMS are silent now.

The voices of several thousand strong in War Memorial Stadium, the Polo Grounds, Balboa Stadium, and Jeppesen Stadium have faded. The days of watching Lance Alworth make acrobatic catches are over.

The memories, however, remain strong.

Retired Kansas City Chiefs wide receiver Otis Taylor still feels the numbing cold of a December game in Buffalo. *San Diego Tribune* sportswriter Jerry Magee remembers departing the Rockpile after a tough loss and hearing the old stadium's mocking rattle, courtesy of a thousand empty beer cans.

Oakland Hall of Fame center Jim Otto recalls the bitterness of the Raiders–Chiefs rivalry that dominated the AFL from 1967 to 1969 and produced three of the league's four Super Bowl representatives. New York Jets linebacker Larry Grantham describes the humiliation the AFL endured in its early years and the absolute feeling of redemption on January 12, 1969, when the Jets upset the NFL's Baltimore Colts in Super Bowl III.

Buffalo guard Billy Shaw remembers the all-pro duels he engaged in with San Diego's Ernie Ladd; and Houston's Charley Hennigan, who set a pro record with 101 catches in 1964, recalls how receivers used to use the goalposts, which were situated in the end zones, to pick off defenders.

The ebullience of Hank Stram is evident as he talks strategy and explains the development of the moving pocket, the tight-end I, and stack defense. Pride surfaced in the voices of two of Stram's ex-players, Jerry Mays and Buck Buchanan, who in the years before their untimely deaths spoke of the camaraderie they felt in being a part of the AFL.

From Al LoCasale, an administrative assistant to Al Davis in Oakland, there was a sense of satisfaction at the league's success in changing the structure of the game. Ask LoCasale about the legacy of the AFL and he quickly responds, "I'm wearing it." When the Raiders won their first Super Bowl in January of 1977, Davis had the old AFL insignia engraved on the side of the Raiders' championship rings.

The AFL, then, was many things to many people, and the history of the league offers a wide range of images.

The AFL was Chiefs mascot "Warpaint" thundering along the sidelines at Kansas City's Municipal Stadium after a K.C. score, while high above the field, the "Wolfpack" cheered on the horse and his Indian rider.

It was all-pro linemen like Gene Upshaw and Buck Buchanan waging a terrific version of trench warfare, while out on the perimeter, Willie Brown was in bump-and-run coverage on Otis Taylor.

It was Joe Namath dropping back amid the dusty swirl of the Shea Stadium infield and snapping deep spirals to Don Maynard and George Sauer.

It was Buffalo head coach Lou Saban shoving his quarterback and future Congressman Jack Kemp into an empty locker during a halftime argument, and it was "The Boston Leaper," an unknown Patriots fan who sneaked onto the field and tipped away the Texans' potential game-winning TD pass.

It was the punishing forearm of Buffalo's 250-pound fullback Cookie Gilchrist, and the record-setting right foot of Jets kicker Jim Turner.

It was Kansas City's "Wild West" offense and Oakland's "Angry Eleven" defense, and it was Curt Gowdy and Paul Christman in the broadcast booth, telling viewers that Texans star halfback Abner Haynes had just fumbled the coin toss in the famous 1962 double-overtime title game.

It was the Broncos' vertically striped socks, and the "AFL-10" patches sewn onto the shoulders of the Chiefs' jerseys for Super Bowl IV.

It was Buffalo's Mike Stratton laying "the hit heard round the world" on San Diego's Keith Lincoln in the '64 title game, and it was the Raiders shocking the Jets four years later in the "Heidi Bowl."

It was Freddy "the Hammer" Williamson predicting he would personally knock out the Packers in Super Bowl I, only to be knocked out himself, courtesy of a Lombardi power sweep; and it was "Broadway Joe" guaranteeing a Jets victory over the Colts two years later, and delivering.

It was Sid Gillman's bow-ties and Hank Stram's red vests.

It was single-bar facemasks and double-post uprights.

It was a blast from the past, pro football being played in high school-sized stadiums, in all the elements, and it was a glimpse of the future, when the AFL opened the first domed stadium in Houston.

Mostly, it was wide-open, entertaining football, a stark contrast at that time to the more conservative NFL.

"It was balls-to-the-walls offense," says Steve Sabol, the executive producer of NFL Films and a football historian. "The AFL was an innovative league, and they had a lot of great players who had come over from the NFL. They had some very good original thinkers in the AFL Sid Gillman, Al Davis, Chuck Noll — and the legacy of their league is the wide-open style of play."

Like Sabol, Joe Horrigan, director of the Pro Football Hall of Fame in Canton, Ohio, believes the AFL's legacy can be found in the new frontiers it forged, on and off the field:

The most obvious and most significant contribution the AFL made to pro football was expanding the game into cities the NFL wasn't in. That alone was a very significant contribution in just growth alone.

Another very significant contribution was in TV. Television dictates the success or failure of pro football, and at the start, the AFL simply wanted to survive, and they knew they had to work together to survive. So the owners shared their revenues and grew together as a league. That's what the NFL is doing today, and they can look back and thank the AFL for that.

AFL offenses were explosive, and since they were challengers to the NFL, they could basically do anything they wanted on the field and not be criticized for it. It became a situation of action-reaction, and the NFL became a part of that [strategic] ebb and flow.

The AFL produced some very, very important people. Lamar Hunt, Ralph Wilson, Bud Adams.... They're the only real league that has challenged the NFL, and won.

Jerry Mays, the defensive captain on the Chiefs' Super Bowl IV championship team, compared the AFL in a 1992 interview to a large, extended family. Because of all the junk we went through, a lot of guys got close," Mays said. "There was a great deal of love in the AFL, a great deal of love on those teams. I had love for John Hadl, Jack Kemp, Ron Mix, Tom Sestak, Joe Namath, Bob Talamini, Winston Hill, and on and on."

Says Curt Gowdy, the Hall of Fame announcer who broadcast AFL games first for ABC-TV and later for NBC, "The story of the AFL, how the league grew and became popular, is one of the best sports stories of all time."

Appendix A

AFL Yearly Standings 1960–69

1960

EASTERN DIVISION

	W	L	T	Pct.	Pts.	Opp.
Houston	10	4	0	.714	379	285
New York	7	7	0	.500	382	399
Buffalo	5	8	1	.358	296	303
Boston	5	9	0	.357	286	349

WESTERN DIVISION

	W	L	T	Pct.	Pts.	Opp.
Los Angeles	10	4	0	.714	373	386
Dallas	8	6	0	.571	362	253
Oakland	6	8	0	.429	319	388
Denver	4	9	1	.308	309	393

Leading Rushers	Att.	Yards	Avg.	TD
Haynes, Dallas	156	875	5.6	9
Lowe, L.A.	136	855	6.3	9
Cannon, Hous.	152	644	4.2	1

Leading Receivers	No.	Yards	Avg.	TD
Taylor, Denver	92	1,235	13.4	12
Groman, Houston	72	1,473	20.5	12
Maynard, N.Y.	72	1,265	17.6	6

Leading Passers	Att.	Comp.	Yards	TD
Kemp, L.A.	406	211	3,018	20
Dorow, N.Y.	396	201	2,748	26
Tripucka, Den.	478	248	3,038	24

Leading Scorer	TD	FG	PAT	Pts.
Mingo, Den.	6	18	33	123

Leading Interceptor	No.	Yards	Avg.	TD
Gonsoulin, Den.	11	98	8.9	0

1961

EASTERN DIVISION

	W	L	T	Pct.	Pts.	Opp.
Houston	10	3	1	.769	513	242
Boston	9	4	1	.692	413	313
New York	7	7	0	.500	301	390
Buffalo	6	8	0	.429	294	342

WESTERN DIVISION

	W	L	T	Pct.	Pts.	Opp.
San Diego	12	2	0	.857	396	219
Dallas	6	8	0	.429	334	343
Denver	3	11	0	.214	251	432
Oakland	2	12	0	.143	237	458

Leading Rushers	Att.	Yards	Avg.	TD
Cannon, Houston	200	948	4.7	6
Mathis, N.Y.	202	846	4.2	7
Haynes, Dallas	179	841	4.7	9

Leading Receivers	No.	Yards	Avg.	TD
Taylor, Denver	100	1,176	11.8	4
Hennigan, Hous.	82	1,746	21.3	
Powell, N.Y.	71	881	12.4	5

Leading Passers	Att.	Comp.	Yards	TD
Blanda, Hous.	362	187	3,330	36
Flores, Oak.	366	190	2,176	15
Kemp, S.D.	364	165	2,686	15

Leading Scorer	TD	FG	PAT	Pts.
Cappelleti, Bos.	8	17	48	147

Leading Interceptor	No.	Yards	Avg.	TD
Atkins, Buff.	10	158	15.8	0

1962

EASTERN DIVISION

	W	L	T	Pct.	Pts.	Opp.
Houston	11	3	0	.786	387	270
Boston	9	4	1	.692	346	295
Buffalo	7	6	1	.538	309	272
New York	5	9	0	.357	278	423

WESTERN DIVISION

	W	L	T	Pct.	Pts.	Opp.
Dallas	11	3	0	.786	389	233
Denver	7	7	0	.500	353	334
San Diego	4	10	0	.286	314	392
Oakland	1	13	0	.071	213	370

Leading Rushers	Att.	Yards	Avg.	TD
Gilchrist, Buff.	214	1,096	5.1	13
Haynes, Dallas	221	1,049	4.7	13
Tolar, Houston	244	1,012	4.1	7

Leading Receivers	No.	Yards	Avg.	TD
Taylor, Denver	77	908	11.8	4
Powell, N.Y.	64	1,130	17.7	8
Christy, N.Y.	62	538	8.7	3

Leading Passers	Att.	Comp.	Yards	TD
Dawson, Dallas	310	189	2,759	29
Parilli, Boston	253	140	1,988	18
Tripucka, Denver	440	240	2,917	17

Leading Scorer	TD	FG	PAT	Pts.
Mingo, Denver	4	27	32	137

Leading Interceptor	No.	Yards	Avg.	TD
Riley, New York	11	122	11.1	0

1963

EASTERN DIVISION

	W	L	T	Pct.	Pts.	Opp.
Boston	7	6	1	.538	317	257
Buffalo	7	6	1	.538	304	291
Houston	6	8	0	.429	302	372
New York	5	8	1	.385	249	399

WESTERN DIVISION

	W	L	T	Pct.	Pts.	Opp.
San Diego	11	3	0	.786	399	256
Oakland	10	4	0	.714	363	288
Kansas City.	5	7	2	.417	347	263
Denver	2	11	1	.154	301	473

Leading Rushers	Att.	Yards	Avg.	TD
Daniels, Oak.	215	1,099	5.1	3
Lowe, San Diego	177	1,010	5.7	8
Gilchrist, Buff.	232	979	4.2	12

Leading Receivers	No.	Yards	Avg.	TD
Taylor, Denver	78	1,101	14.1	10
Powell, Oakland	73	1,304	17.8	16
Turner, N.Y.	71	1,007	14.2	6

Leading Passers	Att.	Comp.	Yards	TD
Rote, San Diego	286	170	2,510	20
Flores, Oakland	247	113	2,101	20
Kemp, Buffalo	384	194	2,914	13

Leading Scorer	TD	FG	PAT	Pts.
Cappelleti, Bos.	2	22	35	113

Leading Interceptor	No.	Yards	Avg.	TD
Glick, Houston	12	180	15.0	1

1964

EASTERN DIVISION

	W	L	T	Pct.	Pts.	Opp.
Buffalo	12	2	0	.857	400	242
Boston	10	3	1	.769	365	297
New York	5	8	1	.385	278	315
Houston	4	10	0	.286	310	355

WESTERN DIVISION

	W	L	T	Pct.	Pts.	Opp.
San Diego	8	5	1	.615	341	300
Kansas City	7	7	0	.500	366	306
Oakland	5	7	2	.417	303	350
Denver	2	11	1	.154	240	438

Leading Rushers	Att.	Yards	Avg.	TD
Gilchrist, Buff.	230	981	4.3	6
Snell, N.Y.	215	948	4.4	5
Daniels, Oak.	173	824	4.8	2

Leading Receivers	No.	Yards	Avg.	TD
Hennigan, Hous.	101	1,546	15.3	8
Powell, Oakland	76	1,361	17.9	11
Taylor, Denver	76	873	11.5	7

Leading Passers	Att.	Comp.	Yards	TD
Dawson, K.C.	354	199	2,879	30
Parilli, Boston	473	228	3,465	31
Blanda, Hous.	505	262	3,287	17

Leading Scorer	TD	FG	PAT	Pts.
Cappelletti, Bos.	7	25	37	155

Leading Interceptor	No.	Yards	Avg.	TD
Paulson, N.Y.	12	157	13.1	1

1965

EASTERN DIVISION

	W	L	T	Pct.	Pts.	Opp.
Buffalo	10	3	1	.769	313	226
New York	5	8	1	.385	285	303
Boston	4	8	2	.333	244	302
Houston	4	10	0	.286	298	429

WESTERN DIVISION

	W	L	T	Pct.	Pts.	Opp.
San Diego	9	2	3	.818	340	227
Oakland	8	5	1	.615	298	239
Kansas City	7	5	2	.583	322	285
Denver	4	10	0	.286	303	392

Leading Rushers	Att.	Yards	Avg.	TD
Lowe, San Diego	222	1,121	5.0	7
Gilchrist, Den.	252	954	3.8	6
Daniels, Oak.	219	884	4.0	5

Leading Receivers	No.	Yards	Avg.	TD
Taylor, Denver	85	1,131	13.3	6
Alworth, S.D.	69	1,602	23.2	14
Maynard, N.Y.	68	1,218	17.9	14

Leading Passers	Att.	Comp.	Yards	TD
Hadl, San Diego	348	174	2,798	20
Dawson, K.C.	305	163	2,262	21
Namath, N.Y.	340	164	2,220	18

Leading Scorer	TD	FG	PAT	Pts.
Cappelletti, Bos.	9	17	27	132

Leading Interceptor	No.	Yards	Avg.	TD
Hicks, Houston	9	156	17.3	0

1966

EASTERN DIVISION

	W	L	T	Pct.	Pts.	Opp.
Buffalo	9	4	1	.692	358	255
Boston	8	4	2	.667	315	283
New York	6	6	2	.500	322	312
Houston	3	11	0	.214	335	396
Miami	3	11	0	.214	213	362

WESTERN DIVISION

	W	L	T	Pct.	Pts.	Opp.
Kansas City	11	2	1	.692	448	276
Oakland	8	5	1	.615	315	288
San Diego	7	6	1	.538	335	284
Denver	4	10	0	.286	196	381

Leading Rushers	Att.	Yards	Avg.	TD
Nance, Boston	299	1,458	4.9	11
Garrett, K.C.	147	801	5.4	6
Daniels, Oak.	204	801	3.9	7

Leading Receiers	No.	Yards	Avg.	TD
Alworth, S.D.	73	1,383	18.9	13
Sauer, N.Y.	63	1,079	17.1	5
Taylor, K.C.	58	1,297	22.4	8

Leading Passers	Att.	Comp.	Yards	TD
Dawson, K.C.	284	159	2,527	26
Hadl, San Diego	375	200	2,846	23
Flores, Oakland	306	151	2,638	24

Leading Scorer	TD	FG	PAT	Pts.
Cappelletti, Bos.	6	16	35	119

Leading Interceptors	No.	Yards	Avg.	TD
Robinson, K.C.	10	136	13.6	1
Hunt, K.C.	10	113	11.3	0

1967

EASTERN DIVISION

	W	L	T	Pct.	Pts.	Opp.
Houston	9	4	1	.692	258	199
New York	8	5	1	.615	371	329
Buffalo	4	10	0	.286	237	285
Miami	4	10	0	.286	219	407
Boston	3	10	1	.231	280	329

WESTERN DIVISION

	W	L	T	Pct.	Pts.	Opp.
Oakland	13	1	0	.929	468	233
Kansas City	9	5	0	.643	408	254
San Diego	8	5	1	.615	360	352
Denver	3	11	0	.214	256	409

Leading Rushers	Att.	Yards	Avg.	TD
Nance, Boston	269	1,216	4.5	7
Granger, Hous.	236	1,194	5.1	6
Garrett, K.C.	236	1,087	4.6	9

Leading Receivers	No.	Yards	Avg.	TD
Sauer, N.Y.	75	1,189	15.9	6
Maynard, N.Y.	71	1,434	20.2	10
Clancy, Miami	67	868	13.0	2

Leading Passers	Att.	Comp.	Yards	TD
Lamonica, Oak.	425	220	3,228	30
Dawson, K.C.	357	206	2,651	24
Namath, N.Y.	491	258	4,007	26

Leading Scorer	TD	FG	PAT	Pts.
Blanda, Oak.	0	20	56	116

Leading Interceptors	No.	Yards	Avg.	TD
Farr, Houston	10	264	26.4	3
Janik, Buffalo	10	222	22.2	2
Westmoreland, Mia.	10	127	12.7	1

1968

EASTERN DIVISION

	W	L	T	Pct.	Pts.	Opp.
New York	11	3	0	.786	419	280
Houston	7	7	0	.500	303	248
Miami	5	8	1	.385	276	355
Boston	4	10	0	.28	229	406
Buffalo	1	12	1	.077	199	367

WESTERN DIVISION

	W	L	T	Pct.	Pts.	Opp.
Oakland	12	2	0	.857	453	233
Kansas City	12	2	0	.857	371	170
San Diego	9	5	0	.643	382	310
Denver	5	9	0	.357	255	404
Cincinnati	3	11	0	.214	215	329

Leading Rushers	Att.	Yards	Avg.	TD
Robinson, Cin.	238	1,023	4.3	8
Holmes, K.C.	174	866	5.0	7
Dixon, Oak.	206	865	4.2	2

Leading Receivers	No.	Yards	Avg.	TD
Alworth, S.D.	68	1,312	19.3	10
Sauer, N.Y.	66	1,141	17.3	3
Biletnikoff, Oak.	61	1,037	17.0	6

Leading Passers	Att.	Comp.	Yards	TD
Dawson, K.C.	224	131	2,019	9
Lamonica, Oak.	416	206	3,245	25
Namath, N.Y.	380	187	3,147	15

Leading Scorer	TD	FG	PAT	Pts.
Turner, N.Y.	0	34	43	145

Leading Interceptor	No.	Yards	Avg.	TD
Grayson, Oak.	10	195	19.5	1

1969

EASTERN DIVISION

	W	L	T	Pct.	Pts.	Opp.
New York	10	4	0	.714	353	269
Houston	6	6	2	.500	278	279
Boston	4	10	0	.286	266	316
Buffalo	4	10	0	.286	230	359
Miami	3	10	1	.231	233	332

WESTERN DIVISION

	W	L	T	Pct.	Pts.	Opp.
Oakland	12	1	1	.923	377	242
Kansas City	11	3	0	.786	359	177
San Diego	8	6	0	.571	288	276
Denver	5	8	1	.385	297	344
Cincinnati	4	9	1	.308	280	67

Leading Rushers	Att.	Yards	Avg.	TD
Post, S.D.	182	873	4.8	6
Nance, Boston	193	750	3.9	6
Granger, Hous.	186	740	4.0	3

Leading Receivers	No.	Yards	Avg.	TD
Alworth, S.D.	64	1,003	15.7	4
Biletnikoff, Oak.	54	837	15.5	12
Denson, Denver	53	809	15.3	10

Leading Passers	Att.	Comp.	Yards	TD
Cook, Cincinnati	197	106	1,854	15
Namath, New York	361	185	2,734	19
Lamonica, Oak.	426	221	3302	34

Leading Scorer	TD	FG	PAT	Pts.
Turner, New York	0	32	33	129

Leading Interceptor	No.	Yards	Avg.	TD
Thomas, K.C.	9	146	16.2	1

Appendix B

Scoring Summaries for AFL Playoff, Championship, Super Bowl, and All-Star Games

PLAYOFF AND CHAMPIONSHIP GAMES

1960 CHAMPIONSHIP

January 1, 1961 at Houston
HOUSTON 24, L.A. CHARGERS 16
Chargers   6   3   7   0 - 16
Oilers   0   10   7   7 - 24
LA-FG Agajanian 28
LA-FG Agajanian 22 (Blanda kick)
HOU-FG Blanda 18
LA-FG Agajanian 27
HOU-Groman 7 pass from Blanda (Blanda kick)
LA-Lowe 2 run (Agajanian kick)
HOU-Cannon 88 pass from Blanda (Blanda kick)
Attendance — 32,183

1961 CHAMPIONSHIP

December 24, 1961 at San Diego
HOUSTON 10, SAN DIEGO 3
Oilers   0   3   7   0 - 10
Chargers   0   0   0   3 - 3
HOU-FG Blanda 46
HOU-Cannon 35 pass from Blanda
HOU-Smith 17 pass from Blanda (Blanda kick)
SD-FG Blair 12
Attendance — 29,556

1962 CHAMPIONSHIP

December 23, 1962 at Houston
DALLAS 20, HOUSTON 17, 2 OT
Texans   3   14   0   0   0   3 - 20
Oilers   0   0   7   10   0   0 - 17
DALL-FG Brooker 16
DAL-Haynes 28 pass from Dawson (Brooker kick)
DALL-Haynes 2 run (Brooker kick)
HOU-Dewveall 15 pass from Blanda (Blanda kick)
HOU-FG Blanda 31
HOU-Tolar 1 run (Blanda kick)
DALL-FG Brooker 25
Attendance — 37,981

1963 EASTERN DIVISION PLAYOFF

December 28, 1963 at Buffalo
BOSTON 26, BUFFALO 8
Patriots   10   6   0   10 - 26
Bills   0   0   8   0 - 8
BOS-FG Cappelletti 28
BOS-Garron 59 pass from Parilli (Cappelletti kick)
BOS-FG Cappelletti 12
BOS-FG Cappelletti 33

BUFF-Dubenion 93 pass from Lamon-
ica (Tracey pass from Lamonica)
BOS-Garron 17 pass from Parilli (Cap-
pelletti kick)
BOS-FG Cappelletti 36
Attendance — 33,044

1963 CHAMPIONSHIP

January 5, 1964 at San Diego
SAN DIEGO 51, BOSTON 10
Boston   7   3   0   0 - 10
San Diego   21 10   7 13 - 51
SD-Rote 2 run (Blair kick)
SD-Lincoln 67 run (Cappelletti kick)
BOS-Garron 7 run (Cappelletti kick)
SD-Lowe 58 run (Blair kick)
SD-FG Blair 11
BOS-FG Cappelletti 15
SD-Norton 14 pass from Rote (Blair kick)
SD-Alworth 48 pass from Rote (Blair kick)
SD-Lincoln 25 pass from Hadl (Blair kick)
SD-Hadl 1 run (Blair kick)
Attendance — 30,127

1964 CHAMPIONSHIP

December 26, 1964 at Buffalo
BUFFALO 20, SAN DIEGO 7
Chargers   7   0   0   0 - 7
Bills   3 10   0   7 - 20
SD-Kocourek 26 pass from Rote (Lincoln kick)
BUFF-FG Gogolak 12
BUFF-Carlton 4 run (Gogolak kick)
BUFF-Gogolak FG 17
BUFF-Kemp 1 run (Gogolak kick)
Attendance — 40,242

1965 CHAMPIONSHIP

December 26, 1965 at San Diego
BUFFALO 23, SAN DIEGO 0
Bills   0 14   6   3 - 23
Chargers   0   0   0   0 - 0
BUFF-Warlick 18 pass from Kemp (Gogolak kick)

BUFF-Byrd 74 punt return (Gogolak kick)
BUFF-FG Gogolak 11
BUFF-FG Gogolak 39
BUFF-FG Gogolak 32
Attendance — 30,361

1966 CHAMPIONSHIP

January 1, 1967 at Buffalo
KANSAS CITY 31, BUFFALO 7
Chiefs   7 10   0 14 - 31
Bills   7   0   0   0 - 7
KC-Arbanas 29 pass from Dawson (Mercer kick)
BUFF-Dubenion 69 pass from Kemp (Lusteg kick)
KC-Taylor 29 pass from Dawson (Mercer kick)
KC-FG Mercer 32
KC-Garrett 1 run (Mercer kick)
KC-Garrett 18 run (Mercer kick)
Attendance — 42,080

1967 CHAMPIONSHIP

December 31, 1967 at Oakland
OAKLAND 40, HOUSTON 7
Oilers   0   0   0   7 - 7
Raiders   3 14 10 13 - 40
OAK-FG Blanda 37
OAK-Dixon 69 run (Blanda kick)
OAK-Kocourek 17 pass from Lamonica (Blanda kick)
OAK-Lamonica 1 run (Blanda kick)
OAK-FG Blanda 40
KC-FG Stenerud 10
HOUS-Frazier 5 pass from Beathard (Wittenborn kick)
OAK-FG Blanda 36
OAK-Miller 12 pass Lamonica (Blanda kick)
Attendance — 53,330

1968 WESTERN DIVISION PLAYOFF

December 22, 1968 at Oakland
OAKLAND 41, KANSAS CITY 6
Chiefs   0   6   0   0 - 6
Raiders   21   7   0 13 - 41

OAK-Biletnikoff 24 pass from Lamonica
(Blanda kick)
OAK-Wells 23 pass from Lamonica
(Blanda kick)
OAK-Biletnikoff 44 pass from Lamonica
(Blanda kick)
OAK-FG Blanda 42
KC-FG Stenerud 8
OAK-Biletnikoff 54 pass from Lamonica
OAK-Wells 35 pass from Lamonica
(Blanda kick)
OAK-FG Blanda 41
OAK-FG Blanda 40
Attendance — 53,605

1968 CHAMPIONSHIP

December 29, 1968 at New York
NEW YORK 27, OAKLAND 23
Raiders   0 10   3 10 - 23
Jets   10   3   7   7 - 27
NY-Maynard 14 pass from Namath (J. Turner kick)
NY-FG J. Turner 33
OAK-Biletnikoff 29 pass from Lamonica
(Blanda kick)
OAK-FG Blanda 26
OAK-FG Blanda 9
NY-Lammons 20 pass from Namath (J. Turner kick)
OAK-FG Blanda 20
OAK-Banaszak 5 run (Blanda kick)
NY-Maynard 6 pass from Namath (J. Turner kick)
Attendance — 62,627

1969 DIVISIONAL PLAYOFF

December 20, 1969 at New York
KANSAS CITY 13, NEW YORK 6
Chiefs   0   3   3   7 - 13
Jets   3   0   0   3 - 6
NY-FG J. Turner 27
KC-FG Stenerud 23
KC-FG Stenerud 25
NY-FG J. Turner 7
KC-Richardson 19 pass from Dawson
(Stenerud kick)
Attendance — 62,977

1969 DIVISIONAL PLAYOFF

December 21, 1969 at Oakland
OAKLAND 56, HOUSTON 7
Oilers   0   0   0   7 - 7
Raiders   28   7 14   7 - 56
OAK-Biletnikoff 13 pass from Lamonica
(Blanda kick)
OAK-Atkinson 57 interception return
(Lamonica kick)
OAK-Sherman 24 pass from Lamonica
(Blanda kick)
OAK-Biletnikoff 31 pass from Lamonica
(Blanda kick)
OAK-Smith 60 pass from Lamonica
(Blanda kick)
OAK-Sherman 23 pas from Lamonica
(Blanda kick)
OAK-Cannon 3 pass from Lamonica
(Blanda kick)
HOU-Reed 8 pass from Beathard
(Gerela kick)
OAK-Hubbard 4 run (Blanda kick)
Attendance — 53,539

1969 CHAMPIONSHIP

Jaury 4, 1970 at Oakland
KANSAS CITY 17, OAKLAND 7
Chiefs   0   7   7   3 - 17
Raiders   7   0   0   0 - 7
OAK-Smith 3 run (Blanda kick)
KC-Hayes 1 run (Stenerud kick)
KC-Holmes 5 run (Stenerud kick)
KC-FG Stenerud 22
Attendance — 53,564

# AFL–NFL WORLD CHAMPIONSHIP GAMES I–IV

SUPER BOWL I

January 15, 1967 at Los Angeles
GREEN BAY 35, KANSAS CITY 10

Chiefs	0	10	0	0	- 10
Packers	7	7	14	7	- 35

GB-McGee 37 pass from Starr (Chandler kick)
KC-McClinton 7 pass from Dawson (Mercer kick)
GB-Taylor 14 run (Chandler kick)
KC-FG Mercer 31
GB-Pitts 5 run (Chandler kick)
GB-McGee 13 pass from Starr (Chandler kick)
GB-Pitts 1 run (Chandler kick)
Attendance — 61,946

SUPER BOWL II

January 14, 1968 at Miami
GREEN BAY 33, OAKLAND 14

Packers	3	13	10	7	- 33
Raiders	0	7	0	7	- 14

GB-FG Chandler 39
GB-FG Chandler 20
GB-Dowler 62 pass from Starr (Chandler kick)
OAK-Miller 23 pass from Lamonica (Blanda kick)
GB-FG Chandler 43
GB-Anderson 2 run (Chandlerkick)
GB-FG Chandler 31
OAK-Miller 23 pass from Lamonica (Blanda kick)
GB-Adderley 60 interception return (Chandler kick)
OAK-Miller 23 pass from Lamonica (Blanda kick)
Attendance — 75,546

SUPER BOWL III

January 12, 1969, At Miami
NEW YORK 16, BALTIMORE 7

Jets	0	7	6	3	- 16
Colts	0	0	0	7	- 7

NYJ-Snell 4 run (J. Turner kick)
NYJ-FG J. Turner 32
NYJ-FG J. Turner 30
NYJ-FG J. Turner 9
BALT-Hill 1 run (Michaels kick)
Attendance — 75,377

SUPER BOWL IV

January 11, 1970 at New Orleans
KANSAS CITY 23, MINNESOTA 7

Vikings	0	0	7	0	- 7
Chiefs	3	13	7	0	- 23

KC-FG Stenerud 48
KC-FG Stenerud 32
KC-FG Stenerud 25
KC-Garrett 5 run (Stenerud kick)
MINN-Osborn 4 run (Cox kick)
KC-Taylor 46 pass from Dawson (Stenerud kick)
Attendance — 80,562

ALL-STAR GAMES 1962–70

1962

January 7 at San Diego's Balboa Stadium

East	5	7	7	8	- 27
West	0	21	14	12	- 47

Head coaches — East: Wally Lemm, Houston; West: Sid Gillman, San Diego
East — FG Blanda 32
East — Safety, Haynes tackled in end zone
West — Stone 45 pass from Davidson (Blair kick)
East — Cannon 34 pass from Blanda (Blanda kick)
West — Haynes 12 run (Blair kick)
West — Kocourek 24 pass from Davidson (Blair kick)
West — Haynes 66 punt return (Blair kick)
West — Norton 10 pass from Davidson (Blair kick)

East — Cappelletti 5 pass from Blanda (Blanda kick)
West — Williamson 53 interception return (kick failed)
East — Hennigan 3 pass from Dorow (Dorow run)
West — Stone 15 run (pass failed)
Attendance — 20,973

1963

January 13 at San Diego's Balboa Stadium

West	7	7	0	7 -	21
East	0	0	14	0 -	14

Head coaches — East: Frank Ivy, Houston; West: Hank Stram, Dallas
West — McClinton 64 run (Mingo kick)
West — Kocourek 11 pass from Dawson (Mingo kick)
East — Hennigan 8 pass from Blanda (Blanda kick)
East — Grantham 29 interception return (Blanda kick)
West — Taylor 20 pass from Tripucka (Mingo kick)
Attendance — 27,641

1964

January 19 at San Diego's Balboa Stadium

West	0	3	14	10 -	27
East	10	14	0	0 -	24

Head coaches — East: Mike Holovak, Boston; West: Sid Gillman, San Diego
East — FG Cappelletti 35
East — Gilchrist 1 run (Cappelletti kick)
West — FG Fraser 19
East — Garron 12 pass from Parilli (Cappelletti kick)
East — Mathis 3 pass from Parrilli (Cappelletti kick)
West — Lincoln 64 run (Fraser kick)
West — Lowe 5 run (Fraser kick)
West — FG Fraser 7

West — Powell 25 pass from Davidson (Fraser kick)
Attendance — 20,016

1965

January 16 at Houston's Jeppesen Stadium

West	7	10	14	7 -	38
East	0	14	0	0 -	14

Head coaches — East: Lou Saban, Buffalo; West: Sid Gillman, San Diego
West — Lincoln 73 pass from Dawson (Brooker kick)
West — Daniels 5 pass from Hadl (Brooker kick)
East — Blanks 5 run (Cappelletti kick)
West — FG Brooker 46
East — Buoniconti 17 fumble return (Cappelletti kick)
West — Lincoln 80 run (Brooker kick)
West — Alworth 7 pass from Hadl (Brooker kick)
West — Powell 17 pass from Hadl (Brooker kick)
Attendance — 15,446

1966

January 15 at Houston's Jeppesen Stadium

Buffalo	10	3	0	6 -	19
All-Stars	0	6	17	7 -	30

Head coaches — Bills: Lou Saban; All-Stars: Sid Gillman, San Diego
Buffalo — FG Gogolak 20
Buffalo — Saimes 61 fumble return (Gogolak kick)
All-Stars — FG Cappelletti 46
Buffalo — FG Gogolak 1
All-Stars — FG Cappelletti 14
All-Stars — FG Cappelletti 32
All-Stars — Lowe 1 run (Cappelletti kick)
All-Stars — Alworth 43 pass from Namath (Cappelletti kick)
All-Stars — Alworth 10 pass from Namath (Cappelletti kick)

Buffalo — Carlton 34 pass from Lamonica (run failed)
Attendance — 35,572

1967

January 21, at Oakland Coliseum
East   0 0 16 14 - 30
West   9 7 7 0 - 23
Head coaches — East: Mike Holovak, Boston; West: John Rauch, Oakland
West — McClinton 31 pass from Dawson (Van Raaphorst kick)
West — Safety, center snap out of end zone
West — Dixon 17 pass from Flores (Van Raaphorst kick)
East — Safety, Dawson tackled in end zone
West — Buchanan 39 fumble return (Van Raaphorst kick)
East — Biggs 50 interception return (Cappelletti kick)
East — Carlton 3 pass from Parilli (Cappelletti kick)
East — Burnett 12 run (Cappelletti kick)
East — Frazier 17 pass from Parilli (Cappalletti kick)
Attendance — 18, 876

1968

January 21 at Jacksonville
East   3 10 0 12 - 25
West   7 14 0 3 - 24
Head coaches — East: Joe Collier, Buffalo; West: Lou Saban, Denver
East — FG Mercer 10
West — Duncan 90 kickoff return (Blanda kick)
West — Frazier 3 pass from Lamonica (Mercer kick)
East — Lammons 35 pass from Namath (Mercer kick)
West — Alworth 9 pass from Lamonica (Blanda kick)
East — FG Mercer 33

West — FG Blanda 28
East — Maynard 24 pass from Namath (pass failed)
East — Namath 1 run (run failed)
Attendance — 40,103

1969

January 19 at Jacksonville
West   3 0 10 25 - 38
East   3 16 3 3 - 25
Head coaches — East: George Wilson, Miami; West: Lou Saban, Denver
East — FG Turner 27
West — FG Stenerud 51
East — Kiick 2 run (Turner kick)
East — FG Turner 16
East — FG Turner 19
East — FG Turner 13
West — Trumpy 6 pass from Dawson (Stenerud kick)
East — FG Turner 18
West — FG Stenerud 30
East — FG Turner 21
West — Dixon 1 run (Stenerud kick)
West — Robinson 1 run (Robinson run)
West — Robinson 1 run (Stenerud kick)
West — FG Stenerud 32
Attendance — 41,058

1970

January 17 at Houston Astrodome
East   0 0 3 0 - 3
West   13 3 0 10 - 26
Head coaches — East: George Wilson, Miami; West: Lou Saban, Denver
West — Post 1 run (pass failed)
West — Alworth 21 pass from Hadl (Stenerud kick)
West — FG Stenerud 38
East — FG Turner 44
West — FG Stenerud 30
West — Livingston 11 run (Stenerud kick)
Attendance — 30,170

Appendix C

AFL Team and Individual Honors, 1960–69

1960

OFFENSE
E-Bill Groman, Houston
E-Lionel Taylor, Denver
T-Rich Michael, Houston
T-Ron Mix, LA Chargers
G-Bill Krisher, Dallas Texans
G-Bob Mischak, NY Titans
C-Jim Otto, Oakland
QB-Jack Kemp, LA Chargers
HB-Abner Haynes, Dallas Texans
HB-Paul Lowe, LA Chargers
FB-Dave Smith, Houston

DEFENSE
DE-Laverne Torczon, Buffalo
DE-Mel Branch, Dallas Texans
DT-Bud McFadin, Denver
DT-Volney Peters, LA Chargers
LB-Archie Matsos, Buffalo
LB-Sherrill Headrick, Dallas Texans
LB-Tom Addison, Boston
DB-Richie McCabe, Buffalo
DB-Dick Harris, LA Chargers
DB-Ross O'Hanley, Boston
DB-Austin Gonsoulin, Denver

1961

OFFENSE
E-Lionel Taylor, Denver
E-Charley Hennigan, Houston
T-Ron Mix, San Diego
T-Al Jamison, Houston
G-Bob Mischak, NY Titans
G-Chuck Leo, Boston
C-Jim Otto, Oakland
QB-George Blanda, Houston
HB-Abner Haynes, Dallas Texans
HB-Billy Cannon, Houston
FB-Billy Mathis, NY Titans

DEFENSE
DE-Earl Faison, San Diego
DE-Don Floyd, Houston
DT-Bud McFadin, Denver
DT-Chuck McMurtry, Buffalo
LB-Sherrill Headrick, Dallas Texans
LB-Archie Matsos, Buffalo
LB-Chuck Allen, San Diego
DB-Tony Banfield, Houston
DB-Dick Harris, San Diego
DB-Dave Webster, Dallas Texans
DB-Charlie McNeil, San Diego

1962

OFFENSE
E-Charley Hennigan, Houston
E-Chris Burford, Dallas Texans
T-Eldon Danenhauer, Denver
T-Jim Tyrer, Dallas Texans
G-Bob Talamini, Houston
G-Ron Mix, San Diego
C-Jim Otto, Oakland
QB-Len Dawson, Dallas Texans
HB-Abner Haynes, Dallas Texans
FB-Cookie Gilchrist, Buffalo
TE-Dave Kocourek, San Diego

272

DEFENSE
DE-Don Floyd, Houston
DE-Mel Branch, Dallas Texans
DT-Bud McFadin, Denver
DT-Jerry Mays, Dallas Texans
MLB-Sherrill Headrick, Dallas Texans
LB-Larry Grantham, NY Titans
LB-E. J. Holub, Dallas Texans
CB-Tony Banfield, Houston
CB-Fred Williamson, Oakland
S-Austin Gonsoulin, Denver
S-Bob Zeman, Denver

1963

OFFENSE
E-Art Powell, Oakland
E-Lance Alworth, San Diego
T-Ron Mix, San Diego
T-Jim Tyrer, Kansas City
G-Billy Shaw, Buffalo
G-Bob Talamini, Houston
C-Jim Otto, Oakland
QB-Tobin Rote, San Diego
HB-Clem Daniels, Oakland
FB-Keith Lincoln, San Diego
TE-Fred Arbanas, Kansas City

DEFENSE
DE-Larry Eisenhauer, Boston
DE-Earl Faison, San Diego
DT-Tom Sestak, Buffalo
DT-Houston Antwine, Boston
MLB-Archie Matsos, Buffalo
LB-E. J. Holub, Kansas City
LB-Tom Addison, Boston
CB-Dave Grayson, Kansas City
CB-Fred Williamson, Oakland
S-Fred Glick, Houston
S-Austin Gonsoulin, Denver

1964

OFFENSE
E-Charley Hennigan, Houston
E-Art Powell, Oakland
E-Lance Alworth, San Diego
T-Ron Mix, San Diego
T-Stew Barber, Buffalo
T-Jim Tyrer, Kansas City
G-Billy Shaw Buffalo

G-Billy Neighbors, Boston
G-Bob Talamini, Houston
C-Jim Otto, Oakland
QB-Babe Parilli, Boston
HB-Keith Lincoln, San Diego
FB-Cookie Gilchrist, Buffalo
TE-Fred Arbanas, Kansas City

DEFENSE
DE-Earl Faison, San Diego
DE-Larry Eisenhauer, Boston
DE-Bobby Bell, Kansas City
DT-Tom Sestak, Buffalo
DT-Ernie Ladd, San Diego
DT-Jerry Mays, Kansas City
MLB-Nick Buoniconti, Boston
LB-Larry Grantham, NY Jets
LB-Mike Stratton, Buffalo
LB-Tom Addison, Boston
CB-Willie Brown, Denver
CB-Dave Grayson, Kansas City
CB-Fred Williamson, Kansas City
S-Ron Hall, Boston
S-Dainard Paulson, NY Jets
S-Fred Glick, Houston
S-George Saimes, Buffalo

1965

OFFENSE
E-Lionel Taylor, Denver
E-Art Powell, Oakland
E-Lance Alworth, San Diego
T-Jim Tyrer, Kansas City
T-Ron Mix, San Diego
T-Eldon Danenhauer, Denver
G-Billy Shaw, Buffalo
G-Bob Talamini, Houston
C-Jim Otto, Oakland
QB-Jack Kemp, Buffalo
HB-Paul Lowe, San Diego
FB-Cookie Gilchrist, Denver
K-Pete Gogolak, Buffalo
TE-Willie Frazier, Houston

DEFENSE
DE-Earl Faison, San Diego
DE-Jerry Mays, Kansas City
DE-Ron McDole, Buffalo
DT-Tom Sestak, Buffalo
DT-Ernie Ladd, San Diego
MLB-Nick Buoniconti, Boston

LB-Mike Stratton, Buffalo
LB-Bobby Bell, Kansas City
CB-George Byrd, Buffalo
CB-Fred Williamson, Kansas City
CB-Dave Grayson, Oakland
S-George Saimes, Buffalo
S-Johnny Robinson, Kansas City
S-Dainard Paulson, NY Jets
P-Curley Johnson, NY Jets

1966

OFFENSE
E-Otis Taylor, Kansas City
E-Art Powell, Oakland
E-Lance Alworth, San Diego
T-Jim Tyrer, Kansas City
T-Ron Mix, San Diego
T-Sherman Plunkett, NY Jets
G-Billy Shaw, Buffalo
G-Bob Talamini, Houston
G-Ed Budde, Kansas City
G-Wayne Hawkins, Oakland
C-Jim Otto, Oakland
C-Jon Morris, Boston
QB-Len Dawson, Kansas City
HB-Clem Daniels, Oakland
FB-Jim Nance, Boston
K-Gino Cappelletti, Boston

DEFENSE
DE-Jerry Mays, Kansas City
DE-Larry Eisenhauer, Boston
DE-Ron McDole, Buffalo
DE-Verlon Biggs, NY Jets
DT-Buck Buchanan, Kansas City
DT-Jim Dunaway, Buffalo
DT-Houston Antwine, Boston
MLB-Nick Buoniconti, Boston
LB-Mike Stratton, Buffalo
LB-Bobby Bell, Kansas City
CB-George Byrd, Buffalo
CB-Dave Grayson, Oakland
CB-Kent McCloughan, Oakland
S-Johnny Robinson, Kansas City
S-Kenny Graham, San Diego
S-George Saimes, Buffalo
P-Bob Scarpitto, Denver

1967

OFFENSE
E-George Sauer, NY Jets
E-Lance Alworth, San Diego
TE-Billy Cannon, Oakland
T-Ron Mix, San Diego
T-Jim Tyrer, Kansas City
T-Harry Schuh, Oakland
G-Bob Talamini, Houston
G-Walt Sweeney, San Diego
C-Jim Otto, Oakland
QB-Daryle Lamonica, Oakland
RB-Mike Garrett, Kansas City
RB-Jim Nance, Boston

DEFENSE
DE-Ben Davidson, Oakland
DE-Pat Holmes, Houston
DT-Buck Buchanan, Kansas City
DT-Tom Keating, Oakland
MLB-Nick Buoniconti, Boston
LB-George Webster, Houston
LB-Bobby Bell, Kansas City
CB-Miller Farr, Houston
CB-Kent McCloughan, Oakland
S-George Saimes, Buffalo
S-Johnny Robinson, Kansas City

1968

OFFENSE
E-Lance Alworth, San Diego
E-George Sauer, NY Jets
TE-Jim Whalen, Boston
T-Ron Mix, San Diego
T-Jim Tyrer, Kansas City
G-Walt Sweeney, San Diego
G-Gene Upshaw, Oakland
C-Jim Otto, Oakland
QB-Joe Namath, NY Jets
RB-Paul Robinson, Cincinnati
RB-Hewritt Dixon, Oakland

DEFENSE
DE-Gerry Philbin, NY Jets
DE-Rich Jackson, Denver
DT-Buck Buchanan, Kansas City
DT-Dan Birdwell, Oakland
MLB-Willie Lanier, Kansas City
MLB-Dan Conners, Oakland
LB-George Webster, Houston
LB-Bobby Bell, Kansas City
CB-Miller Farr, Houston
CB-Willie Brown, Oakland
S-Dave Grayson, Oakland
S-Johnny Robinson, Kansas City

1969

OFFENSE
E-Lance Alworth, San Diego
E-Fred Biletnikoff, Oakland
E-Don Maynard, NY Jets
E-Warren Wells, Oakland
TE-Bob Trumpy, Cincinnati
T-Jim Tyrer, Kansas City
T-Harry Schuh, Oakland
T-Winston Hill, NY Jets
G-Ed Budde, Kansas City
G-Walt Sweeney, San Diego
G-Gene Upshaw, Oakland
C-Jim Otto, Oakland
QB-Daryle Lamonica, Oakland
QB-Joe Namath, NY Jets

RB-Floyd Little, Denver
RB-Matt Snell, NY Jets

DEFENSE
DE-Rich Jackson, Denver
DE-Gerry Philbin, NY Jets
DE-Ron McDole, Buffalo
DT-John Elliott, NY Jets
DT-Buck Buchanan, Kansas City
DT-Tom Keating, Oakland
MLB-Nick Buoniconti, Oakland
LB-Bobby Bell, Kansas City
LB-George Webster, Houston
CB-Willie Brown, Oakland
CB-George Byrd, Buffalo
S-Dave Grayson, Oakland
S-Johnny Robinson, Kansas City

ALL-TIME ALL-AFL TEAM

Chosen by AFL members of the Hall of Fame Selection Committee

OFFENSE

Name	Position	Ht.	Wt.	Teams
Lance Alworth	Flanker	6-0	180	San Diego 1962–69
Don Maynard	Split End	6-1	179	New York Titans 1960–62; Jets 1963–69
Fred Arbanas	Tight End	6-3	240	Dallas Texans 1962, Kansas City 1963–69
Ron Mix	Tackle	6-4	250	Los Angeles Chargers 1960, San Diego 1961–69
Jim Tyrer	Tackle	6-6	274	Dallas Texans 1961–62, Kansas City 1963–69
Ed Budde	Guard	6-5	265	Kansas City Chiefs 1963–69
Billy Shaw	Guard	6-2	258	Buffalo Bills 1961–69
Jim Otto	Center	6-2	248	Oakland Raiders 196–69
Joe Namath	Quarterback	6-2	195	New York Jets 1965–69
Clem Daniels	Running Back	6-1	220	Dallas Texans 1960, Oakland 1961–67
Paul Lowe	Running Back	6-0	205	Los Angeles Chargers 1960, San Diego 1961, 1963–68, Kansas City 1969
George Blanda	Kicker	6-2	215	Houston 1960-66, Oakland 1967–69

DEFENSE

Name	Position	Ht.	Wt.	Teams
Jerry Mays	End	6-4	252	Dallas Texans 1961-62, Kansas City 1963–69
Gerry Philbin	End	6-2	245	New York Jets 1964–69
Houston Antwine	Tackle	6-1	170	Boston 1961–69

Name	Position	Ht.	Wt.	Teams
Tom Sestak	Tackle	6-4	260	Buffalo 1962–68
Bobby Bell	Linebacker	6-4	228	Kansas City 1963–69
Nick Buoniconti	Linebacker	5-11	220	Boston 1962–68, Miami 1969
George Webster	Linebacker	6-4	223	Houston 1967–69
Willie Brown	Cornerback	6-1	190	Denver 1963–66, Oakland 196–69
Dave Grayson	Cornerback	5-10	187	Dallas Texans 1961–62, Kansas City 1963–64, Oakland 1965–69
Johnny Robinson	Safety	6-1	205	Dallas Texans 1960–62, Kansas City 1963–69
George Saimes	Safety	5-11	186	Buffalo 1963–69
Jerrel Wilson	Punter	6-2	222	Kansas City 1963–69

YEARLY INDIVIDUAL HONORS

AFL PLAYER OF THE YEAR
As voted by United Press International

1960-Abner Haynes, HB, Dallas
1961-George Blanda, QB, Houston
1962-Cookie Gilchrist, FB, Buffalo
1963-Lance Alworth, FL, San Diego
1964-Gino Cappelletti, FL-K, Boston
1965-Paul Lowe, HB, San Diego
1966-Jim Nance, FB, Boston
1967-Daryle Lamonica, QB, Oakland
1968-Joe Namath, QB, New York
1969-Daryle Lamonica, QB, Oakland

AFL ROOKIE OF THE YEAR
As voted by United Press International

1960-Abner Haynes, HB, Dallas
1961-Earl Faison, DE, San Diego
1962-Curtis McClinton, FB, Dallas
1963-Billy Joe, FB, Denver
1964-Matt Snell, FB, New York
1965-Joe Namath, QB, New York
1966-Bobby Burnett, HB, Buffalo
1967-George Webster, LB, Houston
1968-Paul Robinson, RB, Cincinnati
1969-Greg Cook, QB, Cincinnati

AFL PLAYER OF THE YEAR
As voted by *The Sporting News*

1960-Abner Haynes, HB, Dallas
1961-George Blanda, QB, Houston
1962-Len Dawson, QB, Dallas
1963-Clem Daniels, HB, Oakland
1964-Gino Cappelletti, FL-K, Boston
1965-Paul Lowe, HB, San Diego
1966-Jim Nance, FB, Boston
1967-Daryle Lamonica, QB, Oakland
1968-Joe Namath, QB, New York
1969-Daryle Lamonica, QB, Oakland

AFL ROOKIE OF THE YEAR
As voted by *The Sporting News*

1960-Abner Haynes, HB, Dallas
1961-Earl Faison, DE, San Diego
1962-Curtis McClinton, FB, Dallas
1963-Billy Joe, FB, Denver
1964-Matt Snell, FB, New York
1965-Joe Namath, QB, New York
1966-Bobby Burnett, HB, Buffalo
1967-Dickie Post, RB, San Diego
1968-Paul Robinson, RB, Cincinnati
1969-Carl Garrett, RB, Boston

AFL COACH OF THE YEAR
As voted by United Press International

1960-Lou Rymkus, Houston
1961-Wally Lemm, Houston
1962-Jack Faulkner, Denver
1963-Al Davis, Oakland
1964-Lou Saban, Buffalo
1965-Lou Saban, Buffalo
1966-Mike Holovak, Boston
1967-John Rauch, Oakland
1968-Hank Stram, Kansas City
1969-Paul Brown, Cincinnati

Index

Abrams, Isaac 195
Abruzzi, Ray 226
Adams, Bud 3, 13, 15, 19–20, 22, 28, 45–47, 50, 59, 64, 75, 83, 160, 163, 257
Adams, Dave 112
Adderley, Herb 160, 174, 194
Addison, Tom 112–113
Agajanian 58–59
Ali, Muhammad 197
All-America Football Conference (AAFC) 8, 17, 21–22
Allen, Chuck 119
Allen, George 117
Alworth, Lance 78, 80–81, 84, 105, 117, 120, 131, 136–137, 149–151, 153, 186, 230, 235, 255
Ameche, Alan 7
American Broadcasting Company (ABC) 5, 17, 226, 257
American Football League (AFL) 4, 5, 8, 11, 14, 18, 20–21, 35–37, 41–42, 91, 96, 106, 108–109, 142, 162, 226, 254–257
Anders, William 195
Anderson, Dave 207, 217
Anderson, Donny 155–156, 193
Angsman Elmer 89
Anti-Trust Action 18
Antwine, Houston 113, 116
Arbanas, Fred 178, 238
Arcuni, Joe 61
Arnsparger, Bill 217
Atkinson, Al 219
Atkinson, George 211–213, 239–240
Atlanta Falcons 221, 227
Auer, Joe 64, 167

Babb, Gene 76
Baird, Bill 239
Baker, Ralph 202, 214, 222

Balboa Stadium 98, 255
Baltimore Colts 4, 7, 8, 10, 13, 42, 82, 101, 211, 216–225, 255
Banaszak, Pete 156, 193, 212
Barber, Stew 130
Bartle, H. Roe 103
Bass, Glenn 131, 136, 151, 170
Bates, Bill 113
Baugh, Sammy 41, 70, 85–86
Bears Stadium 92
Beasley, John 250
Beathard, Pete 240
Beathea, Elvin 229
Behrman, Dave 151
Bell, Bert 11, 13–19, 21–25, 52
Bell, Bobby 82, 167–168, 175, 181, 208, 232–235, 248, 252
Bemiller, Al 130, 151, 171
Bengston, Phil 174–175
Berry, Raymond 9–10, 201
Beverley, Randy 211, 219, 223
Bidwell, Violet 15
Bidwill, Charles 140
Biggs, Verlon 214, 222
Biletnikoff, Fred 142, 144, 183, 189, 193–194, 210–212, 214, 231, 242
Bird, Roger 156, 193
Birdwell, Dan 183, 185, 187–188, 203
Bite, Mike 140, 227–228
Blair, Sam 116
Blanda, George 4, 5, 54–55, 59–60, 62–63, 65–66, 68–69, 72–72, 83–84, 111, 113, 182, 188–189, 211, 236, 243–244, 248
Blood, Johnny 8
Bond, Lyle 78
Boozer, Emerson 156, 189, 197, 199–201
Borman, Frank 156, 195
Boston Braves 20
Boston Celtics 186
Boston College 26, 52

277

Boston Patriots 11, 48, 50, 55, 118, 123, 164, 227
Bourne, Harold (Red) 73-74
Bowman, Ken 190
Boyer, Bill 16, 19
Boyette, Garland 229
Bradshaw, Terry 3
Bratkowski, Zeke 45
Breen, John 40, 45, 47
Brennan, Terry 39
Brodie, John 160
Brooker, Tommy 77, 96
Brookshier, Tom 185
Brown, Aaron 82, 114, 156, 243, 245, 248, 252, 254
Brown, Jim 229
Brown, Tom 193
Brown, Paul 8, 38, 84, 89, 105, 202, 253-254, 256
Brown, Warren 116
Brown, Willie 66, 182, 185-187, 212, 233, 242
Broyles, Frank 80
Bruney, Fred 118
Bryant, Paul (Bear) 139
Buchanan, Buck 5, 66, 78, 82, 167-168, 174, 181, 232-234, 238-239, 241, 247-248, 250, 254-256
Buck, Jack 73, 190
Budde, Ed 244
Buffalo Bills 55, 70, 126, 146-148, 155, 159, 164, 229-230
Buffalo Evening News 25
Buoniconti, Nick 113-115, 118-119, 129
Burford, Chris 44, 123, 170
Burnett, Bobby 164
Burt, Jim 169
Burton, Charles 36
Burton, Ron 49
Butkus, Dick 142, 181
Byrd, Butch 128, 148-149, 164

Caffey, Lee Roy 178
Campbell, Marion 113, 118
Canadian Football League (CFL) 63, 108, 128, 247
Cannon, Billy 45-49, 54-55, 58-59, 62-63, 65, 83, 111, 182, 203, 236, 244
Cannon, Jimmy 17
Capp, Dick 193
Cappelletti, Gino 5, 42-43, 50-51, 99, 112-113, 115-116, 120-121, 203, 236, 244

Carlton, Wray 55, 67-68, 126, 129-130, 133-134, 136, 146
Carmichael, Al 50
Carson, Johnny 214, 226
Castro, Fidel 164
Chandler, Don 192-193
Chicago Bears 9, 14-15, 21, 92, 117, 142-143
Chicago Cardinals 9, 13, 15-16, 45, 181
Christman, Paul 73, 77-78, 175, 256
Christy, Earl 205
Cincinnati Bengals 180
Clarke, Hagood 148-149, 164
Cleveland Browns 8, 14, 54, 89, 112, 202, 211, 216, 248
Cline, Dick 204-205
Cline, Doug 76
Coan, Bert 110, 178
Colclough, Jimmy 50, 112
Collier, Joe 127, 150, 155, 164
Columbia Broadcasting System (CBS) 226
Conners, Dan 183, 185, 242
Continental Baseball League 16-17
Corey, Walt 44
Cosell, Howard 105, 160, 208, 219, 228
Cox, Wally 11
Crane, Paul 204
Crockett, Bobby 169
Culliman, Craig 22
Culp, Curley 232, 239, 241, 247-248, 254
Culver Military Academy 15
Curran, Bob 11, 22
Curtis, Mike 216

Dale, Carroll 174
Daley, Art 163
Dallas Cowboys 14-15, 56, 59-60, 189
Dallas Mercantile Bank 19
Dallas Texans 73-74, 88-89, 96, 103, 123, 233
D'Amato, Mike 214
Danahy, Jack 227
Daniels, Clem 97, 103, 183-184, 235
Davidson, Ben 182, 185, 203, 210-212, 214
Davidson, Cotton 80
Davis, Al 2, 44, 66, 67, 80, 95, 97, 100-102, 108, 144, 157-158, 160-162, 182, 184-185, 187, 189, 194, 199, 203, 207-209, 240, 255-256
Davis, Willie 160, 174

Dawson, Lenny 4, 5, 75–76, 89, 141, 168–169, 175–177, 181, 196, 209, 231–232, 238–240, 243–245, 247, 249–251, 253, 254
Day, Tom 127, 150–151, 153, 164, 183
Dee, Bob 113, 115–116
DeLuca, Sam 110, 205, 211, 215
Denver Bears 216
DeRogatis, Al 219
Detroit Lions 8, 17, 24, 108, 144, 181
Devaney, John 114
Dewveall, Willard 76
Dietzel, Paul 46
Discenzo, Tony 50
Ditka, Mike 160
Dixon, Hewritt 97, 182–183, 189, 192, 203–204, 244
Dorow, Al 55, 70
Dowler, Boyd 174, 193
Dubenion, Elbert 55, 115, 131, 147, 151, 164, 169
Dukes, Mike 76
Dunaway, Jim 126, 153, 164
Durslag, Mel 157–158
Durso, Joe 20, 104

Edgerson, Booker 148
Edmonton, Eskimos 63
Edwards, Jennifer 205
Eischeid, Mike 205
Eisenhauer, Larry 113–114, 116, 227
Eller, Carl 247, 250, 253
Erdelatz, Eddie 39, 42, 112, 184
Ewbank, Weeb 105, 113, 180, 199–200, 210, 212, 218, 221–223, 227

Faison, Earl 66, 68–69, 106, 110, 150
Farr, Miller 189, 229
Faulkner, Jack 91, 101, 108, 185–186
Feldman, Marty 184
Felser, Larry 78–79, 127, 129–130
Felt, Dick 119
Fenway Park 98
Ficca, Dan 67
Filchock, Frank 40, 93
Finley, Bob 74
Fitzgerald, Ed 123
Fleming, Marv 176
Flint, George 15
Flores, Tom 102, 182, 236
Flowers, Charlie 49, 69, 108, 147
Floyd, Don 11

Foss, Joe 30–33, 35–36, 38, 56, 60, 70, 77, 83, 99, 104, 123, 125, 134, 137 145, 156–157
Foster, Bud 78
Fox, Larry 210, 213
Frank Youell Field 93, 97–99, 183
Frazier, Charley 149

Gabor, Zsa Zsa 17
Gabriel, Roman 160
Gallagher, Dick 39, 70
Garrett, Mike 144, 156, 167, 170, 177–179, 231–232, 240, 247, 250–251
Garron, Larry 112, 115–116, 120
Getty, J. Paul 9
Gibbs, Joe 146
Gifford, Frank 9, 55, 82, 175, 190, 228
Gilchrist, Cookie 84–85, 115, 126, 128–131, 137, 146, 155, 256
Gillman, Sid 5, 38, 41–42, 50, 60, 66–67, 71–72, 80, 89, 97, 106–107, 109–110, 113, 117–119, 121–122, 134, 136–137, 145, 149, 157, 160, 163, 180, 183, 185, 230, 256
Gillmore, Connie 12
Givens, Jimmy 117
Gogolak, Pete 136, 151, 159–160
Goldman, Julian 204
Gonsoulin, Goose 92
Goode, Tom 77
Goodman, Murray 204–205
Gordon, Cornell 211
Gowdy, Curt 5, 63, 73–74, 77–79, 96–97, 175, 219, 256–257
Grabowski, Jim 155–156
Graham, Art 111
Graham, Otto 8, 107, 122
Grambling College 232
Grange, Red 139
Granger, Hoyle 156, 188
Grant, Bud 246–247, 253
Grantham, Larry 5, 42, 55, 87–88, 142, 202–203, 208, 214, 218–219, 223, 230, 255
Grayson, Dave 75, 182, 186, 242
Green, Jerry 254
Green Bay Packers 14, 59, 96–97, 108, 112, 155, 172–179, 180, 189–194, 216, 225, 246
Greene, Joe 242
Gregg, Forrest 174, 193
Gregston, Gene 61
Griffing, Dean 28, 40, 92–93
Grigsby, Bill 78, 235, 239, 250, 252
Groman, Bill 54, 59, 62, 64–65, 71, 83

Grosscup, Lee 147
Gunsel, Austin 47
Gutman, Bill 149

Hadl, John 4, 80, 82, 110, 115, 117, 136, 149–153, 230, 257
Halas, George 9, 21–23, 26, 45, 48, 60, 117, 122, 138, 180, 182, 226
Hall, Ron 113
Harmon, Merle 78, 201, 205, 211, 214, 222–223
Hart, Leon 24
Hawkins, Wayne 236
Hayes, Bob 142
Hayes, Wendell 231, 240, 251
Haynes, Abner 44, 56, 73–75, 78, 80, 89–90, 256
Headrick, Sherrill 90–91
Heidi Bowl 203–205
Henderson, John 250
Herman, Dave 201
Herskowitz, Mickey 160
Hess, Leon 104–105, 199
Hicks, W.K. 229
High, Robert 145
Hill, Jerry 219, 221, 223
Hill, Winston 105, 114, 214–215, 224, 228, 257
Hilton, Barron 17–19, 22, 44, 56, 60–61, 161, 163–164
Hilton, Conrad 17, 26, 32, 164
Holmes, Ernie 242
Holmes, Robert 144, 232, 244–245, 247, 252
Holovak, Mike 113, 128, 148, 166
Holub, E.J. 62, 73, 91, 176, 179
Hope, Bob 142
Hornung, Paul 160, 173–174, 190
Horrigan, Joe 5, 187, 256
Houston Astros 15
Houston Oilers 14–15, 50, 58–59, 60, 62–64, 66, 70–71, 73–74, 188, 190, 229
Houston Sports Association 22
Howsam, Bob 13, 15–16, 19, 40, 62
Howsam, Lee 62
Hudson, Bill 66
Hudson, Dick 130–131
Hudson, Jim 202–203, 211, 221, 229
Hull, Bill 75
Humphrey, Hubert 145
Hunt, Bobby 168
Hunt, Bunker 11
Hunt, H.L. 9–10, 12, 18, 56

Hunt, Jim 202–203, 211, 221, 229
Hunt, Lamar 5, 9–13, 14–30, 33, 50, 53, 57, 74–75, 77, 88, 103, 105, 125, 157–159, 162–163, 172–173, 233, 245, 249, 254, 257
Hunt, Lyda 10
Hunt, Margaret 10
Hunt, Stewart 27
Huram, Michael 49
Hurston, Chuck 179
Hurt, Harry III 12
Husmann, Ed 73
Hutson, Don 231

Iselin, Phil 104–105, 199, 227
Ivy, Pop 75, 77, 83, 111
Izenberg, Jerry 196
Izo, George 46

Jacobs, Harry 127, 150, 236
Jamison, Al 65, 73, 111
Janik, Tommy 169
Jeppesen Stadium 97, 255
Joe, Billy 146, 151, 203
Johnson, Curley 219
Johnson, Edwin 15
Johnson, Harvey 84–85, 148
Joiner, Dad 9
Jones, Charlie 78, 175, 215
Jones, Dub 63
Jones, K.C. 186
Jordan, Henry 178, 187

Kaine, Elinor 36, 187
Kansas City Chiefs 4, 12, 103, 142–143, 160, 167, 172–179, 181, 202, 231, 246–254, 255
Kansas City Municipal Stadium 99, 256
Kapp, Joe 147, 247–248, 250–253
Karas, Emil 119
Karras, Alex 181
Kassulke, Karl 251–252
Kaze, Irv 160
Kearney, Jim 144, 245
Keating, Tom 182, 185, 187, 189, 206, 242
Kelly, Leroy 216
Kemp, Jack 44, 58, 66, 71, 82–83, 108, 110, 115, 131, 133–137, 147–148, 150–152, 164, 168–169, 206–207, 236, 256–257
Kennedy, John 116
Kennedy, Robert 195

Kerbawy, Nick 25
King, Bill 78
King, Joe 173
King, Martin Luther 195
Kirkland, Frank 203
Klein, Dave 7
Klein, Eugene 164
Klosterman, Don 49, 80–82, 142, 160–161, 188, 233
Knox, Chuck 105, 200–201, 214
Kocourek, Dave 71, 118–119, 134, 183, 189
Kramer, Jerry 190, 193, 198
Kuharich, Joe 37
Kunz, Calvin 6

Ladd, Ernie 5, 66–69, 101, 106, 109–110, 121–122, 134, 136, 150–151, 170, 233–234, 255
LaGuardia, Fiorello 31
Lambeau, Curley 254
Lambeau Field 190
Lambert, Jack 242
Lammons, Pete 201, 212–213, 222
Lamonica, Daryle 4, 115, 182–184, 189, 192–194, 203–209, 211–212, 214, 231, 235, 240–244
Landis, Kenesaw 21
Landry, Tom 9, 36, 40–41, 173
Lanier, Willie 144, 232, 238–240, 242, 244, 247, 248, 252
Laskey, Bill 185
Lassiter, Ike 185, 188, 203, 210–211, 244–245
Layne, Bobby 24, 108
Leahy, Frank 26, 28, 39, 41, 45, 52–54, 82
Lee, Jacky 65–66, 232
Leininger, Buddy 85
Lemm, Wally 65, 71–72, 75, 83, 111, 180, 188
Levitt, Ed 157
Lillis, Don 104–105, 199
Lincoln, Keith 82, 101, 106–107, 110–111, 115, 117, 119, 121, 131, 134–137, 152, 256
Lindemann, Carl 125
Lipscomb, Gene 48
Livingston, Mike 232
LoCasale, Al 160–161, 255
Lombardi, Vince 100, 155, 173–175, 178–180, 190–194, 196–198, 206, 216, 219, 229, 246, 254, 256
Long, Charley 67
Los Angeles Chargers 32, 41, 53, 58–60, 66, 70, 71

Los Angeles Dodgers 60
Los Angeles Rams 8, 14, 22, 41, 47, 59–60, 167, 186, 191, 248
Louderback, Tom 95
Louis, Joe 197
Lovell, James 195
Lowe, Paul 44, 56, 59, 66, 82, 101, 106–107, 109–110, 118–119, 121, 131, 133–137, 150, 152
Lucas, Richie 149
Lujack, Johnny 45
Lynch, Dick 185
Lynch, Jim 232, 248

McCabe, Richie 55
McCafferty, Don 216
McClinton, Curtis 75, 89, 176
McCloughan, Kent 186, 206
McDaniel, Wahoo 126, 129
McDole, Ron 127, 148, 164, 170
McDonough, Will 78–79, 182
McElhenney, Hugh 23
McFadin, Bud 42–43, 192
McGah, Ed 34, 62, 95, 102
McGee, Max 176–179, 193
McKay, John 167
Mackbee, Earsall 251
McKeever, Ed 39
Mackey, John 217, 219
McMahon, Jim 147
McNamara, Bob 236
McNeil, Charlie 59
McVea, Warren 144, 232, 247, 252
Madden, John 187, 207, 212–213, 231, 236, 240
Madro, Joe 110, 119
Magee, Jerry 61, 71–72, 78, 98, 111, 178, 255
Maguire, Paul 119, 236
Mako, Gene 18
Mara, Jack 52
Mara, Wellington 158–160
Marciano, Rocky 197
Marsalis, Jim 240, 242
Marshall, George 18, 34, 60
Marshall, Jim 247, 251, 253
Martin, Townsend 104–105, 199
Mathis, Bill 201, 203, 213, 228, 236, 239
Matson, Ollie 23, 55
Matsos, Archie 55, 70
Matte, Tom 216, 219, 221
Maule, Tex 7, 9, 53, 54, 60, 79, 137, 173, 178, 195–196, 248–249, 254
Max, Peter 195

Maynard, Don 4, 55, 86, 93, 199–201, 210–213, 218, 220, 222, 228, 236, 256
Mays, Jerry 87, 90–91, 103, 168, 178, 232, 238–239, 242, 245, 248, 254–255, 257
Mays, Willie 49, 55
Menlow College 15
Mercer, Mike 170, 177
Merchant, Larry 160
Meredith, Dudley 169
Miami Dolphins 24, 64, 167
Michaels, Al 29
Michaels, Jay 29
Michaels, Lou 202, 219, 221, 223
Michaels, Walt 105
Michigan State University 17
Miller, Bill 182, 189, 193, 194
Miller, Van 53, 70, 78–79, 134
Mingo, Gene 50, 56
Minneapolis Lakers 16
Minnesota Vikings 90, 91, 216, 233, 246–254
Mitchell, Tom 219, 223
Mitchell, Willie 170, 176–177
Mix, Ron 5, 41–42, 66, 82, 101, 107–108, 117, 150, 236, 257
Modell, Art 180
Montana, Joe 4
Moore, Tom 29, 30, 123–125
Moorman, Mo 251
Morrall, Earl 216
Morris, Jon 67, 114, 166
Morton, Craig 142
Mowatt, Zeke 189, 229
Murchison, Clint 27, 33
Murphy, Bob 78
Murphy, Jack 61
Music Corporation of America 104
Mutual Radio Network 17

Namath, Joe 4, 79, 139–142, 149, 188–189, 196–201, 203–204, 206, 211–213, 215, 217–220, 222–223, 226–228, 232, 239, 240, 256, 257
Nance, Jim 142, 164–167
National Basketball Association (NBA) 16
National Broadcasting Company (NBC) 7, 8, 226, 257
National Football League (NFL) 4, 7, 8, 9, 11, 13, 96, 141, 142, 162
Neiman, Leroy 198
Nery, Ron 66, 69–70
Neville, Paul 25
New England Patriots 48

New Mexico Highlands University 92
New York Giants 7, 8, 14, 17, 96, 117, 125, 142, 159, 160, 233
New York Jets 4, 125, 139–140, 189, 216–224, 225–226, 228, 230
New York Titans 85–88, 91, 100
Newark (N.J.) *Star-Ledger* 7
NFL Films 249
Nicholas, James 211
Nitschke, Ray 174–175, 179, 191–192
Nobis, Tommy 156
Noll, Chuck 69, 101, 217, 236, 256
Norton, Don 119, 134

Oakland Coliseum 98
Oakland Raiders 4, 42, 56, 93, 95, 100–101, 182, 190, 202, 231, 248, 255
Oats, Carleton 244
O'Brien, Davey 18–19
O'Donnell, Joe 131, 151
O'Hanley, Ross 129
Olderman, Murray 228
Oliver, Chip 243–244
Orange Bowl 192
Orr, Jimmy 216, 221, 223, 231, 237
Osborn, Dave 251
Osborne, Robert 34, 62
Otto, Gus 185, 213
Otto, Jim 5, 42, 67–68, 183, 192, 203, 236–237, 240, 255

Pacific Coast League 16
Page, Alan 251, 253
Parilli, Vito (Babe) 45, 47–48, 68, 112, 116, 120, 128, 217, 236
Park, Ernest 153
Parker, Dan 104
Pauley, Ed 22–23
Petitbon, Richie 182
Philadelphia Athletics 20
Philadelphia Eagles 59
Philbin, Gerry 202, 204, 208, 228
Phipps, Gerald 62
Pitts, Elijah 176
Pitts, Frank 144, 232, 239, 243, 250–251
Pittsburgh Steelers 4, 162, 226, 242
Polinsky, Abe 61
Polo Grounds 55, 97, 253
Powell, Art 55, 93, 102, 182, 207
Pro Football Hall of Fame 10
Prudhomme, Remi 250
Pye, Brad 66

Ralbovsky, Marty 196
Ramsey, Buster 39, 70
Rauch, John 213–214
Reeves, Dan (Cowboys) 142
Reeves, Daniel (Rams) 158, 172
Reinsch, J. Leonard 145
Remmel, Lee 178–179
Ressler, Glenn 217
Rice, Andy 144
Richardson, Gloster 144, 240, 244
Richardson, Jesse 113–114
Richardson, Willie 216
Rickey, Branch 16
Ridlehuber, Preston 205
Robinson, Dave 178, 192–193, 234
Robinson, Eddie 232–233
Robinson, Johnny 90, 129, 168, 170, 176, 182, 232, 236, 239, 245, 250, 252
Rochester, Paul 236
Rocky Mountain Sports Enterprises, Inc. 15
Rooney, Art 162, 226
Roosevelt, Franklin 31, 131
Rosen, George 104
Rosenbloom, Carroll 27, 161
Ross, George 102
Rossi, Don 39
Rote, Kyle 219, 223, 238
Rote, Robin 108, 118–120, 134, 137, 149
Roy, Alvin 68, 109–110
Rozelle, Pete 29, 37, 46, 53, 124, 137–138, 145, 158–159, 161–162, 168, 225–228
Rush, Clive 105
Ruth, Babe 22
Ryan, Frank 141
Rymkus, Lou 40, 58–59, 63–65, 111

Saban, Lou 5, 39, 112, 126, 130, 133, 136, 146, 148, 150–151, 154–155, 206–207, 236–237, 256
Sabol, Ed 249
Sabol, Steve 256
Saimes, George 128, 135, 148–150
St. Louis Browns 20
St. Louis Cardinals 83, 140
Sample, Johnny 196, 202, 210–211, 221, 229
San Diego Chargers 106, 117–118, 131, 149–150, 202, 230
San Diego Tribune 61, 71, 98, 111, 178, 255
San Francisco 49ers 8, 14, 22, 44, 163
Sardisco, Tony 62

Sauer, George, Jr. 199, 201, 212, 218, 222, 238, 256
Sauer, George, Sr. 87
Sayers, Gale 142, 143, 144, 181
Scherick, Edgar 123–124
Schramm, Tex 158–162, 225
Schuh, Harry 183
Schulman, Sam 164
Scott, Ray 175, 190
Sears, Jim 59
Senate Anti-Monopoly Subcommittee 19
Sestak, Tom 127, 134–135, 146, 148, 153, 164–165, 257
Shaw, Billy 5, 67–68, 132–133, 136, 146–147, 150–152, 154, 164, 170–171, 255
Shea, William 14, 17
Shea Stadium 256
Sherman, Allie 122–123, 130
Sherman, Rod 240, 245
Sherrod, Blackie 89
Shonta, Chuck 129
Shula, Don 216–217, 221–223
Simpson, O.J. 229–230
Sinatra, Frank 226
Skoglund, H.P. 19, 31
Skoronski, Bob 179
Smith, Billy Ray 217
Smith, Bubba 144, 216
Smith, Charlie 204–205, 214, 243
Smith, Dave 58
Smith, Fletcher 176
Smith, Rankin 146
Smith, Robert 253, 254
Snell, Matt 125, 200–201, 213, 219–220, 222, 224, 228, 239
Snow, Jack 142
Snyder, Jimmy (The Greek) 217
Soda, Chet 34
Southern Methodist University 10
Southwestern Athletic Conference 144
Spadia, Lou 158–159
Speedie, Mac 40, 63, 146
Spikes, Jack 76
Sports Illustrated 7, 132, 137, 248, 254
Spyri, Johanna 203
Starr, Bart 173–179, 190–194, 197
Steadman, Jack 90, 103
Stenerud, Jan 238, 245, 250
Stirling, Scotty 101–102
Stover, Smokey 43–44
Stram, Hank 5, 34, 41, 49, 54, 56, 69, 73–74, 78, 89–90, 97, 169, 174, 178, 185, 200, 231, 235, 241–243, 246, 247–248, 251–256

Stratton, Mike 64, 127–128, 131, 134–136, 146–148, 151, 170, 256
Sugar, Bert 38
Sullivan, Billy 5, 11, 26, 35, 39, 51–52, 70, 116, 122, 161, 165, 172–173
Sullivan, Paul 51
Summerall, Pat 175
"Super Bowl" 4
Super Bowl I (Chiefs–Packers) 172–179
Super Bowl II (Packers–Raiders) 190–194
Super Bowl III (Jets–Colts) 216–224
Super Bowl IV (Vikings–Chiefs) 246–254, 256–257
Svihus, Bob 183–184
Sweeney, Walt 121–122, 150

Talamini, Bob 65–66, 136, 189, 210, 257
Taylor, Elizabeth 17
Taylor, Hugh (Bones) 111
Taylor, Jim 173–174, 176, 190
Taylor, Lionel 5, 51, 56, 92–94, 187
Taylor, Otis 82, 142–144, 167–169, 174, 176, 181, 231–232, 239, 243–244, 251–252, 256
Taylor, Rosey 66
Texas Monthly 12
Texas Rich 12
Thomas, Danny 145
Thomas, Emmitt 232, 238, 242, 244–245
Thompson, Chuck 7, 216
Thompson, Steve 214
Thomson, Bobby 49
Thorpe, Jim 8, 254
Tingelhoff, Mick 250
Tittle, Y.A. 117
Torczon, LaVerne 55
Tracey, John 127–128
Trask, Orville 59
Tripucka, Frank 50–51, 92–94
Tulane Stadium 249
Tunnell, Emlen 233
Turner, Bake 105
Turner, Jim 204, 221, 238, 256
Twilley, Howard 156
Twombly, Wells 124

Unitas, Dorothy 141
Unitas, Johnny 7, 9, 36, 48, 123, 137, 141, 197, 216, 223
University of Alabama 139–141
University of Illinois 233
University of Kansas 15

University of Michigan 233
University of Minnesota 42
University of Mississippi 42
University of Notre Dame 17, 26, 52–53, 233
University of Southern California 167, 229
Upshaw, Gene 183–185, 231, 234, 256

Valley, Wayne 34, 62, 93, 95, 102, 157, 161, 163
Van Brocklin, Norm 8, 79, 81, 234
Veeck, Bill 35
Volk, Rick 216, 219–221

Waldorf, Lynn 28
Walker, Doak 24
Wallace, William 179
Walls, Will 40, 49
Walsh, Bill 236
Walsh, Jimmy 227–228
Walton, Sam 210
War Memorial Stadium 97, 131–132, 168, 255
Ward, Al 33
Ward, Gene 26, 77
Warlick, Ernie 131, 146, 151
Washington, Gene 250
Washington Redskins 17, 18, 41, 59
Waterfield, Bob 81
Webster, George 188, 229
Weisman, Harold 28
Weller, Steve 84
Wells, Lloyd 49, 143–144
Wells, Warren 144, 182, 203, 211, 231, 245
Werblin, David (Sonny) 100, 104–105, 125–126, 139–142, 161, 199
West, Charlie 250
Willard, Ken 142
Williams, Howie 244
Williams, Ted 165
Williams, Travis 193
Williamson, Fred 170, 174, 178, 217
Wilson, George 180
Wilson, Jerrell 82, 169
Wilson, Nehemiah 243
Wilson, Ralph, Jr. 5, 24–27, 70, 85, 99, 138, 155, 157, 161, 172, 229, 257
Winter, Max 13, 15, 16, 19, 22, 225
Wismer, Harry 17, 19–20, 28, 32, 41, 49, 53, 55, 59, 70, 85–88, 100, 104
Wolfner, Walter 13–16
Wood, Willie 174

Woodard, Milt 5, 33, 35
Wright, Ernie 118, 153, 236
Wynne, Angus 27
Wynne, Bedford 27

Yalta 162
Yankee Stadium 7, 8

Yates, Brock 132
Young, Buddy 142, 233
Young, Dick 87

Zeno, Charlie 102
Zimmerman, Paul 78–79, 188

www.ingramcontent.com/pod-product-compliance
Ingram Content Group UK Ltd.
Pitfield, Milton Keynes, MK11 3LW, UK
UKHW041928140426
5217IPUK00014B/370